BIG DEAL

Geoffrey Block, Series Editor

Series Board
Tim Carter   Jeffrey Magee
Kim Kowalke   Carol J. Oja
Dominic McHugh   Larry Starr

Stephen Banfield, Emeritus

"South Pacific": Paradise Rewritten
Jim Lovensheimer

Pick Yourself Up: Dorothy Fields and the American Musical
Charlotte Greenspan

To Broadway, to Life! The Musical Theater of Bock and Harnick
Philip Lambert

Irving Berlin's American Musical Theater
Jeffrey Magee

Loverly: The Life and Times of "My Fair Lady"
Dominic McHugh

"Show Boat": Performing Race in an American Musical
Todd Decker

Bernstein Meets Broadway: Collaborative Art in a Time of War
Carol J. Oja

"We'll Have Manhattan": The Early Work of Rodgers and Hart
Dominic Symonds

Agnes de Mille: Telling Stories in Broadway Dance
Kara Gardner

The Shuberts and their Passing Shows: The Untold Tale of Ziegfeld's Rivals
Jonas Westover

Big Deal: Bob Fosse and Dance in the American Musical
Kevin Winkler

BIG DEAL

Bob Fosse and Dance in the American Musical

KEVIN WINKLER

OXFORD
UNIVERSITY PRESS

OXFORD
UNIVERSITY PRESS

Oxford University Press is a department of the University of Oxford. It furthers
the University's objective of excellence in research, scholarship, and education
by publishing worldwide. Oxford is a registered trade mark of Oxford University
Press in the UK and certain other countries.

Published in the United States of America by Oxford University Press
198 Madison Avenue, New York, NY 10016, United States of America.

Library of Congress Cataloging-in-Publication Data
Names: Winkler, Kevin, author.
Title: Big deal : Bob Fosse and dance in the American musical / Kevin Winkler.
Description: New York, NY : Oxford University Press, [2018] |
Series: The broadway legacies series | Includes bibliographical references and index.
Identifiers: LCCN 2017026450 (print) | LCCN 2017045894 (ebook) |
ISBN 9780199336807 (updf) | ISBN 9780199336814 (epub) | ISBN 9780199336791 (alk. paper)
Subjects: LCSH: Fosse, Bob, 1927–1987. | Choreographers—United States—Biography. |
Musicals—United States.
Classification: LCC GV1785.F67 (ebook) |
LCC GV1785.F67 W56 2018 (print) | DDC 792.8092 [B]—dc23
LC record available at https://lccn.loc.gov/2017026450

1 3 5 7 9 8 6 4 2

Printed by Sheridan Books, Inc., United States of America

"Una más," Bob Fosse's rehearsal mantra, was shorthand for "do it one more time" until it was perfect, no matter how late it was or how exhausted you were. This book is dedicated to every dancer who has ever lined up to compete for a job, sweated through rehearsals and performances, and then did it "una más."

Bob Fosse rehearses Gwen Verdon and William Guske on stage in Chicago during the post-Broadway national tour of Redhead *in 1960. Library of Congress, Performing Arts Reading Room.*

CONTENTS

● ● ●

FOREWORD

• • •

Big Deal (1986), a dance revue set to early song hits that appeared one year before his death, was the title of Bob Fosse's last Broadway show. Although Fosse received a final Tony Award for Best Choreography, the show was not a success. Despite this minor setback, readers of Kevin Winkler's *Big Deal: Bob Fosse and Dance in the American Musical*, the second book in the Broadway Legacies series devoted to a choreographer,[1] will inevitably discover that Fosse (1927–1987), whose career as a dancer began in the later 1940s, was a *huge* deal. For starters, viewers in a variety of formats can savor footage of a young dancing Fosse already exhibiting his instantly recognizable dance moves in "From This Moment On," a number in the film version of *Kiss Me, Kate* (1953), or the priceless *pas de deux* "Who's Got the Pain" with his dancing (and soon-to-be marriage) partner Gwen Verdon in the film adaptation of *Damn Yankees* (1957).

While still in his twenties, Fosse made his initial mark as a Broadway choreographer in *The Pajama Game* (1954), *Damn Yankees* (1955), *New Girl in Town* (1957), *How to Succeed in Business without Really Trying* (1961), and *Little Me* (1962). Beginning with *Redhead* in 1959 and for much of the 1960s and 1970s, Fosse dominated the post–Jerome Robbins generation of Broadway director-choreographers with *Sweet Charity* (1966), *Pippin* (1972), *Chicago* (1975), and *Dancin'* (1978), in addition to an acclaimed film version of *Cabaret* (1972), all of which amply display Fosse's angular, dramatic, often provocative and highly idiosyncratic and seminally influential choreographic style.

In 1973, the same year Secretariat became the first thoroughbred in twenty-five years to win the coveted triple crown in horseracing, Fosse became the first (and to date only) person to win a previously unimaginable triple crown for his work on stage, television, and film: a Tony Award for *Pippin*, an Emmy for *Liza with a Z* (both for direction and choreography), and a Best Director Oscar for *Cabaret*. As Winkler informs us in his introduction, the latter recognition gave Fosse further distinction as "the only star director of musicals of his era—a group that included Jerome Robbins, Gower Champion, Michael Kidd, and Harold Prince—to equal his Broadway success in films."

Shortly after his death in 1987, works first directed by Fosse and now revived "in the style of Bob Fosse" have remained at the center of the popular entertainment universe. *Chicago*, which was overwhelmed by *A Chorus Line* when both shows appeared on Broadway in 1975, came roaring back in 1996 when its Best Revival not only far surpassed its former run but eventually became the longest-running musical to originate in America and the second-longest running Broadway musical ever, behind only *The Phantom of the Opera*. Additional milestones include the musical revue *Fosse* based on Fosse's choreography, which received the Tony Award for Best Musical in 1999, the 2002 film adaptation of *Chicago*—the first film musical to win the Oscar for Best Musical since 1968—and a stage revival of *Pippin* that received the Tony for Best Revival in 2013.

Before completing more than twenty years of service as a curator, archivist, and director for several divisions at the New York Public Library for the Performing Arts, the author of *Big Deal* was a professional dancer who, as a member of a dancing chorus, experienced the life-altering opportunity of being coached by Fosse during a week of rehearsals in preparation for the 1982 revival of *Little Me*. As one of those lucky enough to claim the title of "Fosse dancer," Winkler, the future author of the first comprehensive scholarly study of Fosse's stage, film, and television work, recalled that "the experience of working with him left a tremendous impression" mainly because "he brought a director's eye to staging dance and demanded the same dramatic intent from the dancers as from the actors."

Winkler not only demonstrates an almost uncannily readable knack for describing dance numbers (even in the absence of the helpful glossary he provides) but also places Fosse's choreography in the larger context of the shows and films, explains how everything worked together, and tells the story of how Fosse realized his increasingly independent vision. Interviews with such luminaries as Chita Rivera, Ann Reinking, lesser-known dancers, and a wide array of other knowledgeable witnesses offer fresh opinions and add considerably to the narrative. For me, the most revealing exchange was Winkler's interview with Stephen Schwartz, who in the early 1970s was the young and feisty composer of *Pippin*, fresh from his success as the composer of *Godspell*, more than thirty years before *Wicked*. The interview sheds considerable interpretative light on the fascinating and turbulent artistic and personality conflicts between the talented young composer and his controlling boss, and includes Schwartz's following powerful revelation: "It's only been in retrospect and with my own aging that I've come to appreciate the bigger vision that he brought to the piece, and actually, in an ironic twist, I've become quite an ardent defender of it." As a result of this interview, Winkler is able to demonstrate with conviction that "the conflict between the two strong-willed men ultimately led to *Pippin*'s success."

In addition to presenting readers with the scope and range of Fosse's career, Winkler also places Fosse's vast output within a meaningful social context. Among numerous other fringe benefits provided by *Big Deal* are an illuminating survey of Broadway choreography in the decades before Fosse arrived on the scene (introduction) and an insightful comparison of dance styles and approaches between Fosse and his two primary contemporaries, Jerome Robbins and Gower Champion (chapter 5). Readers also acquire an especially rich history of the women in Fosse's creative and personal life, all dancing partners and significant dancers and actresses in their own right:

- Mary Ann Niles, Fosse's first dancing partner and wife from 1947 to 1952;
- Joan McCracken, Fosse's second wife from 1952 to 1956;
- Gwen Verdon, the featured star in numerous Fosse shows and his third wife from 1960; despite their personal if not professional separation in 1971 and his ongoing affair with Ann Reinking, Fosse and Verdon remained legally married until his death;

- Ann Reinking continued the Fosse legacy in numerous Fosse roles, choreographed the 1996 *Chicago* "in the style of Bob Fosse," and was the conceptual and directorial guiding force behind *Fosse* in New York and London.

Winkler also demonstrates how the Fosse style exerted a profound impact on other realms of popular culture, for example in his persuasive contention that "with the opening sequence of *All That Jazz* Fosse virtually created the modern MTV music video." Winkler also shows how dancing moves in hip-hop and their residue in Lin-Manuel Miranda's *Hamilton* continue the Fosse legacy. And anyone who might doubt Winkler's claim that Michael Jackson's Moonwalk was "a reincarnation of Fosse" need only watch a few minutes of one of several YouTube "mash-ups" of Fosse's moves as the snake in the grass in the film *The Little Prince* in 1974, juxtaposed to reveal a startling resemblance to video performances of Jackson in the early 1980s.

From the "Steam Heat" number in *The Pajama Game* in the early 1950s to Jackson's Moonwalk in the 1980s and the phenomenon of *Hamilton* in the 2010s, the "hunched shoulders, turned-in stance, and stuttering, staccato jazz movements" that mark the "Fosse style" have become indelibly marked in our cultural consciousness and serve as a formidable Broadway legacy. In short, the star of this book was a really big deal. Kevin Winker's *Big Deal: Bob Fosse and Dance in the American Musical* will tell us why.

Geoffrey Block
Series Editor, Broadway Legacies

ACKNOWLEDGMENTS

• • •

Gwen Verdon once described Bob Fosse the filmmaker as using the camera to get inside his dances. My mission statement for this book was to get inside Fosse's choreography, to pull apart the Swiss watch precision of his dances and understand not just their structure but also the wide-ranging sources of his movement vocabulary and to consider them in the context of their shows and films, and in his larger development as an artist.

Speaking with dancers on whom Fosse created his work was the most important way of getting inside his dances, and I thank them for their generosity of spirit in sharing their memories of him: Sandahl Bergman, Candy Brown, Eileen Casey, Suzanne Charney, Cheryl Clark, Lloyd Culbreath, Marilyn D'Honau, Kathryn Doby, Alice Evans, Gene Foote, Gary Gendell, David Gold, Linda Haberman, James Horvath, Patricia Ferrier Kiley, Richard Korthaze, Diane Laurenson, George Marcy, Lenora Nemetz, Michon Peacock, Valarie Pettiford, Mimi Quillin, Lee Roy Reams, Ann Reinking, Chita Rivera, Alton Ruff, Ken Urmston, and Chet Walker. My thanks also to Mindy Aloff, Allen Herman, Mary MacLeod, John McMartin, and Larry Spivack. Extra-special thanks are due Harvey Evans, possibly the best-loved dancer in New York City, who spent an afternoon with me at the Paley Center for Media watching television clips of his work with Fosse and who put me in touch with several dancers I would otherwise never have found. Important Fosse collaborators like Jules Fisher, Gordon Lowry Harrell, Harold Prince, Stephen Schwartz, and Tony Walton graciously answered my many questions. John Sefakis, president of the indispensable organization Dancers Over 40, was an early supporter of my work and helped me reach out to a number of interview subjects.

The Verdon/Fosse Legacy LLC maintains the heritage of these two artists with passion and integrity; I am deeply grateful to this organization for inviting me into its circle through its choreographic workshops. My sincere thanks to Nicole Fosse, Brian Christopher Cummings, and Steve Jones. The opportunity to watch Lloyd Culbreath, Dana Moore, Mimi Quillin, Valarie Pettiford, Lynn Sterling, and others pass on their deep understanding of Fosse's work to a new generation of dancers was invaluable to my research.

As a librarian and archivist, I knew the archival record would yield new ways inside Fosse's dances. But I was unprepared for the breadth and depth of the Bob Fosse and Gwen Verdon Collection at the Library of Congress. This magisterial collection, processed with great care and sensitivity by the late Mary E. Edsall, is a marvel, documenting the evidence of Fosse's life and career in minute detail and offering endless avenues for research. I thank the reference staff of the Library of Congress's Music Division and Recorded Sound Section for their infinite patience with my voluminous requests over the course of several years of research visits and offer special thanks to Mark Eden Horowitz, Robert Lipartito, and Walter Zvonchenko.

I received gracious assistance from Morgen Stevens-Garmon, Theater Archivist at the Museum of the City of New York, and the staff of the Margaret Herrick Library. The staff of the Shubert Archive welcomed me like a returning friend, and I am grateful to Maryann Chach, Reagan Fletcher, Mark E. Swartz, and Sylvia Wang. Jane Klain at the Paley Center for Media was generous and full of great suggestions.

I have always considered the corner of Sixty-Fifth Street and Amsterdam Avenue, where the vast theatrical riches of the New York Public Library for the Performing Arts reside, to be paradise on earth. I was lucky to call it my professional home for nearly twenty years, and the idea for this book took shape while I worked there. Researching it allowed me to savor paradise once more and to reconnect with friends and colleagues. My thanks to Jacqueline Z. Davis, Don Baldini, Amy Russell, Cheryl Raymond, Evan Leslie, Doug Reside, Barbara Cohen Stratyner, and Tom Lisanti, Manager of Permissions and Reproduction Services at the NYPL. In the heart of paradise, the special collections reading room, I could not have had more supportive assistance from Karl Baranoff, Harrison Behl, John Calhoun, Danielle Castronovo, Danielle Cordove, Jennifer Eberhardt, Paul Greenhaw, Jamaal Harris, Tema Hecht, Jonathan Hiam, Tanisha Jones, Bob Kosovsky, Suzanne Lipkin, Louise Martzinek, David McMullin, Charles Perrier, Daisy Pommer, Alice Standin, Annemarie van Roessel, Channan Willner, Jessica Wood, and Arlene Yu. The soundtrack to paradise is provided by the staff of the audio and video playback unit who patiently responded to my every request, and I thank Anthony Arostegui, Doris DeJesus, Michael Diekmann, Johnny Gore, Scott Greenberg, Yvonne Hall, Elena Rossi-Snook, and Nicholas Smeraski. The print delivery team was all fleet efficiency; my sincere thanks go to Brenta Agard, Sylvia Alicea-Felipe, Caleb Cadet, Patricia Darby, Joenique Davis, Pedro Herenandez, Robbie Hicks, Jalen Quashie, Tina Ragoobir, Danielle Rogers (so helpful in navigating off-site deliveries), Sharena Stanley, Brian Weldon, and dear Eydie Wiggins. The staff of the one-of-a-kind Theatre on Film and Tape Archive was always welcoming, and I thank Emily Currie, Michael Hearn, Patrick Hoffman, Steve Massa, Wm. Charles Morrow, Wendy Norris, Sharon Rork, Holly Sansom, Amy Schwegel, Misy Singson, Melisa Tien, and Victor Van Etten. Last but far from least, Jeremy Megraw's detailed knowledge of the library's immense photo collections and his Zen-like demeanor made my photo research much less stressful, and for that, I am very grateful.

Ken Bloom was generous and supportive of this first-time author, as was Andy Propst who shared back-from-the-trenches stories and suggestions. Tim Connell, Mark Frawley, Joe Joyce, Tom Lisanti, Lee Raines, and Carol Schuberg graciously shared contacts to important interview subjects. Charles Kloth and Michael Schiavi read early drafts and offered cogent and encouraging feedback, as did my sister, Kathy Winkler Moore. I could not ask for a more supportive friend than Jim Wilson, who was one of the first people I talked to about the idea for the book. He was always available to read chapters, talk through ideas that were sometimes only partly formed, and offer clear-eyed and caring feedback. We laughed, gossiped, and debated, and in the process he helped me become a better writer.

I thank my editor, Norman Hirschy for his Lana-Turner-at-Schwab's-Drugstore "discovery" of me at the Song, Stage and Screen conference, and for patiently navigating my writing process through some choppy waters. His support and encouragement were essential to keeping me on track. Broadway Legacies series editor Geoffrey Block offered steadfast support and enthusiasm for the project from the very beginning. The MacDowell Colony in Peterborough, New Hampshire provided me a blessed period of writing solitude in a beautiful setting.

Finally, it would have been impossible to complete this project without the unwavering support of my husband, Richard Schneider. He transcribed all my interviews and read (and reread) countless drafts, providing expert copyediting. He spent seven years going alone on field trips, outings, and family events while I stayed home to write or went to the library. He sat through umpteen screenings of *Sweet Charity* and *All That Jazz* with (rarely) a protest. His piano playing in the next room provided the soundtrack for my writing, to the extent that I will forever identify Bob Fosse with the music of George Gershwin and Scott Joplin. He always had dinner ready for me when I finished writing each night. He has sustained me in every possible way. For me, writing and research are full of undefined, private pleasures. I love being by myself, formulating ideas, and working them out on paper. That work is more pleasurable, more exquisitely satisfying, because when I'm done I know on the other side of the door Richard is waiting for me.

GLOSSARY OF DANCE TERMS

• • •

arabesque A position in which the dancer stands on the supporting leg while the other is extended behind the body.

arabesque leap A move in which the dancer leaps with one leg in an arabesque extension.

attitude turn A turn with the working leg held in attitude position, in which the leg in the air is bent at the knee.

barrel turn A rapid series of turns using the arms in a windmill or airplane position.

battement A movement in which the dancer lifts one leg to the front, side, or back and returns it to the supporting leg. A standard high kick is an example of battement.

bell kicks A click of the heels together while in the air.

black bottom A jazz dance sensation of the 1920s consisting of syncopated rhythms, bent knees, crouched torsos, and hip and pelvic movements.

cakewalk A strutting promenade or march, of African American origin, often done by couples.

chaînés turn A turning step executed on pointe or demi-pointe, performed in a series and in a straight line or circle.

changement A jump in which the feet change positions in the air.

cobrahead movement An isolation of the neck in which the head continues to move, giving the impression of a cobra's head turning in all directions.

cooch dancing A sinuous, quasi-Oriental dance performed by a woman and characterized chiefly by suggestive gyrating and shaking of the body.

coupé turn A step in which one foot cuts the other foot away, taking its place, usually done as a transition to, or preparation for, a bigger step.

demi-pointe Supporting the body's weight on the balls of one or both feet, heels raised off the floor.

développé A movement in which the leg is lifted and then fully extended outward.

entrechat quatre A jump into the air with rapidly crossed legs in front and behind.

flick kick A quick in-out kick of the leg.

fouetté turn A turn in which the working leg extends forward and whips around.

frug A popular social dance of the mid-1960s in which the dancers move only their arms and hips while the feet remain stationary.

gazelle leap A leap resembling an arabesque leap, but with the legs bent under and the body and arms arching down, giving the impression of a gazelle in midleap.

grand jeté A long horizontal leap, starting from one leg and landing on the other, resembling a split in the air.

hornpipe A lively dance associated with sailors, typically performed by one person.

jazz run A running jazz walk, in which the body is in plié and the shoulders and arms move in opposition.

jeté A leap in which one leg appears to be thrown in the direction of the movement.

lindy Also called the lindy hop, a form of swing dancing usually done to jazz music.

"mess around" An eccentric dance step in which the dancer places hands on hips, then rotates the hips while shuffling the feet.

mudra A symbolic or ritual hand gesture used in Indian classical dance.

pas de deux A dance for two people.

passé Bending the leg and sliding it to the knee of the supporting leg.

penché A position in which the body is tilted forward from the hip of the supporting leg so that the head is lower than the working leg.

pirouette An act of spinning on one foot, typically with the raised foot touching the knee of the supporting leg.

pirouettes à la seconde A turn with the leg held steady in second position, parallel to the floor.

plié A smooth and continuous bending of the knees outward with the upper body held upright and heels on the ground.

port de bras A movement of the arms through different positions.

relevé A movement in which the dancer rises up onto full point or half point from the flat of the feet.

saut de basques A traveling step in which the dancer jumps and turns in the air with one foot drawn up to the knee of the other leg.

"shave and a haircut" A brief tap step used to punctuate the end of a dance.

shim sham A tap step done with a shuffling rhythm.

shimmy A jazz dance characterized by a shaking of the body from the shoulders down.

snake hips A dance move with sideward foot twisting and resultant hip wriggling.

soft-shoe A form of tap dancing done with soft-soled shoes and at a slower tempo and a more relaxed rhythm.

split jump A jump in which the dancer assumes a split position while in the air.

stag leap A leap with the back leg bent behind, giving the impression of a stag caught in midair.

tour en l'air Literally, a turn in the air.

traveling time step A tap dance move executed while covering space across a stage.

trenches A sliding movement with legs and arms in opposition.

turnout A rotation of the legs at the hips, resulting in knees and feet facing away from each other. *Turn-in* is the opposite, with the feet pointing toward each other.

INTRODUCTION

• • •

In *The Season*, William Goldman's examination of the 1967–1968 Broadway season, he coined the term "the Muscle" to refer to the individual who exerts ultimate power over a production, be it star, director, writer, or producer. "The Muscle," Goldman wrote, is the one person whose ultimate vision gets on the stage, making it "the most prized status you can have on Broadway."[1] That "Muscle" was on full display when the producers of a 1982 Broadway revival of *Little Me* asked Bob Fosse to recreate one of his key numbers from the original production. Fosse had choreographed and co-directed this 1962 Broadway musical, which featured music by Cy Coleman, lyrics by Carolyn Leigh, and a book by Neil Simon, based on Patrick Dennis's satire of tell-all star autobiographies. The "Little Me" of the title was Belle Poitrine, a poor girl who rose to fame as a stage and screen star based on her prodigious figure (Belle Poitrine means "beautiful chest" in French). Directed by Robert Drivas and choreographed by Peter Gennaro, the revival was not playing well in previews. Lack of focus and a sluggish pace were the biggest problems; Gennaro's splashy, energetic dances were well received by audiences. So it was a surprise when the producers announced that Bob Fosse was arriving to restage "Deep Down Inside," a full-chorus, hoedown number in which Belle and the townspeople try to convince the tight-fisted local banker, Mr. Pinchley, that he really was good-hearted, "deep down inside."

As a member of the dancing chorus for this revival, I had the opportunity to witness the galvanizing effect Fosse had on every department of the production. The cast and crew, already exhausted from rehearsing and playing preview performances, were at strict attention for his first appearance at the theater. The women were in full make-up with freshly coiffed hair. Everyone had on his or her best audition outfit. (I even pulled out my special electric blue jazz pants for the occasion.) Fosse arrived early, accompanied by a young woman who steadily supplied him with black coffee and cigarettes, and dance assistant John Sharpe, who had appeared in the original production and had served as dance assistant to Fosse on numerous shows and films.

Fosse worked quickly, teaching steps and creating formations on one side of the stage while Sharpe mirrored his efforts on the other. Previously there had been a disconnected quality to the number, with the chorus standing passively, waiting for its cue to begin dancing. Now there was full engagement with the scene's dramatic intent by all performers. Before, the chorus entered with Belle, and the number started when she got a musical cue and went directly into the song. Now Belle entered alone and the music came in under the dialogue, allowing her to ease into the song. Fosse worked with Mary Gordon Murray, the actress playing Belle, on the intent behind the lyrics, coaching her performance as she started the song in a quieter, more natural style. Next she called the chorus to join her, and Fosse staged us in one large group entering from the wings in superfast, cartoon fashion, instantly establishing the number's mood and movement style. When dancing began, it flowed naturally from the action. The steps were not technically difficult, but they required speed, coordination, and the ability to work together as a unit. The number took on a delicious theatricality, most cleverly when the chorus crawled on our stomachs toward the lip of the stage, singing (in increasingly lower tones), "deep, deep, deep, deep, deep . . . ." Our heads were finally lowered, looking directly down into the orchestra pit, and—wham—on the downbeat, we snapped up, exclaiming, "Deep down inside!"

Fosse worked with us several mornings over the course of a week, but my most vivid memory of his time with the company was not about dance. Instead, it was of the actors approaching him, eager for help and coaching on the script. They recognized that his skill in staging musical numbers included helping actors convey character and motivation through song and dance. For those of us who got to call ourselves "Fosse dancers," even for just a short time, the experience of working with him left a tremendous impression. We saw that he brought a director's eye to staging dance and demanded the same dramatic intent from the dancers as from the actors. For dancers, this is a powerful incentive and helps explain our idolatry of him.

Fosse belonged to a rich lineage of Broadway choreographers who expanded their duties to include directing in the post–World War II era. Perhaps more than any other director-choreographer, he took the concept of "the Muscle," or complete control of his productions, to its furthest extent, eventually eliminating collaborators altogether.

Big Deal: Bob Fosse and Dance in the American Musical considers Fosse's career in the context of changes in the Broadway musical theater over four decades. It examines how each of the important women in his adult life—all dancers— impacted his career and influenced his dance aesthetic. Finally, the book investigates how his evolution as both artist and individual mirrored the social and political climate of his era and allowed him to comfortably ride a wave of cultural changes.

The book draws on the Bob Fosse and Gwen Verdon Collection at the Library of Congress; the personal papers of Harold Prince, Jerome Robbins, Paddy Chayefsky, Fred Ebb, Abe Burrows, and others at the New York Public Library for the Performing Arts; and interviews with key Fosse collaborators and many of the chorus "gypsies" on whom Fosse built his iconic choreography.

Chapter 1 examines the foundation of the Fosse style through his years as a young performer in the waning days of vaudeville, his teenage appearances in Chicago area nightclubs and burlesque houses, and the dance act he formed with his first wife, Mary Ann Niles. Fosse appeared in three films at MGM, the last of which, *Kiss Me, Kate* (1953), featured a short sequence of his choreography that displayed aggressive jazz stylings, burlesque traces, and witty comic touches. It also showed the influence of Jack Cole, the American dancer and choreographer who had created his own dance idiom incorporating movement from Middle Eastern, Indian, Afro-Cuban, and other ethnic dance traditions into an athletic, sexually charged jazz dance style that was highly influential.

Bob Fosse's first four Broadway shows were with George Abbott or Jerome Robbins or some combination of both. *The Pajama Game* (1954), *Damn Yankees* (1955), *Bells Are Ringing* (1956), and *New Girl in Town* (1957) provided him with a high-level apprenticeship that served as a foundation for every Fosse show that followed and are the focus of chapter 2. Fosse was hired as *The Pajama Game*'s choreographer with the proviso that co-director Jerome Robbins serve as a backup, and indeed, Robbins restaged or completed a number of *Pajama Game*'s musical moments. Nevertheless, with his very first Broadway musical, the "Fosse style" was already fully developed, with its hunched shoulders, turned-in stance, and stuttering, staccato jazz movements as exemplified in "Steam Heat."

Damn Yankees introduced Fosse to Gwen Verdon, a former Jack Cole dancer whose performance of Fosse's choreography for "Whatever Lola Wants" proved indelible and led to a professional and personal association that would last the rest of their lives. Verdon and Fosse collaborated on several key shows, including *New Girl in Town*, a musicalization of Eugene O'Neill's *Anna Christie*, on which he fought with director George Abbott and producer Harold Prince over his "Red Light Ballet." Designed by Fosse to show the degradation of Anna's employment in a bordello, the ballet was dismissed by Abbott as "just plain dirty."[2] The ensuing clash led Fosse to sever his ties with both men and determine that he would follow Robbins's example and direct his next show.

Two very different experiences form the basis of chapter 3. At Verdon's insistence, Fosse was hired as both choreographer *and* director of *Redhead*, a musical comedy murder mystery. *Redhead* had the pace and flow of a show fully staged by one person. A seminal project for Fosse, *Redhead* demonstrated that he clearly possessed "the Muscle." His next project was a musical version of Preston Sturges's World War II film satire *Hail the Conquering Hero* (shortened to *The Conquering Hero*). Fosse felt that his contributions as director and choreographer were so integral to the show's creation that he sought, and received, Dramatists Guild recognition as an author. However, his relationship with his collaborators was particularly troubled, and he was dismissed while the show was in out-of-town tryouts. Fosse's experience on *The Conquering Hero* demonstrated that the control he increasingly sought was not always easily negotiated. Following this troubling setback, Fosse contributed choreography to two comedic musicals, and chapter 4 considers his work on *How to Succeed in Business without Really Trying* and *Little Me* as emblematic of Kennedy-era confidence and high spirits.

Opening at the top of 1966, *Sweet Charity* proved a virtual compendium of then-current styles and sexual attitudes, and chapter 5 examines the importance of this key Fosse work on stage and screen. He conceived this American adaptation of Federico Fellini's film *Nights of Cabiria* (1957) as a vehicle for Gwen Verdon, writing several drafts of the show's book before relinquishing those duties to Neil Simon. Nonetheless, in *Sweet Charity* Fosse's authorial voice was much in evidence, and the show pointed to a new direction in his work. Fosse's staging exhibited a new fluidity, and the entire show seemed to dance. *Sweet Charity* was also the vehicle by which he would return to movies, this time as a director. Although full of arresting moments, the film was deemed too busy and full of gimmicky, self-conscious camerawork. *Sweet Charity* was a commercial and critical failure, but it allowed Fosse to explore the camera's potential in presenting dance on film.

The international success of Fosse's film version of *Cabaret* in 1972 kicked off the busiest, most productive decade of his career. Fosse's achievement of the triple crown of show business awards—the Oscar (for *Cabaret*), Emmy (for *Liza with a Z*), and Tony (for *Pippin*), all in 1973—remains unprecedented and nearly impossible to imagine another director repeating. Fosse and the 1970s were made for each other, with the mood of the decade reflected in both his life and his work.

Fosse became the only star director of musicals of his era—a group that included Jerome Robbins, Gower Champion, Michael Kidd, and Harold Prince—to equal his Broadway success in films. The original Broadway production of *Cabaret*, directed by Harold Prince, was a transitional work, joining a conventional narrative to a production concept in which cabaret numbers comment on, and reflect, the story. Fosse's film version jettisoned most of the score for numbers performed only onstage, thus refining the show's use of performance to comment on dramatic reality. The hyperactive camera work he was criticized for in *Sweet Charity* was refined and focused here. *Cabaret* found parallels between the chaos and national crisis of identity in pre-Nazi Germany and contemporary anxieties over the continuing Vietnam War. *Liza with a Z*, starring Liza Minnelli and filmed by multiple cameras before a live audience in a Broadway theater, brought the kinetic energy of a live performance to this musical concert for television. Chapter 6 examines the making of these two seminal films.

Chapter 7 traces Fosse's bitter fights with *Pippin*'s composer and lyricist, Stephen Schwartz, over the show's tone and message. Fosse ultimately prevailed and infused *Pippin* with a dark cynicism. Chapter 8 discusses two back-to-back projects in different media that share similarities. *Lenny* was Fosse's film biography of comedian Lenny Bruce, whose disgust at sexual taboos and political and religious hypocrisies pushed his routines into the area of social satire. *Chicago*, Fosse's "musical vaudeville," unfolded as a series of numbers that conjured popular entertainment acts of the 1920s. Its story of jazz era killers who seek show business celebrity through murder and manipulation of the media was clearly meant to echo the present. Fosse shared co-librettist credit with Fred Ebb on *Chicago*, but the critical response to the original 1975 production focused on Fosse's staging concepts as the dominant production element.

Perhaps inevitably, Fosse dismissed all collaborators on *Dancin'*, an evening of numbers performed to preexisting music from a variety of composers, which is covered in chapter 9. Untethered to a narrative, Fosse was free to create dances around his favorite music, which included classical, swing, rock, and pop. *Dancin'* had moments of startling eroticism, and his ability to sculpt stage pictures with bodies, space, and light was unmatched. But there were also cringe-inducing attempts at comedy and moments of maudlin sentimentality. During the 1970s Fosse's choreographic style moved from traditional musical comedy with touches of antic vaudeville stylings to a more lyrical, self-serious approach that he could not always support. Perhaps to compensate for what he himself admitted was a narrow choreographic vocabulary, his choreography began to take on a self-conscious quality. A sameness crept into much of his work, with similar steps, patterns, and groupings carried over from one show or film to another. Choreographing for character seemed no longer important, and all his dancers appeared to be performing the role of Bob Fosse. It was an iconic style, but one that no longer surprised.

Fosse concluded the decade with his most ambitious film, the nakedly auto-biographical *All That Jazz*, examined in chapter 10. Here Fosse took the movie musical further than anyone had dared—not only in subject matter but also in structure and pacing. Fosse tells this "putting on a show" musical in nonlinear fashion, with surprising juxtapositions, fragments, and time leaps.

When Fosse was working with the cast of *Little Me* in early 1982, no one could have known that his career had already peaked. During the previous decade, his successes led to greater control over his projects, and he now took on for-mal authorship responsibilities. Bob Fosse had achieved that greatest emblem of success: autonomy. But the 1980s would prove to be a fallow period for him, with none of his work connecting with audiences or critics. The era of large-scale, pageant-like British musicals arrived shortly, prioritizing special effects over dance and not requiring the services of a director-choreographer who conceived his shows in terms of movement. Onscreen, blockbusters, sequels, and fantasy films were the popular hits of the decade.

These trends did not serve Fosse well. *Star 80*, his 1983 film about the death of *Playboy* Playmate Dorothy Stratten, which he wrote and directed, was a fail-ure both critically and commercially. Its subject matter was grisly, and Fosse's straightforward presentation of the story offered no resolutions or bromides. When he made his belated return to Broadway in 1986, it was with *Big Deal*, his own adaptation of the Italian film *Big Deal on Madonna Street* (1958). Written, directed, and choreographed by Fosse, with a score made up of standards from the 1930s, *Big Deal* was the purest distillation of his theatrical vision. But its slight story was at odds with the dark, abstract set Fosse demanded, and it suf-fered from a shortage of showstopping dances. *Big Deal* closed after only seventy performances, the first Bob Fosse show to fail on Broadway. Now that he had achieved complete control, Fosse appeared to have lost his sense of timing; for once, he seemed out of step with current trends. These two late-career projects are covered in chapter 11.

When Bob Fosse died in 1987, his influence on a new generation was already being felt, and the concluding chapter traces that influence into the twenty-first century. With the opening sequence of *All That Jazz*, Fosse virtually created the modern MTV music video. His use of editing to fracture time and tell stories in a nonlinear manner has been much imitated by other filmmakers. *Chicago*, revived on Broadway in 1996 and choreographed "in the style of Bob Fosse," is now the longest-running American musical in Broadway history and an international hit. More than forty years after its original production, it is recognized as the quintessential Fosse show.

Chicago's success prompted the creation of *Fosse*, a 1999 Broadway retrospective that further established the Fosse brand. *Fosse* followed *Jerome Robbins' Broadway* (1989), a similar career overview of the work of Fosse's one-time mentor. While Robbins's retrospective featured fully staged scenes, songs, and choreography from his musicals, *Fosse* concentrated solely on his dances, divorced from their shows' narratives. The contrast between the two tributes underscores the differences that defined the careers of these two musical theater visionaries. The strong-willed Robbins provided choreography and direction tailored to the specific demands of each project. The equally strong-willed Fosse imposed his own particular style, dance language, and vision on his projects. The uses to which they put "the Muscle" illustrate two very distinct approaches to the role of director-choreographer as it developed over the previous half-century.

THE MUSCLE: THE RISE OF THE DIRECTOR-CHOREOGRAPHER

The director-choreographer is recognized today as that individual whose overall artistic vision is responsible for melding the various elements of a musical, including songs, scenes, dances, and design elements, into a theatrically satisfying entity. He or she is often the most celebrated member of the creative team, overshadowing the contributions of the composer, lyricist, or book writer. ("The New Bob Fosse Musical" was the only descriptor deemed necessary for promoting *Big Deal* in 1986.) While the designation is relatively new, its roots can be traced back more than a century, to when work assignments for Broadway musicals were strictly segregated. Directors worked exclusively with the actors, creating blocking and shaping performances. Choreographers, or dance directors, as they were then called, worked separately with an all-dancing, no-talking, no-singing chorus line whose dancing was largely ornamental and mostly formulaic, built from a limited repertory of steps assembled to garner maximum applause.[3]

Among the important dance directors of the early twentieth century was Ned Wayburn (1874–1942), a Chicagoan with a background in architecture and mechanical drawing who choreographed and arranged dancers onstage with draftsman-like precision. Wayburn established a school that trained dancers in a mathematically organized set of five basic types of stage dancing: tap and step dancing, acrobatic dancing, exhibition (or ballroom) dancing, modern Americanized ballet dancing, and musical comedy dancing.[4] In describing the latter category, Wayburn defined a surprisingly contemporary polyglot of dance styles and musical tempos that remain relevant today, including ballet, tap, soft shoe, and every sort of ethnic dance.

Wayburn brought this same structured approach to the creation of the dance routine, assigning it a proscribed set of steps in exact sequence designed to elicit the greatest audience response.[5] He staged vaudeville acts and revues for Florenz Ziegfeld (and created the fabled "Ziegfeld Walk" for showgirls negotiating stair-cases while wearing large hats and costumes), gave Fred Astaire his first tap danc-ing lessons, and worked in films, radio, and early television.[6] Wayburn was an early hyphenate—a director-choreographer who expanded his range beyond dance and theater into other media, predating by half a century Bob Fosse's career path.

Wayburn had a British counterpart in John Tiller (1854–1925), whose dance training school turned out a steady supply of "Tiller Girls," lineups of between eight and sixteen dancers whose precision kicks and marching steps gained immense popularity when they were imported to the United States. Their direct descendants today include Broadway chorus lines, the Radio City Music Hall Rockettes, and the tightly drilled unison moves of contemporary hip-hop dance groups. (In *Cabaret*, Bob Fosse linked this military-style precision to Nazism in the explicitly titled "Tiller Girls" number.)

An early prototype for the choreographer-director is the now-forgotten Julian Mitchell (1854–1926), who started his career as a dancer. Mitchell was adept at drawing together the work of set, costume, and lighting designers into elabo-rate, large-scale spectacles like *The Wizard of Oz* (1903) and Victor Herbert's *Babes in Toyland* (1903). Perhaps his greatest contribution to musicals was his creation of the "production number," in which he broke up Tiller's rigid formations into expressive groupings and allowed the dancers to exhibit their personalities.[7]

Seymour Felix (1892–1961) was one of the earliest dance directors to attempt a unification of his work with that of the creators of such shows as Richard Rodgers and Lorenz Hart's *Peggy-Ann* (1926) and *Simple Simon* (1930); Vincent Youmans, Clifford Grey, and Leo Robin's *Hit the Deck* (1927); and Walter Donaldson and Gus Kahn's *Whoopee!* (1928).[8] Well-versed in the full range of high kicks, acrobatics, and "hot" dancing that made up the dance director's repertoire, Felix neverthe-less declared during preparations for *Whoopee!* that these time-worn devices had lost their novelty, and "the important thing today is the so-called 'book num-ber.'"[9] His efforts to realistically integrate dancers into the dramatic intent of a number and engage them in singing and acting marked a small but important step in the development of the director-choreographer.

Jerome Kern and Oscar Hammerstein II's *Show Boat* (1927) is not considered a major dance show, but its show business setting and time span from the 1880s to the 1920s allowed popular choreographer Sammy Lee (1890–1968) to fill it with a wide variety of social and musical comedy dances, from tap to hornpipe, cakewalk to cancan, waltz to burlesque "cooch," and right up to the then-current Charleston.[10] *Show Boat* became the first musical to present controversial subject matter such as miscegenation, alcoholism, and marital abandonment. Theater his-torian Ethan Mordden later wrote, "The breakthrough in choreography obviously depended on a breakthrough in composition . . . as Sammy Lee was so hemmed in by Kern and Hammerstein's conceptual planning that he had no choice but to help them tell the story."[11] The presence and importance of black characters in *Show Boat* offered Lee opportunities to incorporate black social dances into his staging. The joyous shuffle performed by the dockworkers during "Can't Help Lovin' Dat Man" developed naturally out of the moment and engaged historically accurate movement. Lee provided a glimpse of the ways in which choreography could contribute to the integrated musicals to come.[12]

Russian-born George Balanchine (1904–1983), widely acknowledged as the greatest ballet choreographer of the twentieth century, brought several advances to the Broadway musical beginning with Rodgers and Hart's *On Your Toes* (1936). Built around the personalities and intrigues of a touring Russian ballet troupe and a young vaudeville hoofer-turned-composer who creates a new American-style ballet, *On Your Toes* was steeped in dance. The leading role of the troupe's prima ballerina was played by ballet star Tamara Geva, and the show's choreographic demands required that its chorus be filled with classically trained dancers. With *On Your Toes*, Balanchine not only developed the musical's talent pool and introduced dance as a key element in a musical's production, but his demand for credit as "choreographer" over "dance director" forever changed the billing and status of dance creators.

In his next show, Rodgers and Hart's *Babes in Arms* (1937), Balanchine introduced what quickly became known as the "dream ballet" and made it a recognized and valid storytelling device. He became the first choreographer to earn the credit "Entire Production Staged by . . ." for Vernon Duke and John LaTouche's *Cabin in the Sky* (1940), though direction of the book scenes was credited to the show's co-producer, Albert Lewis, and most of the choreography was supplied by Katherine Dunham, one of the show's stars.

Balanchine choreographed more than a dozen musicals during a fifteen-year period as he continued his work in classical ballet. He was not one of the great innovators of Broadway dance. He never truly pushed his choreography to further the narrative but was content for it to keep a genteel distance, and he relied on additional choreographers for many nonballet dance sequences. It was the era of supremacy for composers and lyricists, and his work was always in service to, not in competition with, scores by Rodgers and Hart, Irving Berlin, and others. Nevertheless, Balanchine's influence was immense, and he prepared the stage for the innovations of others.

In *Oklahoma!* (1943), the dances by Agnes de Mille (1905–1993) emerged organically from the narrative, defining character and advancing plot, and mixed ballet and modern dance movements with tap and "character" steps right out of Ned Wayburn's instruction book. It was a new and instantly identifiable movement vocabulary that captured the humor and earthiness of the American West and flowed naturally out of stage movement and blocking. De Mille's choreography proved to be as integral to the telling of this story of love and courtship in the Oklahoma Territory as the contributions of its composer, Richard Rodgers; its lyricist and librettist, Oscar Hammerstein II; and its director, Rouben Mamoulian.[13]

In the act 1 dream ballet, de Mille's staging injected dramatic tension and sexual conflict into its narrative. Laurey dreams that she marries Curly, her good-natured cowboy suitor, who is then killed by Jud, her menacing farmhand, who claims Laurey for himself. The suggestive postcard girls on Jud's wall come to life and mock Laurey, who is both repulsed and excited by Jud and the world of sensuality he represents. De Mille's use of symbolism and psychological inquiry made "Laurey Makes Up Her Mind" unlike any dream ballet created for a Broadway musical. She deepened and developed this template in her later shows and made the dream ballet a site for characters to examine their subconscious feelings through dance and pantomime.[14]

From the beginning of her career, de Mille approached choreography from a dramatist's viewpoint. As she later recalled, "My pieces were not properly dances at all. They were realistic character sketches, dramatic rather than choreographic in form."[15] This dance playwriting approach required that her dancers not only be superb technicians with vivid stage personalities but also bring to their work the rigor and intellect of an actor. De Mille even established a class called "Acting for Dancers" in which she led her students through a series of sensory exercises to enable them to convey character and emotion through movement.[16]

De Mille scholar Kara Anne Gardner describes the choreographer filling her dances with secondary characters "created in movement rather than dialogue."[17] These characters serve to connect the dances and establish a sense of community, and require dancers capable of making distinct impressions in small moments, both comedic and dramatic, throughout the show. It is unsurprising that many of the *Oklahoma!* dancers established important careers based on their work with de Mille. Most notably, Joan McCracken, featured as the Girl Who Falls Down in *Oklahoma!*'s "Many a New Day" ballet, went on to starring roles on Broadway in both musicals and plays and would prove an important figure in Bob Fosse's life and career.

Following the spectacular success of *Oklahoma!*, de Mille applied the same dance playwriting approach to her ballets for Kurt Weill and Ogden Nash's *One Touch of Venus* (1943), Harold Arlen and E. Y. Harburg's *Bloomer Girl* (1944), Rodgers and Hammerstein's *Carousel* (1945), and particularly Alan Jay Lerner and Frederick Loewe's *Brigadoon* (1947), which so thoroughly integrated dance into its storytelling that it is difficult to revive without her original staging. She had flexed "the Muscle" to the extent that she had elevated the choreographer to a comparable position alongside composers, lyricists, and librettists.

Rodgers and Hammerstein entrusted de Mille with the overall direction of *Allegro* (1947). *Allegro* marked the first original project for the team, an allegorical story of a boy from the country who becomes a doctor and, upon moving to the city, grows disenchanted with his life administering to the rich and frivolous. Eventually he returns home to embrace the values of his community. *Allegro* was written and staged as a metaphor for contemporary life and featured a Greek chorus in addition to separate dancing and singing ensembles. De Mille worked closely with set and lighting designer Jo Mielziner to create a seamless blend of dance and musical staging using platforms, treadmills, and drapes. *Allegro* was both a commercial and a critical disappointment, but with it de Mille opened the door for a generation of director-choreographers.

Mark N. Grant writes, "De Mille was the first to draw dance and subtext together so that dance itself was a parallel form of playwriting that fused with blocking and conarrated the book with the music and lyrics. Jerome Robbins (1918–1998) was the second."[18] No one did more to seamlessly meld dance into all elements of production than Robbins, whose story ballet *Fancy Free* (1944) served as the blueprint for his first musical, *On the Town* (1944), with music by Leonard Bernstein, book and lyrics by Betty Comden and Adolph Green, and direction by George Abbott. With his very first show and at the age of twenty-six, Robbins was more than just a choreographer for hire.[19] He would become the most celebrated director-choreographer of his time, everyone's first choice for a new show and the most sought-after "show doctor" for a troubled musical.

George Abbott, the most prolific and practical of directors, had supervised many musicals with dances contributed by important choreographers, including Balanchine (*The Boys from Syracuse* [1938] and *Where's Charley?* [1948]) and Robert Alton (1906–1957; *Too Many Girls* [1939] and *Pal Joey* [1940]), but their work represented a subservient, albeit important, element. Robbins went on to choreograph several Abbott productions while simultaneously creating ballet works, and he learned quickly from the older man about clarity of plotting (Abbott also wrote or contributed to the books of many of his musicals), pacing, and the imperative to cut any song, scene, or dance—regardless of its quality—that slowed a show's momentum. During this period Robbins studied at the Actors Studio and drew on Konstantin Stanislavsky's methods to push dancers to explore and understand the emotional lives of their characters in both his Broadway and his ballet work. Robbins had experienced this working method himself in the ballets he danced for choreographer Anthony Tudor at Ballet Theatre.

Robbins originated the idea for *Look Ma, I'm Dancin'* (1948), like *On Your Toes*, set in the ballet world. He was responsible for bringing onto the project composer and lyricist Hugh Martin and a new playwriting team, Jerome Lawrence and Robert E. Lee, to write the libretto.[20] Robbins choreographed and was also listed as co-director with George Abbott. *Look Ma, I'm Dancin'* not only had the distinction of being the first musical to bill one person as conceiver, choreographer, and director but also was the first instance of a choreographer being credited with a show's conception.

It was with *West Side Story* (1957) that Robbins developed the template for overall supervision of a musical. He conceived the idea for the show: an update of Shakespeare's *Romeo and Juliet* set in New York City. Reflecting the influx of Puerto Rican immigrants settling on New York City's West Side and an outbreak of gang violence across the United States, the story centered on the rivalries between teenage street gangs of Puerto Ricans (the Sharks) and Americans (the Jets). Again Robbins brought together the collaborators: Leonard Bernstein to compose the music, Arthur Laurents, who had never written the libretto for a musical, and finally a twenty-seven-year-old Stephen Sondheim to contribute lyrics.

Under Robbins's leadership, they would create a musical that broke ground in several ways. The violence and racial intolerance would be realistically conveyed, and as in Shakespeare, there would be no happy ending. The story would be told primarily through music and dance rather than dialogue. (According to Laurents, *West Side Story* has the shortest libretto ever for a musical.)[21] Robbins's young cast was made up of dancers required to also sing and act, a startling approach at a time when a strict separation existed between the dancing ensemble, the singing chorus, and the actors.

West Side Story opened on September 26, 1957, with Robbins's name listed twice in the program, first directly under the title ("Based on a conception of Jerome Robbins") and then set apart from the other collaborators in a box, making it easily the most prominent name on the page:

Entire Production Directed and Choreographed by
JEROME ROBBINS

Robbins eliminated the traditional overture and opening vocal number. Instead, he devoted the first ten minutes to a danced prologue that established the enmity between the two gangs and introduced the show's overall movement scheme, which shifted effortlessly from stage blocking to dance and back again. Writing about its 1980 Broadway revival, again directed by Robbins, Frank Rich in the *New York Times* marveled at Robbins's "ability to set almost the entire evening to dance movement,"[22] as in the moment when Maria dons her new dress for the dance and begins to spin in happy anticipation. "Her friends start to spin with her, streamers fall from above, the set changes (without us really registering it) and suddenly we have joined the entire company in the midst of a big number, 'The Dance at the Gym.' It's all happened as fluidly and gracefully as a movie dissolve, with none of the awkward transitional dialogue that usually pockmarked pre-Robbins musicals."[23] *West Side Story* proved decisively that it was a choreographer who could most effectively harness a musical's various elements into an integrated whole and even overshadow the contributions of talented collaborators.

West Side Story was not the only hit musical directed and choreographed by one person playing on Broadway in 1957. Michael Kidd (1915–2007), who danced with Robbins in Ballet Theatre, was the director-choreographer of *Li'l Abner* (1956), based on the popular Al Capp comic strip, which had opened a year earlier. Kidd was a successful and sought-after choreographer, and the satiric athleticism of his dances for *Finian's Rainbow* (1947), *Guys and Dolls* (1950), and *Can-Can* (1953) contributed greatly to their success. Kidd's *Li'l Abner* dances exhibited a muscularity and kinetic energy that propelled the entire show, but they were mostly set pieces that sat alongside a straightforward libretto. Dance critic John Martin contrasted the difference in achievement between the two shows when he wrote, "Robbins has bent Broadway practice to his choreographic will whereas with Kidd the opposite is true."[24]

"I had a vision of theater from which other people went on," Robbins reflected in 1981.[25] That vision was one in which a single individual used movement to align all elements of a musical into an integrated and cohesive entity. It had been slowly coming into focus for more than half a century when *West Side Story* arrived: from Ned Wayburn's codified dance routines and Julian Mitchell's scenic effects and production numbers to Seymour Felix's and Sammy Lee's early attempts at dance integration with narrative; from George Balanchine's introduction of ballet into the structure of musicals and the corresponding requirement for classically trained dancers to Agnes de Mille's danced psychological scenarios that embedded choreography into the composition of musicals. From these antecedents, Robbins built and refined the role of director-choreographer, strengthening "the Muscle" and readying it for a new generation of artists, of whom Bob Fosse would be one of the most assertive and authoritative.

BOY DANCER

• • •

"The show curtain . . . it's my deepest memory of those days in Chicago—
standing, waiting—next to the curtain."

Bob Fosse, 1974[1]

In *All That Jazz*, the teenage Joe Gideon sits backstage in a ramshackle burlesque
theater studying Latin while awaiting the cue to perform his "Tops in Taps" dance
act between the strippers and comics. When the strippers realize just how young
Joe is—that he is in fact a minor—they taunt him mercilessly, rubbing up against
him and forcing his face into their naked breasts. When his cue finally arrives, he
runs onto the stage with the evidence of their provocations obvious to everyone
in the audience. The camera pulls back to show the semen stain on his white trousers, while the audience's cruel laughter mocks and shames him. The sequence is
drawn directly from the experiences of young Bob Fosse during the years he led
a dual existence as a model high school student, popular with his peers and the
pride of his family, while working late nights dancing in burlesque houses in and
around his native Chicago.

Fosse's use of his life as primary source material for his art was a hallmark of
his career. Anecdotes, vignettes, past performances, and chance encounters from
his life repeatedly showed up in his work, but none with more frequency than
his experiences as an underage dancer in second-rate nightclubs and burlesque
theaters in the era leading up to and during World War II.

Fosse came naturally to show business ("I was a home-made talent, just like my
father"),[2] and unlike in many families, he was encouraged to pursue a performing
career. Sadie, his mother, had been a supernumerary in operas. His father, Cyril,
had been a song plugger for music publishers before forming a vaudeville act with
his brother Richard and two other men. The act eventually broke up, and Richard
later died of cancer at the age of twenty-six.[3] Cyril soon left performing, but as
Fosse remembered, "My dad, I think, kind of romanticized about me taking his
place. He was always very anxious and hopeful that I'd be in show business."[4]
Cyril found work as a salesman and eventually went on the road selling Hershey's
chocolates, a job that kept him away from home for long periods of time. Despite
his father's show business past, Fosse would later characterize Cyril as "closer to
Willie Loman than he was to George M. Cohan."[5]

The name Fosse means "the farm by the waterfall," and it was a Norwegian farm that gave Bob Fosse's ancestors their surname, it being the custom of the time for tenants to adopt the name of the farm on which they lived. Born June 23, 1927, on the North Side of Chicago to the Norwegian Methodist Cyril and Irish Catholic Sadie, Fosse was the fifth of six children, and the youngest of four sons. Not only was he nine years younger than his next-oldest brother, but Fosse, who had asthma as a child, would always be smaller and slighter than the others—the little brother in every way. He was given the name Robert Louis, possibly after Robert Louis Stevenson.

In later years, Fosse spun several variations on the story of how he first began taking dancing lessons at the age of nine, always underscoring that his interest in girls led him to class: "I used to hang around with my older sister, mostly because she had two girlfriends and I had a crush on one of the girlfriends. They all decided they wanted to go to dancing school . . . . I said I'm going to dancing school. In three weeks, they quit and I stayed. I started with tap dancing and then studied ballet."[6] His dance lessons at the Chicago Academy of Theater Arts were encouraged by his parents, and the school offered additional benefits. The academy was run by Frederic Weaver, a former vaudevillian who brought in fellow performers for special instruction. As Fosse later recalled, "We'd get clowns from the circus who would teach us tumbling, we'd get old repertory Shakespearean actors who would teach us makeup. It was a marvelous place."[7] Fosse's first performances were given at the academy's recitals and included tap, ballet, and comedy and vaudeville routines learned from Weaver.

By the time Fosse was thirteen, Weaver was acting as agent, manager, and talent booker for Fosse and Charles Grass, another student at the school, in a dance act called the Riff Brothers, named for the "riff," a tap movement combining a forward brush with the front of the foot and a scuff with the heel in rapid succession. Grass later described the four-number act Weaver designed for the two boys: a duet tap number to open, followed by tap solos for each boy (a ballet tap for Grass and an aggressive military-style tap for Fosse to "The Stars and Stripes Forever"). The finale was a "challenge" dance, with each boy executing increasingly difficult steps to which the other responded.[8] The boys performed in white tie and tails, with a costume change to white dinner jackets. The grown-up formality of their attire and the precision of their dancing contrasted strikingly with their extreme youth.

The Riff Brothers's early performances were at lodges, USO shows, and church socials and as featured entertainers in the academy's regular talent showcases (including a performance known as "Bobby Fosse's La Petite Cafe").[9] Their first night as professionals found the two boys racing from theater to theater, finally ending at a beer garden, and splitting sixteen dollars for the night.[10] Many such evenings were spent performing in nightclubs (where the boys lied about their ages or waited outside for their turn to perform), on radio, and as "plants" in amateur contests, in which they were booked to give a professional sheen to the proceedings. Many of their engagements included performances at presentation houses, which featured live acts between film screenings.

"So you're the act that's supposed to keep the cops out. Boy, you must be lousy!" a weary stage manager surmises of the vaudeville act "Rose Louise and Her Hollywood Blondes," booked into a burlesque house in the musical *Gypsy*.[11] That musical's depiction of both the twilight of vaudeville and burlesque's transition to coarse comics and strip acts had been playing out across the United States for some time and represented a particular kind of paid performing opportunity for Fosse and Grass. Burlesque emerged in the nineteenth century as a rollicking form of popular entertainment that included sketches and parodies mocking the rich and aristocratic, songs and dances, circus acts, and elaborate stage effects. With its appeal to a working-class audience, burlesque coexisted alongside vaudeville, whose variety of self-contained music, comedy, and novelty acts generally played to middle-class crowds.

The Chicago World's Fair of 1893 introduced "cooch" or "hootchy cooch" dancing in the person of Little Egypt, who undulated her stomach and shook her hips in time to the music's ragtime rhythms while exposing her midriff. Her *danse du ventre*, or belly dancing act, caused a sensation and made Little Egypt, according to burlesque historian Rachel Shteir, "the putative grandmother of modern striptease."[12] Gradually "cooch" dancing became integrated into burlesque shows, and the display of female bodies took on increased prominence. Family audiences turned exclusively to vaudeville, leaving burlesque as a male-only entertainment.

The Riff Brothers, who were frequently the only "legit" act on a burlesque bill, worked hard, creating new numbers and polishing their act. The black dance acts Fosse saw in Chicago vaudeville houses began to influence him. He loved the jump splits that sent the Nicholas Brothers, Slip, Slap, and Slide, and the Step Brothers leaping off pianos and platforms onto the floor. Fosse later recalled, "They were all over the stage, and I liked that kind of energy that they had."[13] He began to add steps from these acts into the routines he and Grass performed. It was in the rehearsal room where Fosse's perfectionism was unleashed that his lifelong attachment to cigarettes began: "Ever since I was young, cigarettes were identified with work."[14] It was rare to see a photograph of Fosse in rehearsal in later years without a cigarette in his mouth, and he came up with countless ingenious ways to incorporate them into his dances.

It is unlikely that burlesque audiences were appreciative of the Riff Brothers' precision tap skills or viewed them as anything but an interruption to the lineup of strippers. An advertisement for the Gayety Village gives a glimpse of one such engagement. The Riff Brothers are billed fourth, below three headline strippers. "4 Gay Shows Nightly" are promised, with the first show starting at 9:30 p.m.[15] This meant that the boys would finish their performances well after midnight, as Fosse confirmed much later: "I used to work until 3:30 or 4 o'clock in the morning . . . . Then I'd come home and get a few hours sleep, do an hour's worth of homework, and go to school. I'd come home from school, do a little homework, and go to sleep until it was time to go to the night club."[16]

It was during this time that Fosse received his first credit as a choreographer. *Hold Ev'rything! A Streamlined Extravaganza in Two Parts*, presented by Frederic Weaver's Academy of Theatre Arts at a local high school, featured Fosse choreography for a fan dance to the recent hit song "That Old Black Magic," by Harold

Arlen and Johnny Mercer. Rehearsal photographs show the earnest young choreographer intently directing a group of girls in a series of synchronized movements with large ostrich plume fans. It was a motif that Fosse would return to with regularity in his later career in numbers like "All I Care About" for *Chicago* and "Who's Sorry Now?" in *All That Jazz*. Its obvious reference is to Sally Rand, the celebrated fan dancer of the 1930s, but with the fan dance's illusion of peek-a-boo nudity it also conjures images of the burlesque strippers he and Grass watched from the wings.

The Riff Brothers continued to perform as a team, but Fosse also began doing a solo act, sometimes billed as Bobby Riff ("Dancer Par Excellence—Offers Ultra-Modern Tap Modes").[17] Increasingly, nightclubs and strip clubs were the bulk of his bookings, and they took him beyond Chicago on a "wheel," or circuit, that included St. Louis, Peoria, Springfield, and Minneapolis. He later described his act as "straight dancing with jokes."[18] Fosse soon found himself introducing the acts: "I was in a place called the Cuban Village in Chicago when the comic got drunk or drafted, I forget which, and they made me the emcee. I was billed as 'The Youngest Emcee in Chicago.'"[19]

Chicago's "Youngest Emcee" managed to be a model student at the same time he was sharing the stage with burlesque strippers. While he dated several girls at Amundsen High School and maintained a busy schedule of athletics and school activities, he kept his show business experiences mostly to himself.

"That Old Black Magic": Fourteen-year-old Bob Fosse choreographs his first fan dance, a motif he would return to years later. Library of Congress, Performing Arts Reading Room.

During this period Fosse often led an itinerant life, traveling alone to out-of-town bookings in shoddy surroundings, and while he could boast of his travels, his feelings were deeply conflicted, as he later remembered: "I can romanticize it, but it was an awful life . . . . I was very lonely, very scared. You know, hotel rooms in strange towns, and I was all alone, 13 or 14, too shy to talk to anyone, not really knowing what it was all about, and among—not the best people. That's not romantic."[20]

His parents, he recalled, were confident that their straight A–earning, churchgoing son would not be influenced by his surroundings: "My mother misunderstood. She thought you could send a boy of that age into a roomful of naked women and it wouldn't bother him—because he was such a good boy. Obviously, she was wrong."[21] Photographs of Fosse during this period show a good-looking, blond and blue-eyed young man with a dancer's lithe figure, one who appears never to have gone through an awkward or gangly period. At fifteen, a terrified Fosse was named as a co-respondent in a divorce case based on an affair with an older, married waitress during an engagement in Springfield. (He later admitted, "As I got older, it made a good story.")[22]

While his later work could display touches of sentiment and pathos, it was the triangulation of vaudeville, burlesque, and nightclubs that formed the basis of Fosse's aesthetic DNA. Traces of the venues and performances of his youth in Chicago show up in "Hernando's Hideaway," the Fandango Ballroom, the Kit Kat Klub, the basement jazz clubs of *Lenny*, and *Star 80*'s wet T-shirt contests. The performing women, including those who seduced him, were refracted through Lola, Anna Christie, Charity Hope Valentine, Sally Bowles, Dorothy Stratten, and others. Three decades later, Fosse would reflect on both the negative and positive aspects of his performing experiences: "I think it's done me a lot of harm, being exposed to things that early that I shouldn't have been exposed to . . . . The good part is that I learned a lot about show business, particularly about that background. I mean, I really know seedy show business very well."[23]

Fosse was an early and fervent fan of Fred Astaire and later spoke of dancing all the way home after sitting through repeat showings of Astaire's films. Fosse was equally influenced by the work of Paul Draper, the pioneering dancer who created a unique ballet-tap style of dance, often performed to classical music. Draper lifted tap from the more common bent-knee, into-the-floor style, and brought the elevated upper body of ballet to his performances. Fosse later described seeing Draper for the first time when he was fifteen years old: "I think Paul was probably the most elegant performer that I had ever seen . . . . For me, he created a kind of magic . . . a kind of enchantment that stuck in my head for a long, long time."[24] Photographs of the young Fosse in performance display him in poses emulating Astaire's top hat and tails elegance, with Draper's uplifted torso and easy, graceful arm movements.

Fosse graduated from high school with a sizable resume of professional experiences. He had performed in theaters, nightclubs, and burlesque houses before wide-ranging audiences. He had created choreography for both himself and

Teenage Bob Fosse emulating the elegant, pulled-up stance of Paul Draper and Fred Astaire. The microphone poised near his feet indicates a radio performance. Library of Congress, Performing Arts Reading Room.

others. He had traveled and interacted professionally with booking agents, musicians, and managers. He had exercised the discipline necessary to juggle school and work responsibilities. And he was not yet eighteen years old.

"I think of dancing as sheer joy. As exhilaration. As running, as jumping, as athletic. Like a trapeze artist."

Bob Fosse, 1962[25]

Fosse entered the Navy on June 20, 1945, directly after high school graduation. Boot camp coincided with VJ day and the winding down of the war. Fosse was placed in an entertainment unit and sent to New York City to rehearse an all-Navy revue called *Hook, Line, and Sinker*.

The thirteen-man cast shipped off on October 31 to entertain troops stationed across the Pacific, awaiting their final release from service. A Navy press release described the show as an "all-sailor, all-star entertainment combine" with "ex-stars of stage, radio, screen, and nite clubs" and Seaman First Class Robert Louis Fosse as "another pink-cheeked prodigy, [whose] terpischorean [*sic*] endeavors in pre-Navy theatres, hotels, and nite spots have assured him a high place amongst the top dancers of the future."[26] Photographs of *Hook, Line, and Sinker* show a bare-bones production with skits and musical numbers taking off on current popular performers like bandleader Kay Kyser and the Andrews Sisters (a drag routine with Fosse in a brown wig) and pie-in-the-face slapstick. Fosse is prominent, most notably dancing a toreador tap number with flying leaps. With his hat tilted at a rakish angle, and looking trim and athletic in navy whites, he could be Gene Kelly's little brother and is clearly the center of attention.

Fosse mustered out of the Navy on August 9, 1946, in Lido Beach, New York, having spent a total of fourteen months in the service. His performing talents and the happy circumstance of the war's conclusion saved him from seeing active combat like his older brothers. He immediately moved into a YMCA in Manhattan and began auditioning for work. Within a month, Fosse had his first job, as a featured dancer in the ensemble cast of the national tour of *Call Me Mister* for a weekly salary of $150.[27] Composer-lyricist Harold Rome's musical revue centered on the topical issue of returning servicemen adjusting to civilian life. When it opened on Broadway in April 1946, it proved a popular hit and eventually ran a total of 734 performances. Fosse was one of numerous veterans in the touring cast, including Carl Reiner, Buddy Hackett, and William Warfield.

Among Fosse's featured dance moments was a number with effervescent, brown-haired Marion Niles. Like Fosse, Niles had started her career as a child performer, tap dancing on the *Horn & Hardart Children's Hour* radio show. She later performed in nightclubs and before joining the *Call Me Mister* road company had made her Broadway debut in the short-lived *The Girl from Nantucket*. As the tour moved west from its premiere in New Haven, a romance developed, and by the time they arrived in Chicago for a summer stint at the Blackstone Theater, the couple was engaged and Fosse had taken Niles home to introduce her to his family. A reception on the Blackstone stage followed their wedding on August 1, 1947. Niles was twenty-four and Fosse twenty. She would be the first of three Fosse wives who all shared remarkable similarities. Each was older than Fosse, each was a dancer, each was more established in show business at the time they met, and each would play a significant role in his career development.

When the Chicago critics issued their selections for outstanding productions and performances during the 1946–1947 season, Fosse and Carl Reiner were listed among the "Most Talented Young Actors and Actresses" for *Call Me Mister*, with Fosse receiving a backhanded citation as "a tap dancer who reminds you of Paul Draper and is almost as good."[28] Fosse and Niles were most frequently reviewed in tandem, as "a dance team not to be missed."[29] They danced well together and soon began working out routines for a duo act. After the show closed in San Francisco, they returned to New York and began looking for bookings. With Fosse choreographing their routines, they developed an act in the style of Marge and Gower Champion, the popular husband-and-wife team who had established a lighter, less formal style than earlier ballroom dance acts, featuring short narrative dances alongside more traditional ballroom routines.[30] So celebrated were the Champions that Fosse would self-deprecatingly introduce himself and Niles with, "You've heard of the Champions? Well, we're the runners-up."[31] Niles later recalled their act as "second-hand Marge and Gower Champion but with more tap."[32]

"Fosse and Niles" found bookings in the hotel ballroom market, from Montreal to Miami Beach and in New York, on bills shared with vocalists, comedians, and showroom orchestras. The act encompassed an opening tap dance to "Crazy Rhythm," a routine called "Showoff" in which Fosse would sing while Niles danced around him, and a salute to vaudeville performers. The most distinctive moment was "Limehouse Blues," developed by Fosse from one of Niles's solo tap dances. She later described Fosse's staging: "He put drums in it and we did Oriental, East Indian kind of stuff . . . . The lights would go down and here we were in tap shoes doing a shimmy and our heads would go side to side and doing the arms and then we would go back into tap."[33]

Niles's reference to the "Oriental, East Indian kind of stuff" acknowledges the impact of Jack Cole, the pioneering choreographer who blended East Indian, Balinese, and Afro-Caribbean dance techniques to American swing music to create a highly influential style known as jazz dance. At the time of Cole's death in 1974, Gwen Verdon, who had been a leading exponent of his dance style and served as his assistant for several years, remarked, "Jack influenced all the choreographers in the theater from Jerome Robbins, Michael Kidd, Bob Fosse down to Michael Bennett and Ron Field today . . . . When you see dancing on television, that's Jack Cole. In Paris, what they call 'le Jazz Hot' is all Jack Cole."[34]

Cole, who was as exotic-looking as his dances, was in fact born to a pharmacist and his wife in New Brunswick, New Jersey, in either 1911 or 1913.[35] He had a thorough grounding in modern dance through his training with Ruth St. Denis and Ted Shawn's Denishawn company, and he later performed with Shawn's all-male troupe. He also danced with the companies of Doris Humphrey and Charles Weidman before striking out on his own with nightclub appearances that became legendary. Patrons of high-end clubs like the Rainbow Room where Cole established a residency were startled and fascinated by Cole's "swingtime Oriental dance," as dance critic Walter Terry dubbed it.[36] While he absorbed the Asian motifs of St. Denis's work, Cole undertook serious study of Indian dance and incorporated classical Bharata Natyam techniques into his choreography. One of the oldest forms of dance, Bharata Natyam is based on the sculptures of Indian temples, with a codified set of movements emanating from a rigid, upright torso. As dance historian Constance Valis Hill writes, "Cole mastered the technique— the cobra head movements, undulating arms, subtle hip-shoulder isolations, precise 'mudra' hand gestures, and darting eye actions . . . . It was a powerful tool to rivet focus as well as to sexually titillate his audience."[37]

Cole was under contract to Columbia Pictures, where he established a stock company of dancers who took daily classes in a variety of dance techniques and danced in the films he choreographed for the studio. (These films were mostly routine, though he memorably created Rita Hayworth's one-black-glove strip-tease to "Put the Blame on Mame" in *Gilda*.) When that contract ended, Jack Cole and His Dancers returned to the nightclub circuit, introducing "Sing, Sing, Sing" to New York at the Latin Quarter in March 1947. To Benny Goodman's big band arrangement, Cole and three men danced his muscular hybrid of East Indian, African, and jitterbug styles with slides, sharp turns, isolations, leaps, punishing knee drops, and stealthy, catlike walks in deep plié.[38]

Fosse's "Limehouse Blues" looks nothing like the numbers he would become known for, but it offers intriguing traces of both his later work and Cole's influence. Fosse and Niles begin with a series of easy, synchronized tap steps done in unison. A brief partnering sequence features a frequent Fosse step: legs pushing off into an arabesque leap with arms exploding overhead. A tacit section (a sequence in which the music drops out) emphasizes the clarity of their tap sounds. Suddenly, the music goes into a jivey, jitterbug rhythm, and the pair responds with brief swing steps before adding the first glimpse of East Indian motifs, with arms extended and a rapidly vibrating mudra, or hand gesture. Tap steps resume, but now with angular arm and head movements as the pair adopts a rigid formality. With the dancers' palms flattened together above their heads and their necks isolated, their upper bodies remain still while they continue tapping.

Niles, in plié, positions herself in front of Fosse, and their movements simulate a multi-armed Indian statue. During a drum break, Niles executes a slow-motion sequence of arm and cobra head movements, remaining stationary while Fosse does much the same as he travels downstage in an impossibly wide plié. A short promenade in a prayerful pose leads into the final, high-energy sequence with more jumps and a knee slide for Fosse. One last promenade is broken by shrugged shoulders and a "Who, us?" expression, as if it has all been a put-on. Fosse and Niles assume a pose of comic formality suggesting the most aristocratic of East Indian couples as a fanfare concludes the number.[39]

There is little subtlety on display, but Fosse incorporates the East Indian movements seamlessly, introducing them gradually and using them to punctuate the rapid changes in focus and rhythm. Fosse and Niles dance together with precision, and Niles takes the athletic leaps and jumps in stride. The tightly woven, detailed movements danced to a heavily percussive musical accompaniment give a glimpse of Fosse's later choreography.

Variety was mildly encouraging in reviewing their twelve-minute act at the Hotel Pierre's Cotillion Room in New York: "Nice-looking pair with expert terps doing their ballet and taps to consistently okay results."[40] Niles's stage presence and prettiness were often the focus of attention for both audiences and critics, something that upset Fosse. "He wanted to be the personality, the star," Niles later shared with dancer Eileen Casey.[41]

The new medium of television provided additional opportunities for the team and gave them national exposure. By early 1949, Fosse and Mary Ann (who by now had changed her name from Marion) were back on the road in the touring company of *Make Mine Manhattan*, this time with featured billing. *Make Mine Manhattan*, which had opened on Broadway the year before, was another topical musical revue, this one based on rueful observations about life in New York City's most prominent borough.

Performance photographs of the first-act finale, "Saturday Night in Central Park," show Fosse and Mary Ann dancing a pas de deux with elegant, elongated upper-body placement reminiscent of Paul Draper and featuring arabesques, développés, and, most strikingly, Fosse's airborne stag leaps, which seem to suspend him in the air. The choreography was credited to Lee Sherman, but the leaps were pure Fosse, and he would continue to incorporate them into his choreography.[42]

Since appearing in the Broadway company of *Make Mine Manhattan*, Sid Caesar had become a television star on *The Admiral Broadway Revue*, an enormous hit in early 1949 that laid the foundation for the even more popular and influential comedy-variety series *Your Show of Shows* the following year. After their appearance on *The Admiral Broadway Revue*, Fosse and Niles were hired as one of the acts supporting Caesar in a run at the Empire Room of Chicago's Palmer Hotel. The booking was a vindication for Fosse. He was now playing the most prestigious nightspot in his hometown when only a few years earlier he had made the rounds of its shabbier nightclubs and burlesque houses. Fosse and Niles's reviews were consistently favorable, with an added air of tribute to the returning hometown boy.

More nightclub and television appearances followed, and by October, while playing at the Copley Plaza Hotel in Boston (where they were billed as "Dynamic and Original Dancers"), their credits were sufficient for Fosse and Niles to take out an ad in *Variety* touting their recent engagements in nightclubs, television, and musicals.[43] Soon after, producer Dwight Deere Wiman offered the team a spot in *Dance Me a Song*, a new musical revue planned for Broadway. Wiman had produced *The Little Show* in 1929, a smart, intimate musical revue that emphasized sophisticated wit over visual spectacle—a kind of anti–*Ziegfeld Follies*. *Dance Me*

Mary Ann Niles and Bob Fosse in "Saturday Night in Central Park" in the national tour of Make Mine Manhattan. *Library of Congress, Performing Arts Reading Room.*

a Song was an attempt to revisit the *Little Show* format of witty, urbane musical revue, with its title indicating that movement would figure prominently. To head the ensemble cast, Wiman hired dancer Joan McCracken, who had just acted in his production of Clifford Odets's *The Big Knife*.

> "Joan was the biggest influence in my life. She was the one who changed it and gave it direction."
>
> Bob Fosse, 1979[44]

In the "Many a New Day" ballet midway through act 1 of *Oklahoma!* the female dancers enact a gentle, sisterly series of lyrical movements around dressing, grooming, and gossiping. Joan McCracken performed the role of a young tomboy who disrupts the gentle routine through childlike mimicry and exuberant horseplay, punctuated by a series of comic falls, from which she rose with plucky resolve. The impact of her performance was stunning and immediate. From the moment *Oklahoma!* premiered on March 31, 1943, McCracken would always be known as "The Girl Who Falls Down."[45]

Born December 31, 1917, Joan McCracken began dancing lessons with tap and acrobatics at age seven, followed by formal ballet training at the Littlefield Ballet School in her native Philadelphia. Like Fosse's, McCracken's parents were entirely supportive of her desire for a dancing career. Her mother had earlier informed her high school that on her sixteenth birthday, McCracken would be legally eligible to drop out of school, which she did for an opportunity to go to New York and study with George Balanchine at his new School of American Ballet.

After Balanchine rejected the short and fleshy McCracken for a spot in his company, she danced briefly in the ballet ensemble at Radio City Music Hall before joining Eugene Loring's Dance Players. Loring's company focused on his dramatic story ballets, which required the dancers to create characterizations through movement—a true integration of dancing and acting. Michael Kidd, a member of Dance Players, remembered McCracken's distinctive quality: "If she had the slightest little part to do onstage your eye went right to her . . . . Her strong point was her dramatic ability, which I think was a reflection of her personal quality. She was always very expressive."[46]

For *Oklahoma!* Agnes de Mille sought dancers with vivid personalities, strong ballet technique, and acting ability, all of which McCracken had in abundance. She was cast in the dance ensemble with no solos until she was memorably spotlighted in the "Many a New Day" ballet. It was a true star-making moment, which is remarkable given that hers was essentially a chorus role. Having never uttered a word or sung a note onstage, McCracken was now in demand for musical comedy roles and soon appeared as the comedic maid in the Civil War–set *Bloomer Girl* (1944), again for de Mille. Next came the starring role of a Jazz Age gold-digger in the 1920s satire *Billion Dollar Baby* (1945), this time for choreographer Jerome Robbins and director George Abbott. While she never developed anything more than an adequate singing voice, McCracken's gifts for comedy and characterization were a perfect fit for the ballets de Mille and Robbins created for her.

Her biographer Lisa Jo Sagolla asserts that in these two roles McCracken established a new kind of musical comedy comedienne who conveyed character through dance rather than song, "a quirky yet exquisitely trained dancer who was amusingly sexy, childlike, and funny, rather that glamorous and steamy."[47] Sagolla points to other "Joan McCracken types" who followed, such as Carol Haney in *The Pajama Game* and Gwen Verdon in *Can-Can* and her many roles for Fosse.[48] Mary Ann Niles had a similar quality. Clearly, the sexy, dancing comedienne embodied by McCracken held a particular attraction for Fosse both onstage and in life.

McCracken danced in a few films in Hollywood but preferred New York, where she began studying at the Neighborhood Playhouse with Sanford Meisner and Herbert Berghof, determined to establish herself as an actress. McCracken, who was diabetic, was required to be vigilant about her diet and medication. In the days before reliable treatments were available, doctors had warned her that a dancing career would pose hazards to her health. In addition to expanding herself as an artist, a transition to acting roles would reduce her physical stress.

McCracken soon appeared in dramatic roles onstage in *The Big Knife* opposite John Garfield and with Charles Laughton in Bertolt Brecht's *Galileo*. (Gwen Verdon, seeing her in *Galileo*, marveled, "A dancer can act!")[49] She also starred in live television dramas and was a founding member of the Actors Studio. McCracken managed to accomplish what so many other dancers are unable to do, moving from the chorus to starring roles in musicals, and then on to dramatic acting roles. It was therefore curious that she returned to musical comedy with the uneven *Dance Me a Song*.

By the time *Dance Me a Song* finished its out-of-town tryouts in New Haven and Boston and moved on to New York, two things were clear. One, its chances of a long run and critical acceptance were slight (*Variety* referred to its "deadly letdowns," with sketches that ran "from soporific to so-so")[50] and two, the entire company was aware that a romance had developed between the star and one half of Fosse and Niles. As she celebrated her thirty-second birthday, McCracken, who was separated from her husband, dancer Paul Dunphy, plunged headlong into a passionate new affair with the twenty-two-year-old Fosse. With her ballet pedigree, her Broadway stardom, her acclaim as a serious actress, and her rarefied group of artist and writer friends, McCracken outclassed the hoydenish Mary Ann Niles in every way. Since the beginning of Fosse's marriage, he had made little effort to hide his sexual indiscretions. But they were nothing more than diversions. Now it was apparent to everyone that Fosse's interest in McCracken (and hers in him) was serious and that the marriage to Niles had run its course.

Bob Fosse made his Broadway debut on January 20, 1950, when *Dance Me a Song* opened at the Royale Theater. The out-of-town reviews were a preview of the show's reception by the New York critics, and it was gone after thirty-five performances. (Gwen Verdon later noted that *Dance Me a Song* was nicknamed around Broadway as *Drop Me a Bomb*.)[51]

Fosse was now left to negotiate a professional truce with Niles. Regardless of their marital status, they were still tethered to each other through their act. They continued their television appearances, becoming regulars on *Your Hit Parade*, where, as the Lucky Strike Dancers, Fosse created dances in a variety of styles around the week's most popular songs. In August and September 1950, Fosse made his first television solo appearances on *Toni Twins Time, Ford Star Revue,* and *The Jack Haley Show*.

Fosse and Niles were now a seasoned dance team, well regarded if not widely known and acclaimed. Their most high-profile appearances to date came after Dean Martin and Jerry Lewis invited them to appear on their *Colgate Comedy Hour* telecast from Chicago. Fosse and Niles were billed in the credits as choreographers for their old "Limehouse Blues" routine, here embellished with an opening dance ensemble to set the stage for the team's entrance. This was Fosse's first opportunity to choreograph for someone other than himself and his wife, and he drew steps directly from his and Niles's routine for small groupings of two or four.

Fosse and Niles became favorites of the comedy team and were invited back for additional appearances. Their television routines were highlighted by ambitious camerawork and unusual visual motifs. For "Steppin' Out with My Baby," the camera starts on Fosse's feet before pulling back to a full-body shot. Dissolves and changes of camera angles are used frequently. Close-ups of Fosse and another male dancer lighting cigarettes and exhaling smoke into the camera are used to segue from one section to another. For "Get Happy," the camera begins with a close up on a drum, which is then overlaid onto the screen to give the impression of the pair dancing on it. Close-ups of their vibrating hands dissolve to the ensemble's hands shooting out in rhythmic blasts. Pyrotechnics, reminiscent of Astaire's firecracker dance in *Holiday Inn* (1942), are used for visual punctuation.

The two numbers display remarkable similarities. Camera placements, including overhead and stage-level angles, give the numbers visual variety not seen in other dance numbers on the series. Acrobatics by individual chorus dancers are used as transitions. Niles appears as the point of a triangle of three female dancers, an early example of a favorite Fosse grouping. Whether the dancers are in evening wear or contemporary clothes, their dancing is clean and fast. Their repertoire of steps is now identifiable: aggressive tap combined with athletic leaps and jumps, and frequent knee work by Fosse. They were fond of a move in which Niles pirouettes and falls to a crouch so that Fosse can jump exuberantly over her with his legs tucked under him. Fosse had also discovered the rapid series of barrel turns that he would increasingly employ. Fosse used the step as punctuation to an energetic series of steps or as a dynamic finish. While he often dances with his head down as if in deep concentration, Niles plays the sassy soubrette, always sure of the camera's placement. "Steppin' Out with My Baby" shows Fosse aiming for Astaire's elegance, but "Get Happy" is closer to Gene Kelly at his most strenuous. (At number's end, the pair literally jumps into a hole in the floor.) The overwhelming impression these numbers convey is of Fosse trying to fit every step he knows into a single four-minute routine. The results are both exhilarating and exhausting.[52]

These performances marked the end of the professional partnership of Fosse and Niles. Fosse was now living with Joan McCracken, who urged him to rethink his career ambitions. He later said, "I was very show biz, all I thought about was nightclubs, and she kept saying, 'You're too good to spend your life in nightclubs,' she lifted me out of that, and I'll always be grateful."[53] McCracken felt that Fosse had abundant talent but little formal training. At her insistence, he enrolled in classes at the American Theatre Wing in New York City, paid for by the GI Bill. It was here that he received his first formal dance training from Anna Sokolow, Charles Weidman, and Jose Limon, as well as classes in acting, singing, and speech.[54]

McCracken also recommended that he study acting with her former teacher, Sanford Meisner, at the Neighborhood Playhouse. Meisner, a founding member of the Group Theatre, had developed a practical, reality-based approach to acting that drew in part on his training as a musician and held obvious appeal to dancers, whose art is focused on training the body to respond forthrightly to any demands placed on it by choreography.[55] For Fosse, Meisner's classes opened a window to another way of communicating onstage—honestly and simply rather than relentlessly energetic—that would be reflected in his subsequent work.

For an American Theatre Wing showcase, Fosse combined two scenes from William Saroyan's *The Time of Your Life*, playing Harry, a would-be hoofer and comic, a role that had been played previously by two of Fosse's idols: Gene Kelly on Broadway and Paul Draper on film. The role allowed Fosse to draw on his memories of burlesque comics putting over unfunny material with gusto, while at the same time showcasing his tap dancing. An MGM talent scout saw the showcase and arranged for Fosse to repeat the performance as a screen test. On April 19, 1951, he signed a standard seven-year contract with the studio known for turning out the very best movie musicals, the studio of Fred Astaire and Gene Kelly, the "dream factory" of Technicolor song and dance.[56] It was as easy as that.

Fosse's MGM contract and his $500 weekly salary would be delayed until he finished his next engagement, another career first.[57] *Pal Joey*, the 1940 Rodgers and Hart musical based on John O'Hara's *New Yorker* stories, revolved around Joey Evans, a small-time nightclub dancer who is taken up by an older, married socialite. Director Gus Schirmer Jr. packaged a summer stock production to tour tents and playhouses along the East Coast—*Pal Joey*'s first appearance since the Broadway production. Fosse auditioned for and won the title role. The vocal demands were slight (the role was yet another originated by the light-voiced Gene Kelly), and the dancing was easily within his range.

Fosse's background and personal status held similarities with the character of Joey. Like Fosse, Joey was an experienced hoofer, ingratiating and glib on a nightclub floor and expert in the byways of backstage life, particularly with women. Joey and Fosse, both show business veterans by an early age and surrounded by beautiful women, shared the drive to score with as many of them as possible. Like Joey, whose liaison with an older woman gave him entrée to a luxury world, Fosse's affair with McCracken provided a lover-mentor who brought him into her circle of artists and intellectuals and introduced him to wider career possibilities. But where Joey was opportunistic and self-deceiving, Fosse was grateful and clear-eyed: "Joan was incredible to me. She really helped me to believe in myself, and she told me honestly what I had to do. She was in a whole different world."[58]

Fosse had never played a full-length acting role, and certainly not one that was the focus of the entire production. His reviews were mixed. The *Boston Globe* called him "more than creditable when it comes to portraying the cheap, tricky and boastful night club entertainer,"[59] while the *Washington Post* wrote, "Bob Fosse, a slight, blond, puckish fellow, does fine with the character, though he's no Gene Kelly in the other departments."[60] Though Fosse had no way of knowing it at the time, Joey would prove to be his acting summit. He would revisit it often during his prime dancing years, long after he had become a successful director-choreographer, playing it more times than any other actor. Joey Evans remained a touchstone for Fosse, a bridge back to his beginnings and a reference point for his unchecked appetites.

A Broadway revival of *Pal Joey* was now planned, but instead of summer stock Bob Fosse, the producers cast Broadway Harold Lang. Lang was a star dancer with an impeccable ballet background who originated a role as one of the sailors in Robbins's *Fancy Free* and had recently scored a success in *Kiss Me, Kate*. Fosse was chosen as Lang's understudy, though he was treated more as a standby, an actor who is generally not a member of the company but hired specifically to cover a star role. Fosse spent his time backstage waiting for an opportunity to substitute for Lang. Ultimately, Lang never missed a performance, though Fosse departed long before *Pal Joey* ended its 540-performance run.

During his backstage waits at *Pal Joey*, Fosse struck up friendships with two of the show's female dancers, who asked him to choreograph a number for them to be presented at the annual Stage Managers' Club talent show. This yearly show-case of songs, dances, and sketches by chorus members and bit part actors from current Broadway shows was a high-profile insider event that attracted major producers and directors from theater, television, and the movies.[61] Among those in attendance for *Talent '52* was George Abbott, who was there at the urging of his friend Joan McCracken, and film director Stanley Donen. Fosse created a clever set piece for the two dancers, each of whom was shown auditioning for an unnamed Broadway choreographer. By skillful appropriation of identifiable dance traits, Fosse was able to conjure up humorous pastiches of choreography by Agnes de Mille, Jerome Robbins, and Robert Alton. The result was a witty, small-scale gem of dance parody.[62]

Before Fosse left for Hollywood, there was one more television appearance of note. On June 20, just days before his twenty-fifth birthday, he appeared on the live comedy-variety hour *Cavalcade of Stars* in an extended solo dance sequence. Fosse, wearing a suit, bow tie, hat, and white socks—the picture of a young bobby-soxer all dressed up—wanders into a tailor's shop staffed by the June Taylor Dancers and proceeds to raise havoc in the elegant shop. He demonstrates all the tricks he had been perfecting since his first engagements with Niles. Here was a new partnership, but with a chair this time, in a nod to Astaire's celebrated use of props. The full Fosse repertoire is presented—bell kicks, leaps, triple pirou-ettes, barrel turns, and knee slides so strenuous that they take him out of camera range. He also works in tricks with a hat, perhaps as a means of disguising his already-thinning hairline. Jumping onto a broken-legged chair (not so subtly set for the purpose), Fosse falls in a heap and is tossed out of the shop. The premise is not entirely logical, and the routine is just as overstuffed as his earlier choreography, but the number serves as a valedictory dance and closes the chapter on Bob Fosse's New York–based career as a dancer.[63]

> "I got there just as musicals were about to close the doors, but I was there long enough to get a smell of the whole thing."
>
> Bob Fosse, 1969[64]

Shows like *Cavalcade of Stars*—extravagant television showcases for musical and comedy performers broadcast free every night—were part of the reason the movie industry was reeling at just the time Fosse arrived in Hollywood. The musical film, in particular, was vulnerable to the competition presented by television variety shows. That competition, coupled with rising costs, meant a decline in production, even at MGM, the studio most associated with the movie musical. Many stars were being released from their contracts, and films that might previously have had the full weight of studio resources behind them were scaled back.

Such was the case with Fosse's first film, *Give a Girl a Break*. Originally conceived as a starring vehicle for Gene Kelly and Vera-Ellen, it was streamlined to an A-minus budget and, in an ironic twist for Fosse, assigned to Marge and Gower Champion, who had recently joined the studio. The film's director, Stanley Donen, replaced previously cast Carleton Carpenter with Fosse to play opposite new star Debbie Reynolds.[65] Donen remembered Fosse from *Talent '52* and recognized his potential: "In my opinion, he was going to be as good a song and dance man as Kelly and Astaire. I thought Fosse—this guy is going to be it."[66] Together they formed a professional bond, and Donen provided Fosse with his first role model for the possibilities of the musical film.

Donen had started his career as a dancer (including in *Pal Joey*'s original 1940 Broadway production) before going to Hollywood at the age of nineteen, first as a dancer and then as a choreographer. Donen was a low-key innovator of the musical film whose star-filled casts often overshadowed his trendsetting contributions. He helped expand the possibilities for dance on film through his work with Gene Kelly. Together they created *Cover Girl*'s (1944) "Alter Ego" number in which Kelly expresses internal conflict by dancing with a superimposed image of himself—an innovation of synchronized camerawork and dancing. Donen and Kelly co-directed *On the Town* (1949), launching the practice of filming musical numbers on location, and his camerawork ingeniously enabled Fred Astaire to dance on the ceiling in *Royal Wedding* (1951). His most recent film, again co-directed with Gene Kelly, was the triumphant *Singin' in the Rain* (1952).

In *Give a Girl a Break*, Fosse plays the young assistant to Gower Champion's director-choreographer, who is trying to decide among three unknown dancers for the female lead in his new Broadway revue. Fosse spends much of his screen time running errands, distributing sandwiches, and promoting the talents of the dancer played by Reynolds, on whom he develops an immediate crush when she arrives to audition. The slight, eighty-one-minute film has modest virtues, notably the opportunity to examine the contrasting styles of Fosse and Champion, the two future director-choreographers who would dominate the Broadway musical in the post-Robbins era.

Fosse and Champion had much in common. Both were born and raised in Chicago (Champion was eight years older), and both had performed in vaudeville during its final days. But while Fosse toiled as a teenager in burlesque, tapping and emceeing, Champion's stylish ballroom dance act with early partner Jeanne Tyler took him on tours of theaters and hotel ballrooms, and then to Broadway. Both men formed dance acts with their wives, though the Champions were far more successful. Significantly, neither man was ballet-trained, though each had studied classical dance, and each would build his career as a choreographer and director around his own movement vocabulary—Champion, the elegant ballroom glide, and Fosse, the burlesque bump and grind—which would stand them apart from the ballet-based work of de Mille, Robbins, Michael Kidd, and others.

In the film, Fosse dances with Champion only once. In "Nothing Is Impossible" they attempt to encourage the revue's songwriter, played by Kurt Kasner, to come up with a new score. Dancing circles around the thick-waisted Kasner, the two song-and-dance men reveal their differences. The handsome Gower, in sleek slacks and tight shirt displaying his toned musculature, is dashing and thoroughly in charge. The boyish Bob, in dungarees and sweater vest, is eager and ready to please. Gower goes through the vaudeville-style flash steps with assurance and a slight sense of detachment. Bob plays everything full out and with conviction. Show business is serious business for each man, but Champion uses the old routines as a means to an end, while Fosse sees something meaningful in every well-worn bit.

The billing insisted that the choreography was by Donen and Champion, but Fosse's numbers with Reynolds look like variations on Fosse and Niles. Fosse performs the vocal that sets the tone for the charming song and dance number "In Our United State" in a park setting against an MGM-styled Manhattan skyline. He starts with a back flip and ends with a fall into the East River. That back flip was a trick Fosse worked hard to perfect, even traveling back to New York more than once to work with noted acrobatics instructor Joe Price.[67] Fosse would get his money's worth by inserting it in several future numbers. From there, he and Reynolds do Fosse hat tricks (he somersaults into his hat, she cartwheels after it) and some synchronized soft-shoe shuffles. When the music accelerates, they launch into a series of traveling time steps with Fosse's explosive arm accents, the camera following them as they cover the entirety of the vast set. It is a number that Fosse and Niles could have done on television, but here it is less frenetic and more varied. Reynolds lacks Mary Ann Niles's sharp technique, but she keeps up with Fosse, especially in the tap sections, and her lack of virtuosity may have kept him from making the dance more complex. "In Our United State" is a low-key charmer.

The song was used as an instrumental for Fosse and Reynolds's final number together, one imagined by Fosse as a celebration of Reynolds's Broadway success. On a busy, confetti- and balloon-filled rooftop landscape, they do an exuberant variation on their previous number. Donen pulls out all his camera tricks, shooting in reverse so the dancers appear to jump and slide independent of gravity. (It is a trick Fosse adopted much later for "If My Friends Could See Me" in the film version of *Sweet Charity*.) Balloons magically appear and just as magically vanish. It is the danced embodiment of pure joy—of a boy and girl so much in love and so giddy with success that they appear to levitate, an effect similar to that of the love-besotted Fred Astaire dancing on the ceiling in *Royal Wedding*.[68]

It was during the filming of *Give a Girl a Break* that Fosse at last met his idol. Walking with Donen to the studio commissary for lunch one day, they ran into Astaire. As introductions and small talk were made, Astaire noticed a bent nail on the ground and casually used his toe to begin playing with it, eventually executing a riff-like movement with his heel and toe to send it flying off in the distance. It was the kind of casual, mindless act that only the most coordinated and skillful would do and then promptly forget. After the men parted, Fosse told Donen to go on without him, that he didn't feel like eating lunch. An hour later, on his way back to the soundstage, Donen saw Fosse in the same spot, assiduously trying to recreate the effortless toe-heel movement Astaire used to propel the nail. He had spent an hour trying to perfect a step his idol had performed without thinking. Fosse's perfectionism was not born that day on the MGM lot, but his obsessive drive to master even a tiny step or movement would stay with him for the rest of his career.[69]

Fosse recalled his encounters with Astaire at MGM numerous times over the years, helping create a self-deprecating record of his disappointing time at the studio. Another meeting between the two prompted a jaunty "Hi ya, Foss!" from Astaire. ("I thought my heart would jump out of my chest. Fred Astaire at least knew part of my name.")[70] Astaire was filming *The Band Wagon* (1953) at the time, and Fosse got the opportunity not only to watch him rehearse but also to dance for him. "I was so nervous, I was falling all over myself doing it . . . . You can imagine what it's like in a big rehearsal hall and finally there's your idol and you're going to get a chance to dance for him." Astaire's response, according to Fosse, was a noncommittal "That's nice, kid."[71]

When *Give a Girl a Break* wrapped in early December, Fosse returned to New York. With their previous marriages now dissolved, Fosse and Joan McCracken were married at City Hall on December 29, 1952, one day before McCracken's thirty-fifth birthday. McCracken's age had now officially been trimmed to thirty in all publicity, thereby reducing the age difference between the two to a less threatening five years.

MGM thought so little of *Give a Girl a Break* that its release was held up, and the first Fosse film to hit the screen was *The Affairs of Dobie Gillis*. Fosse later ruefully reflected on the studio's assessment of his hairline: "They took one look at me and said, 'Well, he needs a toupee.' Well, of course my heart broke."[72] The toupee was most definitely on display in *Dobie Gillis*, plastered on the front of his head and providing Fosse with a short set of unflattering bangs. His first film gave Fosse considerable screen time opposite one of the studio's emerging stars. But in *Dobie Gillis* his role was secondary, and Debbie Reynolds was leading lady to another dancer from New York. Bobby Van, who grew up in a vaudeville family, shared a similar background with Fosse. Van had been signed to MGM the year before and was having much the same experience as Fosse. The title role in *Dobie Gillis* would be the high point of his own brief time at the studio.

As Van's college roommate, Fosse played a pushier, girl-crazy variation on his previous role and shared a dance number with Reynolds, Van, and Barbara Ruick. "You Can't Do Wrong Doin' Right," set in a campus night spot, begins with a brief Fosse solo, complete with his favorite airborne leap, explosive arms, lots of rhythmic changes in direction, and vibrating hands ("jazz hands," in contemporary parlance). He ends with a saucy midair hip swivel and, perhaps in a tribute to Astaire, a double attitude turn. (The film's official choreographer was Alex Romero, but Fosse's solo carries the hallmarks of his own dance style.) When the others join him, the differences in style and technique between Fosse and Van are obvious. Van is as good a tapper as Fosse, but he dances only with his feet, while Fosse dances with his whole body. The steps seem to shoot up and out through his arms and propel him across the set, while Van's arms hang loosely at his sides. When the two men jump first onto a bandstand and then atop a piano, Fosse flies, while Van works to keep up.

The Affairs of Dobie Gillis could have qualified as the first black-and-white MGM musical in years, except that it was not even a fully formed musical, just a minor league comedy with a few old songs thrown in. But Fosse's next film was a bona fide A budget effort carrying the full weight of the MGM production machine.

Cole Porter's lush, tuneful *Kiss Me, Kate*, in which Shakespeare's *Taming of the Shrew* is performed while the backstage feuds and romances of its tempestuous stars mirror those of Petruchio and Katherine, seemed a natural for the deluxe MGM treatment. (It was also to be the studio's major offering in the short-lived 3D process, the latest screen gimmick designed to compete with television.) *Kiss Me, Kate*'s choreographer was Hermes Pan, who had collaborated with Astaire on his memorable dance routines with Ginger Rogers at RKO in the 1930s—the same ones that sent the young Bob Fosse dancing over fireplugs on his way home from the movies. Here was the first-class musical Fosse had hoped for, but instead of Bill Calhoun, the leading dance role originated by Harold Lang, he was assigned the glorified chorus part of a suitor to Bianca, Katherine's sister, in the onstage *Shrew*. (Tommy Rall was cast as Bill Calhoun, playing opposite MGM contractee Ann Miller.) Fosse had gone from a solid featured role in his first film to this bit part; as he later observed, "My parts were getting smaller. I knew what that meant."[73]

Onstage, "Tom, Dick or Harry" was an amusing double entendre number for the man-hungry Bianca and her three suitors, staged to emphasize Porter's wordplay over movement. With four expert dancers at his disposal (Miller, Rall, Fosse, and Bobby Van, who must have felt the same as Fosse about his diminishing screen assignments), Pan turned "Tom, Dick or Harry" into a showstopper, crowded with buck-and-wing tap steps, split jumps, a solo tap break for Miller, and spots for each suitor. Given sixteen counts of music for showing off, Fosse pulls out his specialty leaps and barrel turns and ends, unsurprisingly, with a knee drop. The number climaxes with time-honored vaudeville applause cues: a series of traveling trenches leading into the old "shave and a hair cut" tap finish. Fosse was used to being the best dancer on the stage or in front of the camera, but here, alongside the prodigious Rall and the vivacious Miller, he dances with an air of joyful competitiveness.

As Hermes Pan's biographer John Franceschina writes, in rehearsals Fosse asked for a chance to choreograph a number in the picture. Pan was impressed both by Fosse's dancing (they both loved knee drops) and by his determination, and so he and musical director Saul Chaplin interpolated "From This Moment On," a number excised from Cole Porter's recent Broadway musical, *Out of This World*.[74] Presented in the next-to-closing spot just before the end of the film, the number was designed as a series of dance duets, first Miller and Rall, then Van and Jeanne Coyne, and finally Fosse and Carol Haney. Miller and Rall are predictably dazzling in their taps and leaps, and Van and Coyne do a quick clog specialty that lasts all of ten seconds.

The number's highlight arrives when the lights drop and the tempo downsizes to a big band fanfare. The cheerful musical comedy dancing of the preceding hour and forty-five minutes is forgotten as a blast of jazz adrenaline jumps off the screen more powerfully than any 3D effect. Haney swings a leg out from the wings and gives a bloodcurdling scream as Fosse zooms out in a running slide that sends him halfway across the stage. Suddenly they freeze, but then pick up the tempo with finger snaps as another blast of brass propels them up and then down into a jazz crouch. They travel with a slow, panther-like strut punctuated by Fosse's "come here, you" nod that elicits a shiver of ecstasy from Haney. Then they are off again in a leap and jazz run that swings them up and around what looks to be an Elizabethan lamp post—Haney on bottom, on her knees, and Fosse on top, wrapped around the post in a broken, rag doll stance. They freeze, but just for a second, as they pick up the pulse of the insistent beat. Fosse jumps down into a one-knee drag with bent elbows and fluttering fingers, while Haney literally crawls on the floor after him. It makes a startling stage picture: the elfin Fosse

Birth of a style: Fosse dancing his own choreography in "From This Moment On" from Kiss Me, Kate. *Metro-Goldwyn-Mayer.*

in tights hungrily pursued by the round-hipped Haney—a jazz Apache dance in miniature.

A series of jazz runs is punctuated by traveling knee slides that change direction as the dancers rise. Finally they hit a pose that seems all but inevitable: legs apart, arms up with wrists hanging limp, shoulders hunched, head gazing down and away from the audience, as they shuffle forward, the rhythm seeming to take over their bodies. Haney points a burlesque bump in Fosse's direction that sends him into his Joe Price back flip. As if to make amends for his earlier cavalier behavior, he ends the flip pleadingly, arms wide open. Haney gives him a grin of acceptance, and off they shuffle in their own private trance.

Fosse and Carol Haney, a former Jack Cole dancer and lately dance assistant to Gene Kelly, appear to be creating a new dance vocabulary in front of the audience. The other couples perform face front, but Fosse and Haney dance off each other, in a narrative at once cocky, insolent, and sexual. This one minute of dance alchemy draws from recognizable elements from Fosse's performing past. The Riff Brothers banter, the Fosse and Niles rhythmic changes, the burlesque bumps, and the Jack Cole slither all coalesce in sixty seconds to lay the foundation for the Fosse style. "From This Moment On" is not just the name of a highlight in his still young career. It serves as a declaration of a whole new career path about to open up for Bob Fosse.

2
APPRENTICESHIP
• • •

"I started with hats because I began losing my hair very early . . . . And I've always been slightly round-shouldered, and so I started to exaggerate that. And I don't have what the ballet dancers call a turn-out, so I started turning my feet in. So I guess that's the style they talk about."

Bob Fosse, 1980[1]

Over the course of his career, Bob Fosse crafted a narrative of his life and work through numerous interviews. In response to frequent questions about his signature dance style, he developed a self-deprecating explanation that pointed to his physical limitations. It was all slightly disingenuous: declaring his basic equipment to be substandard, but with an unspoken acknowledgment of how far it had taken him.

George Abbott's long-time stage manager, Robert Griffith, and a recent addition to Abbott's team, twenty-five-year-old Harold Prince, had optioned the stage rights to the new Book-of-the-Month Club selection, 7½ Cents by Richard Bissell, and intended it to be their first show as a producing team. Bissell, who had run his family's pajama factory in Dubuque, Iowa, brought a Midwestern Damon Runyon–style swagger to his tale of romance between a factory superintendent (Sid) and a member of the sewing assembly line (Babe) set against a battle between the management of Sleep Tite ("The Pajama for Men of Bedroom Discrimination") and its unionized labor force over the wage increase that provided the book's title. Abbott agreed to direct if a suitable book could be written.[2]

At age sixty-six, George Abbott was the grand old man of musical comedy. Prince described him as "six feet whatever tall. Incredibly handsome. Not remotely like a Broadway director. Not Jewish. And everybody was in awe and respectful of him."[3] Mr. Abbott, as everyone called him, began his professional career as an actor before establishing himself as a director and playwright. Abbott directed every kind of play but became known for fast-moving farces (Twentieth Century, Room Service, and his own Three Men on a Horse) and, increasingly, musicals.

Abbott imposed discipline and order on the writing and directing of musicals. He brought a playwright's sense of logic and structure to his direction, and his shows were swift and efficient. He insisted that songs and jokes grow plausibly from the action. Incongruous star turns and fizzy specialty numbers, so much a part of musicals a decade earlier, were banished. Abbott's actors, always cast to type, were required to enunciate their lines and act with honesty even in the most fanciful situations.[4]

His clear-cut, one-man-in-charge approach would come to be called "the Abbott Touch." It established the director as the unquestioned authority whose vision tied all elements together into a coherent and entertaining package, and it was a model that influenced his three brightest successors—Prince, Jerome Robbins, and Fosse—all of whom would work on this new George Abbott musical and carry his lessons decades into the future.

While others expanded the boundaries of the musical, Abbott unapologetically stuck to solidly crafted commercial fare. ("Strictly a formula man," Brooks Atkinson called him.)[5] His prodigious output in the 1940s and early 1950s included *Pal Joey, Best Foot Forward, On the Town, Billion Dollar Baby, High Button Shoes, Where's Charley?, Call Me Madam,* and *Wonderful Town.* He was known for working with emerging talents, who were presumably easier to control than established artists, and he introduced many newcomers in their first shows, including Robbins, Betty Comden and Adolph Green, and later, Jerry Bock and Sheldon Harnick and John Kander and Fred Ebb.

Abbott would introduce a whole roster of new talents on the now-renamed *The Pajama Game* and collaborate with Bissell on the musical's book, emphasizing the comedy and romance of the pajama factory over the labor angle. When Frank Loesser turned it down, he recommended his protégés, the team of Richard Adler (aged thirty-two) and Jerry Ross (aged twenty-seven) to write the score.

Griffith and Prince were soon joined by Frederick Brisson, a veteran agent and producer whose wife, Rosalind Russell, was currently starring in *Wonderful Town.* As the new production team struggled to raise *The Pajama Game*'s $169,000 capitalization, the job of choreographer was still unassigned.

Kiss Me, Kate was released in the fall of 1953, but by then Fosse had asked for and received a six-month leave of absence from MGM in order to return to New York.[6] Over the years, several parties have taken credit for "discovering" Bob Fosse's work on *Kiss Me, Kate* as an audition for *The Pajama Game.* Prince said his wife pointed it out to him.[7] Buzz Miller, who was living with Jerome Robbins at the time, said he persuaded Robbins to see the film with the Fosse number featuring Miller's old Jack Cole colleague, Carol Haney.[8] But most acknowledge that Joan McCracken's aggressive campaign on Fosse's behalf resulted in George Abbott seeing the film at Radio City Music Hall and deeming him acceptable. (McCracken was one of the stars of Abbott's current show, Rodgers and Hammerstein's *Me and Juliet.*)

Harold Prince was concerned about Fosse's lack of experience. Fosse had never choreographed a Broadway musical, never designed dances for a large ensemble, never staged vocal numbers, and never worked with nondancing actors. "I wanted assurance. I mean, it's nice that Joan thinks he's great, but I wanted assurance," Prince recalled.[9] He sought out Jerome Robbins, who, like Abbott, had seen Fosse's work in *Talent '52,* with its satire on Robbins and other choreographers, and felt he had potential. Robbins agreed to serve as a backup for Fosse on the condition that he be listed as co-director.

Fosse's contract and billing reflected his entry-level status among the creative team. "Choreography by Bob Fosse" would be of equal size to the musical director's billing in the advertisements and would follow credits for the set and costume designers.[10] His total compensation was $1,500.[11] By contrast, Robbins's contract offered him maximum prominence and payment for a loosely defined workload. Essentially, he was to clean up and fix any problems with Fosse's choreography. If Robbins changed or rechoreographed three numbers in their entirety, he would receive billing for additional choreography.[12]

Fosse surely felt the pressure to live up to the promise everyone was convinced he had—and to avoid the embarrassment of having Robbins take over should he fail. With *The Pajama Game* he established a preproduction ritual that he continued throughout his career. Logging in hours at a studio by himself, he played the score and even music not related to the show, worked out short combinations of steps, and kept a notebook of his ideas. It was in this manner that his choreography began to take shape. For *The Pajama Game* he gave himself a full eight weeks in the studio to work out every detail of the show's dances, in part to avoid looking unprepared. As he later recalled, "The most difficult thing for me—because I'm slightly shy and inhibited—was to get up in front of people and try to *create* for them . . . . to be stuck for an idea in front of forty people, all of whom are standing, waiting for you."[13]

This planning served him well, as he had responsibility for creating at least nine dances and production numbers, in addition to staging songs and musical scenes. The show's cast included plenty of nondancers like Broadway leading man John Raitt as Sid and Hollywood redhead Janis Paige as Babe. Eddie Foy Jr., one of the Seven Little Foys of vaudeville fame, cast as Hines, the factory "time study man," was more than capable of the soft-shoe steps Fosse gave him and also contributed his own eccentric dance moves. Fosse's biggest asset was his *Kiss Me, Kate* dance partner, Carol Haney, whom he recommended for the show's principal dance role. In early rehearsals, Haney got laughs with her few lines. Soon Abbott fired comedienne Charlotte Rae, who played Hines's girlfriend, Gladys, the boss's secretary, and combined the two roles into a true showcase for Haney.[14]

Haney, who had been dancing professionally since she was fifteen, spent several years performing as part of Jack Cole and His Dancers before accepting a job as dance assistant to Gene Kelly at MGM. Haney worked with Kelly on such films as *On the Town*, *Singin' in the Rain*, and *Invitation to the Dance*, occasionally appearing on screen. Her gamine quality gave her a passing resemblance to Joan McCracken. Haney was a character dancer who would find it difficult to duplicate her onstage success in *The Pajama Game*, and she eventually became a respected choreographer.

Fosse charged through the numbers and impressed the cast and creators with his imaginative and varied routines. With dance arranger Roger Adams, Fosse worked out wonderfully rhythmic variations on a vaudeville soft-shoe routine for Foy and Reta Shaw, an actress of large girth, in "I'll Never Be Jealous Again."

For "Her Is," performed "in one" (in front of the curtain during a scene change), Fosse drew on his burlesque experience for a comic vamp routine for Haney that served as a tryout for "Whatever Lola Wants." The comic payoff was doubled by reprising the number with heavyset actress Thelma Pelish performing identical bumps and grinds.

"Once a Year Day," performed at the Sleep Tite company picnic, gave the first indication that Fosse was bringing something new to his choreography. Fosse devised a full-cast number filled with the exuberance of the company's factory workers on a rare day off. The movements grew naturally and comically out of roughhousing and acting silly. Carol Haney, dragged out by the others to perform, at first tries to run away but finally comes up with a little hop-and-jump step finished with one hand on her head and the other extended forward, giddily exclaiming "Whee!" Others pick up the step, and soon the stage is full of squealing girls running into each other until finally the boys jump up, grab the girls, and the stage explodes in a mad polka.

Fosse fragments the number through changes in tempo and personnel. The result is a mosaic of individual moments conveying a community at play. At one point, the entire cast, holding hands, becomes a human jigsaw puzzle, trying to step over arms and legs without breaking their grasp. Fosse stages crossovers in front for the character actors like Reta Shaw as counterpoint to the general athleticism. Haney is lifted high over the chaos squealing "Whee!," followed by Thelma Pelish, lifted almost as high, doing the same. (Fosse proved adept at creating movement for larger performers like Pelish and Shaw, highlighting their grace

"Whee!" Fosse, with back to the camera, directs the dancers in The Pajama Game's "Once a Year Day." Shirley MacLaine is second from left among the women. Peter Gennaro is third from left among the men. Billy Rose Theatre Division, The New York Public Library for the Performing Arts.

over their girth.) Dance critic Walter Terry called it "a weaving-of-bodies pattern calculated to make George Balanchine (himself a distinguished weaver) jealous."[15]

Haney led the final, climactic sequence that accelerated to the point of exhaustion with the entire cast collapsed on the floor. Fosse found a physicality for these working-class picnic-goers that was recognizable and comic. "Once a Year Day" is rough-edged and rowdy, without a trace of Agnes de Mille–style formality.

Fosse worked clever variations on what could have been standard production numbers. "Hernando's Hideaway," a tango, was performed in pitch black, with the ensemble striking matches to illuminate different vignettes, an idea he drew from match ceremonies at Chicago's Soldier Field.[16] For the "Jealousy Ballet," in which Hines imagines what married life with Gladys would be, Fosse gave the now-clichéd dream ballet a burlesque makeover, with the couple's bedroom invaded by multitudes of men hiding under beds or climbing through windows, all for the chance to romance Gladys, here presented as the world's most lust-worthy vamp.

It was in the nondanced musical numbers that Fosse's lack of experience became apparent. When his ideas for the full-company "7½ Cents" fell embarrassingly flat, Robbins was called in to restage it. Fosse remembered Robbins's diplomacy and later spoke of the importance of that experience: "I think I learned more in a couple of hours watching him stage than I had learned previously in my whole life . . . . He was very sweet about it and as he did the number he would consult with me and ask me what I thought. (I had no opinion at all I was in such awe of the man.) And in two hours he staged this song absolutely brilliantly . . . . I think it was a turning point in my career as a choreographer."[17]

There were other numbers that required Robbins's help, and while Fosse was never in danger of losing his solo credit, Robbins was more involved with the musical staging than perhaps Fosse would have liked known. A list drawn up by Robbins a year after the show opened detailed the extent of his contributions:

1. Helped re-stage the opening.
2. Staged about one half of "Racing With the Clock" and the fade-out of the first scene
3. Worked with Johnny Raitt on NEW TOWN ["A New Town is a Blue Town"]
4. Completely staged "I'm Not At All in Love"
5. Staged reprise of "Her Is"
6. Completely staged "There Once Was a Man"
7. Completely staged "7½ Cents"
8. Completely staged the finale after the dance which opens it
9. Staged the bows and curtains
10. Re-staged "Small Talk" and re-staged the reprise of "Hey There" with Janis [Paige].[18]

Robbins could have invoked his contractual stipulation to share billing for the musical staging, but the dances were clearly Fosse's. He felt differently in 1973 when *The Pajama Game*, again directed by George Abbott, was revived briefly on Broadway. Robbins, who was not credited in the opening-night program, demanded that the program be changed to read, "Musical numbers originally staged by Jerome Robbins and Bob Fosse," and that the song listing would credit Robbins alone with staging "7½ Cents."[19]

One number that required no assistance from Robbins was "Steam Heat." The second act was to open with a big union meeting featuring what Fosse called a "hillbilly entertainment."[20] His ideas failed to please Abbott, who suggested doing a simpler, amateur-style number that promoted the idea of the union. Fosse went to Adler and Ross for song ideas, and they played him a "trunk" song that they originally deemed not good enough for the show. As a songwriting exercise, Adler had locked himself in a bathroom until he came up with a song about something in the room. The resulting song referenced dripping faucets and clanging, hissing radiators.[21] Its syncopated sound effects and rhythmic bounce immediately appealed to Fosse, who put together a new number in just five hours.[22]

"A couple of the cutting room boys has got up an act with Gladys Hotchkiss who's from the front office,"[23] announced the union president before Carol Haney, Buzz Miller, and Peter Gennaro ran on in front of the act curtain to perform their little amateur song and dance. "Steam Heat" begins with an unassuming syncopated beat and immediately establishes its movement vocabulary: a staccato shuffle with traces of vaudeville and cool jazz stylings, ready to explode but always tamped down and brought back to lockstep. Pushing their hats off their heads or away from their chests, the dancers approximated the pajama factory's steam irons, hissing, clicking, clanking, and "boinking" their way through the sounds of their workplace. The number's trickiest hat trick requires each dancer to throw the derby *up* to a hand above the head (easier than it looks if the hat is weighted correctly), and then sink it down onto the head with an exaggerated "sssssss."

The movements drew from Fosse's affection for vaudeville dancer and comedian Joe Frisco. Calling himself the "World's First Jazz Dancer," Frisco hired jazz musicians to accompany his act. Dressed in dapper suit and tie, topped with a derby and sporting a cigar, Frisco shuffled, shimmied, and snake-hipped in a surprisingly provocative style and executed many of the same hat tricks that Fosse wove into "Steam Heat."[24] In describing the number's influences, Fosse said, "He dug his hands deeply into his pockets and sort of hunched shoulders and just chugged along and that was Joe Frisco. I've always loved that step and I love some of the [Jimmy] Durante steps and so it's sort of a combination of Frisco, Durante and me."[25] The "Joe Frisco" and the "Durante" (a shuffle step with hat shimmying just above the head accompanied by a broad showboating grin) are prominent in "Steam Heat," as are variations on rubber-legged dancing from the 1920s. The dancers first rubber-leg across the stage, then return, adding hat tips and foot isolations for a "how did they do that?" effect. The number is filled with surprising rhythmic accents—necks and shoulders in syncopated isolation, the knee slides from "From This Moment On," and a stop-time, foot stomp and hand clap pattern. The dense and detailed dancing performed in perfect precision by the trio produces an almost hypnotic effect.

"It isn't surprising that his style was there at the very start. If you have a statement to make you usually don't develop into it," Robbins later reflected.[26] "Steam

Heat" was a singular distillation of Fosse's past influences, but given a contemporary coolness. The Jack Cole lunges, the vaudeville references and silent movie clowning, and Fosse's own hat and knee work were parlayed into something that spoke of jazz: angular, off-kilter, and filled with the joy of showing off. The signature Fosse hand movements—the broken wrists, the splayed fingers—made their first appearance here. The dancers wore identical black suits and bow ties, black derbies, and black shoes—the formal air broken by white socks under their high-hemmed pants. They looked a bit like Charlie Chaplin's Little Tramp, but they moved like Bob Fosse in triplicate. In one form or another, "Steam Heat" would reappear in every Fosse show.

Most reviewers agreed that they had never seen a dance quite like "Steam Heat." *Dance Magazine* viewed it as a history-maker: "We predict that this number will become a classic, the sort of thing this generation will remember the way a little older generation remembers Fred and Adele Astaire duos."[27] But "Steam Heat" was just the sort of number that Abbott felt slowed down the forward momentum of a show. During the first out-of-town engagement in New Haven, he was determined that it be cut. "Look, the number is just too good. You can't throw it out," Robbins insisted, and the number remained.[28]

When *The Pajama Game* opened at the St. James Theater on May 13, 1954, ovation followed ovation, "Steam Heat" stopped the show, and producers Griffith and Prince, who had hired themselves as stage managers to cut costs on the tightly financed production, felt finally that they might have a success—a feeling that

Buzz Miller, Carol Haney, and Peter Gennaro in The Pajama Game's *"Steam Heat." Photo by Will Rapport. Billy Rose Theatre Division, The New York Public Library for the Performing Arts.*

was confirmed by the opening-night reviews and the lines at the box office the next day. Everyone associated with *The Pajama Game* received accolades, including its debuting choreographer. Richard Watts Jr. in the *New York Post* concluded, "It is in the dancing that 'The Pajama Game' is at its most enlivening."[29] Fosse was a predictable winner for his choreography at the 1954–1955 Tony Awards, and *The Pajama Game* took the top honors for Best Musical. It settled in for a run of 1,063 performances, closing on November 24, 1956, by which time a nationwide tour was playing and a film version was underway.

Robbins's participation in *The Pajama Game* served several purposes. It gave him a big commercial hit with his name listed prominently as co-director (from which he immediately launched into preparations for directing *Peter Pan*). It gave Fosse both a celebrated Broadway choreographic debut and the opportunity to learn from someone Stephen Sondheim called "the best stager of musical numbers—I think in my lifetime, anyway—in the Broadway theater."[30]

Fosse and Robbins maintained a friendship for the remainder of Fosse's life. On opening night, Robbins gifted Fosse with a pair of cufflinks that had belonged to Robbins's father. On *Peter Pan*'s opening night, Fosse returned them to Robbins as a good-luck gesture. The two would pass the cufflinks back and forth on opening nights until Fosse's death.

"I'm confused. I really want to dance or act myself."

Bob Fosse, 1954[31]

This plaintive remark, made just weeks after the triumphant opening of *The Pajama Game*, gives an indication of Bob Fosse's conflicted feelings regarding his new success. A year earlier he had been a struggling nightclub performer and disappointed MGM contract player. Now he was a newly acclaimed Broadway choreographer. But rather than commit immediately to choreograph another show, Fosse held out for a return to Hollywood. He had screen-tested for the role of Will Parker in the film version of Rodgers and Hammerstein's *Oklahoma!* and still harbored film ambitions, his MGM experience notwithstanding.[32] *The Pajama Game* had burnished Fosse's reputation in Hollywood, and he soon signed a film contract with Columbia Pictures to choreograph a new musical version of *My Sister Eileen*.

My Sister Eileen had a long lineage in print, onstage, and in the movies. Ruth McKenney's short stories about the adventures of the Sherwood sisters from Ohio who arrive in New York City to pursue careers first appeared in the *New Yorker*. Ruth, the older, more sensible sister, sought a career as a writer, while the beautiful Eileen was a fledgling actress. The stories were successfully adapted to the Broadway stage by Joseph Fields and Jerome Chodorov in 1940, with Shirley Booth as Ruth. In 1942, Columbia Pictures acquired the film rights, and Fields and Chodorov adapted their play to the screen, with Rosalind Russell as Ruth. In 1953, Fields and Chodorov once again adapted the material, this time as a musical. *Wonderful Town* had a celebrated score with lyrics by Betty Comden and Adolph Green and music by Leonard Bernstein. George Abbott directed, and Rosalind Russell returned as Ruth. Columbia, which still owned the film rights to the play, chose to do a new musical adaptation of the property rather than negotiate with the creators of *Wonderful Town* for a screen version.

Fosse was also assigned the supporting role of Frank Lippencott, the drugstore soda jerk with a crush on Eileen. While the role was similar to his mild-mannered MGM characters, Fosse knew he would be showcased in his own choreography and may have entertained the idea of the film serving as his tryout for the role of Joey Evans in the studio's proposed film version of *Pal Joey*.

Filmed in Cinemascope, *My Sister Eileen* offered Fosse the opportunity to choreograph for the wide screen, though the numbers in the film are striking for their intimacy. With the exception of the concluding "Conga" number with Betty Garrett as Ruth, Janet Leigh as Eileen, and a crowd of Brazilian naval cadets, there were no large-scale production numbers. "Conga," which actually includes very little conga dancing, shows Fosse creating for the screen a big dance number with the same confidence he displayed in "Once a Year Day." He breaks it into discrete sections marked by variations in tempo, groups the dancers into multiple small units, and infuses comic bits to build to an exuberant finish.

"There's Nothing Like Love," a duet between Fosse and Janet Leigh danced in a Greenwich Village courtyard, begins and ends in clichéd fashion, with the couple partnering in typical romantic duet style while the camera circles overhead. But for its middle section, Fosse adds unexpected rhythms and syncopated tap breaks. The couple expresses their growing affection not by dancing into each other's arms but by synchronized finger snaps performed in perfect unison. "There's Nothing Like Love" shows Fosse confident enough to choreograph a quieter, subtler number and willing to upend the notion of what a romantic song and dance could be.

"Give Me a Band and My Baby," performed in a deserted outdoor bandstand, is based on the sounds of trombone, bass fiddle, drum, and cymbal mimed by Fosse, Garrett, Leigh, and Tommy Rall, Fosse's *Kiss Me, Kate* costar. Fosse builds the number around only a few movement themes, including open-armed spins, an exaggerated formal dancing stance, and burlesque shimmies and bumps. (It would not be the last time Fosse placed female-identified movements on himself and other male dancers.) A series of trenches underscores the number's vaudeville flavor. The most distinctive comedic movement requires the dancers to stoop slightly with arms hanging rigidly in front while their knees, held tightly together and in slight plié, move in opposition.

"Give Me a Band and My Baby," like "Steam Heat," is a specialty number, an entertainment with no relation to the plot. (George Abbott probably would have cut it.) Fosse uses repetition to build its small repertoire of movements into an exhilarating dance. Steps are frequently performed in unison and in a straight line parallel to the camera, as if the dancers are on a proscenium stage. "Bob was brilliant with music," Ann Reinking later observed. "He had a great ear and a great sense of composition for dance arranging."[33] With his favorite dance arranger, Roger Adams, who would work with him for the remainder of the decade, Fosse worked out variations in tempos, from Dixieland to ragtime syncopation to stop-time rhythms, which allowed him to fragment the number, starting and stopping, introducing new steps, and breaking the dancers off in solos or groups of two.

Unquestionably, the high point of *My Sister Eileen* is the dance performed by Fosse and Tommy Rall in an alley outside a stage door. The number was built on a series of challenges performed by Eileen's rival suitors. It starts simply, with competitive hat tricks—the very same Joe Frisco tricks used in "Steam Heat." The challenge quickly escalates, with Rall daring Fosse to match his stag leaps, splits, and pirouettes, and soon they are "Durante-ing" back and forth. Fosse's challenge is filled with his signature moves: the knee drop-and-drag from "From This Moment On" and "Steam Heat," a Chaplin walk, and a climactic series of high-velocity barrel turns. Rall responds with jump splits and a double tour en l'air. They reach a temporary détente in a stop-time tap break. Finally, the two come to a stop and eye one another suspiciously, as if each is saving his best trick in order to top the other. Then simultaneously they both execute Fosse's Joe Price back flip, ending on their knees, hats off and arms opened wide, as if saying "ta da!" This challenge dance ends in a draw.

The "Alley Dance," as it has come to be called, is a key number in Fosse's résumé. It gives lie to the idea that his work is tight and contained. It also refutes the notion put forth by Fosse himself that he was a limited dancer. Here he is working in an expansive, muscular mode alongside a dazzling ballet-trained dancer whose every move he matches. Executing his favorite stag leap after Rall does it flawlessly, Fosse appears to get up a head of steam to ensure that he out-does him. But he generously gives Rall the floor to execute virtuosic feats that he could not match. (Rall neatly pulls off a dizzying seven pirouettes.) Solo or in tandem, Fosse and Rall dance hard and prodigiously and make the "Alley Dance" truly memorable.

My Sister Eileen proved pleasant but mediocre, and it disappeared from theaters quickly. But it was an important project in Fosse's career. After appearing in films and contributing in a limited way to their choreography, he had now created an entire film's dances and musical staging. Harry Cohn, head of Columbia Pictures, was impressed enough with Fosse's choreography to offer him a lucrative contract with the studio, but he turned it down and went back to New York.[34]

> "There's nobody who can touch her. And that goes into character, into vulnerability, into a desire to *give* to an audience. When she's on stage, something happens!"
>
> Bob Fosse, 1972[35]

Gwyneth Evelyn Verdon was an exalted name for a child of show business, but one easily reduced to the marquee-ready Gwen Verdon. Even more than Fosse's, Verdon's lineage ran deep through the world of performing. Actors and dancers were among her ancestors, and even her birthplace was the stuff of show business legend. She was born January 13, 1925, in Culver City, California, the home of Metro-Goldwyn-Mayer, where her father, Joseph, worked as a grip and electrician. Verdon's mother, Gertrude, was a dancer with a varied background. Having studied and danced with Denishawn, she now taught its technique in Los Angeles dance schools.

A series of illnesses, including rickets, left Verdon severely knock-kneed as a small child and made walking difficult. Rejecting the advice of doctors to have Gwen's legs broken and reset, Mrs. Verdon prescribed dancing for her daughter, first tap and tumbling, and later ballet and Denishawn technique. Gwen's legs were so deformed that she had to learn ballet in "turn-in" position until her legs straightened and she was able to dance in correct "turnout."[36] When she wasn't in dance class, she was required to wear knee-high corrective boots everywhere, resulting in the unwanted childhood nickname "Boots Verdon."[37]

Her mother's regimen was a success, and by four, Verdon was part of a tumbling act called the Four D'Arcys. By six, billed as "the fastest tapper in the world," she was playing vaudeville theaters and dancing at the Hollywood Bowl. Verdon's mother took an anything-and-everything approach to her daughter's career. As part of Willie Covan and Family, little Gwen joined Covan, a black tap dancer, and his wife, Flo, who was lighter-skinned with red hair and freckles, as their daughter in a "family" tap dance act.[38]

She continued ballet studies with renowned teacher Ernest Belcher, the father of Marge Champion, and at eleven danced a ballet solo in the film *The King Steps Out* (1936). Taking full advantage of her prematurely lush figure, Verdon and her mother lied easily about her age. At fourteen (pretending to be twenty-two), she was appearing in nightclubs as one half of a ballroom dance team called Verdon and Del Valle. Bathing suit modeling and appearances at the Florentine Gardens nightclub in little more than gold body paint (applied nightly by her mother) were all part of her résumé by the time Verdon was sixteen.[39]

Verdon's teenage career path paralleled that of Fosse's and offered ample opportunities for exploitation. But where Fosse's parents were largely absent as guardians for their underage son, Mrs. Verdon served as a vigilant chaperone for her pretty, red-haired daughter and was committed to helping her pursue a dancing career. Thus it was a bitter blow to her when Verdon gave up dancing at seventeen to elope with James Henaghan, a columnist and reviewer for the *Hollywood Reporter* twice her age.

The new bride became pregnant immediately and gave birth to a son, James Jr., just after turning eighteen. A Hollywood gadfly and heavy drinker, Henaghan kept late and inconsistent hours, often disappearing for days at a time. Verdon assembled Henaghan's columns for him and covered shows that he skipped or was too drunk to attend. Eventually the strain and abandonment became too much. Verdon later recalled, "My son was born in March and on New Year's Eve, I said, 'That's it' and I went home to Mama. I took my child, my dog and my cats and left."[40]

Verdon parlayed her experience as Henaghan's "leg man" into work as a columnist and reviewer. But one night, on assignment to review Jack Cole and His Dancers at Slapsie Maxie's, a Hollywood nightclub, the performance awakened in her such a strong desire to return to dancing that she went backstage to introduce herself and ask for an audition. Cole quickly grasped her strengths and weaknesses, as he said later. "She had an adeptness and know-how that showed she had lots of experience but not much real training . . . . And she was very, very young. But she could do anything you showed her."[41]

In 1947, Cole called her to dance in the chorus of *Bonanza Bound*, a new musical he was choreographing. Leaving her son in the care of her parents, Verdon made her first trip to New York City to start rehearsals. At the show's Christmas opening in Philadelphia, the closing notice went up between the first and second acts, and *Bonanza Bound* was gone by the new year.[42] From there, Verdon joined Cole's nightclub dance act, replacing Carol Haney, who left to work as assistant to Gene Kelly at MGM.

Verdon happily studied with East Indian dance masters La Meri and Uday Shankar, and learned the Bharata Natyam techniques around which much of Cole's choreography was based. Cole's caustic personality and punishing quest for perfection were all taken in stride. Verdon, who had learned the discipline of dancing even before she could stand up straight and had fled a chaotic marriage, welcomed the regimentation of life with Jack Cole. She would remain with him for five years as dancer and devoted assistant.

Verdon was at Cole's side assisting on his next Broadway show, *Magdalena*, a lavish spectacle built around the themes of Brazilian composer Heitor Villa-Lobos that had a short run in late 1948. In early 1950, just days before Bob Fosse made his Broadway debut in *Dance Me a Song*, she made her own belated debut in *Alive and Kicking*, a revue for which she also served as Cole's assistant. Dance critic John Martin singled out Verdon as "stunning," but *Alive and Kicking* was yet another disappointment for Cole, and it closed after forty-six performances.[43] Twentieth Century-Fox offered Cole a contract, and after several years of working on unsuccessful shows and traveling with his dance troupe, he opted to return to Los Angeles and the stability of a studio berth.

Cole's Twentieth Century-Fox pictures were no more distinguished than those he made at Columbia—mostly musical biopics and backstage romances. But studio head Daryl F. Zanuck gave him great latitude in designing and executing musical numbers, most of which were stand-alone, show-within-a-show performances with little connection to the plots of their films. Cole favored swooping camera movements and bold colors (hot pink was a favorite), and frequently staged his dances on ramps and across large staircases. He peopled his numbers with dancers from his nightclub troupe, including George and Ethel Martin, Marc Wilder, Matt Mattox, and Buzz Miller. Verdon was front and center in nearly all of them. In the Danny Kaye vehicle *On the Riviera* (1951), as a showgirl in brilliant blue plumage, she is prominent as she sings (in dubbed voice) and leads the dance ensemble. She later essays an East Indian routine, demonstrating immaculate technique. Her detailed hand movements, rigid yet supple torso, and tight isolations are riveting.

The "I Don't Care" Girl (1953), a Mitzi Gaynor showcase, features some of Cole's most inventively staged and filmed dances. "Beale Street Blues" is its highlight, with Verdon dominating the number in swirling pink and a fedora, dancing aggressively and embodying the sharp detail of Cole's choreography. In two Betty

Grable vehicles, she is even more prominent, dancing alongside the star in the floorshow number "No Talent Joe" in *Meet Me after the Show* (1951). Here Cole slowed down the choreographic detail to accommodate Grable, giving a glimpse of the simpler jazz dance style other choreographers would derive from his work. For *The Farmer Takes a Wife* (1953), Cole created a calypso tap number for Verdon and Grable, danced with pie plates on their feet.

Verdon followed Cole to MGM, where he choreographed *The Merry Widow* (1952). His waltzes for stars Lana Turner and Fernando Lamas did not tax his creativity, but Cole staged a raucous cancan number that showed off Verdon as never before on-screen. Instead of the traditional long cancan skirts, the dancers wear black stockings, corsets (with provocative pink panties and ruffled bustles), and wide-brimmed hats. Set against all that black, Verdon's red hair flames off the screen, and the camera spends much of its time trained on her. Winking, flirting with the camera, and slapping a red scarf against the floor, Verdon is a knockout and made the camera's cutaways to Lana Turner entirely unwelcome.

Michael Kidd asked Verdon to come to New York to audition for a role in the new Cole Porter musical *Can-Can* that he was choreographing. Kidd and Verdon had gotten to know each other through the close-knit community of dancers in Hollywood while Kidd was there choreographing *Where's Charley?* (1952) and *The Band Wagon* (1953). Though nervous about her singing, Verdon auditioned and was hired on the spot by director Abe Burrows.

With *Can-Can*, Verdon got a lesson in star prerogatives and theatrical politics. Verdon's role as Claudine, by day a laundry worker but at night a cancan dancer in a notorious Montmartre dance hall, was of secondary importance. But it became clear during rehearsals and out-of-town tryouts that her sensational dancing was drawing focus from French chanteuse Lilo, the highly paid but insecure leading lady imported from Paris by producers Cy Feuer and Ernest Martin. At Lilo's insistence, Verdon's role was substantially cut, and her dances were arranged so that she ended most of them offstage. (For extra humiliation, Lilo made sure that Verdon appeared in the curtain call behind a piece of scenery.) By the time *Can-Can* arrived in New York, a discouraged and worn-down Verdon had reached an agreement with the producers that she would depart as soon as a replacement was hired.

No one, least of all Verdon, was prepared for the audience response to this unknown in a now minuscule role when *Can-Can* opened on May 7, 1953. In the second-act Apache dance, Verdon performed with athletic fury. At its climax, Verdon spies a knife stuck in a large cheese being carried across the stage. With one deft move, she extracts the knife from the cheese, stabs her abusive lover dead, returns the knife to the cheese, and triumphantly exits the stage.[44]

Verdon returned to her tiny dressing room and was changing for her next entrance when she heard a roar go up from the audience: "We want Verdon!" The set was changed and actors were now attempting to continue with the show, but the audience would not have it. Stomping and cheering, they refused to let *Can-Can* continue until they demonstrated their appreciation for the red-headed wonder who had yet to be given an opportunity for applause. Michael Kidd rushed back to her dressing room, grabbed the half-dressed Verdon, and literally pushed her onto the stage to take a bow, where she stood grinning and embarrassed, holding her costume in front of her. For a full seven minutes, *Can-Can* stopped while the audience fell hopelessly and forever in love with Gwen Verdon.

"She came on stage and everybody else disappeared," said Cy Feuer.[45] Verdon's blazing hair topped a delightfully animated face, with a wide mouth and sparkling eyes. It was a true stage face, one that registered every flicker of emotion to the farthest balcony seat. Verdon danced boldly and with athletic confidence and had the muscular legs of a Cole dancer, but those legs supported a figure both luscious and delicate, with expressive, graceful arms and a fluid torso. (Feuer claimed, "No one had a better behind" than Verdon in her prime.)[46] Her acting matched her dancing—direct, focused, and playful. Verdon's voice, which she had seldom been called upon to use, was the delicious topper: hoarse and crinkly, like cellophane, and with a throaty laugh that bubbled with innuendo. She was a sexpot with a sense of humor. The package was perfection.

The idea of a performance so overwhelming that it stops a show cold is part of cherished Broadway lore, but more frequently an invention of movie plots rather than something seen in actual practice. Yet here was a true showstopper, a definitive "star is born" moment that instantly became a Broadway touchstone. Just as Lilo feared, Verdon completely overshadowed her onstage and in the reviews. Her ex-husband's paper, the *Hollywood Reporter*, compared her triumph to that of Mary Martin singing "My Heart Belongs to Daddy" in Cole Porter's *Leave It To Me!* back in 1938.[47]

In the "Garden of Eden" ballet, when Eve takes a bite of the apple, its impact registers both on her face and in her pelvis, as her instant transformation into a bump and grind burlesque queen is tempered by naughty-girl bemusement. Verdon found the dance of the show's title to be vulgar. "Just an athletic display of underwear," she said.[48] "Dance it like a lady athlete," Jack Cole advised,[49] and she did just that, leading the ensemble in Kidd's climactic cancan routine with furious abandon as the curtain came down. Chita Rivera marveled that Verdon was "the perfect mixture of male and female. She was so feminine but she had power. She really showed female dancers that we can be as strong as a guy, but using our feminine attributes also."[50]

Verdon won the Tony Award for Best Featured Actress in a Musical, the Theatre World Award, and two Donaldson Awards, for Supporting Actress (Musical) and Female Dancer. (Carol Haney would win the same two awards the next year.) *Can-Can* was a hit, if not a distinguished one, and ran for 892 performances. But by the time it closed, Verdon had found the role that would secure her status as one of the great Broadway stars of the era.

"People ask if I created Gwen, and I say, 'She was hot when I met her.'"

Bob Fosse, 1985[51]

The players involved in *Damn Yankees* made it almost a sequel to *The Pajama Game*: same producers, same director, same choreographer, same composers, same budget, another Book-of-the-Month Club bestseller, and another

"Dance it like a lady athlete," Jack Cole once advised Gwen Verdon. Here she transmits Cole's strength and athleticism to Fosse in "Two Lost Souls" from Damn Yankees. *Photo by Friedman-Abeles © Billy Rose Theatre Division, The New York Public Library for the Performing Arts.*

collaboration between George Abbott and the book's author on the script. *The Year the Yankees Lost the Pennant*, written by the aptly named Douglass Wallop, updated the Faust legend to a contemporary, baseball-obsessed America. In it, a middle-aged Washington Senators fan sells his soul to the devil for the chance to become the great long ball hitter required to lick those "damn Yankees" and win the pennant for his team. George Abbott began working on the musical's book with Wallop almost immediately after Griffith, Prince, and Brisson purchased the stage rights. He even came up with the new, punchier title.

This time there was no talk of needing a backup, and Fosse's *Damn Yankees* contract reflected his elevated status. He was to receive payments totaling $2,500 by the first public performance, but more important, he would share in the royalty pool, receiving 1 percent of the gross weekly box-office receipts. His billing was now equal to that of the authors and director.[52]

The $162,000 budget for *Damn Yankees*, a bit less than that for *The Pajama Game*, allowed for the hiring of a similarly solid, if not star-laden, cast. Ray Walston, a wry, wiry actor whose résumé included Shakespeare and Tennessee Williams, as well as musicals like the recent *Me and Juliet*, was cast as Applegate, the devil's stand-in. Strapping, big-voiced Stephen Douglass, a replacement for John Raitt in *The Pajama Game*, was a natural for young Joe Hardy, the Washington Senators' star hitter. It proved more difficult to fill the role of Lola, the devil's top seductress, who effortlessly brings men to ruin. As originally planned, Lola was not a star role, and her first entrance did not arrive until late in act 1. Both Mitzi Gaynor and Zizi Jeanmarie turned down the role before third choice Gwen Verdon was approached.[53]

Given the potent theatrical alchemy Fosse and Verdon achieved in their many stage successes, it is surprising to learn that at first each was wary of working with the other. "I don't know her. How do I know we can work together?" Fosse asked producer Harold Prince.[54] For her part, Verdon had a reputation for being demanding. "And I was," she later said. "I couldn't stand bad dancing. I just hated choreography that was like animated wallpaper. It wasn't about anything, but it kept moving."[55] Verdon's standards were high, and her years with Cole had toughened her. Fosse's choreography would have to give her a reason to work with him.

When the two arrived at the Walton Warehouse, a West Side rehearsal studio, there was apprehension all around. "I'm very nervous," he said.[56] "So am I," she replied. "I'm just going to show you this number. I'll just do it," Fosse finally said, proceeding to dance every step of "Whatever Lola Wants," Lola's introductory number. "He was fantastic doing it," Verdon later recalled. "It had such sex appeal and yet it was so funny." All it needed was Verdon's insouciant sexuality and comic spark to complete it, and they immediately set to work. There at the Walton Warehouse Lola was born, and the partnership of Fosse and Verdon was forged.

Lola, the devil's number one homewrecker, first slithers into the Washington Senators' locker room all set to seduce Joe Hardy, wearing a getup described as "a sort of latter-day Sadie Thompson with a rose in her hair."[57] When her hokey, coquettish routine (in overstated Spanish dialect) eventually leads into "Whatever Lola Wants," it is a languid tango, conjuring musty images of Theda Bara and Rudolph Valentino. "I'll give him the standard vampire treatment,"[58] she determines, and it is this premise that Fosse satirizes in Lola's dance. Lola advances on Joe with her foot flexed in comic curlicues. She strips off her gloves and skirt and urges him to "give in" with thunderous hip bumps. Stalking Joe like a bullfighter, Lola pauses ever-so-briefly to scratch her leg. She clutches her throat in mock ecstasy and prances around with exaggerated Egyptian arm movements. She talks baby talk and "poo poo pe doo," drapes herself all over Joe, and crawls on the floor. She shimmies and strikes throat-grasping poses with all the subtlety of a silent movie vamp.

When Lola makes her final attack, Fosse draws on the step he first used in *My Sister Eileen*'s "Give Me a Band and My Baby." Lola pauses briefly with her hands on her hips, as if deciding just which killer move to pull out. She fixes Joe with an intent gaze, stoops slightly with arms hanging tightly in front of her and wrists locked together, and furiously minces toward him with arms and legs in sharp opposition. The effect is hilarious and slightly surreal. When she reaches Joe, she at last strikes the iconic pose that would define *Damn Yankees* and Verdon: in black lace tights cut scandalously high, legs triumphantly apart, and hands confidently on her hips, she belts out, "I always get what I aim for!" Fosse gradually decelerates the tempo (and gets in one more joke—a silly "sexy girl" walk) before the number ends in dramatic fashion with Lola throwing herself across Joe, practically demanding to be ravaged. *Time* magazine caught the sexy/satiric dichotomy Fosse and Verdon created in the number: "She wears a double crown: no one can make sex more seductive, or more hilarious."[59]

"Watch him move. He knows the joke," Verdon would later say of Fosse.[60] It was a joke they both knew and understood: sexuality leavened with humor, which gave it humanity and universality. Fosse's humor was a welcome antidote to Jack Cole's dour intensity, and Verdon's strength and versatility allowed Fosse to stretch as a choreographer. Their connection was immediate, and their affair seemed inevitable. For him, it was talent charged with sex, as he later said: "That alabaster skin, those eyes, that bantam rooster walk. Her in the leotard I will never forget."[61] "I just fell into Bob's work,"[62] Verdon remembered, much as she had done with Jack Cole a decade earlier, and she quickly and unquestioningly transferred her devotion to this new dance master.

While *Damn Yankees* and *The Pajama Game* shared many of the same personnel, the new show went through considerably more difficulties in finding the right mix of elements. One of Fosse's most elaborate numbers was the source of his first instance of conflict with Abbott and the producers. The first act was to end with a danced game of musical chairs led by a character dressed in a Yankees uniform and wearing a gorilla mask. The complicated, full-company number was confusing, and Abbott and Harold Prince urged Fosse to cut it. Instead, he spent valuable rehearsal time trying to refine the number before the New Haven tryout, eventually suggesting that if he played the gorilla, it would work. The number was in the show on opening night (with dancer George Marcy as the gorilla), and as Abbott and Prince predicted, it ended the first act on a baffling note. Prince's remarks to that effect, overheard by Fosse in the next hotel room, sent Fosse into a rage at what he felt was secretive maneuvering around his work.

The ever-practical Abbott suggested cutting the ballet and substituting a simpler number. From the Adler-Ross song trunk came "Who's Got the Pain?," a rhythm number capitalizing on the current mambo dance craze. As with "Steam Heat," a large-scale number was replaced by a simpler routine bearing no relation to the plot. Once again, Fosse created the number quickly, this time with help from Verdon, who received program credit.

"Who's Got the Pain?" was not the revelation that "Steam Heat" had been, but the two dances share similarities. Danced in unison, it gains much of its excitement from the synchronization of movement, in this case of two, rather than three, dancers. (Verdon was partnered by dancer Eddie Phillips.) The number is built around small mambo steps, emphasizing hip and rib cage isolations. Costumes are simple and androgynous (black toreador pants and sneakers, a midriff top for Verdon, a pullover for Phillips). Like the "ssssss" sounds in "Steam Heat," the dancers frequently punctuate the rhythms with a guttural "Ugh!"

The already-recognizable Fosse elements are on display: isolations, shimmies, a Chaplin walk, the use of hats. His favorite traveling step is here: as the dancer's arms lap forward in a swimming motion, the legs swing under and back. The step could be used to travel across the stage or stay in place while giving the impression of moving great distances.

"Who's Got the Pain?" abounds with clever touches. At one point, Verdon balances herself on Phillips's shoulders and leg, then falls backward, hanging from his shoulders, all while continuing to sing. Later, Verdon and Phillips place their backs against each other and slide to the floor, then rise up with bent knees and upper bodies parallel to the floor. Walking back and forth in this position, they look like lazy beachcombers with hats over their eyes, raising them only for an occasional "Ugh!"

Fosse filled *Damn Yankees* with other standout dances that showed his increased confidence working with large groups. A ballpark ballet early in act 1, constructed around the body language of the players, refutes the notion that dancing is for sissies. The number begins with Gloria, a female sports reporter, coining a new name for Joe Hardy: "Shoeless Joe from Hannibal Mo." The Washington Senators take up the chant and repeat it until the melody, in hoedown tempo, kicks in. Stressing athleticism and humor over graceful precision, Fosse creates danced variations on a variety of baseball runs, jumps, and slides, most notably a rhythmic walk in which the players pound their mitts and then airily leap up to catch a fly ball, with backs arching and feet toggling up underneath.

Fosse's players exhibit courtly sportsmanship, tipping their hats and walking on their heels with elbows up in a jaunty gait. Fosse broke his core team of eight dancers into quartets, trios, and duos and staged them in opposition, making simple movements look complex. A trio walks Chaplin-style to center stage for a series of catches; later it returns for a variation with bats—kicking, twirling, and proudly promenading.

The dance has the frequent shifts in tempo that give Fosse's numbers their sense of variety and momentum. The dancing stops while a pitcher juggles balls. A batter hits a fly ball out of the field, to the wonderment of his teammates, all in exaggerated slow motion. The players execute a vigorous bit of Irish step dancing. They execute backward barrel turns, first in small groups, then everyone, before ending with a slide into home plate down at the footlights. Fosse melds dance and baseball without compromising either.

More than any other number in *Damn Yankees*, the next-to-closing "Two Lost Souls" shows Gwen Verdon's influence on Fosse's choreography. In a seedy dive not unlike Hernando's Hideaway, couples dance or slouch at tables. Lola and Joe, out for the night and slightly drunk, soon wind up on the floor. The nightclub denizens slowly join in, snapping fingers and rolling shoulders, creating a cool, beatnik energy. Fosse ignores the convention of keeping everyone facing front; dancers turn their backs to the audience and do unison steps in opposition to the others. Lola begins a dance sequence and is joined by several women, some held up at the knees by a man. The women perform the arm movements while the men dance the floor patterns, giving the illusion of ten-foot-tall dancers. A trio begins a step, which is then picked up by the larger group, some on their knees, others on an upstage bandstand. Unison movement is given texture and variety through Fosse's use of levels and positioning.

The dancers form an amoeba, a large, tightly packed human clump of bodies all executing different steps at various levels but moving together as one unit. Verdon later recalled Fosse's visualization of the amoeba as a giant torso, taken from the art books he collected of painters like Hieronymus Bosch featuring surreal images of freaks and people stuck together with arms and legs jutting out.[63] The amoeba would become a Fosse signature move, useful in a variety of settings. Here it has a languid, late-night quality, and it soon dissolves, leaving Lola at center stage for a solo that shows Verdon mixing Fosse with Jack Cole. While Cole worked most often in plié, "Bob liked everything pulled up," Verdon later recalled.[64] Here they split the difference, with Verdon expertly lunging low and lifting high. Playful and tossed off as it is, the dance illustrates Cole's transmission through Verdon to Fosse. The stiff backs, the horizontal movement, and the formal, elegant quality of the upper-arm work embody Cole's jazz dance style. "Two Lost Souls" builds to a full-ensemble climax of extravagant loucheness as the curtain comes down. (Oddly, the dance does not end or "button," but gives the sense of continuing on after the curtain descends.)

The out-of-town reviews were encouraging. Cyrus Durgin in the *Boston Globe* called *Damn Yankees* "as fresh and unconventional as 'Oklahoma!' was in 1943" and ended a short list of suggested improvements with a plea to the creators: "And bring Gwen Verdon on earlier."[65] Verdon had three major numbers but less total stage time than either Walston or Douglass, and audiences clearly

Social dancing, 1950s. Gretchen Wyler, Gwen Verdon's replacement as Lola, leads the dancers, down on their knees or lifted high, in Damn Yankees' *late-night, louche "Two Lost Souls." Photo by Friedman-Abeles, Museum of the City of New York © The New York Public Library.*

wanted more of her. The authors set to work finding an earlier introduction for Verdon, and Adler and Ross came up with "A Little Brains, a Little Talent," in which Lola humorously describes her professional skill set as a mantrap, punctuating the lyric with baby talk. It was as tightly choreographed as anything else in the show, built around the tiniest of movements. Verdon, in a skintight dress, did little more than small, strategically placed hip undulations, for which Fosse gave her the image of adjusting her panties inside her dress with as little unnecessary movement as possible.[66]

Joan McCracken accompanied Fosse on the show's out-of-town engagements and was at his side on opening night, but it was clear to everyone that the marriage was over. In a replay of *Dance Me a Song*, by the time *Damn Yankees* returned to New York, Fosse had become romantically involved with the star of the show, all in front of his wife.

Each of his wives collaborated with and inspired Fosse at important moments in his career. Niles, the talented tap dancer, was his partner in the act that helped him reach his early goal of a nightclub career. McCracken, the ballet-trained star, expanded his outlook by encouraging him to study acting and other forms of dance, and promoted his potential as a choreographer. But now he was an emerging star himself who no longer needed his wife's mentoring. Verdon, with her Jack Cole training and insouciant sexuality, was poised to be the perfect embodiment of the developing Fosse style.

Damn Yankees opened May 5, 1955, at the 46th Street Theater to generally positive reviews that inevitably compared it to *The Pajama Game*. It was foremost a personal triumph for Verdon, whose notices exceeded those of everyone, including Fosse. *Variety*, noting her earlier acclaim in *Can-Can*, declared that she "demonstrates even greater talent, versatility and personal impact in 'Yankees.' . . .The dancer-singer-comedienne is a genuine star prospect."[67]

Some critics called attention to Fosse's recycling of steps and motifs from his earlier work even as they praised the numbers themselves—criticism that would continue throughout his career. *Variety* observed, "Among the notable dance numbers are . . . a duet by Miss Verdon and Eddie Phillips, called 'Who's Got the Pain?' (slightly reminiscent of 'Steam Heat' from 'Pajama Game') and finally a striking ensemble to 'Two Lost Souls' (a little in the manner of 'Hernando's Hideaway' from 'Pajama Game')."[68] It seemed rather early for such observations to be lodged against the twenty-seven-year-old choreographer.

The show was an even bigger success than *The Pajama Game* at the Tony Awards, winning in nine categories, including Best Musical, with Verdon and Fosse taking the awards for Best Actress in a Musical and Best Choreography, respectively. Unlike *The Pajama Game*, *Damn Yankees* did not immediately take off at the box office. Less than a month after opening, the show's advertising and billing were altered to shift their focus from baseball to sex. In recognition of her star-making performance, Verdon was promoted to above-the-title billing. With her promotion, the producers took the opportunity not only to change the poster from baseball green to devilish red but also to swap its image of Verdon in a baseball jersey and cap to her triumphantly sexy Lola pose, in black lace and tights.

That alteration had an immediate impact on sales, keeping the show running for 1,019 performances.

During *Damn Yankees*' run, Verdon became one of the rare dancers to claim the cover of *Time*. She was now officially a Broadway star, a box-office draw whose next career move was much anticipated. And it was fully expected that her next show would again be choreographed by Bob Fosse.

> "In those days, I was still jumping back and forth between being a performer and I wasn't quite sure whether I liked being a choreographer that much."
>
> Bob Fosse, c. 1980[69]

Over the summer of 1955, while Verdon performed in *Damn Yankees*, Fosse reprised *Pal Joey* in summer stock. It was the first of several returns he would make to this role, though none of these appearances led to further acting opportunities. Harold Prince later observed, "Bobby was terrific. He had great charm. But he was eaten by wanting to be a performer, and he just didn't have it. And it frustrated him totally."[70]

Joan McCracken was also away that summer, touring as a guest artist with Ballet Theatre, dancing the role of the Cowgirl in Agnes de Mille's *Rodeo*. By now, she had developed symptoms of heart disease related to her diabetes, which was exacerbated by a lifelong smoking habit. She left the tour prematurely and soon suffered successive heart attacks and a case of pneumonia that kept her hospitalized for a lengthy period. Fosse, now deeply involved with Verdon, was less available to McCracken, either physically or emotionally, at this fragile time.

In December, the *Colgate Variety Hour* staged a tribute to George Abbott, with numbers from several of his shows, including *Damn Yankees* and *The Pajama Game*. Fosse appeared twice, first as straight man (executing a rather stiff ballet barre) to Nancy Walker in the lead-up to a comic ballerina number from *Look Ma, I'm Dancin'*, and later in an original dance number with Peter Gennaro called "Senors Loco," to music by his trusted dance arranger, Roger Adams. Introduced by Abbott as a dance about "two charming fellows who go for a day in the country and have a terrible time," it was an early attempt at a story dance within a rhythmic "Steam Heat"/"Who's Got the Pain?" framework. Looking dapper in identical black pants with suspenders, white shirts, and caps, and carrying canes, Fosse and Gennaro are a good match, their slim-hipped swivels closely synched.

"Senors Loco" begins slowly, as arm and torso movements in opposition give way to Chaplin walks and off-balance turns. Charlie Chaplin goes Mambo with Fosse and Gennaro's hyperactive hips augmenting their flat-footed walk. Eventually the walk is done in a very deep plié, then rising up to a Joe Frisco step in which one foot inches along in toe-heel traveling movements without leaving the floor, while the other trails along in a slow, circular movement. The step would become a favorite of Fosse's, and it makes its debut here. They comically embrace for a mock tango before arriving in the country and taking to the water.

Soon they are scooping water with their caps, and Fosse throws the contents of his cap into Gennaro's face, initiating a none-too-convincing fight. A sword duel with the canes follows. Fosse does a brief Mexican hat dance around his cap.

Bending over to pick up the cap, Fosse uses the old vaudeville trick of placing his sword/cane under his arm with the "blade" behind him, accidentally stabbing Gennaro as he sneaks up from behind. Gennaro returns the stab, and they drop to their knees, roll on their backs, and stick their legs up like dying insects. The number ends with Fosse clumsily dragging Gennaro, on his knees, offstage, while he twirls his cane as a baton and Gennaro strums his like a guitar.[71]

As a story dance, "Senors Loco" lacks coherence. The relationship of the two men is unclear, its conflict awkwardly set up and staged, its resolution bizarre. "Senors Loco" shows Fosse struggling to use his already identifiable choreographic style to create a narrative.

He was on much safer and satisfying ground performing a song and dance with Carol Haney to Irving Berlin's "I Love a Piano" on Ed Sullivan's television show in early 1956. Fosse, in tux and straw boater, looks like a young, jazzy Fred Astaire, and he and Haney exhibit the same raffish chemistry they had in "From This Moment On." After a charming and playful vocal, Fosse and Haney dance an easygoing soft-shoe. They launch into a series of 1920s dance steps, including shimmies, snake hips, and the black bottom, climaxing with a cakewalk. The old vaudeville applause-getter of one dancer holding a hat at increasing elevations while the other kicks ever higher is given new life by Fosse and Haney. Attitude and energy made period dancing look contemporary. "Keep It Hot" (later called the "Hot Honey Rag") from *Chicago* would borrow heavily from this routine, with similar impact.[72]

It was a surprise to see Fosse's name appear in advance news reports as co-choreographer for *Bells Are Ringing*, alongside director-choreographer Jerome Robbins. *Bells Are Ringing* was made to order by Betty Comden and Adolph Green, writing for their old friend and fellow revue performer Judy Holliday, who had since attained Broadway and movie fame in Garson Kanin's *Born Yesterday*. With music by Jule Styne, *Bells Are Ringing*'s slight story hinged on the involvement of Holliday's Ella Peterson, a telephone answering service operator, with her varied clients. The billing for this new Robbins-Fosse collaboration read, "Dances and Musical Numbers Staged by Jerome Robbins and Bob Fosse."

Mostly, Robbins did the musical staging of songs, while Fosse attended to the dances. "Hello, Hello There!," a full-cast number set on a subway, brought back unkind memories of Fosse's experience with "7½ Cents." When Fosse's staging failed to lift the number, Robbins again came to the rescue, as dancer Frank Derbas remembered: "Bobby had us all shaking hands on the subway, and Jerry would have us reach out and put our hands way over our heads in a big circle [and] bring them down to shake hands. When you've got thirty people [onstage] that's what you need to see."[73]

Fosse's major contribution to *Bells Are Ringing* was "Mu-Cha-Cha," another "Who's Got the Pain?" reworking, given the flimsiest of plot setups. While Ella is dressing for a date, two friends teach her the latest dance sensation, the cha-cha. After a chorus of the song and a brief dance, Holliday exits, leaving Peter Gennaro, Ellen Ray, and the dance ensemble to continue. Featuring the kind of tight, close choreography now associated with Fosse, "Mu-Cha-Cha" was a

"Tight trousers, etc." Ellen Ray and Peter Gennaro dance "Mu-Cha-Cha" in Bells Are Ringing. *The hinge, in plié and on demi-pointe, remained a favorite Fosse stance. Photo by Friedman-Abeles © Billy Rose Theatre Division, The New York Public Library for the Performing Arts.*

high-spirited retread, with hip swivels and generic Latin flavor. *Dance Magazine*'s critic dismissed it as "tight trousers, etc."[74]

Bells Are Ringing was a popular hit, playing 924 performances. For all its success and the warm relationship that Robbins and Fosse enjoyed (the cufflinks were once again exchanged on opening night), it is surprising to learn how unhappy Robbins was with Fosse's work on the show. In a letter to dancer Tanaquil Le Clercq soon after the opening, he wrote, "One terrible part of the show is that Bob Fosse, who did most of the dances, managed to eke out a bad second hand version of dances I have already done, so that it looks like I have just copied myself and repeated badly what I once did well."[75]

By the time *Bells Are Ringing* opened on November 29, 1956, Fosse was in California, working on his next project. *The Pajama Game* and *Damn Yankees* were both acquired by Warner Brothers, and as with the Broadway productions, the two films form a matched set of production and personnel, including Fosse adapting his choreography to the screen. Originally Abbott was to produce the film version of *The Pajama Game*, in association with Griffith, Prince, and Brisson, and

Stanley Donen, who had danced in Abbott's *Pal Joey* and *Best Foot Forward* years earlier, would direct. To persuade Abbott to share his staging ideas from the theater, Donen offered Abbott the credit of co-director. Abbott accepted on the condition that Donen share co-producer credit with him, and the arrangement was carried over to *Damn Yankees* the following year.[76]

Warner Brothers produced both *The Pajama Game* and *Damn Yankees* on tight budgets and swift shooting schedules.[77] Shooting moved so quickly because, with notable exceptions, both films were peopled with their original Broadway casts. For *The Pajama Game*, Doris Day replaced Janis Paige as Babe for box-office assurance, but the rest of the cast and many of the dancers came directly from New York ready to perform for the cameras.

The "Jealousy Ballet" and "Her Is" were early victims of the need to reduce a two-and-a-half-hour stage show to an under-two-hour film. But even "Steam Heat" was not entirely safe. In a telegram to Fosse before filming began, Harold Prince wrote, "Evidently Steamheat [*sic*] is not definitely eliminated from movie but has been postponed because of budget difficulties. Situation has nothing to do with Carol's health."[78] (Haney had been discovered to be suffering from diabetes.)

Happily, Carol Haney and "Steam Heat" were part of the finished film, and the wide, clean camera angles capture this "in performance" number perfectly. *The Pajama Game* was unusual among musical films of this period in eschewing MGM-style glamour to portray its smoky union halls and dingy factory workrooms. The surprisingly gritty photography by Harry Stradling highlighted "Once a Year Day," the film's biggest and most photographically innovative number. Donen and Fosse spent a week filming it in Los Angeles's Hollenbeck and Griffith Parks.[79]

Fosse blew up the number, filling the park with an expanded ensemble of eighty dancers, while maintaining its loose, improvised quality. His staging concepts were all there, including the human jigsaw puzzle (in even larger proportions), the crossovers, and the character bits. But the camera pulled up and back to show the full scope of the group movement. Long, expansive traveling shots captured Haney leading the dancers through the park, seemingly for miles. Donen and Fosse built the number to its climax by splintering movement through editing. Quick cuts and odd angles (with the camera above, beneath, or embedded among the dancers) captured the picnickers leaping, doing stunts, and rolling down a hill. No less than Jean-Luc Godard praised Fosse's ability to heighten everyday movement into an original dance style and hailed the number as one of the best in any musical, applauding Donen, with help from Fosse and Stradling, for composing "a wild and ravishing kaleidoscope."[80] *The Pajama Game* made its first appearance, appropriately, on Labor Day weekend 1957 at Radio City Music Hall.

A year later, *Damn Yankees* went through much the same rushed schedule, this time due to a pending film union strike. Warner Brothers heartthrob Tab Hunter, as Joe Hardy, joined the entire original Broadway company, including Gwen Verdon, who now returned to films as a star. One other notable addition to the cast included Fosse himself, who, appropriately enough, danced "Who's Got the Pain?" with Verdon. In a letter to George Abbott, Robert Griffith informed the director, "I have negotiated with Bobby Fosse about doing the Mambo and the terms are as follows: one blond toupe [*sic*] for one week's work. I consider these excellent terms."[81]

Their performance of "Who's Got the Pain?" is the only example of the two dancing together in a feature film, and Fosse's perfectionism is much in evidence. Patricia Ferrier Kiley, who assisted Fosse on the dances, remembered him ordering her to monitor their performance to make sure the pair was in perfect sync: "He said, if we're not together, if we miss anything, you've got to stop the filming."[82] More pointedly, Fosse and Donen argued over the lighting of the number. As Verdon later recalled, "Bob wanted it black, with a real vaudeville spotlight, and Stanley said, 'It'll look like the black hole of Calcutta.' "[83] Fosse's concept won, and the resulting number has an unexpected dramatic intensity. Fosse and Verdon in their yellow tops and white sneakers glide through the screen's inky blackness. The two are indeed together throughout the dance, their very breathing seemingly in sync, and the movement, now so calibrated to their bodies, joyful and effortless. Fosse and Verdon danced together later on television, but this Technicolor duet captured them at a perfect moment as true collaborators— flying high and in love.

Flying high and in love, Fosse and Verdon dance "Who's Got the Pain?," a number they originally choreographed together, in the film version of Damn Yankees. *Warner Bros.*

Much of *Damn Yankees* had a flat, studio-bound visual quality, but as with *The Pajama Game*, location work brought an added dimension to a large dance number. Filming "Shoeless Joe from Hannibal Mo" in a baseball stadium gave the movement space to expand. At one point, the ball players dance on, and then jump from, the top of the dugout roof. The dancers' runs and pitches looked perfectly natural in a real playing field. Once again, Donen and Fosse pumped up the excitement with a series of quick cuts—close-ups of players chanting "Joe!" and shots of them somersaulting, diving, and whipping up clouds of dust leading to the final full-cast slide.

"Two Lost Souls" was an anomaly in the film's brightly lit visual palette. Its smoky, diffused lighting made the number glow with carnal energy. The rich pastels of the dancers' costumes made Verdon, in black, even more prominent as the camera tracks her across the floor. Fosse's staging of the dancers on elevations, and the deep-focus photography, created a cast-of-thousands effect. Verdon remembered how Fosse "used the camera like another dancer," and at one point, wearing a shoulder-held camera, he "got in the dance with us," giving the number a greater sense of intimacy.[84]

Damn Yankees got slightly better reviews than *The Pajama Game* when it was released in September 1958. Calling it "a first class musical film," Bosley Crowther in the *New York Times* sang the leading lady's extravagant praises: "Her appearance in the best role in this picture is a major screen event of the year. Miss Verdon . . . is an absolute natural for films, a superlatively talented dancer and a sparkling comedienne."[85] However, more than one reviewer noted the camera's unkindness toward Verdon, including Crowther, who pointed out, "She may not be too good looking, by the measuring tape of Hollywood."[86] The animated features that carried all the way to a theater balcony photographed rather sharply in close-up, especially next to the creamy-skinned Tab Hunter. Verdon, like Ethel Merman, Mary Martin, and Carol Channing, had a face better suited for the stage than the screen, and *Damn Yankees* would be her only starring film role.

The Pajama Game and *Damn Yankees* represent the early, joyous flowering of the Fosse style, and both reflect an easygoing postwar optimism. Their working-class settings, in a Midwest factory town and the suburbs of a sleepy Washington, DC, were gently shaken up by Fosse's choreography, unpretentious yet cocky, with its vaudeville touches and satiric sexiness.

Within their conventional frameworks, *The Pajama Game* and *Damn Yankees* push the limits of the musical film in ways that would influence Fosse when he eventually took his place behind a camera. Donen's location work, theatrical use of lighting, and editing that pumps added energy into the dance numbers give suggestions of both his earlier work with Gene Kelly and later Fosse films like *Sweet Charity* and *Cabaret*. He stands alongside George Abbott and Jerome Robbins as an important early influence on Fosse's development as an artist.

"I didn't like the way directors had the power to ruin my dances—or throw them out altogether. A director would say, 'You've got to cut that!' Well, he was the boss, so I thought, 'You've got to be the boss, if you want to protect the integrity of the work.'"

Bob Fosse, 1972[87]

It was Doris Day who set in motion the events that led to Bob Fosse's next musical, the show that convinced him it was time to become a director himself. Day told George Abbott that MGM had an exciting score by Bob Merrill for a contemporary retelling of Eugene O'Neill's *Anna Christie*, set on California's Monterey coast. Intrigued, Abbott and the Brisson-Griffith-Prince producing team heard the score and agreed that it would be their next musical project. Merrill was a hugely successful songwriter of pop hits such as "How Much Is That Doggie in the Window?," and he now joined the list of young talents given their first opportunity in an Abbott show. (The team of Jerry Adler and Jerry Ross had come to an abrupt and tragic end when Ross died at age twenty-nine of a chronic lung infection months after *Damn Yankees* opened.)

O'Neill's Pulitzer Prize–winning 1921 drama centered on a woman embittered by her former life as a prostitute who struggles to rehabilitate herself. Recovering from tuberculosis, Anna arrives at New York's waterfront to stay with her father, an alcoholic barge captain whom she has not seen since he sent her to live with relatives when she was a young girl. She meets a rough-edged seaman who begins to melt her hardened view of men, but he violently rejects her when he learns of her past. Ultimately he comes to understand Anna's desire to put her past behind her and start over and, as he embarks on a sea voyage, promises to return to her. The role is most closely identified with Greta Garbo, who uttered Anna's famous opening lines—"Gimme a whiskey—ginger ale on the side. And don't be stingy, baby"—in her talking film debut in 1930.

Bob Merrill's score was the starting point for the production, but since it had been written for a present-day setting, much of it had to be jettisoned. In the end, Merrill wrote an entirely new score, retaining only two of his original songs.[88] Abbott did his own adaptation and pushed the setting from the 1920s back to the turn of the century. "The clothes were prettier in 1900," he flatly stated.[89] Indeed, Rouben Ter-Arutunian's lavish turn-of-the-century costumes, including a garish "sporting woman" turnout for Anna's first entrance, and colorful waterfront sets made for a sumptuous production and pushed the budget up to $242,750.[90] Bob Fosse was considered such an integral part of the creative team that the producers were willing to postpone rehearsals until he had enjoyed a six-week vacation following the filming of *The Pajama Game*.[91]

Gwen Verdon actively campaigned to play Anna in order to stretch herself beyond the sexy comedienne roles that had brought her success. "I wanted them to realize that I'm not Lola," she later said.[92] It was decided early on that Fosse's dances for the waterfront floozies and barroom denizens would swirl around, but never engage, Anna. Harold Prince expressed concerns that having Verdon in the role would automatically raise audience expectations for a dancing Anna: "I said, 'Gwen, you're a terrific actress. I'd love to have you play Anna Christie. But you cannot dance. Anna Christie doesn't dance.'"[93] Verdon agreed, and an initial reading prompted encouragement from Abbott. A disappointing singing audition was followed by intense vocal training, after which a final audition won Verdon the role in the now-retitled *New Girl in Town*.

New Girl in Town was to be a serious musical play from the producers, director, and choreographer of *The Pajama Game* and *Damn Yankees*, and starring the delectable Lola—an ambitious extension of everyone's talents. Rehearsals began on March 1, 1957, with George Wallace as Mat, the sailor who first loves and then rejects Anna; Cameron Prud'homme as Chris, Anna's father; and celebrated character actress Thelma Ritter in the expanded role of Marthy, the blowsy wharf rat who is Chris's long-time consort. The role was enlarged to such a degree that Ritter would share above-the-title billing with Verdon.

Verdon was "a natural," a major talent with immense charm and a vibrant personality. But acting O'Neill—even musicalized O'Neill—required more, and Verdon approached her new role with serious intent and a dancer's discipline. She had already begun classes with Sanford Meisner, the acting teacher Fosse had earlier studied with at Joan McCracken's recommendation, and she now began private coaching sessions. Fosse viewed Verdon's studies as a way for her to grow as an actress and also to cope with Abbott's directorial practices, as he later recalled. "George Abbott is the kind of director that requires almost immediate results . . . . so I thought that she needed another influence so that she could also give Abbott what he wanted . . . and then fill it in underneath, and Sandy, I believe, could give her that."[94] Verdon herself was more succinct: "I wanted to show that musical theater acting *is* acting, like in straight O'Neill."[95]

New Girl in Town did not lend itself as easily to dance as his previous shows, and it carried a feeling of Fosse grasping for movement opportunities. He devoted considerable preproduction time to devising walks, steps, and bits of movement that could be combined and executed by groups of various sizes, remembered Patricia Ferrier Kiley.[96] For his first period show, Fosse created robust, rowdy dances. The burly waterfront milieu was established at the very top of the show with "Roll Yer Socks Up," as sailors were welcomed back to shore by the local prostitutes. "It was big choreography, not all that tight stuff," remembered dancer Harvey Evans, particularly a lift in which the women flipped themselves over the sailors' arms.[97] Photographs show the sailors dragging the women by their legs across the stage as others leap and perform handsprings.

"The Sunshine Girl," a barbershop harmony number, gave Fosse a chance to again evoke Joe Frisco. With cigar firmly chomped, dancer Eddie Phillips (Verdon's "Who's Got the Pain?" partner) snake-hipped and chugged across the stage. The dance was superfluous, in line with previous Fosse specialties, but it added humor and eccentricity to the somber story.

For "The Check Apron Ball," performed "in one," Fosse devised ingenious staging that brought the cast, all dressed in outlandishly colorful fancy dress, across the front of the stage from left to right, individually and in small groups. Once they were offstage, they dashed back to stage left and re-entered in other groupings, giving the impression of an endless cast. For each reappearance, Fosse designed different movements to delay the inevitable discovery that it was the same dancers, and he created additional humor through selective repetition. A focal point for the number was a heavyset cast member in a garish suit, always recognizable when he came back around. By his third appearance, the audience would break into applause, according to Harvey Evans.[98]

In New Haven for its first tryout engagement, audiences for *New Girl in Town* waited through a long first act before Verdon lifted a toe to dance. "There Ain't No Flies on Me," the first-act finale set at the Check Apron Ball, included four dance variations—"Cakewalk," "Jelly Roll," "Promenade," and "Soft Shoe"—and Verdon was prominent in all of them.[99] Photographs of the soft-shoe trio of Verdon, Harvey Evans, and Harvey Jung show that despite Anna's long dress and the men's period suits, the number featured distinctive Fosse touches, including hats, flexed feet, and detailed hand work. The "Jelly Roll" was another eccentric dance sequence with Eddie Phillips.

Anna, falling in love with Mat and warmly welcomed by the locals, begins to soften and enter the spirit of the party. She steps forth and performs a dance of great pride and happiness, presenting herself in her new role as a woman of decent character. Verdon described it as "a dramatic moment. The dance was being presented as something very special and I had to convince the audience that I was very special."[100] Fosse emphasizes the performative nature of Anna's dance by basing its movement on that of a show pony, proud and high-stepping. Each sequence is preceded by a bow or presentation of arms, as if Anna is trying out variations on her new persona. She begins by loosening her hair and letting it fall into a ponytail, which she shakes and twirls. To a grand, swirling melody, Anna bows and paws at the ground, while executing elegant port de bras. She circles around herself while rotating her upper torso. A double-time pony step leads into a cakewalk sequence with Anna now partnered by a male dancer. She circles the stage in a series of stag leaps, first alone, then joined by the male dancer, before ending with a curtsy and bow as he kisses her hand and the partiers cheer and applaud. In the "Pony Dance," as it has become known, Fosse set to dance the very moment when Anna sheds the burden of her past and declares that she deserves to be happy and in love. It was the joyous, emotional high point of *New Girl in Town*, and when he first saw it performed, George Abbott himself wept.[101]

A full-cast cakewalk with Verdon at the center immediately follows and brings the first-act curtain down at a peak of excitement. Fosse engineers a stunning staging moment when the entr'acte ends with the same cakewalk music and the curtain rises on the company still dancing, as if they had never stopped throughout the intermission. Only then does the number reach its conclusion. The device, breathtaking in its simplicity, continues the narrative without a break, making the show appear to be performed in one seamless act. Fosse was clearly thinking as a director.

If Abbott wept when he saw the "Pony Dance," he was dry-eyed when it came to the second-act ballet Fosse and Verdon had devised. Following Mat's rejection of Anna when he learns of her past, she thinks back to her days in a bordello, conjuring her fellow whores and their various customers. A decade and a half after Agnes de Mille's "Laurey Makes Up Her Mind" in *Oklahoma!*, dream ballets were now both a staple and a cliché. (Fosse's "Jealousy Ballet" in *The Pajama Game* was a comic riff on the practice.) But the impulse behind "Red Light Ballet" in *New Girl in Town* is dramatically sound and theatrically practical. Anna's rejection by Mat just at the moment of her greatest happiness is a reasonable starting point for her to re-examine her former life. Meisner had helped Verdon build her performance by drawing on her own childhood experience of wearing corrective boots. Verdon remembered, "Even after I was able to take those shoes off, I was afraid something would stick out and give me away. For Anna, I think, 'I'm trying to be a lady but now people look at me and still think I'm a prostitute. Something gives me away.'"[102] Verdon's observation is played out by a character known simply as the Masher, who follows Anna, trying to remember where he has seen her before. It is a reminder that her past is never far away, with the Masher figuring prominently in her tortured remembrance.

After a long first act, the second act was barely forty-five minutes and short on musical moments. A ballet would provide a much-needed dance spot in the lead-up to the plot's conclusion. It was also a pretext to get the show's dancing star dancing once more—and in the mode that most theatergoers favored for Verdon. At last, the bewitching dance star could strip off her long skirts and perform with the unbridled sexuality of her earlier roles.

The "Red Light Ballet" is a lost piece of choreography, but through examination of photographs and remembrances of its dancers, this signal work in the Fosse canon comes into focus. A bare stage, set with only straight-backed chairs and a staircase leading offstage, is broken by sinister slashes of light. The only music is the throbbing of a double bass. Anna joins the other prostitutes draped suggestively across the chairs or on the floor spread-eagled—flagrant poses demonstrating the exotic menu of sexual opportunities to be found upstairs. As the men enter, the women twirl into a lascivious cancan, hoisting their skirts to show off their crotches or bending over to expose their rumps. Anna is the center of attention, the cheekiest, most provocative of whores. A young boy on his first trip to a whorehouse is held by his belt as he leans forward and Anna teases and licks at his face, sending him into a frantic nerve tap with his foot that quickly takes over his entire leg. One by one, the men carry the women up the stairs, leaving Anna alone with the Masher. He and Anna, now stripped to a corset, dance an erotic pas de deux that includes a feigned performance of oral sex and climaxes with Anna's backward leap from the staircase into his arms. Carrying her over his shoulder like a captured deer, the Masher slowly ascends the stairs as the ballet ends.[103]

The nineteenth-century prostitutes of the "Red Light Ballet" bear some similarity to the Postcard Girls in the dream ballet from *Oklahoma!*. But where de Mille deconstructs the cliché of the good-time, cancan-dancing saloon girl through striking stylization—a "broken doll" posture renders them listless and sexless—Anna and her sister prostitutes are energetic and alive with sex, if only for the selling.[104] Fosse brings his own stylization to the movement, arranging the women in impossible, off-center postures on the chairs, with flexed feet and dresses hanging over their heads. (One dancer was staged on

In "Red Light Ballet" from New Girl in Town, *Fosse evokes the broken-doll postures of Agnes de Mille's* Oklahoma! *Postcard Girls. At center, John Aristides as the Masher and Gwen Verdon as Anna Christie. Library of Congress, Performing Arts Reading Room.*

the floor, on her shoulder with bent legs up in the air.) The effect, simultaneously erotic and unsettling, is one he would adapt later for "Mein Herr" in *Cabaret.*

Fosse leavens his first dramatic story ballet with his own brand of humor (the seasoned burlesque gag of a shaking leg comically signifying an erection) and uses lighting and sound effects for texture. A lobsterscope (a slitted, rotating disc that spins in front of a spotlight) gave the movement a hypnotic, slow-motion quality. The women hiss and make kissing sounds as they entice the men. More ambitiously, Fosse attempts to show what Anna could never tell Mat—that as much as she hated being a prostitute, it also had rewards. The ballet's early, raucous moments present Anna as an enthusiastic whorehouse employee. She and the other women tease and provoke the men, guiding their every move. Anna may have contempt for them, but she exerts control in a way she does nowhere else. Only later with the Masher does she experience the disgust she has described to Mat.

Abbott's concern about the explicit nature of Fosse's choreography began in the rehearsal hall long before the show's first out-of-town tryout in New Haven. He later wrote, "I made no protest against this number, nor did my associates, until we saw it before an audience. Then the cold, shocked reaction of the viewers made us realize that the sequence was just plain dirty."[105] Even Fosse admitted that the audience sat silent and no one applauded. But while his response was to work to improve the ballet, Abbott and the producers emphatically wanted it out. More than fifty years later, Prince still bridled at the remembrance of it: "It was a filthy dance with whores lying on their backs, with fans on their feet, fanning themselves, and so on. And George and I just hated it."[106]

Abbott and Prince's view of the ballet was similar to Mat's of Anna: the display of her vibrant, lively sexuality led them to dismiss its representation of her soul-crushing humiliation. To be fair, Fosse provided mixed signals. The excitement and humor of the early portions of the ballet, along with its explicit choreography, may have made it difficult for Abbott and Prince (and others) to see the point he hoped to make. Verdon may also have inadvertently affirmed Abbott and Prince's viewpoint. In her studious desire to give an honest, raw performance, she sometimes allowed her breast to pop out of her corset when she was carried up the stairs at the climax of the ballet.[107]

The producers used the show's move to Boston to cut the ballet and discard the staircase, a key element of the number. Both Fosse and Verdon were furious with the decision and fought to have the ballet restored, thus setting up two camps within the company: Fosse and Verdon (and the dancers) versus Abbott and the producers. Fosse was already unhappy with Abbott's adaption, later saying, "He was trying to make another 'Pajama Game' out of O'Neill. . . . I thought the show should be rougher, more animal-like, a little stronger in language, stronger all around, stronger in emotions and he kept pulling it away from that."[108] He also had not forgotten the overheard Harold Prince discussion of *Damn Yankees*' first-act finale number during its out-of-town tryout. Once again, Fosse felt that others were dictating his creative decisions.

Fosse created a tamer version of the ballet, but according to Abbott, "though the new dance started off differently it somehow seemed to end up as the same old peep show. That ballet was like a disease—I couldn't eradicate it."[109] The tension and anxiety created by the conflict were distressing to everyone, especially Verdon, who was rehearsing during the day, performing at night, and working after the show with Fosse on the new ballet. Exhausted, she missed four performances at the end of Boston run, and because no single woman in the company was deemed qualified to cover her role, four were needed to take her place: one to sing and act, and the other three to perform her dances.[110] It was a reminder, along with the sellout business the show was doing out of town, just how much the success of *New Girl in Town* fell on the slender shoulders of its star.

" 'New Girl' has been tougher to get into shape than 'Pajama Game' and 'Damn Yankees,' "[111] Abbott said with understatement as his seventy-sixth Broadway production prepared to open at the 46th Street Theater on May 14, 1957, at a record ticket price of $9.20. Abbott's adaptation was deemed a disappointment, unable to reconcile O'Neill with the requirements of a musical. Even its breezy title placed *New Girl in Town* at odds with its dramatic source material.

Criticism of its adaptation aside, *New Girl in Town* received generally favorable reviews driven by its two stars, particularly Verdon. Not since Joan McCracken had a dancer received comparable notices for her acting. Brooks Atkinson in the *New York Times* wrote, "Miss Verdon gives a complete characterization from the slut to the woman—common in manner, but full of pride, disillusioned but willing to believe, a woman of silence and mysteries. It would be an affecting job on any stage. Amid the familiar diversions of a Broadway musical jamboree, it is sobering and admirable."[112]

Verdon dominated the reviews, but Fosse's ambitious work was given its due, with several reviewers commenting on his ability to creatively recycle old dance forms. In a lengthy review in *Dance Magazine*, Leo Lerman declared, "The best thing about *New Girl in Town* was Bob Fosse's contribution," noting how "Fosse utilizes as he has before, vaudeville dance, social dance, and ballet. He has a neat way of changing an old soft-shoe routine into a bright shiny new design . . . . Fosse manipulates within the period, artfully touching it with a '57 look."[113]

Eventually, Fosse persuaded Abbott to let him reinstate about 80 percent of the original ballet, but this time the dancers performed to accelerated tempos, and with a fuller musical accompaniment. This new, sped-up version of the "Red Light Ballet" was put in the show on June 23, Fosse's thirtieth birthday, and remained for the rest of the run with no further controversy. Fosse later said, "It taught me a lesson. It makes people very nervous if you get too graphic, too sensual with slow, serious music. They don't mind if it's moving."[114]

Based on Verdon's appeal and her acclaim as Anna, *New Girl in Town* settled in for a year's run. She and Thelma Ritter tied for the Tony Award as Best Actress in a Musical, giving Verdon a three-three average—a Tony Award for each of her Broadway appearances. So dependent was this so-so show on Verdon's star power that when she left after ten months to film *Damn Yankees*, there was considerable consternation about finding a replacement. Carol Haney was briefly considered, and Sheree North, a dancer who had lately been in films as a Marilyn Monroe type, was sought because of her marquee appeal. Eventually, a non-star, dancer-singer Evelyn Ward, was hired and played the final two months of the run.[115]

Joan McCracken was also briefly considered for the role with the proviso that she be replaced by an ensemble member for Anna's dances, a sad acknowledgment that the forty-year-old was no longer in adequate health to dance.[116] A decade earlier, McCracken might well have played the tragic, dancing Anna Christie. But the idea of the now-diminished McCracken following the dynamic Verdon, who had long since replaced her in her husband's affections, must have been devastating for McCracken to consider.

New Girl in Town paid back its investment and made a small profit, but it did not tour and never became a standard revival title—just one of many shows of its period that played a season and was forgotten. But there was a bigger reason for its disappearance. Without choreography to lift and expand its story, and without a star dancer with the vulnerability and depth to play its fragile heroine, *New Girl in Town* is merely watered-down O'Neill. Fosse and Verdon, more than any of their colleagues, were responsible for its success; without them, the show had little reason to be produced.

With mentors Abbott and Robbins, Fosse had been the most diligent of students, learning how to stage numbers, integrate song and dance into narrative, and machine-tool a struggling show into a hit. But on *New Girl in Town* he was painfully reminded that the director is the final arbiter. If Fosse wanted his vision alone to be realized onstage, he would have to move beyond choreography and become a director himself. In five years Bob Fosse had choreographed four hit Broadway shows and three films and had won two Tony Awards. More important, he had established himself as a singular, indispensable part of each project. His apprenticeship complete, he was now positioned to take full control of his next show, expanding on the lessons he had learned from Abbott and Robbins.

3
UNCLE SAM RAG
• • •

"But finally you want control. You want the show to move a certain way from start to finish, and that's why we became directors, choreographers like Michael [Bennett] and Jerry and Tommy [Tune]. We had to be able to control it."

Bob Fosse, 1985[1]

Just months after *New Girl in Town* opened, *West Side Story* arrived on Broadway, establishing Jerome Robbins as the premier musical theater director-choreographer. With *New Girl in Town* and the battles with George Abbott behind him, Fosse sought a vehicle that he could mold and shape into his own directorial statement, similar to Robbins.

The Works was the name Dorothy and Herbert Fields gave their musical murder mystery set in a London wax museum and involving a Jack the Ripper–style killer. Completed in 1947 after the opening of *Annie Get Your Gun*, which featured the Fieldses' libretto, it was put aside as the siblings worked on other projects. Over the next ten years a number of producers, including Rodgers and Hammerstein, expressed interest in producing *The Works*, which was proposed as a vehicle for stars as varied as Mary Martin and Beatrice Lillie. Albert Hague, composer of the recent *Plain and Fancy*, was brought in to work on the score, with lyrics by Dorothy.

Bob Fosse and Dorothy Fields shared an agent who facilitated Fosse's participation in the new show, which in turn sparked the interest of Gwen Verdon. By now, Verdon was both audience favorite and critics' darling, and had "the Muscle" to pick her next project and demand director approval.

Fosse and Joan McCracken had divorced in 1956, but he and Verdon were in no hurry to marry. They were, however, anxious to continue working together. An audition of *The Works* was set up for Verdon, along with Fosse and producers Robert Fryer and Lawrence Carr. After listening to Fosse's ideas about the book and score, Fryer and Carr shrewdly offered him the job of director, knowing this would make the show more attractive to their sought-after star.[2] Fosse remembered it differently years later: "Gwen really backed me—she believed in me . . . . she simply said, 'He's my director. *Bob Fosse's my director.*' "[3] Like Mary Ann Niles and Joan McCracken, Gwen Verdon was the latest woman in Fosse's life to facilitate a new career opportunity for him.

The summer of 1958 was devoted to tailoring the show to Verdon's particular talents. By this time, Herbert Fields had died, and screenwriter Sidney Sheldon, who was recruited by the Fieldses to work with them on the book, had returned to Hollywood. To continue the revisions, Verdon suggested David Shaw, who had written *Native Dancer*, her dramatic television debut in 1954, in which she played a waitress who wants to be a ballerina. *The Works* soon became *Redhead*, not only a reference to the crimson hair and beard of the murderer but also a tribute to the musical's new star.

Fosse had his own very specific ideas for *Redhead*. Pages of notes indicate his thoughts on everything from the show's romance to its murder suspect. "*Don't trick audience*," he admonished. "Murderer must at some time if even only momentarily seem guilty before the climax."[4] He was already forming ideas for an opening that would most effectively establish the murder mystery tone of the evening.

After the overture, the curtain rises on a black stage, with a single light shining on a beautiful girl making up before her mirror. As she hums a sprightly tune, a man enters on the other side of the stage. Suddenly a purple scarf appears in the darkness, seeming to float through the air toward the girl. The scarf is wrapped violently around her throat and pulled tight. Her screams ring out until she collapses dead. She falls out of the light, and her face is replaced by that of the killer, his red hair and beard glowing brightly. As the lights fade, the tune the murdered girl was humming is taken up by the orchestra and leads into the next scene. The authors acknowledged the value of Fosse's ideas when, just prior to rehearsals, they agreed to pay him 1 percent from their combined royalties for all subsidiary rights "in consideration of the contributions which you have made and are making to the book . . . consisting of your conceptions, ideas and material."[5]

Verdon's Essie Whimple is a mousy, twenty-nine-year-old spinster living with her two maiden aunts and creating grisly exhibits for their London waxworks museum. Essie, an orphan who was abandoned by her actor father, sees visions. Her latest, in which she falls in love with a big, handsome stranger (weighing "14 stone"), comes true when she meets Tom Baxter, an American performing a strongman act in a local music hall. To be near Tom, Essie fabricates a vision of the killer coming after her, and she hides out at Tom's theater. After a makeover reveals Essie as a bewitching redhead, she is given a spot in the show, and Tom begins to fall in love with her. But her wax depiction of the opening murder is too close to reality, and the murderer eventually pursues and tries to kill her. A series of disguises and mistaken identities follow, climaxed by a frantic chase across London and the revelation of the murderer's identity. Essie and Tom are then reunited and ready for matrimony.

Verdon's standing in the theater, and particularly among her fellow dancers, was now at a peak of respect and adoration. "Dancers love another good dancer, and she was the epitome of what one aspires to in dance," remembered Patricia Ferrier Kiley.[6] "There was no one who came near to touching her as a dancer, actress, singer, or leading lady when dance was the focus of the show. You could do a freeze frame on a dance number, no matter how fast and tricky it was, and her line would be perfect," said David Gold.[7] "We worshipped her," Harvey Evans recalled. "She was the best dancer doing one of the best choreographer's work."[8]

It was in a rehearsal hall that Fosse and Verdon first forged their bond, and now they worked for hours, chain-smoking and feeding off each other's energy as they created *Redhead*'s dance numbers together. Fosse later claimed, "The happiest times I ever had with Gwen were when we were working together. They stimulated all sorts of things. I mean they were fun, we had our own jokes about rehearsals, we had something in common, I think it even affected sex."[9]

For Fosse, Verdon's innate understanding of his choreography and her ability to second-guess and frequently expand on his ideas made her the perfect vessel for his work. As he later observed, "The thing that impresses me most about her is her enthusiasm, her desire for perfection, and endless energy. Whenever I have an idea, I'll kind of fumble my way up to it with an 'Ah, I think we should . . .' and she'll say, 'Oh, I know exactly what you mean,' and she's off to the races."[10] As with Jack Cole, Verdon brought selfless devotion to Fosse's work (even rehearsing the dancers in his absence) while exemplifying the best of it in her performance—and all of it intensified by her love for him. "Sure Bob is tough," she later reflected. "But I get a much bigger kick out of pleasing him in rehearsal than I do an audience in a performance . . . . He's pleased not because you've met his needs but rather that you've achieved something *you* thought impossible."[11]

Together, Fosse and Verdon turned Essie Whimple into a whirligig who not only metamorphosed from dowdy old maid to ravishing star but joyously tried on new and daring personas as the far-fetched plot required. The full range of Verdon's dancing and comedic skills was showcased in charm songs, pantomime numbers, a mock-Spanish revel (a reminder of Lola), romantic duets with her leading man, and every type of dancing—with no one to tell Fosse what to cut or change.

Midway through act 1, Essie disguises herself in a man's suit and takes shelter from the killer in the music hall where a vaudeville troupe is in residence. When Tom suggests she join the show, Essie auditions before the skeptical crowd with a song she claims her father had once performed. "'Erbie Fitch's Twitch," a patter song done in cockney dialect, is a number Charlie Chaplin might have performed in a musical comedy. In baggy suit and derby, and sporting a cane, Verdon conjures both the humor and melancholy of Chaplin's Little Tramp.

"I think he's been the greatest influence on my work," Fosse said of Chaplin, whose iconic movements he had referenced many times before.[12] The balletic grace and indomitable spirit of the Little Tramp surely connected with the boy who danced his way through rough burlesque houses and nightclubs, performing for bored or drunk audiences and picking his way through dingy backstage dressing rooms. Fosse internalized the Little Tramp's waddling walks and graceful pivots, and they came out in some of his most comic and poignant work.

The incongruities of the Little Tramp's appearance (baggy pants, tight jacket, oversized shoes) and his oddly elegant physicality can be discerned in the Fosse silhouette, which blended disparate vaudeville and jazz elements with movements forged from his own physical shortcomings. (The Little Tramp's hat and ever-present cigar also found their way into the Fosse signature.) Chaplin's creation responded to even the most humiliating or physically taxing circumstances with resilience and poise. Fosse's ability to reveal the humanity beneath the most outlandish or degrading moments has a direct parallel to the Little Tramp. Whether rubber-legging and dragging across the stage on their knees in "Steam Heat" or acting out a sex-for-pay scenario in the "Red Light Ballet," his dancers always maintain a core dignity.

To accompany the song's chorus, Fosse devises a movement pattern made up of shifts in balance and focus, finger and elbow pointing, shoulder hunching, and cane twirling. Essie performs it twice, but sensing that her act is not being well received, she pauses awkwardly and acts out an old routine her father did with a late-arriving audience member. Essie finally launches into the chorus a third time, now in tongue-twisting double time and with the movement pattern at the same rapid pace. It is a sure applause-getter and ends the number on an exhilarating high. "'Erbie Fitch's Twitch," a specialty number given the flimsiest of excuses for inclusion, displays the Chaplinesque quality at the heart of Verdon's most boisterous performances.[13]

Fosse and Verdon channel Charlie Chaplin in Redhead's *"'Erbie Fitch's Twitch." Photo by Friedman-Abeles © Billy Rose Theatre Division, The New York Public Library for the Performing Arts.*

Fosse and Verdon revisited the tango rhythms of "Whatever Lola Wants" for "The Pick-Pocket Tango" and made it both an eleven o'clock showstopper and a plot-driving sequence that led into *Redhead*'s climax.[14] Essie, again in disguise, this time as a London barfly, has been jailed along with a group of women from the notorious Green Dragon Pub. Desperate to escape, she affects a Spanish accent and entices the guard to dance a seductive tango with her. The women, snapping and hissing, keep up the Spanish rhythms as the dance intensifies. Essie extracts the key and stands triumphantly over the guard, who lies prone and bare-chested at her feet. She and the guard, now in thrall to Essie's exotic impersonation, continue dancing as she surreptitiously opens the door to the cell and releases the women. With the cell now empty, Essie whirls him inside, locks the door, and briskly exits. The guard, still caught up in the dance and now behind bars, is left alone to exclaim, "Olé!"

With dance the focus of Fosse's staging, *Redhead* had a core group of sixteen dancers, in addition to a singing chorus. Fosse was beginning to redefine not only how a dancing chorus looked but also how it functioned, much as de Mille and Robbins had done. *Redhead*'s dancers were all sizes and ages and came from varied backgrounds. A *Dance Magazine* photo essay touted the individuality of *Redhead*'s dancing ensemble, including its senior member, Kazimir Kokich, a former leading dancer with Ballet Russe de Monte Carlo; waiflike Patti Karr, who had appeared in two previous Fosse shows; Liane Plane, a former soloist with Ballet Theatre; Kevin Carlisle, who had his own modern dance company; and Dean Taliaferro, a young dancer making her Broadway debut.[15]

By now, Fosse's reputation meant that his dance auditions were packed with New York's best dancers, and on *Redhead* his standards became more demanding. Margery Beddow, who was among more than four hundred women at *Redhead*'s first dance audition, recalled the combination Fosse used for his final elimination: "changement [literally 'changing,' as the feet change positions during a jump in the air] into a grand plié and, from the deepest part of the plié, jump up into an air split, landing in fifth position. Twice."[16] To better display Fosse's newly required classical dance technique, rehearsal wear changed. As Harvey Evans remembered, "The difference between *New Girl in Town* and *Redhead* was that suddenly we all had to wear black tights in rehearsal."[17]

The black tights requirement was reflected in the costumes for *Redhead*'s most ambitious dance number. The lengthy "Essie's Vision" was less a dream ballet than a "divertissement," according to Fosse, with no plot purpose.[18] Composed of five sections all orchestrated on variations of Essie's introductory number, "Merely Marvelous," it was the ultimate showcase for Verdon's dance versatility and unflagging energy.

Essie, about to perform with the music hall troupe, has another of her visions and leads the entire dancing ensemble (her "Dream People") through jazz, can-can, gypsy, military, and music hall sequences, all presenting her (and Verdon) as "a Star dancer of extraordinary ability."[19] Verdon seldom left the stage, and when she did, she returned in breathtaking fashion. For the gypsy variation with the men, she jumped from an offstage table onto a trampoline, from which she flew onstage into the arms of two dancers. She cartwheels, beats a tambourine, does the splits, and even presents herself as a strongwoman, lifting a dancer held up by wires. "It was a ball buster," David Gold remembered.[20] Harvey Evans said, "We would come off ready to vomit, it was so exhausting."[21] But Verdon loved the ballet, calling it "the greatest fun I've ever had. It's kind of like the way I thought a circus was when I was a child."[22]

"Essie's Vision" was the longest continuous dance sequence Fosse had yet choreographed, and it overflowed with theatrical invention. He began to incorporate stylized theatrical elements that pulled the show out of its time and locale and underscored a sense of performance for its own sake. The star and the entire dancing ensemble appear in nonperiod black tights and leotards (Verdon, appropriately enough, also wore bright red boots), with accessories added as needed. In one section, hats are flown in on wires, and the dancers pluck them as if from out of the air. This marks the first appearance of what would become Fosse's costume trademark: black derbies and white gloves.

The stage is cleared, freeing it up for the dancers but also setting it in limbo, far removed from Edwardian England. Fosse uses banners and placards to announce each section. The "March Militaire" section is introduced with a seemingly endless banner ("And Now for That Grand Lady with Her Grand Corps . . . More to

Verdon enters in spectacular fashion, via trampoline, in Redhead's *"Essie's Vision." Left to right, the dancers with faces visible are Noel Parenti, Harvey Evans, Dale Moreda, and Kevin Carlisle. Photo by Friedman-Abeles © Billy Rose Theatre Division, The New York Public Library for the Performing Arts.*

Follow . . . Isn't It Grand?") introduced by Essie, who then slips behind it and reappears at the end as if she had been carrying it from both ends.

"Essie's Vision" is not the only instance of Fosse beginning to play with time and space in his staging. In "Behave Yourself," Essie's two maiden aunts prepare her for a date with Tom Baxter by dispensing contradictory advice on proper comportment. As Essie and Tom rendezvous in his apartment, the aunts continue to monitor her behavior while outside the scene. Thus Essie's date becomes a performance available for critique.

Full-cast rehearsals for *Redhead* began November 24, 1958, though Fosse had brought his dancers in three weeks earlier. The first-time director wanted the dance numbers substantially worked out before the others arrived, so that he could concentrate his energies on working with the actors. Margery Beddow remembered Fosse telling the dancers, "Now tomorrow all those actors are going to come in here, and they're going to want to know what their motivation is. The first actor who says that, I want you to all stand up together and say, 'Because Bobby says so!'"[23]

Fosse, still anxious to advance himself as a performer, was originally set to play the role of the murderer, but with an extended workload, he relinquished the role to actor Leonard Stone. Richard Kiley, cast as Tom Baxter, brought a ringing voice and imposing physique to the role. Kiley had a varied background in films, television, and theater, having introduced "Stranger in Paradise" in *Kismet* and played Stanley Kowalski in *A Streetcar Named Desire* on tour. He was not shy to question Fosse's direction, but he was also quick to realize that Fosse brought additional skills to his new role. Too often in musicals the transition from dialogue to song was awkward. Fosse brought music in under the dialogue and encouraged Kiley to speak the first few lines of a song, thereby smoothing the segue from speaking to singing.[24]

To give himself additional support, Fosse hired Donald McKayle as associate choreographer and assigned him "Uncle Sam Rag," a full-ensemble number and the only one not to feature Verdon. Fosse intended "Uncle Sam Rag" as a satire on polite British attempts to approximate the vigorous slang and dance styles of ragtime America. McKayle's efforts to stage it lacked style and period authenticity, and he was unable to smoothly integrate the dancers and singers. As the company left for New Haven, Fosse took it over and staged it himself. He broke his cast into small groups executing the precise movements described in the lyrics ("knock knees," "shake your shoulders," "a low dip and wiggle, if you have got one") with "Ascot Gavotte"–style formality. As the cast, wearing American flags atop their heads, glided across the stage, reciting the latest American expressions ("hot dog!" "wham, bam, thank you ma'am!"), each group wove intricate patterns that mirrored the song's three-part counterpoint. It was also the first use of what Verdon called "Fosse's whisper singing,"[25] in which the cast whispers lyrics, drawing the audience in by forcing them to listen intently. The last-minute staging of "Uncle Sam Rag" represented a new peak for Fosse. Here he divides a stage full of more than twenty dancers and singers into endlessly shifting formations, combining attitude, stylization, and humor.

Fosse's *Redhead* staging resembled less a book musical than a series of songs and musical numbers interrupted by bits of plot. Working again with production designer Rouben Ter-Arutunian, Fosse made sure the scenery could be easily banished to open up the stage for his dances, and he seamlessly worked those set changes into his staging. In a particularly breathless transition, a brawl in the Green Dragon Bar is interrupted when the police arrive. As the women are gathered together for arrest, the set disappears and the bars of a jail cell fly down in front of them, instantly establishing a new locale.

Fosse's use of stagecraft also paid homage to *Redhead*'s penny dreadful elements. Following the grisly curtain-raiser murder, he ended the first act with Essie, alone onstage and calling Scotland Yard to report the murderer when a man enters. "Miss Whimple? I understand you know who murdered Ruth," he says. She drops the receiver in terror as he approaches, a large shadow slowly filling the back wall of the stage as Essie freezes in terror and the curtain comes down.

The practice of staging a number "in one," in front of a curtain or drop while the upstage set is changed, had provided occasions for showstoppers like "Steam Heat." But this long-established custom also slowed transitions between scenes, and Fosse looked for ways to do without it. When Essie meets Tom and sings of her desire to be married ("The Right Finger of My Left Hand"), it is in a spotlight while the pandemonium of a chase goes on behind her. When the chase ends and the set is changed, she simply turns and enters the scene.

On *Redhead*, Fosse began his practice of pushing against the traditional boundary of the proscenium. At one point, Essie jumps over the orchestra pit, circles through the audience, and comes back onstage.[26] When she disrupts a music hall number because she thinks she sees the murderer sitting in a theater box, the box is in the actual theater *Redhead* is playing.

Redhead began a triumphant out-of-town tour in New Haven on December 20 and continued through Washington, DC and Philadelphia. The star's now-established box-office appeal, plus positive reviews that dubbed the show "An Evening with Gwen Verdon,"[27] led to sellout audiences and built strong word of mouth ahead of *Redhead*'s Broadway opening. As Fosse worked to focus and tighten his first show as director-choreographer prior to its Broadway opening, personal behaviors that would soon become commonplace began to emerge. In the wake of his breakup with Joan McCracken, he had begun seeing a psychiatrist who prescribed amphetamines to help him cope with guilt over a number of issues, including his treatment of McCracken, as well as anxieties about his work and his early, disturbing experiences in show business. Amphetamines, or speed, enabled him to avoid those feelings as he worked late into the night and still be focused for rehearsals the next morning. Soon he was also relying on the barbiturate Seconal to help him come down from the amphetamines in order to sleep. Fosse would continue to alternate Seconal and amphetamines like Dexedrine and Benzedrine for a number of years.

"It makes you care about detail," Fosse said with understatement about his attraction to amphetamines.[28] Good reviews and sold-out audiences could not convince him that *Redhead* was in adequate shape. Nervous and jumpy from the drugs, Fosse spent hours rehearsing the dancers, sometimes on their day off, always finding the tiniest of details to refine. *Una más*—one more, as in "do it one more time"—was his mantra, much dreaded by his exhausted dancers. Fosse demanded that they always rehearse "full out," or at performance level, and never merely mark the steps. "He worked the shit out of us out of town," Harvey Evans remembered. At one endless rehearsal for "Essie's Vision," dancer Kevin Carlisle finally exploded, "What are you trying to do, kill us?" Only after intervention by the producers did Fosse reluctantly lighten his demands on his dancers.[29]

Boasting a million-dollar advance, *Redhead* sailed into the 46th Street Theater on February 5, 1959. As expected, the reviews were love letters to Verdon while offering more measured praise for her vehicle. Richard Watts Jr. in the *New York Post* summed up the consensus: "Without her, I am not so sure it would be much more than rather pleasant entertainment. But it decidedly isn't without her, and she transforms it into something delightful."[30]

Lamenting the construction of *Redhead*'s libretto while commending Fosse's ability to paste over it with his staging, Brooks Atkinson appeared to open the door for Fosse's later ambitions by suggesting, "Perhaps in the future all musical comedies should be written by choreographers."[31] However, no critic gave Fosse the unalloyed praise that he received from his star. Soon after the opening, Verdon gave a backhand to George Abbott when she claimed, "What I got from Bob Fosse was direction like I've never had in my life."[32]

In a weak season for musicals, *Redhead* coasted to a sweep of the 1958–1959 Tony Awards, easily besting *Flower Drum Song* and the French revue *La Plume de Ma Tante*. Its six awards included ones for Verdon (her fourth, a record at the time), Fosse for his choreography (his third), and the show itself as Best Musical. At the time, directors of musicals and plays were grouped together, and Fosse was shut out of the nominees' circle. A week after the show opened, *Variety* reported that it was on track to pay off on its investment by June, thanks to the show's strong box-office performance and its modest budget. Capitalized at $300,000 (half of which was provided by NBC, allowing its affiliate RCA Victor to record the cast album), it was brought in for an even more modest $216,000.[33]

With the success of *Redhead* falling squarely on her delicate shoulders, every effort was made to ease the burden on Verdon as she settled in for a long run. Verdon had occasionally been criticized for vocal shortcomings (*Variety* paused in an otherwise rave review to remark, "She hasn't much of a voice"),[34] though she could always be heard in an era before body microphones. But singing came in a decided third among her triple talents. According to Dorothy Fields's biographer Charlotte Greenspan, in order to pace Verdon's vocal requirements in *Redhead*, all her solo singing was scheduled in the first part of the first act. Thereafter she sang only in duets and ensembles, devoting her energies to her dances—a clever and skillful approach to husbanding the star's resources.[35]

To avoid the problems encountered on *New Girl in Town*, the producers made sure a standby for Verdon was in place for the opening. Allyn Ann McLerie was a well-regarded dancer-singer-actress who had danced with Ballet Theatre and played opposite Ray Bolger in both the stage and film versions of *Where's Charley?* She had been in the original casts of de Mille's *One Touch of Venus* and Robbins's *On the Town* and was the leading lady of Irving Berlin's *Miss Liberty* in 1949. A dancing comedienne not unlike Verdon and Joan McCracken, she was a strong standby for a triple-threat star.

When Verdon twisted her ankle before a matinee performance six months into the run, she limped onstage before the curtain to announce that McLerie would take her role. Cleverly diffusing the audience's disappointment, she said, "I'm sorry for the accident, but at least this will give me my first chance to see the show. I hope you'll stay and see it with me."[36] After taking a specially placed seat on the aisle, she watched the show in its entirety, signing autographs at intermission. Despite McLerie's talents, substituting for Verdon was a thankless job. As *Variety* noted, "Her dancing is fine, her acting has charm and her singing is likeable . . . . But Miss McLerie, in the inevitable comparison to Miss Verdon, lacks the electricity and personal magnetism of the star."[37]

So clearly was Verdon *Redhead*'s raison d'être that it seemed impossible for the show to continue without her, and indeed no replacement was sought when she left in March 1960. The show closed its profitable run of 452 performances and launched an immediate tour that took Verdon and most of the original cast to Chicago, Los Angeles, and San Francisco through the summer.

The tour's itinerary allowed Fosse to visit his family in Chicago and for Verdon to see her father when the show arrived in Los Angeles. (Her mother died during the run of *Damn Yankees*, and her son Jim, now seventeen, was in boarding school in Connecticut.) During the show's Chicago run, on April 2, Fosse and Verdon were quietly married, but they did not disclose their marital status until several months later. Because they were already living together and had decided that they wanted to have a child, marriage was strictly a legal formality—something hardworking theater people did on a day off so as not to disrupt their stage routine.

"Now we have four really tip-top musicals in town—'My Fair Lady,' 'West Side Story,' 'The Music Man' and the one which opened last evening at the 46th St. Theatre, 'Redhead,'" proclaimed John Chapman in the *New York Daily News*.[38] With Gwen Verdon cavorting across the stage in Fosse's endlessly imaginative numbers, Chapman's opening night enthusiasm was reasonable. But while the other three titles entered the musical theater repertoire, regularly revived and adapted into beloved films, *Redhead* quickly disappeared. A London production with Verdon (and with Fosse finally playing the role of the murderer) never happened, nor did a proposed film version starring Verdon and Kiley. After the luster wore off on this latest Fosse-Verdon vehicle, its jerry-rigging became obvious. Like *New Girl in Town*, *Redhead* only worked through the combined combustion of its director-choreographer and star.

Fosse's first statement as director-choreographer placed him alongside Jerome Robbins, and not only in billing that duplicated Robbins's for *West Side Story*. While Robbins worked with superior material to create an integrated, emotionally charged musical, Fosse took a script both vague and convoluted and a pleasant but forgettable score, and developed them into a credible musical comedy driven by a succession of dazzling numbers, simultaneously crafting a vehicle for the particular and varied talents of his star. He had assumed control of every production detail, supervising the contributions of writers and designers, and defining the content and look of his very first directorial effort. All that was left was to solidify this initial success with another hit show.

> "Oh God, was I ever eager, pushy, needy, scared, hungry, confident. I felt there was nothing I couldn't do."
>
> Bob Fosse, 1985[39]

Two projects during the fall of 1959 showed Fosse stretching himself as a choreographer and experimenting with staging ideas that he would later develop more fully. He returned to television to choreograph and co-direct, with Kirk Browning, "The Wonderful World of Entertainment," an episode of *Ford Startime*, a weekly series of variety spectaculars. The ninety-minute color extravaganza featured songs, dances, film clips, comedy routines, and dramatic play excerpts tracing a loose survey of entertainment trends since 1927, from vaudeville and silent movies to present-day rock and roll and television. Fosse staged a number of song medleys for Kate Smith and Polly Bergen, and Bergen joined Eddie Foy Jr. and young Eddie Hodges in short interludes as a vaudeville family act. He also created an amusing reverse striptease for hostess Rosalind Russell, who functions as a living mannequin while the male dancers dress her in various high-fashion styles from over the years. The finale features the dancers cavorting around a lineup of the new 1959 Ford automobiles.[40]

The brief three-week rehearsal period left little time for inspired staging, and Fosse fell back on steps and movement patterns that had worked for him before. One of several brief dance sequences interspersed throughout the show, "Let Me Entertain You," from the just-opened *Gypsy*, looks as if the dancers from "Essie's Vision" had run off and joined the circus. In black tights, white gloves, clown make-up, and hats, they move around the soundstage in a Fosse amoeba, here done in a slow, insinuating style. The dancers stay deadpan, their singing breathy and staccato, ending with a hushed "Yes, sir!" This "Let Me Entertain You" looks like Fosse working out ideas he would refine for "Magic to Do" in *Pippin*, but the slightly sinister approach is jarring for such a fleeting, crossover number.

Fosse's most ambitious undertaking for the show was "The Streets of Laredo," a narrative dance that satirized the conventions of the western genre. A conglomeration of *Shane, High Noon*, and decades of B movie westerns, "The Streets of Laredo" stars Tommy Rall as its laconic cowboy hero dressed in white. The cowboy sets out to rid a frontier town of bad guy Black Bart (in black, of course), played by John Aristides, from *Redhead* and *New Girl in Town*.

Fosse showcases Rall's considerable balletic skills, incorporating double tours en l'air, multiple pirouettes, and "fling leaps," in which Rall jumps and flings his leg up and around himself while in the air. Fosse manages to disrupt all this athleticism with his own brand of rhythmic accents. The choreography elsewhere drew on the examples of others. Fosse's jaded dance hall girls appear to have wandered in from Agnes de Mille's *Oklahoma!* dream ballet, and his cowboys exhibit the strenuous athleticism and knee work of Michael Kidd's current *Destry Rides Again*. He revisits the "Pony Dance" from *New Girl in Town* for some high-kicking cakewalks. Fosse's center of gravity here begins to show signs of shifting to the pelvis as his cowboys anachronistically swerve and swivel their hips.

Rall takes time out from saving the town to fend off the advances of an eager young country girl, and though their pas de deux is conventional in dance terms, it is punctuated by voice-overs of the talkative girl making a case for marriage ("I'm a very good cook! I mend, sew, milk cows, churn butter, make apple pie, shear sheep, chop wood, and I'll make a very good mother!") while the cowboy merely replies, "Yep." When Black Bart is finally vanquished and Rall walks off into the sunset alone, the girl follows along, continuing her long-winded pitch. The dialogue, as well as the wry narration throughout the number, was by the show's writer, Larry Gelbart, and proved to be the wittiest element of "The Streets of Laredo."

"A terrible piece of showbiz junk," lamented critic and Fosse champion Clive Barnes when he saw it for the first time in 1999.[41] With its uneven tone and flagrant borrowings from the frontier ballets of de Mille and Eugene Loring, "The Streets of Laredo" is dismaying, though no worse than most quickly assembled numbers on 1950s television. But its ambition outweighs its faults. Fosse stages a lengthy story ballet featuring chorus and soloists, and requiring multiple camera setups, all within the frenzy of a fast-paced rehearsal period. His future efforts with this form always involved comedy, and in that regard, "The Streets of Laredo" is an important step.

No sooner had "The Wonderful World of Entertainment" aired on October 6, 1959 than Fosse was contracted to "doctor" *The Girls against the Boys*, a musical revue starring Bert Lahr and Nancy Walker that was struggling in its Philadelphia tryout.[42] In an effort to give the revue some cohesion, Fosse came up with the idea of vaudeville-style introductions and exhortations by the actors to each other. As dancer Buzz Halliday recalled, "The curtain would come down between a number and a sketch and I would get the word from the stage manager to call out to Dick [Van Dyke], 'Hey, Dick, get ready for the next sketch! These people are waiting!'"[43]

Fosse would continue the practice in later shows, using narrators to announce scenes and songs, directing characters to step out of scenes to comment on them, and having actors address each other by their real names. Taking the audience behind the footlights, showing them the hard work and effort of performance, was theatrical truth telling for him.

"I know I'm good, but they [George Balanchine and Jerome Robbins] talk to God. When I call God, he's always out to lunch."

Bob Fosse, 1984[44]

Hail the Conquering Hero was writer-director Preston Sturges's satire of hero worship, small-town politics, and mother love, released by Paramount Pictures in 1944, during the height of World War II patriotism. Woodrow Lafayette Pershing Truesmith is the milquetoast son of a World War I marine who died a hero's death in combat. His mother maintains a shrine to the fallen hero, and Woodrow is raised with every expectation that he will follow his father's example. But after enlisting, he is quickly discharged due to chronic hay fever. Ashamed and unable to face his mother, Woodrow gets a job in a shipyard and arranges for cards and letters in his name to be sent from the Pacific to his mother and sweetheart. When he tells his story to a group of marines, they call Woodrow's mother, concocting a story of his brave exploits, and send him home, where he is cheered by the entire town as a returning hero. The more he protests his unworthiness, the more he is celebrated as a great man. Woodrow finally confesses the truth and prepares to leave town in shame. But his honesty in the face of humiliation focuses the town's citizens on the true meaning of courage and honor, and Woodrow is finally hailed as an authentic hero.

Fosse saw *The Conquering Hero* (as it was renamed) as a project to be developed by him in much the same manner as *Redhead*. Musicalizing the Preston Sturges film would allow him to make a sharp-edged, satirical statement on American values as pertinent as Robbins's more sober portrayal of inner-city race relations.

To underscore his centrality to the show's creation, Fosse demanded unique contract terms. He would be paid no fee for his services as director-choreographer, instead receiving 3.5 percent of the gross profits until recoupment of the show's $300,000 budget, at which point his share would jump to 4 percent. But 2 percent of that fee would be credited to Fosse as an author, and he would sign a Dramatists Guild contract entitling him to share with the other authors in subsidiary rights. Fosse would also receive 7 percent of the producer's share of profits and would commit to raising 7 percent of the budget.[45]

Fosse's demands continued. He wanted a guarantee of seven to eight weeks of rehearsals with the dancers, which would necessitate a concession from Actors Equity, since union rules at the time allowed for reduced rehearsal salaries for up to six weeks. (Robbins had demanded and received an unprecedented eight-week rehearsal period for *West Side Story*.)[46] His billing would read, "Entire Production Directed and Choreographed by Bob Fosse" in the same type size as the authors' names and would appear in a box—and he would designate its placement. As a letter describing the terms of his contract stated, "He wants approval of just about everything in the production, with the words 'not to be unreasonably withheld' added."[47]

The creative team, essentially writing to Fosse's specifications, included book writer Larry Gelbart, who had worked alongside Neil Simon, Woody Allen, and Mel Brooks crafting jokes and sketches for Sid Caesar on television, and had supplied the witty voice-over dialogue for Fosse's "The Streets of Laredo," and the songwriting team of composer Moose Charlap and lyricist Norman Gimbel, responsible for the score of the recent flop *Whoop-Up*. Many of Fosse's core team of dancers were back, and with Verdon constantly at his side, he had the highest-profile dance assistant on Broadway.

Fosse had originally wanted to play Truesmith himself, according to dancer Richard Korthaze, but as with *Redhead*, was persuaded that taking on the role would be too great a burden alongside his work as director and choreographer.[48] Eventually the role went to Tom Poston, a popular television and stage actor. Poston's low-key, befuddled style was deemed appropriate for the bumbling Truesmith, though Fosse would find fault with his performance through rehearsals and tryout performances.

Those rehearsals were unusually tense, with Fosse at odds with everyone. He immediately established an adversarial relationship with his collaborators. His insistence that *The Conquering Hero* make a political statement caused difficulties with Gelbart, who recalled, "Bobby was getting ideas for the first time, ideas that had been around a long time . . . . and he kept pushing intellectual and political points that I thought were passé, but he was very enamored of them because they were new to him, so a lot of friction was from trying to accommodate stuff that you didn't believe in."[49] Nor was Fosse above revising Gelbart's work without his permission. When Gelbart arrived to hear new dialogue being read by Poston, he asked who wrote it. Fosse implied that he was its author: "You were off fucking around somewhere. *Somebody* had to make the changes."[50]

Fosse continued to take Dexedrine, which kept him wired and working late into the night. "He's a real moon baby—he likes to work at night," Verdon later observed. "That's when he gets psyched out . . . . If the night is when demons are created, that's when it happens for him, and it's those demons that may be responsible for his incredible visions."[51] For the dancers, this made for a replay of the endless and repetitive rehearsals many had endured on *Redhead*. Margery Beddow recalled, "His energy became so erratic and energetic that no one could keep up with him."[52]

In the midst of all this tension, Fosse was creating some of his most inventive dance numbers. In "The Campaign," Truesmith spouts a tongue-twisting flow of campaign banalities ("milk, babies, old ladies, hot dogs, puppy dogs, etc.")[53] with the rhythmic cadence of modern rap music. According to Beddow, Fosse himself supplied the lyrics, further alienating Norman Gimbel.[54] The dancers respond to each of Truesmith's words and phrases with a wild mix of hopping, jitterbugging, and Spanish dancing as his promises drive them into a state of voter frenzy. Fosse melds dialogue and dance into a pointed satire on political campaign sloganeering and the gullibility of the electorate.

The Conquering Hero's most ambitious choreographic statement was a war ballet designed to skewer the idea of American exceptionalism in war. Fosse's notes indicate his conception of a comic ballet combining both dance and narration (not unlike "The Streets of Laredo") and "based on the manufactured and fantastic feats of heroism by Woodrow," according to an early script synopsis.[55] Fosse tells it as a series of vaudeville sketches, each with introduction, dance specialty, and comic payoff leading to a blackout. Originally told by one of the marines who brought Truesmith home, it later evolved into a phone conversation by Truesmith's mother proudly describing her son's battle triumphs.

The Japanese enemy is "cunning . . . shifty . . . ruthless . . . plain nasty . . . . But most of all taught since childhood infancy to KILL!"[56] As played by the female dancers brandishing machine guns, knives in their teeth, and thick bullet belts, they stay close to the ground in plié as they execute mock Kabuki movements. Sometimes they crawl on their bellies. Fosse's notes also outline "a kind of rumba" movement for the Japanese, with "wiggles, squirms," to emphasize that "they were dirty."

The Americans, by contrast, are "clean-cut . . . clean-living . . . clean-minded boys from Main Street U.S.A . . . . In other words they were full of brotherly love." The male dancers leap onstage in golden costumes, with gold dust sprinkling their hair, performing a lyrical "dance of love and comradeship." Not having been trained all their lives to kill, the Americans are frightened by war, and some cry for their mothers. "They don't teach you to fight dirty at the Y.M.C.A. So in the

Fosse, on ladder, rehearses the female dancers, playing Japanese soldiers, in The Conquering Hero's *controversial ballet, "The Battle." Left to right: Margery Beddow, Shellie Farrell, Patricia Ferrier, Reby Howells, Betty Linton, and Marlene Dell. Photo by Friedman-Abeles, Museum of the City of New York © The New York Public Library.*

beginning, 'Our Boys' made a few small errors." Fosse stages a slapstick sequence of the American soldiers' ineptitude in combat: picking up the wrong end of a rifle, mistakenly aiming machine guns at each other, and accidentally setting off a hand grenade.

Woodrow Truesmith arrives assuming that "everyone is a good egg until proven a bad egg." When he extends his hand in friendship to the Japanese, he is promptly flipped, kicked, and jumped upon. "Then the Enemy made a fatal error. They touched at the very foundation of American ideals . . . at the very thing that Woodrow held most sacred." A Japanese soldier steps forward to pantomime "BABE RUTH GO TO HELL!" At this, Truesmith is roused to action and performs a comic "flash act" of his war skills: grenade juggling and shooting tricks (under the leg, behind his back, using a mirror). Fosse's detailed, bar-by-bar notes indicate specific percussion instruments to accompany each trick. Within seconds, the Japanese fall.

Truesmith not only vanquishes the enemy but also entertains his army buddies. On a makeshift stage, he tells jokes, pulls a rabbit out of his hat, and performs a soft shoe. As he dances, the Japanese sneak in, kidnap the Americans, and take their places in the audience. Two of them jump onstage and join Truesmith in a Fosse trio, spinning plates on their bayonets—a demonstration of their multitasking sneakiness. When Truesmith finally notices, he pulls the pin from a grenade, places it on the stage, and does a soft shoe shuffle into the wings. The Japanese applaud his exit before being blown up.

"The Phillipines [sic]! . . . Wake Island! . . . Battaan [sic]! . . . Corrigidor [sic]! . . . Tarawa! . . . Gaudualcanal [sic]!" A procession moves across the stage as Truesmith drives the Japanese backward across the Pacific in a series of dance steps, acrobatics, gun tricks, and "nasty faces, mean looks, etc." (The role of Truesmith in the ballet was played by dancer William Guske.) At last, the enemy is brought to its knees as Truesmith strikes a noble pose in front of an American eagle drop.

No one complained about Fosse's broad caricaturing of the Japanese, but in a repeat of his experience with "Red Light Ballet," the ballet came under intense criticism by the producers. Producer Robert Whitehead called it "just unpleasant and unfunny" and complained about the marines' costumes and movements, fearing that they would be interpreted by audiences as "effeminate."[57] Their "dance of love and comradeship" (balletic, airy, and a trifle fey) may have been considered too uncomfortably homoerotic.

The ballet was in place when *The Conquering Hero* played its first out-of-town engagement in New Haven on November 19, 1960, starting a grueling three-city tryout that prompted Larry Gelbart to coin one of the most repeated show business one-liners: "If Hitler's alive, I hope he's out of town with a musical."[58] The reviews were encouraging and affirmed Fosse's approach. "The musical is really a tribute to Bob Fosse . . . . a rousing entertainment, sparked by his exceptionally fascinating dance patterns," enthused the *New Haven Journal-Courier*.[59]

With Fosse receiving strong reviews for his work, it might have been expected that his colleagues would rally around him, but by now factions had formed: the producers and writers on one side, and Fosse (with Verdon) on the other. Wired and exhausted, but convinced that only his vision was valid, Fosse alienated the very people he needed to help him bring in a successful show. Moose Charlap later said, "We all found it impossible to achieve the close collaboration with him that is required between authors, director and choreographer."[60] In creating a musical, Gelbart remembered, "A lot of egos have to be checked at the door, all the differing objectives have to meld. Bob Fosse's ego would have required a *double* door. His objective was to do *everybody's* work."[61]

The company moved on to Washington, DC, and further turmoil. The day after the opening, Fosse was still unhappy with Tom Poston's performance and suggested that he be fired and replaced—by Fosse. That evening after the show, Fosse auditioned for Whitehead and the writers. All agreed he was wrong for the role—more Pal Joey than Woodrow Truesmith—and, equally important, could not continue as director if he wanted to replace the leading man with himself. The authors met with Whitehead privately and were clear in their demands, as Charlap stated later: "At that meeting we told Mr. Whitehead that we, as authors, felt it impossible to continue with the Play unless Mr. Fosse's role as director and choreographer was terminated."[62]

Fosse was immediately replaced by director Albert Marre and choreographer Todd Bolender, and the show continued on to Philadelphia. Fosse returned to New York and on December 7 filed a complaint with the American Arbitration Association, thereby initiating a legal skirmish of more interest and importance than the show on which it was based.

In a telegram to the *New York Times*, Fosse asserted that he had been fired rather than voluntarily withdrawn, as stated by the producers. His attorney informed him that by firing him, the producers had broken the contract that required all artistic decisions to be approved by Fosse. Thus, he was within his legal rights to remove all his dances from the show. Fearing that this would disrupt the production, he instead sought written assurance that "if any part of a dance or a ballet, meaning concept, steps, accompanying dialogue, etc. was used the dance would be done in its entirety, not in some mutilated form." When this was refused, he proposed that the producers could alter any of his dances as they chose, with the exception of two key numbers—the war ballet and the campaign rally. This too was denied. With recollections of his fights with Harold Prince and George Abbott still fresh, Fosse then sought arbitration "to enforce my rights by restraining the producers from changing these ballets without my consent."[63]

Fosse's concern was never about money. He had, after all, taken no fee and was working only for a percentage of the show's anticipated earnings. Rather, he argued that Whitehead's altering of dances that had been acclaimed by critics and identified with his name was tantamount to changing the work of a playwright or composer, and would damage his professional reputation. (Fosse's telegram quoted extensively from out-of-town reviews praising these two numbers.) Fosse sought only to establish his rights to his own choreography.[64]

The Conquering Hero finally opened January 16, 1961, on Broadway at the ANTA Theater with no director or choreographer listed. It was, as Larry Gelbart said, "as though someone had left the show in a basket under the marquee. An orphan nobody wanted."[65] Many of the show's dismissive reviews commented favorably on Fosse's dances. *Cue* magazine called the two disputed numbers "superb" and declared the war ballet worthy of a life beyond the show.[66] *Dance Observer* called the choreography, even in bastardized form, "the finest work that Mr. Fosse has done for Broadway."[67] *The Conquering Hero* was gone after only seven performances, but the reviews made clear that Fosse's dances were its high point.

Six months later the arbitrators returned a unanimous decision in Fosse's favor, awarding him six cents, the full contractual compensation he was owed for the use of his numbers during the show's brief run.[68] The decision carried implications for other choreographers and artists whose work was not documented by traditional print methods and therefore deemed easy to alter or replace. But this victory could not erase the fact that Fosse had suffered a very public and acrimonious firing. (Robert Whitehead joined Harold Prince on Fosse's list of untrustworthy producers.)

The Conquering Hero, with its commentary on war and American values and its ambitious comic ballets, was meant to establish Fosse as the equal of Jerome Robbins. But the "Muscle" he had flexed so effectively on *Redhead* was stymied by a different set of circumstances and collaborators. Fosse's track record as director-choreographer was now compromised, and as the 1960s began, he would need to re-establish himself.

4
COMIC RELIEF
• • •

In the six months between arbitration hearings and the final decision in Fosse's *The Conquering Hero* complaint, there were no offers to direct or choreograph, but the spring brought an opportunity to return to the stage in a production of *Pal Joey*. It would be a reunion with director Gus Schirmer Jr. and leading lady Carol Bruce from Fosse's first summer stock *Pal Joey* ten years earlier. New York's City Center offered seasons of low-cost revivals of popular Broadway musicals. Rehearsal time was brief, and runs lasted no more than two weeks. Still, it was a chance for Fosse to perform for the first time on a New York stage a role for which he had always felt a kinship.

The choreographer for *Pal Joey* was Ralph Beaumont, a former dancer who had partnered Gwen Verdon in *Can-Can*. But in dance terms, Fosse was "the Muscle" and staged his own numbers. Dancer Billie Mahoney recalled the generous amount of rehearsal time Fosse used for a number with himself and the ensemble: "There were eleven dance numbers in the show and more than half of the rehearsal time was spent on that one dance. And the other choreographer resented it a bit." Nevertheless, Fosse's relentless drilling paid off. "Every night that applause went on and on and you think, 'Boy, it is worth it!'"[1]

Fosse's showcase moment in *Pal Joey* was an interpolated dance solo Verdon dubbed "The Narcissistic Tango." With a cigar hanging from his lips, a preening Joey smoothed his hair and admired himself in a mirror before executing some mild flamenco steps. Fosse affected a Spanish dancer's rigid upper body and tight wrists above the head but eventually retreated into his comfort zone with leap turns and knee work, climaxing with his favorite barrel turns. Nothing in "The Narcissistic Tango" was particularly original, but it was a genuine star turn that showed Fosse at his most confident.[2] Audiences loved Fosse's performance, and *Pal Joey* broke the City Center house record for ticket sales, leading to a three-week extension.[3]

> "They had to seem like people in an office. That put a certain number of restrictions on me and removed a number of dance conventions as well. No dancing on the desks, for one thing."
>
> Bob Fosse, 1972[4]

Shepherd Mead's 1952 bestseller, *How to Succeed in Business without Really Trying*, was a cheeky instruction manual on how to get ahead in the corporate world. Mead, a vice president at the giant advertising agency Benton and Bowles, drew on his own experiences to advise on rising from mailroom to executive boardroom through flattery, image spinning, and the innocent exposure of rivals' weaknesses. The book was also a satirical reflection of postwar corporate culture set in the World Wide Wicket Company, a massive corporation ("big enough so that nobody knows *exactly* what anyone else is doing")[5] devoted to the making and marketing of a product that was never identified.

A few years after its publication, the book was adapted by Jack Weinstock and Willie Gilbert as a play that went unproduced. When producers Cy Feuer and Ernest Martin read it, they were quick to see its potential as a musical comedy. They soon signed Abe Burrows to work with Weinstock and Gilbert to adapt the play into a musical libretto. Composer-lyricist Frank Loesser, whose association with the producing team went back to *Where's Charley?* and *Guys and Dolls*, was their first choice to write the score. Initially Loesser felt that the light, satirical show would not offer opportunities for the soaring melodies and grand set pieces of his most recent shows, *The Most Happy Fella* and *Greenwillow*. However, after securing a producing stake, Loesser joined *How to Succeed*'s creative team, and the bright, bouncing score he created proved a perfect fit for the script.

With Feuer and Martin, Burrows, and Loesser reuniting for the first time since *Guys and Dolls*, the show's $300,000 capitalization fell easily into place. Burrows fashioned Mead's book and Weinstock and Gilbert's play into a tightly constructed comedy mixing big business machinations with just enough office romance to allow Loesser to write a few love songs, one of which, "I Believe in You," was sung by J. Pierrepont Finch to himself. Its gallery of stock characters was straight out of burlesque. Along with young go-getter Finch (played by Robert Morse), there was pompous J. B. Biggley, the company president (Rudy Vallee); Rosemary, a young secretary in love with Finch (Bonnie Scott); Bud Frump, Biggley's scheming nephew who owes his job to nepotism (Charles Nelson Reilly); the buxom Hedy LaRue, Biggley's secret mistress assigned to the steno pool despite her lack of secretarial skills (Virginia Martin); and several others. The broadness of the characters and comedy was reinforced in the show's cutout sets outlined in cartoon strip black and resembling panels in the Sunday funnies.

In the decade since Mead's book appeared, a whole subgenre of books and movies had taken up issues of postwar corporate life in America. *How to Succeed* had an earlier corollary in Billy Wilder's film *The Apartment* (1960). C. C. Baxter (played by Jack Lemmon), an office drone in a large national insurance company, rises up the corporate ladder by letting executives use his apartment for extramarital trysts with girls from the office. After falling in love with one of those girls, and realizing that his hard work and intelligence would never serve him as well as the availability of his apartment, he turns his back on a promotion and quits (and, in the bargain, ends up with the girl). C. C. Baxter was the flip side of J. Pierrepont Finch who, far from being bothered by the moral shortcuts he takes to success, was a comic dervish of deviousness. *The Apartment* ultimately traded its acerbic realism for a sentimental, boy-gets-girl fade-out, while *How to Succeed* skillfully trod a fine line of lighthearted bemusement all the way to Finch's appointment as chairman of the board. As *Time* magazine put it, "Abe Burrows might have tossed satiric vitriol at the corporate image; instead, he paints a mustache on it."[6]

How to Succeed was never envisioned as a big dance musical, and a star choreographer was not required. At a trade show, Cy Feuer saw a dance number with just the spoofing humor *How to Succeed* required. It was the work of Hugh Lambert, a dancer who had recently been active choreographing television variety shows. He was promptly signed as *How to Succeed*'s choreographer.

Lambert quickly choreographed "The Yo Ho Ho," a pirate dance number that lampooned television variety shows and strongly resembled the dance Feuer had seen. But when he began work on "Coffee Break" and "Paris Original," ensemble numbers that relied more on staging than dancing, he was stymied.[7] No one wanted to let an inexperienced choreographer jeopardize what looked to be a sure hit. After two weeks of rehearsal and only one completed number, a call went out to Fosse. Still smarting from his own dismissal from *The Conquering Hero*, and perhaps seeing parallels between Lambert and himself on his first show, Fosse agreed to join *How to Succeed* not as Lambert's replacement but to do "musical staging," a title created to describe his role in the show and one that gave him equal billing alongside Burrows. As Fosse later recalled, "Between Frank and Abe Burrows and Cy Feuer they thought they could stage all the vocals. Well, staging vocals is a very different thing. And they discovered that they couldn't."[8] Lambert remained and kept his credit as choreographer, but "The Yo Ho Ho" was his only contribution to the show and its only example of a stand-alone dance.

Fosse's input was immediately apparent when the curtain rose on the cast frozen in midgesture like corporate puppets on strings. "That's how I saw a way to focus the action, to stop it suddenly or to underline it. First I got the idea for the opening, and then suddenly we saw other places where it could be used, too. So it became an over-all look," as he described it to *Dance Magazine*.[9]

When Fosse began staging "Coffee Break," he further set the tone for the show's physicality. As he explained, "I took it to its extreme, treating coffee as if it were a drug—as though people needed a coffee *fix*. The show was like a cartoon anyway, so careful exaggeration was in order for the dance."[10] When the office workers line up at a large urn for their morning coffee and discover it to be empty, the word is passed down the line in disbelief until a wail erupts and they collapse in collective frustration like a line of dominoes. Fosse creates a comic dance of drug withdrawal to an "ominous cha-cha" (as the orchestration was marked),[11] sending the dancers staggering across the stage and worshipping at the shining urn. An increasingly frenzied chant of "no coffee" even sent one of the dancers jumping into the orchestra pit—the latest example of Fosse's pushing against the proscenium boundary.

The days of Fosse needing help from Jerome Robbins to stage songs were long over. Fosse had, in fact, become a master of moving large groups of singers and

"No coffee!" In How to Succeed in Business without Really Trying's *"Coffee Break," caffeine withdrawal drives one office worker to end it all by jumping into the orchestra pit, "which distressed the violinists," Gwen Verdon recalled. Photo from the show's London production in 1963, courtesy of Daily Mail/Solo Syndication.*

actors around the stage. He later explained, "Basically, you have to restrict movement. To keep it on a simple level . . . and to work with a smaller vocabulary. And to make sense for the actor. Not just to sing a song, but to give them an image to think of, something to play while they're singing a song."[12]

The eleven o'clock number in *How to Succeed* is "The Brotherhood of Man," Fitch's disingenuous reminder of the unwritten code of business ethics. Building from Finch's solo to a fervent, revivalist dance for the World Wide Wicket executives, the number demonstrates Fosse's precision in staging a large-scale number involving both dancers and singers. He seamlessly moves the performers around the stage as they execute simple hand-clapping patterns side to side, up and down, and in opposition to each other, with changes of focus to add variety. Fosse pulls the dancers forward for more complicated steps that build on the same patterns, weaving them in and around the singers. Robert Morse had a quirky, loose-limbed way of moving that Fosse exploits in his dance break, giving him an exaggerated Chaplin walk and double-timing it for comic effect. Fosse's staging makes "The Brotherhood of Man" exactly the rousing showstopper required to bring the musical into its final scene.

One month after beginning rehearsals, *How to Succeed* opened a five-week try-out in Philadelphia. The reviews were strong and the crowds large. *Variety* called the Loesser score "a continuously clever fusion of words and upper case music that is nearly irresistible," but deemed the dancing "the weakest part of the production" and urged the producers to add more numbers to the first act.[13]

"A Secretary Is Not a Toy," originally sung by Rudy Vallee as a warning to his executives about proper treatment of the women they employ, featured some of Loesser's most delicious wordplay, but no one was satisfied with it when the show opened in Philadelphia. Several unsuccessful staging efforts left the creative team flummoxed until, at the end of a late-night conference, Fosse suggested turning it into a "giant soft shoe."[14] He and Verdon, who once again served as Fosse's uncredited assistant, completely overhauled the number, reconceiving it as a series of short stanzas using the entire ensemble in small groupings, with over-lapping entrances and exits, and changing its tempo from lilting waltz to jazzy, syncopated soft-shoe.

Feuer loved this new approach, but it was a radical reinterpretation of Loesser's song and needed his approval before it could proceed (Loesser being "the Muscle" on this show). When Fosse and Verdon nervously performed the number for Loesser, he declared, "Jesus Christ, it's brilliant. I'm gonna have to rewrite the whole thing."[15] Loesser rewrote large portions of the song to accommodate the new rhythm structure, and it became the dance needed to buoy the first act. (Fosse returned to this episode later with "Take Off with Us" in *All That Jazz* in which Joe Gideon reshapes a composer's work to give it an entirely different tone and perspective.)

The rhythmic click-clack of a typewriter sets the tempo as Fosse begins with one of his familiar trios at center stage. Three men snap their fingers, swivel their wrists, and beat out a syncopated rhythm on their thighs, their movements as tight and streamlined as their business suits. Their exit is overlapped by a group of secretaries entering with small skips mimicking a typewriter's carriage return. One group after another enters, dances a short sequence, and exits, building a montage of office movement.

Fosse sends the dancers sliding, gliding, skipping, and swooping across the stage. At one point, with heels together and feet turned out, they remained glued to the floor as they shuffled side-to-side. Sandpaper rhythms, finger snaps, and syncopated whistling provide a bouncy setting, but the dancing is constrained. The dancers' jumps are tight and pulled up under them, as if reflecting the constricted gender roles of the workplace. (Needless to say, there are no women among the executives.)

Fosse saves his most satiric steps for the number's finale. As the stage is emptied, a line of dancers slowly enters from either side doing a repurposed step from *Bells Are Ringing*'s "Mu-Cha-Cha," on their toes and in plié, with knees bent and bodies leaning back at a sharp angle. In the earlier number the move was slightly risqué, pushing the hips forward and accentuating the pelvis. Nothing so provocative is on view here. The dancers are wedged together like typewriter keys, their bodies rigid, with only their heads turning out to emphasize a lyric, then snapping back in place. Cartoonish and creepy, it is the physical embodiment of the cookie-cutter corporate environment.

Working with Fosse proved to be an exhilarating experience for eighteen-year-old Donna McKechnie, dancing in her first Broadway show. She later recalled his requirement that all the dancers create names and character histories for themselves: "Each time we made an entrance or exit, Fosse wanted us to know why—where we were coming from and where we were going . . . . Bobby encouraged each of us to bring our individuality into everything we did onstage. Even when we danced in unison, he wanted to see individual points of view."[16]

"The New Frank Loesser and Abe Burrows Musical" swept triumphantly into the 46th Street Theater on October 14, 1961, and reaped unanimously glowing reviews. Confusion over the credits for Fosse's "musical staging" and Lambert's "choreography" led most critics to give Lambert more recognition than warranted, but Leo Lerman in *Dance Magazine* was adamant about Fosse's importance to the show's success: "Without his special talents the musical would not move as swiftly, nor make its stinging—albeit intensely comical—points as brilliantly."[17]

The full ensemble, wedged together like typewriter keys, at the conclusion of "A Secretary Is Not a Toy" in How to Succeed in Business without Really Trying. *Donna McKechnie is second from far left. Photo by Friedman-Abeles © Billy Rose Theatre Division, The New York Public Library for the Performing Arts.*

How to Succeed was an immediate hit, the most successful Broadway musical since *My Fair Lady*, with sold-out houses well into its third year. It won not only the New York Drama Critics' Circle Award for Best Musical but the Pulitzer Prize for Drama, making it only the fourth musical at that time to do so.[18] *How to Succeed* won a near clean sweep of the 1961–1962 Tony Awards and easily bested *Carnival, Milk and Honey*, and *No Strings*, its competitors for Best Musical. Owing to the confusion over his and Lambert's credits, or perhaps because his work was so fluently integrated into the overall direction of the show, Fosse's name was missing from the choreography category.

How to Succeed ultimately played 1,417 performances. It spawned two American road companies and productions in London, Paris, Berlin, Stockholm, and Melbourne, Australia. Fosse's musical staging was recognized as a foundational element of the show's success everywhere it was presented. "Producers in the rest of the world have found it impossible to produce this show without to some extent using the musical staging, choreography or dances created by my client," wrote Fosse's agent, Jack Perlman, to the producer of a Johannesburg, South Africa, production that was found to have reproduced his work without proper payment or acknowledgment.[19]

How to Succeed had a salutary impact on Fosse both financially and creatively. It was his most successful show up to this time, running longer and earning him more than *The Pajama Game* and *Damn Yankees*. It was also a refreshingly easy assignment. Fosse did no preproduction work, having joined after rehearsals were underway, and he estimated that his total time spent on the show was no more than five or six weeks.[20]

The show's producers and creators were a tonic after his experience on *The Conquering Hero*. Burrows, Loesser, and Feuer were plainspoken and no-nonsense, with a shared vision for the show and a deep appreciation for what Fosse, in very short order, brought to it. Fosse and Burrows shared a particular camaraderie, one of many friendships Fosse would enjoy with writers. Burrows was a funny and effusive presenter of Fosse's *Dance Magazine* Award the year after *How to Succeed* opened. After reading the award citation ("To Bob Fosse: He creates musical comedy movement that is uniquely stimulating. Its viewpoint is of today and yet it has the impudence and economy of top flight vaudeville"), Burrows agreed with its sentiment and offered his own description of Fosse's art: "The goal of vaudeville was to hit the audience between the eye quickly and knock it down with energy. Fosse does that, but he does something else, too. He treats his work with the creative care and precision that we associate only with top flight ballet."[21]

None of the show's creators were involved in the 1967 film version, which featured a number of actors from the Broadway and touring companies, including Robert Morse and Rudy Vallee. Adapted and directed by David Swift, the film was a virtual remounting of the show, down to the stage-like sets and face-front direction, as if the proscenium was just off camera. Dancer Dale Moreda, from the Broadway cast, who also staged many of the foreign companies, recreated Fosse's work. "Coffee Break" was filmed but not used. "A Secretary Is Not a Toy" was seen in truncated form, but the bright, flat lighting showed off Fosse's dance groupings, and at least some of the number's straight-faced comic tone survived. *How to Succeed* premiered at Radio City Music Hall and received generally positive reviews, but in the year of *The Graduate* and *Bonnie and Clyde*, its coy sexuality and mild pokes at corporate life made it seem like a relic from an earlier era, which, in truth, it was.

Fosse barely had time to think about the successful Broadway opening of *How to Succeed* because he was already working on his next project. *Seasons of Youth* was a musical variety hour whose lightweight premise was a celebration of youth. Fosse not only choreographed the dances and musical numbers but also appeared as part of the show's musical repertoire company. He was charmingly low-key in a brief "Just in Time" with singer Jill Corey. Elsewhere he was pleasant but forgettable, evoking memories of his MGM days. His key assignment was two numbers with Miss Barrie Chase (as she was billed), making her first appearance since being partnered with Fred Astaire on his acclaimed television specials.

"I Don't Think I'll End It All Today" is a tongue-in-cheek calypso number by Harold Arlen and E. Y. "Yip" Harburg from their recent musical, *Jamaica*, that finds Fosse and Chase enumerating all the reasons not to commit suicide ("So many slim hips still to be swung"). Dressed in black shirts and pants, and wearing straw boaters, they run through by-now-familiar Fosse moves—the Chaplin walks, the mambo steps, the knee work—but here Fosse tightens everything up. He breaks the dance into short movement phrases, with each ending in a freeze ("pretty pictures," as he later referred to them in *All That Jazz*). Fosse and Chase lock down their lower bodies while only their ribcages keep time to the beat. Elsewhere, they stand stationary while rotating their necks. The ballet-trained Chase's long, clean line and legato phrasing highlight Fosse's sharp isolations and anticipate Ann Reinking's later performances of his choreography.

"I Don't Think I'll End It All Today" starts as yet another retread of "Who's Got the Pain?" and "Mu-Cha-Cha," but Fosse finds new variations on old steps. He pares down the movement and creates striking juxtapositions of the two dancers' bodies. There is new clarity to Fosse's choreography that points to the future. And Fosse is as energized by dancing alongside Chase as he was by Tommy Rall and Verdon. "I Don't Think I'll End It All Today" is the undeniable highlight of *Seasons of Youth*.

The other major number for Fosse and Chase is an elaborate audition sequence intended to demonstrate the passion and determination of a young dancer. "Suzy Glockenspiel" is first seen practicing at a ballet barre as a narrator (voiced by Fosse) describes her dreams of dancing on Broadway. Donning a straw hat and toting a suitcase, she heads for New York and auditions for a tough, impatient producer (also voiced by Fosse). She demonstrates her versatility by performing cancan, flamenco, and ballet sequences, all accompanied by quick-cut costume changes. Ordered to present "interpretive-type dancing," Chase executes a demure bump-and-grind. For her singing audition, she does a snippet of "I Could Have Danced All Night," and is ordered to sing it higher. As she does, Chase jumps higher and higher and is finally lifted by (clearly visible) strings up to the ceiling, at which point the entire sequence loses any semblance of reality. Ultimately, she is rejected, and the number ends on a bittersweet note as she dons her hat and picks up her suitcase, presumably going forward to try again, thanks to youthful hope.

Once again Fosse attempted a story ballet, and once again he borrowed from other sources. There are traces of both the "Born in a Trunk" sequence from the 1954 film *A Star Is Born* and Gene Kelly's "Broadway Rhythm" ballet from *Singin' in the Rain*, but neither Fosse nor Chase brings them to life. The tone shifts awkwardly between hard-bitten and whimsical, and the hopeful ending is unearned.

Fosse's real accomplishment with *Seasons of Youth* was behind the camera. Producer-director Joseph Cates was often missing, and Fosse was more than happy to step in as unofficial director. According to songwriter Ervin Drake, who contributed original songs to the special, "Everything on that screen was a choice he made, even the camera work, which he wasn't credited for."[22] Fosse gave the show a trim, uncluttered look. Unfortunately, his tireless work came to very little. Just ten days after the opening of *How to Succeed*, ABC broadcast *Seasons of Youth* to dismissive reviews. "Sluggish and draggy," the *Boston Globe* called it, and *Newsday* felt the commercials were livelier than the show itself.[23] Nevertheless, this forgotten relic of 1960s variety television gave Fosse the opportunity to step (uncredited) into the director's chair.[24]

Just as he finished *Seasons of Youth*, Fosse was hit with devastating personal news. In the early morning of November 1, 1961, Joan McCracken suffered a heart attack and died in her sleep. Though it had been five years since they divorced, Fosse had stayed in touch with McCracken, sometimes calling her in the middle of the night when he was unable to sleep due to his drug consumption. McCracken's health had worsened in the years since their marriage, and she had long since stopped dancing. She continued acting, but her last stage performance was in 1958. McCracken had long ago shaved five years off her age in the public record, and all her obituaries dutifully gave her age as thirty-eight rather than forty-three.

Just before *All That Jazz* was released in 1979, at a moment when Fosse was at the very peak of his success, Gwen Verdon reflected on Joan McCracken and the impact of her death on him: "He can have half a million in the bank, all the Tonys, Oscars, and Emmys one human being can amass in a lifetime, and all he lives with is the fact that Joan McCracken died so young on him. Years from now, you'll read how Bob enhanced so many lives, which he did. But I'm going to tell you Bob's real tragedy: Nobody, not one of us, except Joan, was ever able to enhance his."[25] Her reference to McCracken having "died so young on him" is misleading, since Fosse had left her for Verdon. In the same interview Verdon insisted that she and Fosse had waited to marry until after McCracken's death, when in fact their marriage had occurred more than a year before. Perhaps she was referring to Fosse's guilt over leaving McCracken, but Verdon's comment that only she was able to enhance his life points to McCracken's larger influence.

It was McCracken who persuaded him to study acting and the wider world of dance. She was the first to recognize and promote his talents as a choreographer and to hold him to a higher standard for himself. And yet Fosse had abandoned her for Verdon at just the moment when her health worsened and she needed him most.

Fosse's mourning took the form of a short story in which he grappled with his guilt. *Cleveland, U.S.A.* is set in a burlesque house identical to the ones Fosse had played as a young dancer. The narrator tries to blot out his grief over a failed relationship with a woman in New York by losing himself in the cheap entertainment of baggy pants comics and tired strippers. Fosse filled the story with pungent details familiar only to someone steeped in the milieu: the comic's forced and unfunny routines, a bruise on the stripper's thigh, "the stench of senile lust" pervading the atmosphere.

The narrator appears to be in a business requiring travel, not unlike Fosse, the young nightclub hoofer. The burlesque performance and his familiarity with and contempt for it resemble the kind of show business world McCracken encouraged Fosse to aim beyond. As he watches, he seems to see it through her eyes, and his anger turns outward: "It all seemed so wrong. She was wrong. Cleveland was wrong . . . . He hated her. He hated them all."[26]

In *Cleveland, U.S.A.* Fosse works out his conflicts in words rather than movement. It was his first sustained piece of writing, and it would not be the last time he chose show business as the lens through which to interpret his life experiences. Fosse the writer matches Fosse the minimalist onstage. In just a few pages, he establishes the story's theme and setting, withholding just enough information to maintain the reader's curiosity. His use of minute details that humanize those he observes echoes his choreography. *Cleveland, U.S.A.* is both a howl of pain and an attempt by an artist to express himself in a new medium.

> "You know, I never can find an over-all idea for a show. It comes to me piece by piece, and then, if I'm lucky, the pieces fit together and a style emerges. But it happens by trial and error."
>
> Bob Fosse, 1963[27]

Even before *How to Succeed* opened on Broadway, Feuer and Martin had settled on their next show. When they read the galleys for a forthcoming book by Patrick Dennis, the author of *Auntie Mame*, the producers immediately envisioned it as a musical. Dennis's new book was a spoof of "as told to" celebrity biographies, but with a twist. *Little Me: The Intimate Memoirs of That Great Star of Stage, Screen, and Television Belle Poitrine as told to Patrick Dennis* was told in both words and photographs. More than 150 photographs illustrated the outlandish and risqué life story of the title character, from the poverty of her early life in Venezuela, Illinois, through war, jail time, movie stardom, multiple marriages, scandal, and redemption.

Auntie Mame's great success surely figured in the decision of Feuer and Martin to option *Little Me* for the stage. Neil Simon had just had a breakout hit with his first play, *Come Blow Your Horn*; more pertinently, he had spent three years writing for Sid Caesar's television hit, *Your Show of Shows*. Simon would apply his sketch comedy skills to Belle Poitrine's episodic tale, substituting gags and one-liners for the book's deadpan camp and shifting the focus from Belle to the seven men she meets and marries, most of whom die under comic circumstances. And it was Simon who insisted that only Sid Caesar could create a star turn out of the seven roles—a strenuous tour de force comparable to Alec Guinness's multiple roles in the film *Kind Hearts and Coronets*. But this would be eight times a week within the disciplined confines of a large-scale Broadway musical.

Caesar, who had not done a Broadway show since *Make Mine Manhattan* in 1948 (the same show in which Fosse and Niles had toured), had spent his television years improvising within a story framework and now feared he would be unable to harness his volcanic comic instincts and stay within the parameters of the script—imperative when music, scenery, and quick changes are timed to dialogue cues. Eventually a solution was reached whereby Caesar would have license to ad lib during rehearsals, and if his contributions were agreeable, they would be added to the script. Caesar's comic instincts served the show almost too well. "The trouble was he was always liable to be right," Feuer jokingly lamented.[28]

By the time *Little Me* was published, the new Feuer and Martin musical starring Sid Caesar was already announced. The team of Cy Coleman (music) and Carolyn Leigh (lyrics) would write the score, observing Caesar's dictum that he would sing no more than three songs.[29] (Counting reprises, Caesar sang twice that number by opening night.) With Fosse's contribution to *How to Succeed* still fresh in their minds, the producers offered him the job of choreographer and, along with Feuer, co-director. When Fosse asked why he was not offered full director credit, Feuer replied, "Because I can handle Caesar."[30] Fosse handled Caesar just fine, and directing lead-in scenes to the show's eighteen musical numbers meant that his imprint would be all over *Little Me*.

Fosse was an early and loyal member of the Society of Stage Directors and Choreographers (SSDC), formed in 1959. But two years later, the League of New York Theatres still refused to acknowledge the society, maintaining that its members were independent contractors, not employees, and thus had no standing as a bargaining agent. Fosse made recognition of the society one of the conditions of his signing, and on February 20, 1962, Feuer and Martin became the first Broadway producers to recognize SSDC when they signed him to co-direct and choreograph *Little Me*. The agreement was the first crucial step in other Broadway managements recognizing the society and the eventual ratification of a contract between the league and SSDC.[31]

"A Fosse show" was by now synonymous with "a hit show," and auditions for *Little Me*'s ensemble of fifteen dancers and eleven singers were fiercely competitive, even for those who had worked with him before. "You sort of knew you were going to get it, because you knew that he liked what you did. But you never really knew," remembered David Gold. "He was very tough. He made you work for every job."[32] By now Fosse had created a standard movement sequence for singers, as Feuer remembered: "He used a set of moves and poses and hand gestures—a test to see if they had two left feet or two left hands . . . . They'd all sing 'Yankee Doodle went to town, riding on a pony, stuck a feather in his hat and called it macaroni . . .' And while they sang, they pretended to stick feathers in their hats, performing elementary steps in time to the tune. He called it moving, not dancing."[33]

Virginia Martin, the original Hedy LaRue in *How to Succeed*, won the role of Belle over better-known actresses like Edie Adams, Tina Louise, and Dorothy

Provine. While the show's focus had shifted to its star comic, Belle was onstage as much as her seven suitors and carried the weight of the show's music. She shared the role of Belle with Nancy Andrews, as an older version of the character.

Before rehearsals began, Fosse and Verdon learned that Verdon was pregnant. Since her marriage, Verdon had refused all stage offers, limiting her activities to serving as her husband's assistant and occasional television appearances. One such appearance occurred on June 5, when she and Fosse guest starred on *The Gary Moore Show*, singing and dancing to "I Wanna Be a Dancin' Man," a song originated by Fred Astaire. They were warm and playful with each other as they made their way through an easygoing vocal and soft-shoe before launching into a fast-paced Dixieland strut. It was state-of-the-art Bob Fosse 1962—the angular arms, the flexed wrists, the double-time traveling footwork while the upper body moved at its own tempo, rolling and weaving. While Verdon danced confidently out to the camera, Fosse cast a look of endearment at his partner. It was mutual admiration, and the two shared a rare intimacy in dance.

After the stylization of *How to Succeed*, the bawdy, revue-like format of *Little Me* was a return to Fosse's early show business days. He would fill the musical numbers with vaudeville and burlesque tropes—both verbal and physical— learned firsthand in his youth. Fosse's preproduction work on *Little Me* was extensive and included not only designing the choreography but also creating scenarios and writing dialogue for the dances. His notes for *Little Me* show a keen ear for one-liners, puns, and show business references that synced perfectly with Neil Simon's comedy.

With "Poor Little Hollywood Star," Fosse showed his impatience for ballads. His notes include a list of four points that Belle's rueful consideration of the price of fame had to accomplish:

1. Show 7 yrs of "so-called culture pictures"
2. Show Belle as have [*sic*] little or no talent
3. The studio losing money
4. Be a good no.[34]

Fosse devised a series of marquees and banners advertising the ludicrous titles and images of the culturally uplifting films that brought Belle movie stardom, including *Mrs. Abe Lincoln* (with Belle in a stovepipe hat); *Scarlet Letter*, featuring a photo of Belle in cheerleader's uniform sporting a giant A (an image taken from Patrick Dennis's book); and "*Kong-Kong—A story of a primitive love that did much to combat the deep-rooted prejudice against apes in this country.*" None of Fosse's titles made it into the final script, but the concept remained. The laughter that greeted Simon's hilarious new titles ("Belle Poitrine in *Ben Her*," "Belle Poitrine as Joan of Arc in *Flaming Youth*," and "Belle Poitrine in *Hello Quo Vadis, Hello, with Free Dishes*") nearly drowned out the plaintive Coleman-Leigh song. Fosse accomplished his four points, including making it "a good no.," and it was not the last time that he would subvert a composer's intentions for a ballad.

Fosse's dance notes were filled with his "greatest hits" of steps from previous shows: "jumps from 'New Girl,'" "'tempest fugit' girls step in 'Pajama Game,'" and various walks ("Penguin walk," "'Secretary' walk," "a little Red Buttons," "chugs" from "Garry Moore"). For "Dimples," Belle's vaudeville act capitalizing on her notoriety after being acquitted of murder, he included a "[Joe] Frisco pants pull," a "baseball walk" (from *Damn Yankees*), and "sort of a Chaplin walk." "Dimples" features a chorus line of baggy-pants policemen and Belle in form-fitting prison stripes sexily swinging a ball and chain (a move director-choreographer Susan Stroman used years later in *The Producers*).

A sight gag highlight comes when the policemen carry Belle sideways behind a screen where another female dancer is waiting. As Belle's head is pulled out from one side of the screen, the other dancer's feet are pulled out from the opposite side, giving the illusion that Belle has been stretched like taffy.[35] One intriguing note references a "Harland Dixon step."[36] Dixon was a tap dancer who appeared in vaudeville and Broadway musicals and specialized in eccentric dance moves, including one in which he kept his arms rigidly locked to his sides while twisting his shoulders.[37] Fosse would revisit this "Harland Dixon step" later in *Sweet Charity*'s "Rich Man's Frug."

"I've Got Your Number" is a song and dance of seduction for George Musgrove, a boy from Belle's hometown who becomes a tough Chicago gangster. The role is small—a vest pocket Joey Evans limited to one number. Fosse cast Swen Swenson, who had recently danced Michael Kidd's strapping "Whip Dance" to acclaim in *Destry Rides Again*. (Verdon thought her husband would like to play George himself, but his experience with *The Conquering Hero* had put Fosse off adding to his workload.)[38] Fosse attempts something rare and potentially disturbing in "I've Got Your Number": a male striptease not unlike "Whatever Lola Wants." The dance has to be sexually aggressive enough to make Belle's capitulation believable while not upsetting the sensibilities of a 1962 Broadway audience.

Fosse had previously used burlesque-style "girly" movements in choreography danced by men ("Give Me a Band and My Baby" in *My Sister Eileen*, for example), but in a spoofing manner. "The Narcissistic Tango" in *Pal Joey* showed him fully capable of choreographing a strutting peacock dance for a man that left no question of his intentions toward a woman. Nevertheless, Fosse may have been revealing his own skittishness when he went out of his way to praise Swenson as "articulate and masculine."[39]

Just as Lola stalked Joe Hardy in "Whatever Lola Wants," "I've Got Your Number" is driven by George's relentless pursuit of Belle, and even though he sheds only jacket, tie, and sleeve garter, the effect is riveting. As the song's brassy vamp kicks in, he pulls his hat low over his eyes, sizing her up as he runs his fingers across her waist from behind. George whips his jacket across the floor and advances on Belle with what one reviewer termed "a stallion's lust strut."[40] He takes off his tie, wraps it around Belle's neck and draws her close. He dances atop a table and knee slides around the stage, but always advances again with the strut, the pelvis leading with a hard focus on Belle.

George removes his sleeve garter while doing "snake hips," a dance move originated by plantation workers and later popularized by vaudeville performer Earl "Snake Hips" Tucker. A lower-body shimmy, it emphasizes loose hips and jelly-like legs, giving the impression the dancer has no skeleton.[41] Fosse also incorporates what he calls a "swimming combination,"[42] another vaudeville dance move in which the arms go limp and flow out to the side of the body in opposition to each other. When performed with snake hips, the effect is loose-limbed and leering. At last, charging on Belle with a "sticatto [sic] mambo move," George picks up the overwhelmed girl and carries her offstage. Fosse came up with several spoken interjections for George and Belle between song verses, but only his exit line for Belle as she succumbs is retained: "Oh well . . . it's wartime."[43]

Just as Verdon kidded sex, Swenson brings a welcome dose of humor that leavens the aggressive sexuality. Swenson himself captured the number's fine line when he observed, "Bob wanted the women to like it. But he didn't want the men in the audience to be offended. He insisted upon the tongue-in-cheek approach, with good humor and with nothing sleazy or offensive. I think men identify with it."[44]

Fosse's dance numbers for *Little Me* overflowed with comic invention. The Buchsbaum Brothers, two theatrical agents, persuade Belle that show business awaits her in "Be a Performer," a fast-talking vaudeville turn that the young Riff Brothers might have learned from Frederic Weaver. (The "Be a Performer" and "Dimples" sequence, charting Belle's transition from murder suspect to vaudeville star, is a capsule preview of *Chicago*.) In "Boom Boom," Val Du Val (Caesar), a Maurice Chevalier–style entertainer, performs a night-club floor show number complete with chorus girls. As part of his research, Fosse watched old kinescopes of Caesar's television shows and learned that he had often used fake taps for comic effect. As a recording played, Caesar would mime with great virtuosity, and only moderate accuracy, a complex tap routine. Fosse incorporates a "nerve tap" (a series of rapid taps with the motion emanating from the vibration of the leg) into the "Boom Boom" dance break during which Caesar points his foot but remains motionless as a frantic "nerve tap" recording plays.[45]

The idea for "Rich Kids' Rag," the show's widely acknowledged dance highlight, originated with Fosse, searching for a dance opportunity early in the show. At the sixteenth birthday party for Noble Eggleston (Sid Caesar), the richest boy in town, his equally rich friends bounce, flounce, and thumb their noses in a burlesque of dance class proprieties set to a series of ragtime themes.

The dance's defining physical trait is its knock-kneed stance ("Jerry Lewis knees,"[46] Fosse called them) with the legs in demi-pointe, supporting the body's weight on the balls of the feet with heels raised. Fosse establishes the knock-kneed profile up front by highlighting just one couple center stage who dance a variation before being joined by the others for what one critic called "an animated cartoon [that] converts awkwardness into a ballet."[47]

A full complement of Fosse movements are poured on as the kids roll their shoulders, isolate their heads and wrists and hips, and shift focus to the percussive dance arrangement. A Fosse amoeba crosses the stages, punctuated by teacup pinky fingers. The boys pick the girls up and swing them into place like rag dolls. Their dance, performed with utmost seriousness, is frequently interrupted as they break into bashful giggles and goofy grimaces. Adult dancers playing youngsters in frilly dresses, knickers, and knee socks doubles the comic effect.

In "Rich Kids' Rag," Fosse marries its giddy high spirits to the tremendous fluidity of his staging. The couples dance in Fosse's trio formation before splitting off in all directions as others take their place for a new variation. A small group executes a short sequence of steps, which is then taken up by others in a danced version of a musical "round." This layering of movement gives the impression of a much larger ensemble than the number's six couples, as does another favorite Fosse trick. As dancers exit into an upstage wing, the first ones off re-enter quickly from the downstage wing and cross the stage. The last dancers off then tack onto the group, making their numbers appear greater than they really are.

"Rich Kids' Rag" was a sensation from its first public performance. Norman Nadel in the *New York World-Telegram* called it "the choreographic coup of the season."[48] It even inspired dance critic Walter Terry in the *New York Herald Tribune* to declare, "If this delicious bit ever gets exposed nationally via television, I can't see why it shouldn't move, in adapted form, off the stage and on to the dance floors of the country as a communal replacement to the Twist."[49] Years later, Verdon recalled Fosse's bemusement at the number's perceived social commentary: "People would say to him, 'Oh, you've made such a comment on society kids.' And he'd turn away and say, 'I didn't know I was making a comment, I was just trying to think of something to do.'"[50]

Little Me opened its out-of-town tryout in Philadelphia, where *How to Succeed* tried out successfully the previous year, and if anything, the critical and box-office response was even more enthusiastic. Only a few critics noted that the nonstop

Social dancing, 1920s. Little Me's "Rich Kids' Rag." The couple at center is Barbara Sharma, a favorite Fosse dancer and, back to the audience, future choreographer Michael Smuin. Photo by Friedman-Abeles © Billy Rose Theatre Division, The New York Public Library for the Performing Arts.

hilarity inevitably gave way to a second-act letdown. The morning after the opening, three hundred people were lined up at the box office, and *Little Me* broke previous Philadelphia sales records set by *My Fair Lady*, *Guys and Dolls*, and *West Side Story*.[51]

In size, complexity, and length, *Little Me* was a big show, featuring multiple settings (seventeen in the first act alone) and lavish and diverse costumes for a cast of forty (Caesar himself had twenty-eight changes in just the first act).[52] Its nearly three-hour running time required trimming and fine-tuning rather than wholesale changes. "Real Live Girl" was a Caesar solo in his role as nearsighted doughboy Fred Poitrine. When Caesar refused to sing multiple verses of the song, Fosse hit on the idea of reprising it for Fred's fellow doughboys, but with a difference. "Everything in the show was getting a ride out and big finishes, so I said I'd do something soft," he reasoned.[53]

Working with dance music arranger Fred Werner, Fosse actually sneaks into the number before the song even begins. As the homesick soldiers anticipate Belle's arrival, their hushed interjections of "real, live girl!" segue easily from dialogue to song. The gentle waltz is transformed in the dance break to a soft-shoe, danced up on the toes, in a nod to Paul Draper. Syncopated whistles and finger snaps punctuate a tacit section. *Time* singled it out, noting that its "gestures of front-line camaraderie and foot-slogging are subtly altered to create a balletic lyric of loneliness."[54] (Gwen Verdon recalled that Fosse was so happy with the number's reception the first time it was performed that he did cartwheels in the back of the theater.)[55] Arriving near the end of a long first act, "Real Live Girl" was an oasis of quiet charm amid *Little Me*'s strenuous comedy, and it was Fosse's favorite number in the show.

There was tremendous interest in Sid Caesar's return after a self-imposed hiatus from his television show, with New York newspapers and national magazines doing feature stories on the show. *Newsweek* even put Caesar in all seven of his characters on its cover. *Little Me* opened on November 17, 1962, at the Lunt-Fontanne Theater, directly across the street from *How to Succeed*. Based on advance ticket sales and opening night reviews, Feuer and Martin had every reason to expect that they would have twin hits on Forty-Sixth Street for the foreseeable future. Among the daily newspapers, *Little Me* received four unqualified raves and three favorable notices.[56] As expected, the show was a personal triumph for Sid Caesar. (Several critics worked variations on "Hail Caesar!" into their reviews.) But two threads ran through the reviews: one, its savvy staging could not overcome a sense that *Little Me* was too glib, and two, Bob Fosse was critical to its success.

In *Dance Magazine*, Leo Lerman made clear his opinion of Fosse's development as an artist and the status he now enjoyed: "Despite the ubiquitous Mr. Caesar, Bob Fosse is—at least for this viewer—the star of the show . . . . Fosse lifts an ebullient TV review [*sic*] sort of show into the realm of musical comedy art . . . . Bob Fosse has become one of Broadway's top ranking choreographer/directors; the other is, of course, Jerome Robbins."[57]

Little Me was not Fosse's first "show business musical" (*Redhead*, with its music hall setting, earns that designation). But in all his shows, characters are at their most vivid when in the act of performance, whether at a union meeting or on a World War II battlefield. The act of showing off in front of an audience is part of every Fosse show, and the setting mattered less than the opportunity. Show business as a lens through which to view the world would increasingly inform Fosse's stage and film projects. At its darkest, Fosse's show business reflects his own conflicted feelings about it—how it robbed him of his youthful innocence or the way he could so easily manipulate audiences through dazzling staging. But in *Little Me* the tone is sunny, even joyful, as he approximates the styles and conventions of vaudeville and burlesque to tell Belle's up-from-nothing show business story.

Little Me was an immediate sellout, joining *How to Succeed* as one of the top-grossing shows on Broadway well into 1963, even after a newspaper strike severely limited advertising opportunities in the days before television commercials for shows were commonplace. However, business began to trail off in the spring, with some speculating that Caesar's return to television during this time had siphoned off audiences who could see him at home for free. (Each week on his night off, Caesar taped a new half-hour series, *As Caesar Sees It*, with the first show airing on November 25, just a week after *Little Me*'s opening.)[58]

In a tie with *Oliver!*, *Little Me* received ten Tony Award nominations, including two for Fosse for direction (with Feuer) and choreography. But *A Funny Thing Happened on the Way to the Forum* proved to be a juggernaut that won Best Musical, Best Actor in a Musical (with Zero Motel besting Caesar), Best Book (Burt Shevelove and Larry Gelbart over Neil Simon), and Best Director (Fosse's old mentor, George Abbott). In the end, *Little Me* received only one award when Fosse took home his fourth Tony for choreography over the work of his old friend Carol Haney in *Bravo Giovanni*.

As summer approached, *Little Me* continued to struggle. In June, Sid Caesar collapsed from exhaustion onstage during the first act, compelling his standby, Mickey Deems, to continue the performance.[59] Given the star's fatigue and the continued lackluster box-office numbers, Feuer and Martin finally did what once would have been unthinkable. They closed *Little Me* on June 29, 1963, after only 257 performances at a 40 percent loss on production costs of $355,765. In an effort to earn back some of its costs, plans were immediately announced for a tour with Caesar and many of the original cast.[60] The tour kicked off in early 1964 and played for six months, but it did not succeed in wiping out the losses.

A London production starring television personality Bruce Forsyth, and with Fosse's staging recreated by dance assistant Merritt Thompson, opened late in 1964 to an avalanche of glowing reviews, most of which predicted a long and profitable run. The British more readily embraced *Little Me*'s episodic format and broad comedy, and seemed not to care about its lack of heart. Neil Simon rewrote parts of the book, shrewdly moving the action to England, where class differences were better understood. But this production also closed early, though at 335 performances it exceeded the Broadway run.[61]

Despite the view that *Little Me* was underappreciated when it first appeared, subsequent Broadway revivals fared even less well than its 1960s productions.[62] It may be that Fosse's choreography and direction, with Feuer, made the best possible case for a musical that, despite its exuberant score and gag-filled book, left audiences cheated by its lack of romance or relatable characters.

Little Me and *How to Succeed* marked a joyous high point in Fosse's career. Catching the buoyant optimism of the Kennedy "Camelot" years, they demonstrated his mastery of comic musical staging. After *The Conquering Hero*, Fosse's experience on these two shows was blessedly free of offstage drama. Tough, good-natured show business confidence marked his collaborations with Cy Feuer, Abe Burrows, Frank Loesser, Neil Simon, and Cy Coleman, and he would work with most of them again.

Little Me and *How to Succeed* also marked an ending of sorts. It was the last moment when their "gags-and-girls" routines could be performed without irony. As the 1960s progressed, shifts in attitudes toward sex and the role of women in the workforce would make the winking sexism of both shows look antediluvian and offensive. (Revivals of *How to Succeed* always place it squarely in its original time period.)

"Bob Fosse is, I think, at the point of experience and promise at which Jerome Robbins was before he did *West Side Story*. How much time will elapse before he will be given the opportunity to do an all-dance show?" wrote Leo Lerman on the occasion of Fosse receiving the *Dance Magazine* Award.[63] Fosse had done eight shows in eight years, with his last two defined, to a significant degree, by the overall physicality of his staging. He was now ready to create a musical in which dance would drive song and story and bring together all theatrical elements to express his singular vision.

5
RHYTHM OF LIFE
• • •

"I was in a good position then. But I made some dumb choices on projects that knocked me out of the box for a few years."

Bob Fosse, 1974[1]

The brightest spot for both Fosse and Verdon in the period following *Little Me* was the birth of their daughter, Nicole, in March 1963. Shortly after Nicole's arrival, Fosse once again returned to the role of Joey Evans in another City Center revival of *Pal Joey*. Fosse's performance displayed maturity and confidence when *Pal Joey* opened its two-week engagement on May 29, 1963. Richard P. Cooke in the *Wall Street Journal* noted, "Although George and Ethel Martin are credited with the choreography in the Playbill, Mr. Fosse seems to have injected much of his own grace and sense of timing into the excellent dancing ensemble."[2] The Martins, former Jack Cole dancers and colleagues of Verdon, stepped aside for Fosse to create his own numbers. His dance notes for "Happy Hunting Horn," an upbeat ode to the joys of girl chasing, give clues to the precision and athleticism he demanded from the female dancers as well as himself. "Some light soft shoe-ish movement" with "Astaire like elegance" continues with the "Flip over from 'Roll Your Sox' [*sic*]," before progressing to "3 girls hold 3 girls with leg up—B. [Bob] does Baseball slide thru legs," and finally, "Bob back jump off chair."[3]

Fosse was nominated for a Tony Award as Best Actor in a Musical. Although he lost the award to Bert Lahr in *Foxy*, the recognition was a fitting cap to what would be his last dance with Joey Evans. Now thirty-five and with thinning hair (his hat stayed more tightly lodged on his head this time), Fosse would soon be too old to play the charming young rotter. While bidding farewell to Joey, he was already launching his next project.

On April 26, 1963, the *New York Times* carried an announcement of some possible upcoming Fosse projects, including *Funny Girl*, insisting it was "almost definite on Mr. Fosse's agenda."[4] The musical biography of comedienne Fanny Brice, to be produced by David Merrick and Brice's son-in-law Ray Stark, featured a book by screenwriter Isobel Lennart, music by Jule Styne, and lyrics by Bob Merrill, the composer-lyricist of *New Girl in Town*. The show had suffered a recent setback with the departure of Jerome Robbins as director-choreographer. Barbra Streisand, the twenty-year-old Brooklynite who was quickly establishing herself as a powerful and emotive singer with a comic personality not unlike the young Fanny Brice, and who had recently been praised for her small role in *I Can Get It for You Wholesale*, was the firm choice of Stark and Styne for the lead role. Robbins, who recognized Streisand's talents as a singer and comedienne, strongly favored Anne Bancroft, whom he felt would be more capable of finessing the troubled script. At an impasse, Robbins withdrew and made it clear that his considerable work with Lennart on the script was not to be used without his participation.[5]

From rowdy burlesque houses to the Broadway stages of Ziegfeld's *Follies*, the trappings of Fanny Brice's story mirrored those of Fosse's career, and the show business setting offered potential for the kind of boundary-pushing theatrical staging he had brought to *Redhead*. In accepting the assignment to replace Robbins, Fosse had two hurdles to overcome. One, Robbins's legal threats meant that the script would require an overhaul to eliminate any of his contributions. Two, still smarting from his experience on *The Conquering Hero*, Fosse wanted assurances that he would not be replaced out of town and that no one but him could alter his dances. Fosse offered to work without pay and without a contract until Stark and Merrick were comfortable with him in this role.[6]

Barbra Streisand was officially signed to play Fanny Brice in July. Fosse would later claim that he had been responsible for casting her, though with Robbins gone, she was the clear favorite.[7] Nevertheless, she was signed during Fosse's tenure on *Funny Girl*, and as he and Lennart reshaped the script, Streisand emerged as the show's "Muscle."

The script Robbins devised with Lennart began with Fanny disrupting a dance number in a vaudeville house before being fired. Lennart created a new opening scene with Fanny entering her dressing room, studying herself in the mirror, and sardonically uttering, "Hello, gorgeous" before making up for one of her comic Indian numbers. Fosse's ideas for the scene start while the overture is still playing. Fanny enters and crosses the stage as a dressing room unit moves in. She steps onto the unit as the overture ends and studies herself for a long moment before saying her now-classic first line. Fosse cuts the application of the Indian make-up, instead focusing on Streisand's face and giving her a true star entrance.[8]

Robbins conceived "People Who Need People" (later shortened to the simpler "People") for Fanny, Nick Arnstein, her future husband, and Dave (later renamed Eddie), Fanny's friend from her burlesque days, as "a love song sung by three people."[9] Lennart and Fosse reimagined the moment as a Fanny solo, showcasing Streisand in the show's hit ballad.[10] Robbins later acknowledged that one of Fosse's best ideas (though later eliminated) was to show Nick gambling in pantomime on one side of the stage while Fanny, in a cinematic montage effect, sang the ballad "Who Are You Now?" on the other side.[11]

Ray Stark enjoyed keeping the creative team off balance. In conversations with Fosse, he referred to others as easily replaceable, and Fosse deduced that Stark was saying similar things about him.[12] While Fosse's contract provided the sought-after assurances that he would not be replaced or have his dances tampered with, he was apprehensive over what he called "an atmosphere of distrust" imposed by Stark and held off signing it.[13]

Around this time, Stark contacted Cy Feuer and Ernest Martin to gauge Fosse's capabilities. When Feuer and Martin answered in the affirmative but questioned the lateness of his inquiry, Stark responded that Fosse had not yet been signed. While technically true, this underscored for Fosse what he later described as Stark's "inclination to 'do me in.'"[14] Stark's behavior was an affront to Fosse's good faith offer to begin work without compensation, especially since Stark had sought him out specifically for the job. Fosse demanded confidence and trust from his producers, and when they were breached, his rejection was swift. He bolted *Funny Girl* for an offer from the more agreeable Feuer and Martin to direct and choreograph their new musical, *I Picked a Daisy*.

In withdrawing, Fosse was much more generous than Robbins, assigning to the producers "all suggestions, material, ideas and other contributions" he had made during his *Funny Girl* tenure.[15] Fosse's staging ideas for Streisand's entrance and his concept for "People" were retained by his successors and proved indelible moments for both the show and the star's growing legend. Garson Kanin came on board as *Funny Girl*'s director, with Carol Haney doing the choreography. Ultimately, Jerome Robbins was brought back as production supervisor, and *Funny Girl* became a long-run hit and, later, a popular movie. Had Fosse stayed with the show, it might have been the vehicle for his debut as a film director. Instead, he walked away after working five months without salary or financial stake, but with enough of his fingerprints remaining to offer a tantalizing glimpse of what Bob Fosse's *Funny Girl* might have been.

"You should have got Stanislavsky to direct this, not a simple Norwegian boy."
Bob Fosse, 1965[16]

I Picked a Daisy, which was soon retitled *On a Clear Day You Can See Forever*, had nearly as many personnel changes as *Funny Girl*. Burton Lane had only recently joined the production after composer Richard Rodgers withdrew in frustration from waiting for lyricist-librettist Alan Jay Lerner to provide him lyrics for the songs. And Fosse again replaced another director-choreographer, this time Gower Champion.[17] Alan Jay Lerner succeeded Feuer and Martin as producer of *On a Clear Day*, but he was no faster in delivering material. After his experience on *Funny Girl*, Fosse was understandably frustrated by the continued delays, which dragged on for more than a year. As he later recalled, "I decided that *if* I was a director, then I had to work. I couldn't develop my craft just by sitting around for two years; I had to get to work with actors. So I took the first show that was offered me."[18]

That show was Frank Loesser's *Ex-Lover*, based on Sam Spewack's *Once There Was a Russian*, a one-performance flop in 1961. Budgeted at $450,000, *Ex-Lover* was to be a lavish musical adaptation of Spewack's comedy of court intrigue involving Catherine the Great, who recruits John Paul Jones, the young naval hero of the American Revolution, to lead the Russian army against the Turks. The naive Jones finds himself embroiled in a triangle romance, sharing Catherine with her consort, Admiral Grigori Potemkin. As usual with a Frank Loesser show, he was the undisputed "Muscle." He not only wrote the score and co-produced with

Allen B. Whitehead but also joined Spewack in writing the book. With Loesser the main selling point, the extravagant show was cast with low-wattage stars. Both Alfred Marks and Hy Hazell were British performers making their first American appearances as Potemkin and Catherine, respectively. John McMartin, who had made his Broadway debut in *The Conquering Hero*, was cast as Jones.

In his haste to accept the assignment, Fosse did something he never did before or after: he neglected to read the script, a decision that almost immediately caused him concern. As he later recalled, "Once I'd heard the score and read the book, I knew we had trouble. But I still thought I could pull it off."[19] Eighteenth-century Russian dances were hardly in Fosse's choreographic repertoire, and his notes show him struggling to Russianize his movement style. A list of various walks include "Mambo shoulder shake . . . Russian style," "Marcel Marceau walk Russianized," and "Russian Dan Dailey (excentric) [sic]."[20]

The now-renamed *Pleasures and Palaces* was less notable for Fosse's choreography than for his staging ideas and infusions of humor. After the overture, the curtain rose on an empty, darkened stage. The faint sound of marching boots could be heard in the distance. As the marching grew louder, it was punctuated by a series of stamps, claps, and finger snaps performed in counterpoint. The sounds and rhythms grew more intense as drums and cymbals joined in. Dancer Kathryn Doby remembered, "And then the lights came up very, very gradually. We arrived on stage, still doing these rhythms, but now mixed with marching and kick steps."[21] The full orchestra opened up to herald the arrival of Potemkin's army, played by the entire ensemble (including the women, dressed as soldiers and sporting mustaches). This simple yet striking opening showed Fosse's theatrical imagination at full throttle.

The Fosse trio can be applied to any style or period, including Russian Cossack dances in Pleasures and Palaces, *here featuring, left to right, Kathryn Doby, Barbara Sharma, and Leland Palmer. Photo by Friedman-Abeles © Billy Rose Theatre Division, The New York Public Library for the Performing Arts.*

Another large-scale dance demonstrated the army's haplessness. ("The fuck up army," dancer Richard Korthaze remembered it being called.)[22] Fosse spoofed the gravity-defying acrobatics of the Moiseyev and Bolshoi companies and filled the dance with gags at least as old as vaudeville. A dancer leapt from a platform in a full split accompanied by sound effects of his pants ripping. Three men danced a variation, each with a knife in his teeth. After their dance, they pulled the knives from their mouths, with one pulling out his false teeth. Dancers in mid-jeté crashed into each other. Korthaze remembered being outfitted with a toupee: "And when I took a bow before going offstage, the wig fell forward."[23] Notwithstanding the Russian acrobatics, the dance bore similarities to the antics of the incompetent American soldiers in Fosse's "The Battle" ballet in *The Conquering Hero*.

Pleasures and Palaces was scheduled for a single tryout engagement, at Detroit's Fisher Theatre, where it opened on March 11, 1965, to reviews that faulted not only its score and book but also its uneven tone. Labeling it "lesser Loesser," Jay Carr in the *Detroit News* criticized its indecision about whether to be "'Admiral on the Roof'" or "'A Funny Thing Happened on the Way to the Imperial Palace.'"[24] Calling Fosse's choreography "adequate," Carr went on to add, "But now that we've seen what the Moiseyev troupe can do, the standard Broadway translation of Cossack fare no longer quite fills the bill."[25] (Igor Moiseyev's precision-drilled troupe, with its flamboyant, theatrical folk dances, had created a sensation in recent American performances on tour and on television.)

Fosse, with Verdon by his side, immediately got to work on improvements, though nothing short of a major overhaul of its book would have made the show work. Loesser, for whom *Pleasures and Palaces* would be his last completed show, wanted to close and cancel the New York opening. Fosse refused to give up, even offering to invest his own money to fund a continuation of the tryout to Boston.

"Tears of Joy," a late second-act song for Potemkin, Catherine, and members of the court, was particularly troublesome. Originally staged as a period court dance, the number fell flat. As the tryout continued, Fosse took the number in the direction of satire, as a takeoff on court decorum. His notes show him working out the sounds and rhythms of crying: "Sniff—Huh? Sniff—Huh? Huh, Huh, Huh, Sniff." Elsewhere, he tried variations such as "One long constant baby cry" and "Cry with hiccup." He even looked to his daughter for ideas, jotting down, "Nicole quivering lips cry."[26]

"He tried to find the humor in it and the number started working," remembered Kathryn Doby. But before he could complete this new version of "Tears of Joy," the closing notice went up. There would be no Boston engagement, and Saturday night, April 10, would be the final performance of *Pleasures and Palaces*. Ordinarily following the posting of a closing notice, all rehearsals are canceled, but as Doby recalls, "The dancers said we have to let Bob finish this number. We can't just leave it like that. So the scheduled rehearsal happened, Bob finished the number, and we did it for him. It never went into the show, but he finished the number that Thursday. That's the kind of loyalty the man inspired."[27]

That final rehearsal before the show closed brought Fosse a valedictory. Alone on the stage with no producers or writers present, no stars or stage managers,

Fosse and his dancers paid tribute to each other, as ensemble member Alice Evans remembered. After performing "Tears of Joy" one last time, "the dancers, those who had been in *Little Me* and other shows with him, proceeded to do other numbers from those shows."[28] This spontaneous performance was the purest, most meaningful way for them to say "thank you." "It was just a very touching afternoon, because we were all crying and so was he. It was just beautiful," Evans said.[29] In a sense, this moment marked the birth of the "Fosse dancer": fiercely loyal, keenly aware of his legacy, and willing to work endlessly to help him achieve his vision and burnish their own skills. In each of his following shows, the "Fosse dancer" would play an increasingly significant role.

> "There was a moment of great happiness, and I wanted to give Gwen something wonderful. I wanted to give her the best show she ever had."
>
> Bob Fosse, 1985[30]

Sweet Charity was Fosse's conception from the very beginning, the first true "Bob Fosse show." It was his idea to adapt Federico Fellini's film *Nights of Cabiria* to the musical stage and transform its little Roman streetwalker into a Times Square "taxi dancer." While Neil Simon was ultimately listed as librettist, the show's shape and sequence were set by Fosse. Similarly, much of the score by Cy Coleman and Dorothy Fields was written to order for the song slots assigned in Fosse's original adaptation.

Fosse shaped the libretto to emphasize dance as the driver of the narrative, and his direction took fluid, cinematic staging further than ever. Working with set and lighting designer Robert Randolph, Fosse employed state-of-the-art lighting and scenic effects. At times the action appeared to float in the air in Randolph's ingenious elevator and parachute ride scenic effects. While many of the numbers grew directly from the plot, Fosse interrupted the narrative for non-plot-related dances that commented on current fads and showcased his choreographic invention—a direct strike at the integrated Rodgers and Hammerstein model of his earlier shows. His choreography became lean and sinewy, more stylized and angular than ever, and it gave off a frank sexuality not seen since "Red Light Ballet" from *New Girl in Town*.

Seeping through the wisecracks, comic set pieces, and hopeful, if not happy, ending were darker intimations regarding sexuality, aging, and the loneliness of urban life that marked *Sweet Charity* as more daring than the cheerful musicals dominating mid-1960s Broadway like *Hello, Dolly!*, *High Spirits*, or *Fade Out—Fade In*. By 1966, postwar feminism and the sexual revolution were well underway. At the very moment when birth control pills were introduced, Helen Gurley Brown published her bestseller, *Sex and the Single Girl*, which encouraged single women to enjoy sex before marriage without guilt. Women were joining the workforce in numbers greater than any time since World War II. Beatnik culture was evolving into the hippie movement and, with it, recreational drug use. Discotheques and group analysis were fashionable.[31] The urban origins of these social changes were reflected in *Sweet Charity*, making it feel right of the moment.

It was a given that any potential Verdon project would be not only directed and choreographed by Fosse but written by him as well. Fosse's many friendships with writers may have stoked his writing ambitions. Fosse met Paddy Chayefsky in 1959 and later joked that he had been required "to audition for twelve years" to be Chayefsky's friend.[32] Chayefsky, one of the most successful writers to emerge from the 1950s era of live television drama, was the author of *Marty*, *Middle of the Night*, *The Catered Affair*, and others. A big, bearish Jewish intellectual with a garrulous personality, Chayefsky was the polar opposite of the small, wiry, high school–educated, and quieter Norwegian-Irish Fosse. Their friendship was forged on a passion for baseball and an even greater disdain for showbiz phoniness. Fosse gravitated toward men who were as eloquent with words as he was with his feet.

Fosse's interest in writing was also consistent with his urge to exert more control over his projects, as he readily acknowledged: "There's a strange thing, and I'm not sure it's good, but it's always been a problem. When I was an actor or a dancer, I was dissatisfied with the choreographer. When I was a choreographer, I was always slightly dissatisfied with the director, and so I kept wanting more and more positions so I would only have to answer to myself."[33] Fosse could have added the role of librettist to the list of collaborators he wished to eliminate.

Among his writings from this period are random poems, sketches, and outlines for film or stage projects. Their topics center on show business and sex, particularly the pursuit—mostly comic—of beautiful women by breathless, besotted men. Fosse was aware of the limited opportunities dancers face as they age, particularly women. His outline for a story of the downward trajectory of a dancer sketches a bleak future and displays Fosse's intimate understanding of the milieu she inhabits:

Coda for a Dancer
1. Auditioning—compete against young girls
2. Working in a show (flop or fired)
3. Child—foster home—mother takes care of—husband gone
4. Love with younger man—beautiful
5. Talked into—dirty movie—nude pictures? Going out with someone important—in need of money
6. Realization there's no future . . . .
7. Working in a cheap niteclub in Pa.—strip?
8. Give child to a couple who love it and can take care of it—goodbye to child.
9. Death? Abortion? Drugs?
10. Date with unattractive man[34]

The fate of this unidentified dancer might have led her to the setting for Fosse's most ambitious writing to this point. He had for some time been compiling detailed notes for a show to be called *Dance Hall*, two one-act musicals. Dance halls, where men paid to dance with women selected from a stable of hostesses, flourished in cities around the United States in the 1920s and 1930s but dwindled in popularity after World War II. Only a few remained in operation in New York

City by the 1960s. The term "taxi dancer" derived from the fact that, as with taxi drivers, the women were paid only for the amount of time spent with a customer, generally the length of one song.

Fosse's notes form a blueprint for *Sweet Charity*, as he describes the faded elegance of a Times Square "Tango Palace" with photographs of its hostesses displayed by the front door.[35] He lists the cost of tickets (fifty cents a dance or one dollar for a brief conversation with a hostess), the clientele (soldiers, sailors, married men, college kids, conventioneers), the ages of the hostesses (between sixteen and forty-five), their length of employment (mostly short-term, but a few as long as ten to twelve years), and their payment system (commission only, 50 percent of the cost of dance tickets and 25 percent of drinks).

Dance Hall was just one of several potential properties for Verdon being discussed with Robert Fryer and Lawrence Carr, producers of *Redhead*. Another was a musical version of *Chicago*, Maurine Watkins's 1926 comedy of corruption in the newspaper and justice system. Verdon was enthusiastic about the property, but it was abandoned when the producers were unable to strike a deal with the now-reclusive Watkins.[36] A musical adaptation of Truman Capote's *Breakfast at Tiffany's* offered an intriguing opportunity for Verdon to portray Holly Golightly. Fryer and Carr gave up their option on the property when Capote expressed concerns that Verdon, thirty-nine at the time, was too old for the role of the runaway Texas bride who reinvents herself as a Manhattan cafe society party girl.[37] Christopher Isherwood's *Berlin Stories* was briefly considered. Fosse's response, highly ironic in view of its eventual successful musical adaptation as *Cabaret* and his later film version, was "We don't quite see it as a musical."[38]

Vivian Shaw, the ex-wife of David Shaw, who had worked on *Redhead*, suggested the Fellini film *Nights of Cabiria* as a possible property for Verdon. Fellini's wife, Giulietta Masina, brought a tragicomic, Chaplinesque quality to the bedraggled but indomitable character of Cabiria, an aging, small-time Roman prostitute. The film begins and ends with Cabiria's near death at the hands of men in whom she has unquestioningly placed her trust.

The appeal of *Nights of Cabiria* as a vehicle for Verdon is easy to understand. There are notable similarities between Masina's screen persona and the roles associated with Verdon. In *La Strada* and *The White Sheik* (where Cabiria made her first, brief appearance), Masina embodied a spiritual innocence that remained resilient against the cruelties of the world. Similarly, the humanity of Verdon's Lola and Anna Christie shone through their outer sensual trappings.

Music and dancing are a source of emotional release for Cabiria, and Fosse was quick to see the possibilities in a dance-driven musical adaptation. In Americanizing *Nights of Cabiria*, he turned to his earlier *Dance Hall* idea. Judging that a prostitute would be unpalatable as the central figure in a Broadway musical comedy, he transferred the setting to that of a faded New York dance hall and boosted his American Cabiria up a few steps in respectability (and legality) by making her a taxi dancer. She still sold her body but only to dance, drink, and talk with customers. This distinction between hooker and hostess was intentionally murky, with the clear implication that the exchange of money for more than dancing was always in the air.

Perhaps owing to his idea of *Dance Hall* as two one-act musicals, Fosse envisioned his American *Cabiria* as needing other properties to pair with it. A number of properties were briefly considered for pairing with the *Cabiria* musical, including one-acts by Elaine May and Martin Charnin. Fryer and Carr encouraged Fosse to write the book for both musicals, but, apprehensive about writing on his own, Fosse wanted a collaborator. Charnin joined him for a short time to work on the *Cabiria* musical.[39] Later, Hugh Wheeler rewrote a portion of the script but then withdrew, citing his insecurities in working on a musical.[40] (Wheeler later overcame these insecurities to become a leading librettist for musicals such as *A Little Night Music* and *Sweeney Todd*; he also contributed to the script for Fosse's film of *Cabaret*.) By this time, Cy Coleman and Dorothy Fields had joined the project as composer and lyricist.

It was soon apparent that as a one-act, the *Cabiria* story was rushed, needing more time to develop Cabiria's relationship with Oscar, who only appeared two scenes before the end. Fosse pressed on with a new two-act version and soon had both a first draft and a new title, *Sweet Charity*, reflecting the change of name for its lead character.

The stylized theatrical elements Fosse had used at least as far back as *Redhead* were already in place. Film techniques like stop action, dissolves, and the use of an iris (in which a diaphragm is set in front of the lens and is then opened or closed to begin or end a scene, or to focus attention on a particular detail) were specified in the script. Signs and placards introduced scenes and served as dramatic punctuation. The first scene ends not with a blackout but with Charity simply walking from one set into a new one while she continues speaking.

Despite its cheery new title, Fosse's script is plodding and grim, with a notable lack of humor. Charity is as tough and abrasive as Cabiria, but she lacks the humor and humanity that deepened the film character. When a rival streetwalker taunts her, Cabiria launches into a fight, demonstrating the assertive side of her nature. In an analogous scene, Charity initiates a nasty fighting and screaming match with her ballroom co-workers, and the effect is sour and mean.

Making Charity a taxi dancer rather than a prostitute is not exactly an even switch and actually diminishes the character in a way that Fosse may not have intended.[41] Cabiria's purity of spirit and faith in love transcend the brutality of her life and imbue her with a heroic quality. Charity, the taxi dancer, is a "noodle-headed nitwit,"[42] as one critic later described her, with a trusting nature that has led her to a string of opportunistic losers, the last one's name a tattooed scarlet letter on her arm. Cabiria's existential quest for some sense of purpose in her life is largely absent in Charity, who is merely, as one of Fosse's signs tells us, "A girl who wanted to be loved." In making her at home on the musical comedy stage of 1960s Broadway, Fosse lowers the stakes for Charity.

Fosse struggled with how to characterize Oscar and arrange his rejection of Charity without making him a potential murderer, as in the film. When Charity finally tells Oscar about her occupation and the men in her past, he insists that it doesn't matter and asks her to marry him. But at the last moment, he undergoes an abrupt change of character and confesses that his "neurosis" won't allow him to put aside the thought of Charity's past involvements. Instead of being pushed, Charity loses her balance and falls in the water. Oscar ignores her money and runs away, promising to send help and dithering about being a terrible person.

Fosse, realizing that comedy was the missing ingredient in his musical comedy, once again reached out to a writer friend for help, sending the script to Neil Simon, who was in Rome working on a film. Simon immediately saw that Fosse had underestimated the script's problem. "It *desperately* needed humor . . . . I sat down and spent one long night removing the lines that didn't work and inserting new and what I hoped were funnier lines."[43] After receiving the revisions back in New York City, Fosse was so pleased that he flew to Rome to play Simon the score and persuade him to do a full revision. Simon reluctantly agreed, with the understanding that "Bert Lewis," Fosse's literary pseudonym, would remain the credited book writer.

An article appearing in *Variety* just before rehearsals began revealed the financial arrangements for *Sweet Charity*. The $395,000 budget included a fee of $3,500 for Fosse, along with a weekly royalty of 4 percent of weekly grosses. Demonstrating how essential Verdon was to the enterprise, her contract guaranteed her $5,000 weekly and 8 percent of the weekly gross, later increasing to 11 percent.[44] While *Sweet Charity's* budget was less than that of *Pleasures and Palaces*, it was indicative of the steady rise in Broadway production costs. A decade earlier, *The Pajama Game* and *Damn Yankees* were economically produced for less than $170,000 each. The lavish *New Girl in Town* came in under $245,000. *How to Succeed*, comparable to *Sweet Charity* in terms of cast size and physical production, cost 25 percent less just four years earlier.

One area where these increasing costs were felt was in reduced cast sizes. The combined singing and dancing ensembles in *Pleasures and Palaces* numbered twenty-nine, the same as *Sweet Charity's* entire cast. *Pleasures and Palaces* was the last Fosse show to have full, and separate, singing and dancing ensembles. Fosse may not have mourned this turn of events, however. *Sweet Charity's* eighteen-member chorus was made up predominantly of dancers who could sing, giving him a sizable dance ensemble.

Within the confines of a "cattle call" audition with hundreds of dancers competing for a limited number of jobs, Fosse established a more respectful environment than many of his peers. Kathryn Doby, who danced in *Sweet Charity* and later assisted Fosse, remembered, "I auditioned for choreographers who would just sit out in the audience and let the assistants handle the audition, and never say anything to the dancers. Bob was a lot more involved and up onstage himself. If somebody was a terrific dancer, but wasn't right for the show, he would always tell them, 'For this show we're looking for something else. But keep it up, you were wonderful. And thank you for coming.'"[45] David Gold, who danced in several Fosse shows including *Sweet Charity*, recalled the key attributes Fosse looked for at auditions: "He liked dancers with a core ballet technique because they had a strong spine and a cleanliness of line. But he would never use people where the ballet technique showed through. He didn't want it to be the thing that you're concentrating on. He wanted you to be involved in what the dance was about."[46]

"[Gwen] was at her peak in *Sweet Charity* because she was old enough to know what to do, and her body was young enough to cooperate."

Bob Fosse, 1986[47]

The dancer Fosse was most excited about working with was his wife. Since *Redhead*, Gwen Verdon had been a popular guest star on television variety programs, appearing frequently on Garry Moore's and Perry Como's weekly shows, and was practically a semiregular on *The Danny Kaye Show*, dancing and clowning with her old Twentieth Century-Fox colleague. Marriage and fatherhood had not lessened Fosse's interest in other women, but it was in the rehearsal studio that his and Verdon's personal and professional partnership began a decade earlier, and *Sweet Charity* would be a happy return to the place where they were most compatible.

"This was to be my present to her on her return to Broadway, so I tried to get into the show everything that Gwen could do so well," he later said.[48] *Sweet Charity* would be the ultimate Verdon showcase, highlighting her singular talents as a dancer and comedienne fully capable of heart-tugging pathos. Verdon, who would turn forty-one just before the show opened, may have sensed that the role would be the culmination of her career as Broadway's star dancer. With shared goals, they worked closer and more creatively than ever before.

Weeks before the cast assembled, Fosse and Verdon began creating a dance language for Charity. Her physicality was suggested to them by the women behind the make-up counter at Bloomingdale's, whose feet burned from standing all day. To relieve the pressure, they cocked the hip of one leg while sharply flexing the heel of the other, pushing down into the floor.[49] From this image Fosse and Verdon created the iconic Charity pose used to promote the show. With her little black dress, heart-shaped tattoo, and purse held over her shoulder by a strap made of rope, it was a silhouette as distinctive as Chaplin's Little Tramp. The Chaplin image was underscored by Charity's costume. Amid the show's colorful swirl, Charity would remain in the same black dress most of the evening.

"Just kind of junkin' around," Verdon called the pigeon-toed, knock-kneed frug, at once loose-limbed and angular, that introduces Charity at the very top of the show.[50] Its aimless and self-effacing quality quickly defines the character as one quite different from the film's Cabiria. From a pitch-black stage, designer Randolph opens up a giant, jagged iris revealing Charity in silhouette against a hot pink background. As she dances, a series of signs appear. "The Adventures of Charity, the Story of a Girl Who Wanted to Be . . . ," they read, followed by a final, valentine-like "Loved."[51] Coleman's jazzy, syncopated theme sounds like Charity—playful and meandering. "Charity's Wish," as the prologue is called, establishes the show's stylized look and format. It is Charity's own private reverie, occurring outside the narrative, and its presentation at the beginning of act 1 alerts the audience that the show will take similar side trips to explore the character's imagination.

In Sweet Charity, *Gwen Verdon is first revealed in the Charity silhouette through Robert Randolph's iris-like opening and his dramatic backlighting. Photo by Friedman-Abeles © Billy Rose Theatre Division, The New York Public Library for the Performing Arts.*

By the time the full cast assembled on November 1, 1965, Neil Simon's rewrites had significantly changed the tone of the show. He eliminated much of the script's grit, making it lighter and considerably funnier. Simon softened Charity, making her a not-very-bright New York City dame whose street smarts evaporate at the first possibility of love. "Your big problem is you run your heart like a hotel—you got guys checkin' in and out all the time," she is breezily told early on. With her bursts of oddly formal dialogue ("Say, do you think I could have some small article of personal apparel?"), this Charity resembles a Damon Runyon doll in search of one special guy.

Simon, who was claustrophobic, had once been stuck in an elevator with his wife, and now he used that experience as the basis for Charity's introduction to Oscar.[52] As Charity talks Oscar through his nervousness, Simon establishes him as a comic neurotic—another New York type—obsessed with the idea of female purity, who tries but ultimately fails to accept all the men who have come before him in Charity's life. The change in Oscar's character better positions him to abandon Charity in a less villainish manner.

Charity once again falls in the lake and is deserted, but she emerges to see a full-dress Good Fairy who tells her that her dreams will come true that very night. She turns to exit and, unseen by Charity, on her back is a sign advertising a new television show called *The Good Fairy*. Her faith in love restored, Charity dances off to her theme music as a sign announces, "And so she lived . . . hopefully . . . ever after." The ending is more flippant than upbeat and treats her like a patsy. Just like Fosse, Simon lowers the stakes for Charity, and this new ending would never entirely satisfy audiences or critics.

Predictably, Fosse cast many of his long-time dancers, some of whom went straight from *Pleasures and Palaces* into *Sweet Charity*. After *The Conquering Hero* and *Pleasures and Palaces*, John McMartin was back for his third Fosse show, cast as Oscar, and he would bring sensitivity and nuance to what could have been a stereotypical character. Next to Verdon, the veteran performer in the cast was Helen Gallagher as Nickie, one of Charity's dance hall friends. Gallagher had danced for Jerome Robbins in *Billion Dollar Baby* and *High Button Shoes* and for Agnes de Mille in *Brigadoon*. She won the Tony Award for her featured role as Gladys in the 1952 revival of *Pal Joey*. In 1959 she had turned down the opportunity to stand by for Verdon in *Redhead*. Now she accepted the same assignment in *Sweet Charity* along with a supporting role and prominent billing. As Helene, another dance hall hostess, Fosse cast Thelma Oliver, a young African American actress who had made a few off-Broadway appearances and had recently gained notoriety in Sidney Lumet's film *The Pawnbroker*. Her hiring was a small but not insignificant example of color-blind casting as there is no indication in the script of Helene's race.

Surrounded by so many dancers and actors with whom he had worked amiably in the past, Fosse found rehearsals remarkably congenial. Nevertheless, his intensity and precision in the rehearsal room were more evident than ever. David Gold remembered, "Once he said, 'In a show like this, every minute and a half something has to work. And if it doesn't work after a minute and a half, then whatever happens three minutes later had better be twice as good, because that's the level of dynamic needed.' And that accounted for the level of detail in his work."[53] Dancer Suzanne Charny likened Fosse's work to that of a visual artist: "He was like a painter with a piece of canvas. He started making the sketches first and then he knew where he wanted to put the shading as he went along—for characters as opposed to dancers doing a step."[54] Charny also recalled a funny example of Fosse's all-business approach to rehearsals. When cast member Ruth Buzzi asked if she could come in the next day an hour late, Fosse snapped, "There'd better be a damned good reason." "Yes," Buzzi explained, "I'm going to City Hall to get married." Following a long pause, he replied, "Okay. But come back right after."[55]

Simon's script made *Sweet Charity* a true New York show, with sequences set in Coney Island and Times Square, at the 92nd Street Y, and in the new clubs that were changing New York nightlight in 1965. Verdon remembered visiting Arthur, a newly opened celebrity discotheque, with Fosse: "We went there and we saw all these people. Mrs. Kennedy . . . Sybil Burton . . . and this funky music was playing . . . and it was just so elegant. But they really thought they were swingin' it around like the kids do. Well, Bob thought that was funny."[56] His observations formed the basis for "Rich Man's Frug," one of the longest pure dance numbers he had yet undertaken, and provided him the opportunity to spoof the laid-back jet-setters who frequented clubs like Arthur.

"Rich Man's Frug" became the centerpiece of the Pompeii Club scene, giving Verdon one of her few chances to get offstage. Fosse's notes for the "High Society Slop," as he called it early on, feature numerous celebrity references that made their way into the final number. A "Marion Marshall walk" (Marshall was a starlet married for a time to Stanley Donen) was the basis for the female dancers' behind-the-back sway-armed walk. The male dancers' walk was built on a "Danny Kaye traveling step" (an exaggerated straight-legged walk with hips distended) with "elbows held in back, Robert Montgomery style" (the pulled-back posture required for the tight-fitting tuxedos the actor wore in 1930s drawing room films).[57]

Taking off from current popular dances like the Watusi, the monkey, and the frug, Fosse came up with his own variations, including "The Race" ("Marcel Marceau with bumps"), "The Mess" ("snake hips stuff"), "The Punch," a variation on boxing moves, and "The Kasi Moto," whose description seemed to defy execution ("Turned in with plié—bent over—then walk").

A "vulgar ascot gavotte" is how one critic described "The Aloof," the first of three movements that made up "Rich Man's Frug."[58] The Pompeii's denizens are led by one of Fosse's trios, in this case two men, and a woman whose violent whipping of her lengthy ponytail jolts the nonchalant atmosphere. The women walk with one leg stretched forward while the other is in deep plié, leaning back with arms dropping directly to the floor. When they come to a stop, the effect is that of a deadpan right triangle. In contrast, the men are upright in their Danny Kaye walk and Robert Montgomery elbows, nonchalantly smoking. The chain-smoking Fosse uses cigarettes and their smoke for punctuation, timing each puff and exhale to a count. The humor derives from the contrast between the ultracool attitudes of the dancers and their sudden Watusi- and frug-styled outbursts, followed by their immediate snap back into composure.

Fosse's satire is bolstered by his stage pictures, which carry the formal elegance of a George Balanchine ballet. The dancers group together at center, then effortlessly peel out into a straight line across the stage. When all are in place, they turn their backs to the audience and walk upstage, the black of their tuxedos and cocktail dresses punctuated only by the women's pale, swaying arms. When they reach their destination, each dancer in sequence, starting from the center, opens out to the audience in a large frug-like arm gesture. The effect is that of a dark and glittering fan opening up before our eyes.

"The Punch" evolved into "The Heavyweight," the number's second movement, named for the recent heavyweight title match between Floyd Patterson and Muhammad Ali. Structured around the formalities of line dancing, the dancers make two lines, in the center of which they perform Fosse's variations on boxing positions like "The Cover-up" (arms held in front of the face to block a hit), "The Jab" (a quick, straight punch), "The Overhand" (a semicircular vertical punch thrown from overhead), and the victorious two-hands-clasping-above-the-head swing. A coy rotation of the wrist at the waist takes the viewer off guard while the other hand knocks out the opponent. The dancers throw their limp arms around their torsos in rapid motion before unwrapping to deliver a punch.

In the wittiest touch, the dancers partner up and, with foreheads touching, spar as if the other is a punching bag, their punches accented with pelvic contractions. This section ends with the dancers in a tight line, moving as one opponent trading punches with the lead Frug dancer. She executes a brief "mess around" before delivering the final knock out punch, sending the entire line collapsing like a row of dominoes.

"The Big Finish" concludes the number in a gospel-like uptempo mood, with call-and-response vocal exhortations. Fosse draws on the moves of vaudeville's Harland Dixon as he locks the dancers down like stiff-legged robots and sends them traveling across the stage shoulder to shoulder with their bodies and arms rigid. They explode into a free-for-all before the music abruptly stops. One last riff sends them into a momentary frenzy before they freeze back into their original postures, ending as they began, impossibly aloof and above it all.

With "Rich Man's Frug," Fosse creates a six-minute ballet, unattached to *Sweet Charity*'s plot, which could be excerpted and performed by a dance company. He uses movie, sports, and celebrity references to create his own dance language, mixed with variations on the very dances he is satirizing. The satire of "Rich Man's Frug" carries a jolt of cultural immediacy, right down to its orchestrations: its wailing guitars were among the first electric instruments used in a Broadway pit.

Social dancing, 1960s. The too-cool "Rich Man's Frug" in Sweet Charity. *Left to right: Michael Davis, David Gold, Kathryn Doby, Barbara Sharma, John Sharpe, Lee Roy Reams, and Charlene Ryan. Photo by Friedman-Abeles © Billy Rose Theatre Division, The New York Public Library for the Performing Arts.*

"Big Spender" is less a dance number than an amalgam of music, dialogue, and staged movement. Fosse staged this introductory number for the Fan-Dango Ballroom employees as a weary lineup behind a downstage railing, assigning the audience the role of customer. "Big Spender" is full of sharp musical accents, and its brazen fanfare came to define the show's musical pulse. Revealed upstage in silhouette and turned away from the audience, the women's posture is extreme: arched backs, cocked hips, turned-in feet. They slowly back their way downstage in a travesty of a sexy walk—effortful, exhausted, but still trying to allure. Each turns in sequence and offers her own well-worn come-on: "Hey, mister, can I talk to you for a minute?," "Hey, good-looking, I like your hair," and so forth until one final, desultory, "Let's have some fun." (The lines were based on actual enticements from the hostesses that Fosse had heard while visiting the dance halls, recalled Diane Laurenson, who danced in the 1986 revival.)[59]

Fosse arrays the dancers across the railing in angular postures both comical and disquieting—pigeon-toed with feet rolled over on themselves, spread-legged, straddling the railing, not unlike those of the whores in "Red Light Ballet." But where they were rambunctious, the Fan-Dango employees are beaten down. The number's most striking quality is its reliance on stillness. Fosse stages the song's first stanza with the women contemptuously staring down the very customers they try to entice—an "antimovement" approach that allows the audience to focus on individual dancers. Even belting out "Hey, big spender!" they remain frozen, too tired or bored to move. In this, they form a sisterhood with Agnes de Mille's sullen and sexless Postcard Girls from the dream ballet in *Oklahoma!*

As the women sing "Spend a little time with me," Fosse encouraged them to treat the word "me" as a kiss being thrown at the customer, according to Laurenson.[60] Bursts of brass and percussion break the stillness as the women retreat from the railing and throw themselves into violent, orgiastic moves as if trying to escape their surroundings, before returning to the controlled passivity of their commercial enterprise. Their description of the pleasures they can offer is reduced to "fun," "laughs," and "good time" recited over and over, as if on a loop, with each word punctuated by the rhythmic pounding of their blistered feet. When the women rush to engage the attention of an unseen man, they form a particularly roiling version of a Fosse amoeba. Undulating and lunging in all directions, they travel like a giant Medusa across the stage before breaking out for a final exhortation. Finally, spent of what energy they had, the women return to their blank and frozen postures along the railing, as the number ends with one last brass flourish.

"Before I started my choreography," Fosse said later, "I spent a great deal of time observing what really went on in the remaining half-dozen dance halls in New York. They are as close to prostitution as anything you can find."[61] The proximity of prostitution to dance hall hostessing is always present in "Big Spender." The lineup of dancers for selection by customers is little different than a gallery of prostitutes at a brothel. Dorothy Fields's lyrics make no mention of dancing, drinking, or conversation, but plenty of veiled promises of the special services the women provide ("I can show you a good time"). Significantly, Charity is the only Fan-Dango employee not in the number, marking her as different from the

The Fan-Dango Ballroom workers form a Fosse amoeba to stalk a potential client in "Big Spender" from Sweet Charity's *1986 Broadway revival. Left to right: Mimi Quillin, Jan Horvath, Christine Colby, Allison Williams, Allison Reneé Manson (hidden), Kirsten Childs, Bebe Neuwirth, Jane Lanier, Alice Everett Cox (partially hidden), and Stephanie Pope. Photo by Martha Swope © Billy Rose Theatre Division, The New York Public Library for the Performing Arts.*

others and less likely to be in what is otherwise referred to as "the 'extracurricular' business."

Despite the success of "Big Spender," Fosse was not at first sure how to stage it, as Verdon later remembered. In a scene that would find its way into *All That Jazz*, Fosse retreated to a rehearsal room where Verdon was working. Unable to come up with an idea for the number, he lamented, "They think I'm terrible." Verdon chased him out of the room with a chair, like a lion tamer, telling him to do anything to get the number started and then refine it later. During the creation of *Sweet Charity*, he got himself into a state of anxiety such that his nerves were raw and sensitive. "Like a safe cracker's fingers," Verdon said. It was only then that he could create.[62]

In *Sweet Charity*, Verdon seldom left the stage, but it was not quite the marathon role that Essie had been in *Redhead*. Fosse strategically arranged scenes and numbers in which Verdon could get offstage and prepare for her next entrance. The scene in the apartment of Italian film star Vittorio Vidal brought together all aspects of Verdon's persona. When Vittorio's estranged girlfriend returns unexpectedly, Charity is shuttled into a closet from which she enacts a series of comic pantomimed responses to their reconciliation. The moment allowed Fosse to act on his dislike for ballads. As Vittorio sings the extravagant "Too Many Tomorrows," Charity lights a cigarette, only to realize that the smoke through the keyhole will give away her presence. Instead, she blows her cigarette smoke into a clear garment bag, unzipping the bag and exhaling before quickly zipping it back up, even tapping at her cheek to ensure that all smoke goes in the bag. Coleman's ballad serves merely as background music for Charity's antics, expertly mimed by Verdon. (Verdon recalled that Fosse once said to Coleman, "This has got to be a ballad. Do you think you can write it in an up tempo?")[63]

Earlier in the scene, Charity fears that the girls from the Fan-Dango will not believe she has spent the evening with a famous movie star, and she asks for a souvenir to prove they were together. Neil Simon came up with the idea of Vittorio running out of the room to retrieve various props from his film roles—a top hat, a cane—which are then used by Charity in a dance number. Coleman and Fields delivered "If My Friends Could See Me Now," which not only served as the basis for a showstopping Verdon solo but also gave insight into her simple, guileless character. The little taxi dancer who cannot believe that "the highest-brow, which I must say is he, should pick the lowest-brow, which there's no doubt is me," feels no need to seek money or other favors from her wealthy date but only wishes that her friends could see her in his exalted company.

The number's pretext is as flimsy as that of *Redhead*'s "'Erbie Fitch's Twitch," and the results are just as exhilarating. Arranged in three sections, it starts with Charity singing to Vittorio's autographed picture and "junkin' around," with good-natured burlesque bumps. She turns her back to the audience and twists her hips as she sails across the floor, conveying Charity's earthiness and free spirit.

Vittorio returns with a flattened top hat that Charity at first finds puzzling ("What a beautiful black thing"). He shows her how to make it pop into full height, leaving Charity—and Fosse—to execute a seemingly endless number of hat tricks. Charity pops it open against her rear end, on top of her head, through her legs and, to a stripper beat, as a stand-in for pasties and a G-string. Fosse fills the sequence with burlesque flourishes like a Groucho Marx walk and low comedy sound effects.

At last Vittorio returns with the prop that will make "If My Friends Could See Me Now" a true top-hat-and-cane number. Charity plants a tender kiss on the top of the cane as the tempo slows to a cakewalk. She strikes an alert pose in profile, the cane standing at her side. She marches forward, but the cane remains in place. As she holds onto it as if it were Vittorio himself, her body becomes elongated, even reaching up on tiptoes in one final effort to maintain contact. Her free hand flexes in time to the music before touching the top of her hat and, in a perfect grace note, lovingly circles its brim. Verdon's control and timing give the moment a nearly mechanical precision that allows every movement to register. As the tempo accelerates, Charity teasingly vamps, in a nod to "Whatever Lola Wants," and channels Charlie Chaplin with stiff-legged, flexed-feet walks, interjecting a joyous wave to the audience. Turning her back, Charity gives one last hip wiggle, displaying the ease with which she uses her body and reminding audiences of

Verdon's sinewy musculature and ripe curves. With her hat down low over her face and with a loose-legged strut, she winds up the number in showboating fashion, ending downstage on one knee with arms outstretched, just like countless performers on the stage of the Palace Theater where *Sweet Charity* played.[64]

Neil Simon's contributions to *Sweet Charity*'s script finally led to his assuming full credit for the book by the time the show opened its first out-of-town engagement in Philadelphia on December 6, 1965. The change happened so late that advance advertisements, including the first *New York Times* ads, still listed "Bert Lewis" as the book writer. The Philadelphia opening was the success everyone had hoped for, and within days *Sweet Charity* sold out its entire two-week engagement.

As always, Fosse set to work fixing and tightening the show. John McMartin remembered Fosse rehearsing the elevator scene with him and Verdon in a shower stall in one of the dressing rooms: "He wanted to get as authentically as possible the feel of that claustrophobic setting. He was very precise in directing physical movement for an actor, which is unusual."[65] Complaints that Verdon had no second-act dance number led Coleman and Fields to quickly write "I'm a Brass Band" in order to get the star dancing one last time.

As Charity and Oscar make plans to marry, she fixes on the words no one has ever said to her. The lights fade on Oscar as Charity steps out of the scene and into a spotlight and marvels, "He loves me! Someone loves me!" Joy overwhelms her as she jumps and twirls around the stage in wild abandon before settling down to sing. The brief solo that follows is the most lyrical dance moment in *Sweet Charity*. Beginning with hands touching and then circling above herself (an "Agnes DeMille gesture," according to Fosse's notes).[66] Verdon executes a series of port de bras, développés, and coupé turns, as eight male dancers appear upstage in silhouette. A cymbal crash abruptly breaks the mood, and the men suddenly become a high-stepping marching band. Once again, Fosse demonstrates his ability to break a group of dancers into seemingly endless small units popping out of the wings and crisscrossing the stage. At one point, military precision gives way to a loose Dixieland jam session as Charity and the men travel across the stage. As the first men exit, they immediately form a lineup that begins entering from directly upstage as the rest of the men continue into the wings. The final men then join the line, giving the impression of a never-ending ensemble.

Charity leads her brass band in a drum break, the men's movements keyed to the percussive beat. They march in tight formation behind her, adopting a mambo step here, pumping their arms like pistons there. With Charity as drum majorette, the group moves with military regimentation. An "about-face" sequence, repeated over and over, brings applause. Charity exclaims, "That's me!" as the men surround her in one final, meticulous stage picture before exiting in a salute. Charity picks up her suitcase, labeled "Almost Married," and toddles off to her presumed happy ending.[67]

Fosse takes "I'm a Brass Band" out of the show's setting, placing it in Charity's imagination—a colorful utopia filled with music and men. "Big Spender" establishes location and character. "Rich Man's Frug" is witty satire. "I'm a Brass Band" is, in Fosse's words, "a dance of sheer elation and joy"[68] that gave the star the requisite eleven o'clock showstopper.

"I'm a Brass Band" was in place when the show opened at Detroit's Fisher Theater just in time for Christmas. The main change in Detroit was the second-act opener, "Give Me a Rain Check," a gospel number performed at the Rhythm of Life Church that refused to come alive for the audience. Coleman and Fields wrote a replacement number named for the song's setting. "Rhythm of Life," recalled Coleman, "was inspired by Bach with a lot of interweaving polyphonic musical lines and was quite a challenge for Dorothy. She worked at it like a jigsaw puzzle and put the lyric together one phrase at a time."[69] (The church leader's name, Daddy Johann Sebastian Brubeck, wittily combined the song's classical and jazz motifs.) Fosse's staging for the full-ensemble "Rhythm of Life" cleverly parallels the song's structure. Each phrase is introduced by a small group executing a simple series of steps with stoned, beatnik cool. Fields's staccato lyrics find the ideal physical embodiment in Fosse's wrist, arm, and head isolations. Eventually, the puzzle pieces of Fosse's choreography merge with Coleman's Bach-like musical lines and Field's interweaving lyrics to create a rousing and highly satisfying climax.

Sweet Charity, with a hefty million-dollar advance, arrived on a Broadway that had changed since Fosse's last show. In a roundtable discussion shortly after its opening, pointedly titled, "Is the Director-Choreographer Taking Over?," Fosse held forth about those changes and why he favored them: "I think there's been a kind of restlessness with our theater, a kind of groping around . . . . And one of the things that we've started groping at is style. We've thought that we've become too conventional in the way we do things and that we should become more visual . . . . and I think that turning toward the director-choreographer has come out of this restlessness."[70]

Not all choreographers were able to bring that sense of movement and style to their direction. The work of hyphenates like Jack Cole and Michael Kidd was indistinguishable from shows with separate directors and choreographers. Cole never found a way to effectively integrate his striking dances with their narratives in his two shows as director-choreographer, *Donnybrook!* and *Kean* (both 1961). While his choreography was as muscular as ever, Kidd's work as a director never achieved the fluidity of Robbins or Fosse, and he was unable to overcome mediocre material in shows like *Wildcat* (1960), *Subways Are for Sleeping* (1961), and *Ben Franklin in Paris* (1964). However, in Fosse's absence, two director-choreographers had elevated staging to a new dominance. But each flexed this "Muscle" in very different ways.

In *Bye Bye Birdie* (1960), *Carnival* (1961), and *Hello, Dolly!* (1964), Gower Champion, Fosse's old MGM costar, brought a streamlined approach to the staging of conventional musicals that was similar to Fosse's work on *Redhead*. Working closely with set and lighting designers, he created seamless transitions between scenes, trimmed dialogue to move more quickly into song, and staged book scenes with dance-like precision. Like Fosse, Champion was unafraid to push past theatrical conventions. For *Carnival*, he did away with the theater curtain and overture, beginning the show with carnival workers entering a bare stage and erecting a circus tent that served as the playing area for the show. At the end, they dismantled the tent, leaving the stage as bare as they had found it. For *Hello, Dolly!* he broke free of the proscenium by installing its famous passerelle around the orchestra pit.

Hello, Dolly!, Champion's biggest hit, "[used] dance as a means of determining the magnitude and characterization of the musical," according to his biographer John Anthony Gilvey.[71] *Hello, Dolly!* was as dance-filled and fast-paced as any Fosse show, but there were marked differences in their work. Fosse was fond of numbers that allowed both him and his cast to show off, with only a tangential connection to the plot, while Champion's numbers almost exclusively drove the narrative. (Even his splashy title number from *Hello, Dolly!* served a plot purpose, establishing the esteem in which Dolly is held by her friends at the Harmonia Gardens.) The difference between "Rich Man's Frug" and *Hello, Dolly!*'s "Put On Your Sunday Clothes" is the difference between the two men's approaches to ensemble staging. Fosse increasingly broke his dancers into small units executing endless variations on similar steps, while Champion was at his best with large ensembles in simple, unison movement. Fosse was drawn to material with an edge of dark satire, most suitable for adult audiences, whereas Champion's shows were family-friendly. Fosse's shows bristled with the humor and sexuality of the burlesque stages of his youth. Champion's work had the silky polish of one of his and Marge's ballroom routines. "His work was very comedic, and very light, very colorful, very smooth—the Hollywood approach," recalled Chita Rivera, the star of *Bye Bye Birdie*.[72]

Having already brought *Funny Girl* to its successful opening, Jerome Robbins returned later in 1964 with his biggest hit, *Fiddler on the Roof*, based on stories by Sholom Aleichem. As in *West Side Story*, Robbins's staging melded the work of the librettist Joseph Stein, composer Jerry Bock, and lyricist Sheldon Harnick into a unified whole. Robbins's collaboration with his design team, which included scenic artist Boris Aronson and lighting designer Jean Rosenthal, complemented but did not overshadow his work with the writers, and his conceptual staging was propelled by the narrative, not the reverse. "*Fiddler*," wrote musical theater historian Larry Stempel, "struck a fine balance between the book-based past of Broadway musicals of the postwar era and their concept-driven future."[73]

Much like *Fiddler*, *Sweet Charity* was a bridge between Fosse's George Abbott–Jerome Robbins apprenticeship and his dance-dominated concept musicals in the following decade. To herald this ascendance, his lofty billing now read, "Conceived, Staged and Choreographed by Bob Fosse," as if the standard "Directed and Choreographed" credit was too puny to describe his far-ranging accomplishment.

The Palace Theater's return as a legitimate theater after years as a movie house and the excitement of Verdon's return in a splashy new musical made *Sweet Charity*'s opening on January 29, 1966, a media event. The critical response was enthusiastic, if not ecstatic, summed up by *Variety*'s observation: "In a season that has thus far been devoid of a major musical smash hit, 'Sweet Charity' is good enough, but by no means a triumph."[74]

Verdon was lauded for her performance, with reviews resembling home-coming cheers. "She seems ageless and more poignantly magnetic and capti-vating than ever" was *Variety*'s reverent description of her appeal.[75] Kevin Kelly acknowledged the iconic character that the Fosse-Verdon partnership had produced: "As created by Fosse and executed by Miss Verdon, 'Sweet Charity' is a humdinger. If Simon's book fades in the memory, his heroine will remain front and center, I think, for a long, long time, a new girl in the history of the American musical comedy."[76]

For Fosse, the reviews acknowledged *Sweet Charity* as a high-water mark in his career and affirmed his use of dance to push the show's narrative. *Saturday Review*'s Henry Hewes called the show "total choreography, a musicalized story conceived in dance images, in which even the dramatic conversations are per-formed as precisely designed movement."[77]

The role of Charity distilled the essence of Verdon's appeal, endearing yet resil-ient, and ebulliently comic. That she was older than in her last Broadway appear-ance gave the character's eternal search for love an added poignancy. Cary Grant, visiting her backstage, summed up what made her performance so indelible: "I really don't understand how you do it, but when you are terribly happy, you make me cry. And when you cry, you make me happy."[78]

Sweet Charity immediately became a sellout hit, with Verdon the focus of numerous newspaper and magazine profiles. Much of the coverage focused on the strenuousness of her role and her status as "The Sexiest Granny in Town."[79] (Verdon's son had recently married and made her a grandmother.) *Sweet Charity* received nine nominations, the most of any show, for the 1965–1966 Tony Awards. In addition to Best Musical, it earned nods for Verdon, John McMartin, Helen Gallagher, Coleman and Fields's score, Irene Sharaff's costumes, Robert Randolph's sets, and two nominations for Fosse for his direction and choreogra-phy. (Neil Simon was not eligible for a nomination as the Tony Awards suspended the award for book of a musical from 1966 through 1970.) In the end, Fosse won his fifth Tony for Best Choreography, *Sweet Charity*'s sole prize of the evening. Verdon's loss to Angela Lansbury for *Mame* marked the first time she had been nominated but failed to take home the award.

In December, a Las Vegas company starring Juliet Prowse opened at Caesar's Palace in a one-act, ninety-minute version performing twice nightly. The show, with Fosse's direction and choreography restaged by original cast member Eddie Gasper, was so well-received that its original sixteen-week engagement stretched to twenty-six. Part of the show's trimming included a revised, happier ending for Charity, which was momentarily considered for the Broadway production but never used.[80]

Variety reported that *Sweet Charity*'s final costs had ballooned from its original $395,000 to nearly half a million dollars.[81] The Broadway production was still sell-ing well when Verdon was in the show, but the demands of the role led to her fre-quent absences. Standby Helen Gallagher went on numerous times for the star, during which earnings fell off. By the time *Sweet Charity* entered its second year, royalty cuts were in place to keep the show running.[82]

To ease the burden of performing her taxing role eight shows a week, Verdon had begun occasionally cutting vocal numbers. When an audience member wrote a letter complaining that he did not get his money's worth because of the cut, Verdon calculated the number's monetary value to the show and sent him a check for forty-two cents.[83] Eventually, "You Should See Yourself," Charity's first number, and "Where Am I Going?," a second-act ballad, were removed from the Playbill's song list.[84] An exhausted-looking Verdon was featured in a *Life Magazine* story about the demands of long-run musicals on their stars, claiming she would never do another Broadway show.[85]

At the end of June, Verdon entered the hospital for a medical procedure, and Helen Gallagher took over the role permanently, along with star billing, expecting to play it through the show's scheduled closing at the end of August. But without Verdon, the show ran only three weeks and closed early, on July 15, 1967, after 608 performances. *Sweet Charity* ran longer than either of the last two Gwen Verdon vehicles, but for a show that generated so much excitement and received generally good reviews, it showed surprisingly little endurance at the box office without its original star.

Sweet Charity launched a national tour in September 1967 with Chita Rivera as Charity. A month later, a London production starring Juliet Prowse arrived, again staged by Eddie Gasper. As with *Little Me*, the British critics were more enthusiastic about the show than their US counterparts; they particularly praised the score, which had been received somewhat dismissively by New York critics. *Sweet Charity* even won the *Evening Standard* Theatre Award for Best Musical over *Fiddler on the Roof* and enjoyed a run of 474 performances. The American national tour was far less successful despite positive reviews for the show and Rivera. Fosse had been in favor of a national tour, against the judgment of the producers, as producer Joseph Harris noted in a letter to Fosse. Calling the tour "a fiasco," Harris complained that its losses "completely wiped out any profits we had and put us in a losing position."[86] After engagements in Boston, Chicago, and Toronto, the tour collapsed in early 1968.

Sweet Charity became a staple on the summer stock circuit and has been produced as far away as Japan and Australia. It has proved to be a durable Broadway title, having returned twice, the first time in a virtual reproduction of the original by Fosse himself in 1986. A 2005 revival directed by Walter Bobbie gave Charity a new, self-empowered ending in which she sends Oscar away (and avoids a dunking in the lake). Wayne Cilento created new choreography that was heavily indebted to Fosse's original conceptions. In 2016, the New Group, an off-Broadway company not known for producing musicals, mounted a fiftieth anniversary production directed by Leigh Silverman and choreographed by Joshua Bergasse, featuring a twelve-member cast and ensemble in a small black box staging, and stressing the grittier aspects of Charity's world. *Sweet Charity* also remains a favorite with British audiences, having been produced twice in the West End since its original London production.

Regardless of the fresh directorial or choreographic statements attempted in these revivals, each has labored in the shadow of Fosse's original template.

Starting as a germ of an idea in the mind of Bob Fosse, Charity and her little black dress have become as recognizable around the world as Nellie Forbush's oversized sailor suit or Peter Pan's green tights and tunic.

> "I think I can say truthfully that directing 'Sweet Charity' gave me the most exhilarating time of my life."
>
> Bob Fosse, 1969[87]

The record-breaking box-office performance of film versions of *The Sound of Music* and *My Fair Lady*, and the Walt Disney original *Mary Poppins* jolted Hollywood and set the major studios on an accelerated program of producing big-budget, wide-screen movie musicals.[88] *Sweet Charity* was deemed a natural for similar treatment, and Universal Pictures acquired the motion picture rights for $500,000 in October 1966. (Before the deal for the film rights could proceed, a lawsuit brought by Martin Charnin over his contribution to *Sweet Charity* during his early work with Fosse had to be settled.)

The film was planned as a starring vehicle for Shirley MacLaine, who claimed that she convinced the studio to hire Bob Fosse as the film's director.[89] No one knew *Sweet Charity* better than Fosse, who was the logical person to translate it to the screen. Having already directed the musical numbers for *My Sister Eileen*, *The Pajama Game*, and *Damn Yankees*, Fosse was anxious to assume overall responsibility for a musical film, despite trepidations. As he later recalled, "I didn't think I was quite ready to direct, but I felt I'd never get another chance, so I jumped in and directed it."[90]

Gwen Verdon, the woman for whom Fosse had created the show and who was crucial to its success, was never seriously considered for the film. Verdon's only substantial film role had been in the screen version of *Damn Yankees* a decade earlier. Now in her early forties and with no profile in films, she would not have been the studio's choice to headline what was planned as a multi-million-dollar production. Verdon would join other Broadway stars like Ethel Merman in *Gypsy*, Carol Channing in *Hello, Dolly!*, and Angela Lansbury in *Mame* in losing the chance to recreate on film one of her most famous roles.

MacLaine's image as an actress and her song-and-dance background made her not just the best but also the only choice for the role among current Hollywood stars. Not incidentally, she also had a history with both Fosse and Verdon. Back in 1954, MacLaine had been on the verge of handing in her notice to *The Pajama Game* in order to go into *Can-Can* as Verdon's understudy. Instead, she was pulled from the chorus to go on for an injured Carol Haney, was spotted by Alfred Hitchcock and producer Hal Wallis, and began a successful film career. MacLaine's most acclaimed roles were women who occupied the fringes of conventional morality, from good-hearted floozy (*Some Came Running*) to wistful single girl in love with a married man (*The Apartment*) to business-minded prostitute (*Irma la Douce*), all of whom shared traits with Charity Hope Valentine. MacLaine had danced only occasionally in her films, and the dance demands of the role required her to begin getting in shape months before shooting began.

Sweet Charity was assigned to Ross Hunter, Universal's top producer, who was finishing up production on the studio's big-budget original musical *Thoroughly Modern Millie*. He in turn hired the celebrated Oscar-winning screenwriter I. A. L. Diamond, whose collaborations with director Billy Wilder produced classics like *Some Like It Hot* and *The Apartment*. Diamond's "step outline" moved *Sweet Charity* closer to the grit and pathos of *Nights of Cabiria*.[91] Hunter was unhappy with Diamond's approach and quickly replaced him with Peter Stone. In addition to his work as a Broadway librettist, Stone specialized in screenplays for star-driven films like *Charade*, starring Cary Grant and Audrey Hepburn. His screenplay split the difference between the Fellini original and the Broadway musical comedy. This new "Cabiria-Charity" invited the camera in close to reveal "a character of more substance, more vulnerability," he insisted.[92]

Ross Hunter had made his reputation with sleek, glamorous romantic comedies and melodramas like *Pillow Talk* and *Imitation of Life*. Hunter intended to put his glossy touch to Charity, further scrubbing her up for the movies and earning a G rating. Fosse later described one of the conflicts among the filmmakers: "There was quite a fight about whether Charity could say 'Up Yours.' I felt if she couldn't then we might as well make *Mary Poppins* all the way. I got upset about the innuendos, not about Charity's straight talk."[93] Eventually Hunter withdrew, citing "serious and irreconcilable differences in the artistic approach to the filming of 'Sweet Charity' between the director and me."[94] Universal replaced Hunter with Robert Arthur, a long-time producer for the studio.

Sweet Charity's casting created tension between the studio's desire to hire high-profile movie names for even small roles and Fosse's preference for stage performers. Casting notes offer a fascinating glimpse of Hollywood star casting choices circa 1968. For the role of Oscar, Alan Alda was an early favorite, along with Robert Redford, Tony Franciosa, Anthony Perkins, and Alan Arkin. Among those rejected were Robert Duvall ("too sinister"), Eli Wallach ("too old"), Dean Jones ("too young"), and Richard Chamberlain ("Can he be funny?").[95] Fosse's choice was John McMartin, the original Oscar from Broadway; after a screen test with MacLaine, she too was enthusiastic about him, though to secure the role, McMartin was obliged to sign a contract binding him to Universal.[96]

The roles of Nickie and Helene attracted several recognizable and unusual names. Mitzi Gaynor was sought for Nickie, along with Juliet Prowse, then onstage in the lead role in London. Ironically, both Chita Rivera and Rita Moreno, who had played Rivera's original role of Anita in the film version of *West Side Story*, were also considered. For Helene, Thelma Oliver, from the Broadway company, and Paula Kelly, who was currently playing the role in London, were top contenders, as were singer Nancy Wilson and Nichelle Nichols from television's *Star Trek*. Ultimately, Fosse chose Chita Rivera and Paula Kelly. By prevailing with McMartin, Rivera, and Kelly, all of whom were making their screen debuts, Fosse flexed his "Muscle" in hiring the stage veterans of his choice.

Fosse approached his debut as a film director with diligence, screening a variety of films—not all of them musicals—to learn camera technique. Films directed by his old friend Stanley Donen, such as *Charade*, *Arabesque*, and the recent *Two for the Road*, were particularly instructive. Fosse observed Donen's practice of using sunglasses, mirrors, and car windows for reflection shots. He adopted Donen's practice of switching between blurred backgrounds and clear foregrounds for visual punctuation. For *Sweet Charity*, Fosse would create photomontages, sometimes panning and zooming across the images, a device later popularized by documentary filmmaker Ken Burns.

The work of directors Robert Wise and Jerome Robbins on the film version of *West Side Story* fascinated Fosse, especially their use of color and light to take the story out of its stage origins and into the realm of cinema. He marveled at the photographic effects they achieved: "Beginning of dance in gym— go to Red . . . how?"[97] "Everything blurred and fuzzy, except one person or object . . . how?" Elsewhere, he found shots that would serve as templates for *Sweet Charity*: "Long shot after Oscar leaves Charity. Example: after rumble," and "Extremely high shot end of 'Where Am I Going?'—She should be alone." This appears to be a reference to *West Side Story*'s final crane shot of Maria alone with the body of Tony after he is killed. Fosse was concerned about the often-jarring transition from dialogue to song in musicals and observed Robbins's methods. "Sing a bit of song acapella, then stop vocal, bring in underscore." (In contrast, after screening Mervyn LeRoy's film version of *Gypsy*, Fosse warned himself, "Watch out for choreographed gestures in book song. Make them appear as unstagey as possible.") Finally, Fosse screened his source, *Nights of Cabiria*, and noted, "Last shot smiling and crying in tight." He would use a similar shot of MacLaine as the film's final image.

With the largest budget Universal had devoted to a film since *Spartacus* in 1960, *Sweet Charity* began filming on January 29, 1968, the two-year anniversary of the show's Broadway premiere. Counting dancers, bit players, and extras, *Sweet Charity*'s cast numbered nearly five hundred. This New York–based story would be filmed mostly at Universal studios in Burbank, California, complete with a backlot recreation of Central Park. For his first film, Fosse had everything he wanted: a substantial budget, the confidence of a major studio, a cast of his choosing (including the dancers, nearly all of whom were from the show's Broadway and road companies), and a new, more supportive producer.

Robert Surtees, the director of photography, had photographed everything from the 1959 remake of *Ben-Hur* to contemporary films like *The Graduate*. Fosse was an apt pupil, quizzing the veteran cinematographer constantly and challenging him "[to let me] stick my curious eye into the viewfinder of his Panavision cameras."[98] (Fosse quickly gained his own viewfinder that he wore around his neck at all times.) Gwen Verdon passed up the opportunity to make her dramatic debut in Tennessee Williams's new play, *The Seven Descents of Myrtle*, in order to be at her husband's side on the film, serving as dance captain, costume consultant, and general sounding board. In perhaps the ultimate act of selflessness, she even coached Shirley MacLaine on the intricacies of Fosse's choreography.

Fosse was as obsessed with minute detail in this new medium as he had been in the theater, and he drove his film cast and crew relentlessly. ("He can go from sweet to Hitler in five seconds," Cy Coleman once joked.)[99] Supported by Verdon and several assistants who already knew the dances thoroughly, Fosse was free to concentrate with Surtees on reconceiving the numbers for screen, sometimes using five or more cameras to capture every angle, and always trying something different.

Fosse made "Big Spender" a self-contained set piece that powerfully establishes the dance hall milieu. As the music vamps, a lone customer examines the Fan-Dango's mirrored billboard, lighting a cigar to the beat of Cy Coleman's now-familiar vamp and ascending the stairs to the ticket booth. After buying his dance tickets from a blowsy cashier who could be a former hostess herself, he opens the ballroom door to find the hostesses frozen in place, draped across a railing. The camera zooms past the women to land on the customer's face as he looks them over like so much merchandise. A series of quick shots shows the women coming to attention at the presence of a new customer, looking up from their newspapers and, in a particularly knowing gesture, placing their cigarettes on the rim of an ashtray, the better to be retrieved in the event they are not chosen. The women's well-practiced "come-on" lines are shot in a slow pan as the customer walks along the lineup. Finally, Rivera and Kelly turn and join the others (with Rivera clutching the railing like a spider setting her web), as the camera pulls back to reveal all ten women in place.

From Stage to Screen: A Director's Dilemma, a promotional short about Fosse and the making of the film, shows him blocking camera movements for "Big Spender" with an ensemble of twelve women. Unable to bring the camera in close enough to capture expressions on all the women's faces, he reduced the lineup to ten. His close-ups of the women in their garish make-up brought the number closer to the spirit of Fellini.[100] As the women begin singing, the camera pulls back to reveal the customer's table in the foreground. An ashtray holds his cigar, and a glass of beer is poured and paid for, marking the hostesses as third in line for his attention.

The Appaloosa, a forgotten film starring Marlon Brando and directed by Sidney J. Furie, was an unexpected source of ideas for "Big Spender," including the use of slow overlap dissolves, "so that the overlapping pictures make a point or visual effect."[101] When the women form the amoeba and travel along the railing, Fosse adds movement by employing dissolves to double and triple the image. "Don't be afraid of feet shots if they have some meaning. 'Big Spender'—legs?" he challenged himself, and indeed the "fun, laughs, good time" section is sharply edited to emphasize the interplay between each phrase, with close-ups of the women's feet pounding the floor. Extra energy is pumped into the final, frenzied dance section through fast cutting, with the camera often placed in the middle of the dancers, then quickly pulling back to return to the lineup in full frame. Fosse shoots the dancers from above and below, isolating torsos and arms, or places the camera behind them, offering their perspective of the customer. He boldly employs theatrical lighting to highlight Rivera and Kelly as the number concludes. Fosse holds the image only a moment, then uses the customer's back as he stands to form a "wipe" that brings the film back to the reality of dialogue.

Dance in films generally followed the example established by Fred Astaire, who demanded that his directors "film the dancers full-frame, without close-up; keep reaction shots to a minimum; run the dance in as few takes as possible, preferably just one."[102] In the 1952 *Moulin Rouge*, set in the world of nineteenth-century artist Toulouse-Lautrec, director John Houston brought the camera in close enough to the Montmartre cabaret dancers to isolate legs, arms, and derrieres, showing perspiration and make-up traces to capture the effort and immediacy of the performances. "It was a new way of shooting dancing," Fosse later marveled. "The Astaire-Kelly movies were always full figure. 'Moulin Rouge' was the first time I saw the shot of a leg or the quick flash of a face in a pirouette. It was very exciting. It's the film I've imitated most of all."[103]

Another who may have influenced Fosse was his former wife, Joan McCracken, who in 1946 penned her thoughts about the motion picture camera's potential to capture dance for *Dance Magazine*. "Why not photograph what can't happen on stage?" she asked. "If there were people to take full advantage of the opportunities the camera offers and the stage does not, the back would not only be photographed, but the front, side, top, and bottom all at once. Think of how nice that would be in the case of a pirouette . . . . How interesting to see the different mood and rhythm of one dancer expressing the conflict of two driving energies, and dancing them both at the same time. Dancing is movement and the movies could make it move even more if the stage were forgotten."[104]

McCracken's observations sounded lofty in the 1940s, but more than twenty years later, a new generation of directors like Mike Nichols with *The Graduate* and Richard Lester with his Beatles films, *A Hard Day's Night* and *Help!*, were disrupting the traditional grammar of filmmaking with quick cuts, freeze frames, long tracking shots, and the use of handheld cameras. French New Wave directors like Jean-Luc Godard and François Truffaut, in turn, had influenced them. Godard's startling jump cuts in *Breathless* and Truffaut's freeze-frame ending for *The Wild Child* were radical approaches to editing and visual storytelling. Fosse, determined that his debut film would not be in the older mode of musicals, eagerly employed many of these new techniques in *Sweet Charity*.

When Shirley MacLaine later said that Fosse "took the camera apart and put it back together," she could have been referring to "If My Friends Could See Me Now."[105] Onstage, it was a song and dance showcase for its star. For the film, Fosse made it a showcase for his cinematic bag of tricks. He begins by cutting from a long shot of Charity sitting on the coffee table in Vittorio's lavish apartment to a medium shot and then a close-up, all cued to the song's first three words: "If . . . they . . . could . . . ." Fosse time shifts between lines in the song, with Charity seen briefly in short takes throughout the apartment, eating lobster and drinking champagne, lounging on the luxurious bed, and looking out one, then another, window, all in the same frame, courtesy of a jump cut. Following Vittorio's delivery of his collapsible top hat, Fosse creates a quick-cut montage of Charity experimenting with various methods for popping open the hat, all leading into the dance break. As Charity romps across the room, Fosse reverses the film, allowing her to repeat her walk over a chair and to magically jump backward from the floor to a platform. These gestures carry a hint of desperation and are oddly out of character for a choreographer who always pushed his dancers to dance with honesty at their peak physicality.

The excessive camera activity is tamped down for the number's final hat-and-cane sequence. Charity focuses the apartment's lights to create a spotlight and then steps into it with great pride. As Coleman's slow cakewalk begins, the camera focuses on the shadow of Charity's extended teacup fingers holding her hat. It pulls back to reveal her not in Vittorio's apartment but inside a giant spotlight on a darkened soundstage, its only decor the apartment's elaborate crystal chandelier. As she hits the final pose, down on one knee with arms outstretched, she is returned to the apartment, her reverie complete. Fosse's direction seamlessly whisks Charity from the realism of the star's bedroom to a stylized performance space where she is free of the Fan-Dango Ballroom and dishonest boyfriends and worry about her future. Her return to the apartment is bittersweet, even with a movie star waiting for her.

Sweet Charity's roots in Fellini are on display in "Rich Man's Frug." The vast emptiness of the Pompeii Club and its dead-eyed inhabitants recall his alienated *La Dolce Vita* jet-setters.

The sequence begins with the screen dominated by the heads of two models in profile. Their parting gives the impression of a stage curtain opening on the action. Fosse uses on-screen titles to introduce each dance section but does not shy away from theatrical flourishes. The dancers are frequently posed in tableau, as if waiting to make their entrances. He is unafraid to pull back and show a full-stage picture. Much of the dancing is framed by foreground movement. Nightclub patrons drape the front of the stage. Waiters and other dancers make their way in front of the crowd at center stage. Large Roman-themed statues and fire displays are used to fill the outside edges of the widescreen image.

Fosse's camera is at its zoom-happiest in this number, crashing into the dancers' faces, then flying back out. Fight punches are aimed directly at the camera. Verdon recalled that Fosse, wanting to be "in the middle" of the dance during its climax, sat in a shopping cart holding a camera as she pushed him among the dancers.[106] His immersive camerawork was augmented with strobe lights, film negative exposures, and tinted color saturations. The number ends, appropriately, with a zoom out to a full-stage picture.

The frustrations of the dance hall hostesses at their dead-end existence are given voice by Charity, Nickie, and Helene in "There's Gotta Be Something Better Than This." Onstage, the number starts in their dressing room, but the scenery is soon removed to give the women a full stage on which to perform some of Fosse's most athletic and rangy choreography, as this becomes another number set in limbo. For the film, Fosse deftly moves the song from the dressing room to the ballroom, where the hostesses and their customers stand frozen in place, as if on a stage set, allowing the three women to comment on them unseen.

From the ballroom the women drift up to the building's roof, where they confide their lofty career goals (receptionist, hatcheck girl). As each woman describes her dream job, Fosse whips his camera around to place her in another part of the set, visual shorthand that breaks up what could have been static speeches. When it is Charity's turn to describe her plans, Fosse's camera whips the trio back downstairs to the ballroom behind the "Big Spender" lineup. On the downbeat signaling the number's dance section, and in a single, breathtaking cut, Fosse instantly returns them to the roof. Much of the dance section is shot in the Fred Astaire mode, with all three dancers in full frame, showing off the razor-shape precision of Fosse's choreography. (Flanked by the expert Rivera and Kelly, MacLaine works harder here than in any other dance sequence and acquits herself admirably.) Long tracking shots follow the women across the expanse of the roof, and the camera highlights the number's triangular formation. Fosse raises his camera high above the trio to capture a moment of joyous sisterhood as they sing the song's final note, then pulls back as they jeté forward and strike a triumphant pose in the sculpted moonlight.

Because of its Latin-flavored rhythms and the obvious soundstage rooftop setting, "There's Gotta Be Something Better Than This" has been unfairly compared to *West Side Story*'s "America." In a film brimming with striking dance numbers, it is a clear highlight, its inventive camerawork imbuing it with unexpected emotional heft.

There was indecisiveness from both Fosse and the studio over the film's conclusion. A happy ending with Charity and Oscar splashing in the lake was shot, as was a new, bittersweet scene in which Charity, after Oscar's rejection, encounters a group of flower children in Central Park who spark in her a renewed faith in love. She heads out of the park and disappears down a busy street, like Charlie Chaplin in *City Lights*, crushed but not defeated, and ending the film on a poignant but hopeful note. Ultimately it was this conclusion that was chosen for the film's final cut.[107]

The production moved to New York City for a month of location shooting, during which Fosse filmed *Sweet Charity*'s most ambitious number. Onstage, "I'm a Brass Band" was an Agnes de Mille–like dream ballet that gave danced expression to Charity's joyful emotions. It remained so for the film, even as Fosse opened the number up to iconic locales across New York City, making it a private playground for Charity and her brass band of male dancers.

As Charity exclaims "Someone loves me!" Fosse spins the camera from Times Square to Shea Stadium, where unseen crowds cheer as she takes a bow. For the song's first verse, Fosse places MacLaine in an open-topped car as it rides across the Manhattan Bridge and films her from below, giving the effect of Charity floating in the clouds. The locale changes to the fountain at Lincoln Center as Charity performs the number's lyrical dance prelude. A crashing cymbal sends the camera spinning to a new location, this time the East Thirty-Fourth Street Heliport. Smooth tracking shots follow Charity and the men across the open-air space. When a new group of dancers joins Charity, the location abruptly switches again, with the men appearing to jump all the way down to Wall Street. ("Tie steps or movements not necessarily locales," Fosse reminded himself regarding *West Side Story*'s cutting from one locale to another, sometimes in the middle of a dance step.)[108]

Onstage, the brief Dixieland jam session sent the dancers exiting into the wings before immediately returning in regimented formation, all in an approximation of a cinematic cross-fade. On film, as Charity and the dancers loosely improvise, Fosse literally fades to a new shot of their military-style arrangement on a different street. During the number's drum break Fosse's camera remains stationary to let the rhythm sink in, even to the point of pushing MacLaine to the screen's margins.

After the number's whirlwind of activity, Fosse keeps his camera still for the last shot as Charity receives a final salute from her band and marches off. As the drums fade, she disappears into the empty canyons of Wall Street, a tiny dot on the Panavision screen as she happily heads toward her future with Oscar. The moment touchingly captures Charity as a small speck of humanity in a large and impersonal city. "I'm a Brass Band" was the final number Fosse shot for *Sweet Charity*, and its conception and execution give it an emotional charge that makes Oscar's rejection a few minutes later all the more powerful.

Fosse was in his creative element during filming, soaking up knowledge from Surtees and the film technicians just as he had from George Abbott and Jerome Robbins on his first Broadway show. The limitless possibilities of the camera fascinated the detail-obsessed Fosse, and the six months spent filming *Sweet Charity* had been among the most invigorating of his life. On his very first film he had been given nearly unprecedented control of a property he knew better than anyone. Whatever the critical and commercial response, *Sweet Charity* would be exactly the film he wanted to make.

> "Look, how can you make an honest film, a good film, about a hooker when you have to get a G rating?"
>
> Bob Fosse, 1974[109]

Fosse interrupted his editing of *Sweet Charity* in October to stage a pair of dances for Gwen Verdon for her appearance on a Bob Hope television special. If the movies were not interested in her, Fosse made sure these two complementary numbers presented Verdon as the star dancer she remained. Working in tight trio formation with Lee Roy Reams and Buddy Vest, both fresh from filming *Sweet Charity*, Verdon demonstrated that she remained the greatest interpreter of Fosse's work.

Lalo Schifrin's elegiac theme from the recent film *Cool Hand Luke* is the setting for the first dance, built around gentle flamenco variations. Proud and pulled up, the three dancers snap their fingers and clap their hands in intricate opposition to the soft guitar and woodwind accompaniment. Fosse revisits the elegant pony steps from *New Girl in Town*, sending the dancers on a gentle saunter, then drawing them up into a proud stallion-like pose before dropping them softly to their knees. Somber and elegant, with sharp movements segueing effortlessly into more lyrical steps, the dance takes on a hypnotic intensity. "Cool Hand Luke" is performed in moody shadows with faces barely visible. Yet when the dancers lower their heads and swivel softly across the floor, her expressive hips mark Verdon as the number's focal point.

The bouncy, mariachi-flavored sound of Herb Alpert and the Tijuana Brass became nationally popular in the mid-1960s and was exemplified by their recording of Sol Lake's "Mexican Shuffle." It was a sound Fosse would favor for the musical scoring of *Sweet Charity*, and he previewed it in Verdon's second dance. Where "Cool Hand Luke" is sober and introspective, "Mexican Shuffle" is joking and impudent. Verdon and company drop their cigarillos on the ground, and the act of stubbing them out leads into a lackadaisical twist before snapping back into a more rigid stance. They chug across the soundstage, languidly rotating just one shoulder, then looking back and teasing the viewer as they shake their hips to the beat. Walking away from the camera, they give a quick finger twirl in the air, almost as an afterthought. They rouse themselves to a series of Fosse's favorite kicks, in which the dancer swings the leg, slightly bent and at waist height across herself, with the force of the swing turning her around rapidly. They drop to the ground and scoot back in a pushup position, shaking their hips and beating the floor, as if protesting their lack of gravity. At last weary of their tease, they slowly return to their opening position, with Verdon standing above the two men as they resume their siesta.

"Cool Hand Luke" and "Mexican Shuffle" point to a new look and tone in Fosse's choreography and give a preview of his work in the coming decade. Both are marked by their minimalism, with movement tightly contained and drawing its power from the dancers' uniformity and control. The tiniest of gestures registers sharply, as when a small pelvic flex by Reams and Vest is echoed one beat later by Verdon. The hip and pelvis isolations later associated with Fosse are now set. The all-black costumes that would become identified with Fosse are also in place. Overt humor is downplayed and character is de-emphasized, as the dancers assume blank-faced expressions throughout, though Verdon's natural ebullience comes through.[110]

As *Sweet Charity* was assembled in the cutting room and postproduction labs, it was evident to everyone that Fosse had not only created a striking film musical but also proved himself a director of real warmth and sensitivity in his work with actors. MacLaine's dancing may be a studious approximation of Verdon's original stylings, but she creates a new Charity, alternately tough and crushingly vulnerable, streetwise yet gullible.

When *Sweet Charity* was sneak-previewed in December, the overwhelming majority of audience preview cards rated it "Excellent" or "Very Good."[111] "It's the 1969 *West Side Story*—but better, I loved every minute of it," raved one audience member. Another predicted it would be the "biggest hit since 'Sound of Music.'" But there were complaints about both the film's length ("Second half was too long and tedious. Cut out band sequence!") and its bittersweet ending.

Most of the criticisms were aimed at what one exasperated audience member called the film's "psychedelic photography." The opening credits set the frenzied pace as Charity romps through midtown Manhattan with the camera zooming and freezing at regular intervals, and the screen tinting red and lavender. In the very first number, "My Personal Property," a new song written by Coleman and Fields for the film, Charity and her fiancé Charlie spend the afternoon together. As they visit a series of locations in Central Park, the camera zooms in, quickly dissolves, and then cuts to another shot before zooming out to bring the picture back into focus. A variety of park views are captured in quick sequence, including a spectacular panorama of New York City's skyline, but as one audience member succinctly put it, "The focusing in and out on the scenes was hard on the eyes."

Fosse was the first director to also be solely responsible for the choreography of a musical film since Busby Berkeley in the 1930s, and he lobbied the Directors Guild to have both duties listed together in his screen credit. While the guild acknowledged multiple duties such as "Written and Directed by" or "Produced and Directed by" on a single card, they turned down Fosse's request, perhaps considering choreography a lesser artistic expression and not worthy of listing with the director's credit. After a second request, approval was granted, and when "Directed and Choreographed by Bob Fosse" flashed on the screen, it was the first time the dual credit had ever been acknowledged on one card.[112] (Fosse downplayed his choreographic contributions to *Cabaret* and *All That Jazz*, with that credit on a separate card and not highlighted in advertisements.)

Sweet Charity underwent few adjustments before a splashy advance screening for industry trade papers that outdid themselves in acclaiming the film. The *Hollywood Reporter*'s headline gushed, "Universal's 'Sweet Charity' Smash: One [of the] All-Time Boxoffice Champions."[113] *Variety* predicted that *Sweet Charity* would "become one of the memorable artistic and commercial successes of this generation."[114] *Sweet Charity* was a state-of-the-art roadshow attraction in its world premiere in Boston on February 11, 1969. Presented in Technicolor and 70mm Panavision ("With Full Dimensional Sound"), its 157-minute running time accommodated an overture, intermission, entr'acte, and exit music.[115]

Universal rolled out an unprecedented promotional campaign for the film, fully expecting it to surpass the studio's current top grosser, *Thoroughly Modern Millie*. But after its ecstatic response from the Hollywood trade papers, *Sweet Charity* faced harsh criticism from the East Coast critics, much of it centered on Fosse's hyperactive camera. Perhaps the most damning review, not least because it was so high-profile, was that of Vincent Canby in the *New York Times*, who dismissed it as "a long, noisy and, finally, dim imitation of its source material," adding, "Fosse struggles unsuccessfully to find the cinematic equivalent to the show's spare, almost cartoonlike style . . . . the movie alternates between the painfully literal and the self-consciously cinematic."[116]

But other reviewers had quite the opposite reaction. Maria Harriton in *Dance Magazine* enthused, "Not since *West Side Story* has dance been given the opportunity of contributing so much ambience to a film, and *Sweet Charity* proves even more than its predecessor that the choreographed camera and the kinetic impulse generate a vibrant and viable cinema style."[117]

Sweet Charity's appearance followed soon after *Finian's Rainbow*, *Funny Girl*, *Star!*, *Oliver!*, and *Chitty Chitty Bang Bang*, resulting in a glut of big-budget musicals, and it fell victim to both viewer fatigue and changing tastes. When it opened on Broadway at the top of 1966, *Sweet Charity* was bracingly current. By the time the film opened three years later in a cinema landscape dominated by frank, adult fare like *Midnight Cowboy*, *Easy Rider*, and *Alice's Restaurant*, *Sweet Charity*'s contemporary flourishes could not keep it from appearing out of touch. Its flower power hippies and dance hall "hostess" who must hide her occupation in order to attract a respectable marriage prospect (a contrivance easier to accept onstage) were corny, G-rated anachronisms. (Tellingly, the flower children in the final scene were introduced in the script with a strict note: "It is important that these are clean-cut, scrubbed, attractive 'Flower Children'—not the unkempt, unwashed 'Hippie' image.")[118]

The film was trimmed and its intermission eliminated when it went into general release in October, much earlier than planned. Universal tried a new approach to its advertising campaign, pushing the "prostie angle," as *Variety* put it.[119] Ads now proclaimed, "Men called her 'Sweet Charity,'" and the dance hall lineup was heralded with "meet the pros" and "swingers all . . . men were their business." "They dig the way they live," the viewer was reminded in an awkward attempt to make the film sound hip.[120] Nothing worked, however, and *Sweet Charity* was out of theaters by the end of the year, having earned only about $4 million in the United States and Canada.[121]

The film received three Academy Award nominations, for Best Costume Design, Best Art Direction–Set Decoration, and Best Music, Score of a Musical Picture (Original or Adaptation). In the latter two categories, *Sweet Charity* lost to *Hello, Dolly!* The contrast between the films is noteworthy. *Hello, Dolly!*, directed by Gene Kelly and choreographed by Michael Kidd, is confident, conventional Hollywood musical filmmaking. Its dances are photographed full on in bright, spacious settings that fill every inch of its Todd-AO widescreen. It ignores the photographic innovations made by a new generation of directors, and indeed, Kelly and Kidd could have turned out the same film fifteen years earlier at MGM.

Sweet Charity, for all its excesses, reflects recent cinematic innovations. Fosse was at the vanguard in applying new techniques to the filming of dance and exploring the possibilities that the camera held for presenting dance on film. In his next film he would refine these techniques, harnessing them to powerful effect and expanding the potential of the film musical genre.

WILLKOMMEN

• • •

For a dancer, timing is everything, and Bob Fosse's timing in the 1970s was impeccable. It was the "Fosse Decade," during which his choreography and, indeed, his entire theatrical aesthetic, became set, formalized, and more easily recognizable, in part because of his wide-ranging successes. *Cabaret* and *All That Jazz* introduced him to movie audiences that had never seen his work onstage. *Liza with a Z* delivered the Fosse dance moves to a big television viewership. *Pippin* and *Dancin'*, his two longest-running stage musicals, enjoyed multiple productions around the world.

Cabaret placed Fosse at the epicenter of America's cultural changes. The political and social turmoil of pre-Nazi Germany and the shifting sexual and ethnic identities of its characters found parallels in America's anxieties over the ongoing Vietnam War, new sexual permissiveness, and identity politics. Historian Bruce J. Schulman declared that the rapidly developing Watergate scandal "added fuel to a widespread cynicism about politics, politicians, and government itself as an instrument of the collective good."[1] Fosse's work in the 1970s captured this turmoil and upheaval, with both *Pippin* and *Chicago* shot full of sarcasm and scorn toward government, war, and the justice system.

As historians Beth Bailey and David Farber point out, "It was during the 1970s, not the 1960s, that sex outside marriage became the norm and illegal drugs became commonplace in middle America."[2] Journalist David Frum provided a litany of the decade's debauches: the mainstream popularity of sexually explicit books like *The Happy Hooker; Penthouse*, with its explicit photographs and full-frontal nudity, outsold *Playboy*; live sex shows dotted Time Square; and pornographic films like *Deep Throat* and *The Devil in Miss Jones* reached into middle America.[3] This hedonism was reflected in all of Fosse's 1970s projects through his increasingly frank and erotically charged choreography and representations of drug use.

"If it's a flop, I'll want to put my head in the oven. If it's a success, I'll want to keep it there," Fosse confided to Shirley MacLaine just before *Sweet Charity*'s premiere, crystallizing the push-and-pull of his feelings about show business achievement.[4] Based on the film's box-office performance, Fosse was able to quickly remove his head from the oven, but no one was there to offer him another job. Fosse was stubborn, however, and rather than return to Broadway, where his stock remained high, he resolved that his next project would be another film.

Fosse had been without representation since 1962, when his long-time agency, MCA, acquired Universal Pictures and divested its talent agency to avoid anti-trust penalties. A legal skirmish over unpaid commissions left Fosse with a feeling toward agents similar to his distrust of producers. Since then, his attorney, Jack Perlman, had negotiated his contracts. But if he was serious about staying in the movie business, he needed movie representation, and the small but pugnacious Creative Management Associates (CMA) would provide the kind of push needed to help him get his first post–*Sweet Charity* film. "I know that all of us working together will produce the most exciting results for you," CMA head David Begelman reassuringly wrote Fosse at the time of his signing.[5]

In the meantime, Fosse retreated to New York, where, since the mid-1960s he had occupied an office at 850 Seventh Avenue, midway between the theater district and his Central Park West apartment. Paddy Chayefsky had an office there, and so did Herb Gardner, who joined the ranks of Fosse's writer friends. Like Chayefsky, Gardner was a New York City–born Jew with a fierce intellectualism. He had enjoyed a Broadway hit before he turned thirty with *A Thousand Clowns* in 1962. Together, Fosse, Chayefsky, and Gardner formed a show business triumvirate at 850 Seventh Avenue.

Fosse spent the latter part of 1969 working on two potential films: *The Eagle of Naptown*, with a screenplay by playwright Steve Tesich, who would become another of Fosse's writer friends, and *Burnt Offerings*, an upscale suspense-horror film in the vein of *Rosemary's Baby*. (A decade later, *The Eagle of Naptown*, retitled *Breaking Away* and directed by Peter Yates, would become an acclaimed box-office hit.)

His work on these film projects left little time for dance, and Fosse stayed true to his plan not to accept any Broadway offers before he had made a second film. However, this did not stop him from choreographing for his wife. During these months he staged dances for two Gwen Verdon appearances on Ed Sullivan's Sunday night variety hour, each giving an indication of his mood at the time. "Mexican Breakfast," performed on June 1, 1969, by Verdon, with dancers Marie Lake and Dee Erickson, is an upbeat continuation of the numbers he had created for her a year earlier for the Bob Hope special.

To a similarly jaunty Tijuana Brass–style arrangement, Verdon leads the trio in a synchronized compendium of echt Fosse moves. The hyperactive pelvis is in place, marking a permanent addition to the Fosse vocabulary. Verdon and the two women rhythmically pump their torsos while languidly undulating their arms. Elsewhere they lock themselves down, legs rigid, and continue to pump. Verdon later said, "With Bob, if there was a part of your body that could move independently of another part—whether it was a shoulder, a finger, a neck, your ear, anything—your pelvis—he would move that in time with the music because he would often say, 'I don't want to know that you're just dancing to the music because your feet go up and down in time. I want the beat to be visual.'"[6]

In "Mexican Breakfast" everything is isolated. The dancers raise their arms above their heads, turn their backs and freeze, with only a twitchy leg still in motion. Or they stand still, hips percolating, and look away from the audience, only to turn back slowly and acknowledge it with a mocking head nod. Dressed in sporty pantsuits, Verdon and company dance like the hippest suburban car pool moms. The dance has a happy, energetic feel that brings a cheerful close to Fosse's 1960s output and is a welcome change from his increasingly all-black numbers.[7]

On February 1, 1970, Fosse and Verdon were back, with Verdon leading an ensemble of six male dancers in "A Fine, Fine Day." A song and dance number rather than a recorded instrumental like "Mexican Breakfast," it proved to be a by-the-numbers exercise for Fosse, filled with steps and signifiers from other, more inspired dances. The derbies and hip isolations are present, as is the whispered stop-time section. Its marching band strut recalls "I'm a Brass Band." The loose, frug-like steps come directly from Charity's "junkin' around" dance vocabulary. Fosse reaches back to "Mu-Cha-Cha" and "A Secretary Is Not a Toy" for a tight, traveling lineup of Verdon and the dancers on their toes and in plié.[8] "A Fine, Fine Day" is Fosse at his most distracted, but by this time he had other, bigger things on his mind. A few days after the Sullivan show, a brief trade paper blurb announced Fosse as the director of the planned film version of the Broadway musical, *Cabaret*.[9]

> "I wanted to prove that given the right material—I thought it was the mate-rial that I was taking the blame for—that I could make a successful movie musical."
>
> Bob Fosse, 1980[10]

Cabaret was the latest adaptation of characters and events from Christopher Isherwood's *Berlin Stories* (1945), based on Isherwood's experiences living in a boarding house in early 1930s Berlin. His characters cope with life in Germany's capital as the freewheeling Weimar Republic gives way to the rise of Hitler and the National Socialist movement. One of the boarding house residents is Sally Bowles, a determinedly daring English girl who remains oblivious to the political turmoil as she sings in a local club at night and pursues her ambition to become an actress by day. In adapting some of Isherwood's stories to the stage as *I Am a Camera* in 1951, John Van Druten downplayed the shadow of Nazism, making the play a genteel comedy dominated by the eccentric Sally, played by Julie Harris on Broadway and in a later film adaptation.

Producer-director Harold Prince was not interested in a musical adaptation of *I Am a Camera* built around Sally Bowles (as the proposed musical for Gwen Verdon would undoubtedly have been). Prince had produced two Jerome Robbins shows, *West Side Story* and the recent *Fiddler on the Roof*, and those experiences influenced Prince as he moved into directing. Robbins was unafraid to take on serious subject matter in a musical, and his staging concepts allowed his shows to resonate beyond their settings. This was a director's musical theater very differ-ent from the George Abbott stand-and-deliver style.

With *Cabaret*, Prince had something much larger in mind, and his colleagues, librettist Joe Masteroff, the composer-lyricist team of John Kander and Fred Ebb, and scenic designer Boris Aronson, enthusiastically followed his lead. "What attracted the authors and me was the parallel between the spiritual bankruptcy of Germany in the 1920s and our country in the 1960s," Prince said, citing the murders of Malcolm X and Medgar Evers and the venomous resistance of white southerners to integration and the passage of voting rights for blacks.[11] (To highlight that parallel, Aronson would devise a large mirror facing the audience, forcing them to view their own complicity in the story.)

Prince and company altered Isherwood's stories in several ways. Isherwood had not addressed his own homosexuality in his earlier stories, and the character was neutered in *I Am a Camera*. Fearing that Broadway audiences would not accept the character if he were gay or bisexual, in *Cabaret* he became a love interest for Sally and was renamed Clifford Bradshaw. Fraulein Schneider, Isherwood's anti-Semitic landlady in the stories, is here relieved of her prejudice and given a middle-aged romance, with Herr Schultz, a Jewish shopkeeper. With four leading roles of equal size, *Cabaret* became an ensemble show no longer centered on Sally Bowles.

A series of cabaret numbers were scattered throughout the evening and led by the Emcee, the epicene host at the Kit Kat Klub where Sally now performs. This new character, suggested by an outrageously rouged and lipsticked dwarf master of ceremonies that Prince had seen at a tiny nightclub in Germany during his army service, took *Cabaret* in an ambitious new direction. The jolly cabaret turns, staged by Ron Field, become more disturbing as the evening continues, commenting on the plot as they reflect the country's growing violence, venality, and prejudice, with the Emcee coming to embody Germany and its descent into Nazism.

The Emcee's last number directly follows a scene in which Fraulein Schneider breaks off her engagement to the kindly Schultz because she fears the consequences of marrying a Jew. In the gentle soft-shoe "If You Could See Her through My Eyes," the Emcee sings of his devotion to his beloved, a dainty, girlish gorilla. The song turns maudlin and sentimental as he begs for understanding of their love. But at the last minute, he turns it into propaganda by leering at the audience and hissing, "If you could see her through my eyes / She wouldn't look Jewish at all."[12] The line was misinterpreted by many at the time as inferring that all Jews look like gorillas, when the authors' intention was to highlight how thoroughly entrenched overt anti-Semitism had become in Germany. (Under pressure, the line was changed to "She isn't a meeskite at all," "meeskite" being Yiddish for ugly. In later productions, as well as the film version, the original line was restored.)[13]

Cabaret was a benchmark in the development of what was soon to be called the "concept musical," in which metaphor trumps narrative as a storytelling device. Rodgers and Hammerstein's *Allegro* in 1947 and the following year's *Love Life*, with a score by Alan Jay Lerner and Kurt Weill, are often cited as early examples of the form. *Allegro*'s story of a young doctor's life was staged as a metaphor for contemporary American society. *Love Life* used vaudeville, circus, minstrelsy, and other entertainment forms to depict American marriage over 150 years, enacted by a central couple that remains the same age throughout the show. Musical theater historian Larry Stempel identified *West Side Story* and *Cabaret* as later examples in the continuing development of the concept musical: "Here artistic priority belongs less to the writers than to Jerome Robbins and Harold Prince . . . . Their point of departure was not an existing script to be realized onstage so much as a vision or stage idea that in turn helped shape the script's development."[14]

It was *Cabaret*'s direction and design that gave it power. Prince worked with lighting designer Jean Rosenthal to create a curtain of light to separate what he called "realistic numbers performed in the cabaret for an audience onstage and metaphorical numbers illustrating changes in the German mind."[15] This area they deemed "limbo," creating a new metaphoric use for the old downstage "in one" strip in front of the curtain—only now the curtain is made of light. The show's climax comes late in the second act when Sally sings the title song and, midway, leaves the Kit Kat Klub and steps through the light curtain, rejecting the real world and giving herself over to a world of chaos. Despite Prince's theatrical reach, *Cabaret* turned out to be two shows that never entirely united. One was a conventional musical, and the other a further development of the concept musical: abrasive, confrontational, set in the past but evoking the present.

The arrival of *Sweet Charity* at the beginning, and *Cabaret* at the end, of 1966 accelerated the evolution of the concept musical. *Sweet Charity* had a conventional, linear structure, but as conceived by Fosse it used dance to define character and drive the story. A concept musical only in the loosest sense, it looked ahead to the more theatrically stylized, metaphoric musicals that Fosse would soon stage. *Cabaret* reflected the lessons learned from Jerome Robbins and pointed to the more fully realized concept musicals Prince would undertake in a few years with Stephen Sondheim.

Cabaret was a breakthrough for the team of Kander and Ebb, who essentially wrote two scores, one filled with traditional ballads and character songs, the other composed of nightclub numbers that carried the astringency of Kurt Weill. Kander and Ebb were the latest young writers to work with George Abbott when they were hired to write the score for *Flora, the Red Menace* in 1965. The show had only a brief run, but it introduced them to nineteen-year-old Liza Minnelli, the daughter of Judy Garland and film director Vincente Minnelli. Minnelli forged a lasting professional relationship with the team that would shape her career.

Kander and Ebb lobbied hard for Liza Minnelli to be cast in *Cabaret*, but Prince was adamant that Minnelli both sang too well for the minimally talented Sally Bowles and could not believably play a British girl. He opted for Jill Haworth, a young English actress making her stage debut. But the breakout star of *Cabaret* turned out to be Joel Grey. The son of comedian Mickey Katz, Grey grew up in show business and, like Fosse, had been performing since he was a boy. Grey's Emcee, who started the show as a merry, glad-handing host but grew more sinister as the evening continued, was a wholly original and troubling creation that became the face of *Cabaret*.

Cabaret was the hit of the 1966–1967 Broadway season, winning both the Tony Award and New York Drama Critics' Circle Award for Best Musical. It would run 1,165 performances and spawn a London company and two national tours. Its film rights were eventually acquired in a co-production arrangement with Allied Artists and ABC Pictures.[16] Cy Feuer was hired as the film's producer, with a budget set at just under $5 million.[17]

Prince turned down an offer to direct the film because he was already involved in producing and directing the new Stephen Sondheim musical, *Company*. At a dinner party, when Prince mentioned that the film still was without a director, Fosse pounced. "Bobby cornered me in the room and asked me how I did *Cabaret*. Every moment of it. And I explained it all to him," Prince said.[18] Fosse wasted no time in contacting Cy Feuer, one of the few producers he trusted. They had remained friendly since *How to Succeed in Business without Really Trying* and *Little Me* and during the tumult of *On a Clear Day You Can See Forever*. Fosse had, in fact, stepped in as uncredited general supervisor on *Walking Happy*, produced by Feuer and Martin, directed by Feuer, and choreographed by Danny Daniels in late 1966.

Feuer was enthused by the idea of Fosse directing *Cabaret*, but both ABC Pictures and Allied Artists wanted a marquee director, not one whose last film was a failure. Feuer was obligated to see others but assured Fosse that he was his only choice. Fortunately, all the illustrious directors Feuer approached turned down the project, including Billy Wilder, Joseph L. Mankiewicz, and Gene Kelly.

For Feuer, there were several attractive aspects to Fosse's directing the film. One, having worked with him on several projects, Feuer knew that Fosse's extensive preparations and strong work ethic would help *Cabaret* stick to its tight budget and shooting schedule. Two, after the failure of *Sweet Charity*, Feuer reasoned that Fosse would be anxious to prove himself and, thus, easy to control. Finally, Feuer was determined to eliminate all songs outside the Kit Kat Klub.[19] He had absolute confidence in Fosse's ability to stage the remaining cabaret turns, later recalling: "As I saw it, if one or two of the numbers didn't work, we had a flop. On the other hand, if all eight worked and the picture was a little short on dramatic direction, we could still have a hit. My bet was on the numbers. I had to protect the musical numbers. And there is nobody better on musical numbers than Bob Fosse."[20]

Before Fosse was signed, Feuer made several important decisions that would later be attributed to Fosse. Feuer's idea to limit the musical numbers to just those taking place on the nightclub stage would make *Cabaret* less a movie musical and more a dramatic film with musical sequences. Feuer hated the secondary romance between Fraulein Schneider and Herr Shultz and wanted it replaced with a subplot involving younger characters. He also rejected the musical's central heterosexual romance and wanted the Isherwood character edged closer to the author's own sexuality.

Screenwriter Jay Presson Allen was hired by Feuer with the proviso that she return to Isherwood's stories for the plot's source material.[21] "The Landauers" supplied a new subplot focused on Fritz Wendel, a fortune hunter who pursues Natalia Landauer, the daughter of a wealthy Jewish family. Fritz eventually reveals that he himself is Jewish, and the couple is married. The musical's American Clifford Bradshaw became British Brian Roberts and was made bisexual (a "switch-hitter," as Feuer called him).[22] He and Sally would have a romance, but each would also become involved sexually with Max, a handsome and wealthy German baron based on the character of a rich American who first appeared in "Sally Bowles."[23] Working closely with Feuer, Allen constructed a screenplay out of these disparate stories, finding new spots to fit the cabaret numbers. The elimination of the book songs meant that only Sally among these characters would sing and perform, thus making her the focal point of *Cabaret*. Liza Minnelli was signed early on, and with her at last playing Sally, the character became American.

Feuer's concept for the film was fully embraced by Fosse. *Cabaret*'s numbers would occur only in the context of performance, a move Fosse felt was long overdue, as he later explained: "I had to break away from the reversed stage-to-movie musical mold. Or movie musicals that just copy conventions of the stage . . . . Today I get very antsy watching musicals in which people are singing as they walk down the street or hang out the laundry . . . in fact, I think it looks a little silly."[24] By juxtaposing the numbers with the book scenes and, more important, intercutting dramatic moments into the numbers, Fosse—and Feuer and Allen—would create on film the concept Prince brought to the stage.

Fosse was unhappy with the very script that satisfied Feuer, Allen, and ABC and asked his writer friends Neil Simon, Paddy Chayefsky, and Robert Alan Aurthur for their feedback. (Like Chayefsky, Aurthur had started out writing for live television in the 1950s but was now a screenwriter and director.) They found the script to be arch and superficial, with too much important action happening offscreen and with a leading character who needed to come into sharper focus. Allen, whose contract required her to deliver a first draft and only one rewrite, soon left for another assignment, and playwright Hugh Wheeler was brought in to pick up where she left off.[25] Fosse considered Wheeler's contributions "close to a *total* re-write," as he stated in an impassioned letter to the Writers Guild arguing for him to share the final screenplay credit with Allen.[26] However, Allen took advantage of a Writers Guild ruling stating that if two-thirds of a film's construction remains unchanged, the first writer who worked on the film receives sole credit regardless of the contribution by another writer. Wheeler's work did not disrupt *Cabaret*'s construction, which had been determined from the start by Feuer. Allen refused to share credit with Wheeler, which led to his billing in the final credits as "Research Consultant" and effectively cut him out of any awards consideration.[27]

Joel Grey had already been signed to repeat the role of the Emcee before Fosse joined the project, something that did not entirely please the new director. Eventually, after coaching Grey to scale his performance down for the camera, Fosse and the actor worked together congenially. While the role was not appreciably larger than onstage, Grey, with Fosse's help, deepened the character. Through a series of mostly silent shots of the Emcee offstage—some of them inserts lasting only seconds—Grey reveals a dark degeneracy that is truly frightening.

A point of major contention was Fosse's choice of a cinematographer. He insisted on Robert Surtees, from *Sweet Charity*, but Feuer and the studio resisted for several reasons. With a budget characterized by Feuer as "a very tight collar,"[28] hiring a cinematographer in Europe would be cheaper than bringing over an American. Also, Surtees was identified with *Sweet Charity*'s overindulgent camerawork. The issue was still not resolved when Fosse and Feuer went to Germany to scout locations. At dinner one night in Munich, Feuer agreed to support Fosse in his campaign for Surtees. But afterward, Fosse heard Feuer in the hotel room next door, on the phone with ABC Pictures president Martin Baum, contradicting what he had just said at dinner. Fosse scribbled down what he heard, as Feuer declared, "I don't want Surtees on the picture."[29] While Feuer had always expressed confidence in Fosse's abilities, now he confided, "I've been wrong about his work with actors too," and revealed concerns about Fosse's "insecurity." Finally, he stated the words that sealed his fate with Fosse: "Don't worry. I can control him."

It was a repeat of Fosse's experience overhearing Harold Prince in the next room during the out-of-town tryouts for *Damn Yankees*. Once again, he was confronted with evidence of a producer's duplicity, and his sense of betrayal knew no bounds. Fosse confronted Feuer the next morning, accusing him of lying while always planning to force another cinematographer on him and telling Feuer that if he wanted him off the film, he would have to fire him. In the end, Fosse stayed, and British cinematographer Geoffrey Unsworth, who had photographed *2001: A Space Odyssey* for director Stanley Kubrick, was hired. But Fosse completely froze out Feuer. Feuer's was the latest name to join the list of producers who had disappointed Fosse with what he saw as deception and dishonesty. And he held a grudge. "He was a black and white man. You were either a friend or an enemy. And he moved me from friend to enemy," Feuer later said.[30]

Cabaret began its swift seventy-five-day shooting schedule at Bavaria Studios in Munich at the end of March 1971. Fosse relied on his youthful experiences in Chicago-area nightclubs and burlesque theaters to create the look and feel of the Kit Kat Klub. He insisted on a tiny stage no more than ten by fourteen feet, one that could accommodate only six dancers, and a cramped backstage dressing room area. ("The real backstage that I knew was a jungle," he said.)[31] Ralph Burns's musical arrangements were written to approximate the sounds of a small onstage band. These self-imposed restrictions extended to Fosse's staging of the numbers, as he tried to make them entertaining yet distinctly second-rate.

Determined to portray the social and political climate with absolute accuracy, Fosse poured over research materials on Berlin between the wars. He relied heavily on the work of George Grosz and Otto Dix, artists who depicted with blunt honesty both the decadence and the brutality of life in Berlin during the Weimar era. "I've always been terribly dissatisfied with Hollywood extras, that same lollypop look over and over," Fosse said.[32] He set off with his assistant director, Wolfgang Glattes, scouting clubs and dive bars in search of faces that would accurately represent the period. Gwen Verdon soon arrived to offer general assistance, and she too was enlisted in the search. Fosse's persistence paid off. When the film opened, *Saturday Review*'s Hollis Alpert noted, "With an instinct for faces that rivals that of Fellini, he has collected dozens that would have served just as well for the sketchbooks of George Grosz."[33]

Even with the elimination of all book songs, the film still contains ten musical spots, the same number as *Sweet Charity*. "Willkommen," with its now-familiar vamp, is the cheery welcome, in three languages ("Willkommen, bienvenue, welcome"), to the Kit Kat Klub and its performers. In the film's first minutes, Fosse establishes the kind of musical *Cabaret* will be, and the way in which the musical numbers will intersect with the world outside the Klub's doors. The mirror that once greeted audiences from the stage is here a mottled, silver foiled wall that emerges out of the blackness as the credits end. The Emcee intrudes on the reflection, unctuous and strutting beneath the stage's crimson canopy. Fosse's first cutaway from the stage to the audience is to his recreation of Otto Dix's painting, *Portrait of the Journalist Sylvia von Harden* (1926), depicting a sharp-featured, independent woman drinking alone in a cafe. The image conveys a self-determination that would soon be snuffed out by Hitler's regime, and its inclusion at the very top of the film serves as a marker for the coming downward spiral.

Cutting from the Emcee to shots of Michael York as Brian Roberts arriving in Berlin by train immediately establishes Fosse's strategy of interlacing music with dramatic reality. The Emcee sings "Willkommen" as much to Brian as to the cabaret audience.

Fosse fills the Kit Kat Klub's chorus line with a motley assortment of women not quite young and not quite pretty, but who give off a heated sexuality. Most of the dancers were cast locally, and sensing that they would have difficulty adapting to his style, Fosse brought over Kathryn Doby and Louise Quick (both from the stage and film versions of *Sweet Charity*) to serve as examples for the others and, as Doby recalled, "pull it up a little bit."[34] Alluring yet sordid, the dancers' stage presence is troubling—a visual rebuke to the Emcee's insistence that "each and every one [is] a virgin." Their costumes are a jumble of old teddies tarted up with sequins and midriff sailor suits, all finished with black stockings and garters. (For an added dash of realism, Fosse forbade the dancers from shaving under their arms, a most unpopular directive, but one that added to the gaminess of their appearance.)

Fosse breaks the small group into even smaller units, creating a pigeon-toed trio at the center of the stage, framed by two others bouncing their rumps at the audience. They slowly come together, indolently swaying their pelvises, making lazy curlicues with their fingers up to the sky in a filthy-looking gesture. But they are also capable of forming a disciplined lineup, with angular shoulders and precision kicks, and for just a moment, the dancers exhibit the polish of a Broadway chorus line.

The Klub's assorted variety acts—magician, contortionist, female impersonator, dwarf ventriloquist, a pair of beefy mud-wrestling sisters, and American chanteuse Sally Bowles—could have stepped out of Fosse's own nightclub past. They perform Fosse's tacky, step-touch, jazz-hands choreography with the committed hard sell of the second-rate. With lights bursting around the stage, the number's climax achieves a tawdry excitement.

Broadway's "Willkommen" was startling for its time, but with a cast of thirty and its jazzy, big band sound, it also met the requirements of a large-scale opening number. Without altering its structure, Fosse pares the music and dance to their essentials, creating a hothouse atmosphere that establishes the seductive Kit Kat Klub and foreshadows the darkness beneath its frivolity. The number begins to sketch in the character of the Emcee, whose mincing byplay with the dancers and orchestra is broken up by glimpses of crude and overbearing behavior. Fosse sets Sally's position in the Klub's hierarchy as just one among the other acts, barely noticed, and given no special placement.

Onstage, the bouncy "Don't Tell Mama" introduced Sally as a madcap whose employment at the Kit Kat Klub was a risqué secret from her family. Kander and Ebb kept the song's introductory vamp but replaced it with the specially written "Mein Herr," which sets forth Sally's preferred image of herself as an insatiable femme fatale. The number starts offstage, as Sally makes up in a tight, overstuffed dressing area while the Emcee introduces her with a vulgar joke. She deposits her cigarette with a disinterested stagehand and steps onstage with a flourish. She must navigate past the Emcee, who whispers something at her, perhaps a reminder that this special number with the chorus is a favor for which she

The motley entertainers of the Kit Kat Klub strike an exultant pose in Cabaret's *opening number, "Willkommen." Emcee Joel Grey is held aloft center, while Liza Minnelli, second from right as American chanteuse Sally Bowles, is merely one among many. ABC Pictures–Allied Artists.*

now owes him. Before presenting herself as a worldly woman who lives only for pleasure, she must first contend with squalid backstage conditions and workplace harassment.

"Mein Herr," with its four minutes of highly concentrated dance, camerawork, and editing, is the ne plus ultra of Fosse film numbers. Starting with shots of the dancers in silent tableau, capturing their off-kilter body language, he pulls back to reveal a full-stage picture with Sally at its center. Unsworth's photography is at its most velvety and voluptuous, showcasing Minnelli in close-ups and sensuous full-body shots, her milky skin glowing in the smoky darkness. Her all-black costume, including bowler hat, stockings with garters, and sequined choker, was completed with Fosse's own black vest worn without shirt or bra. Minnelli is frequently photographed off to the side of the screen or framed between the dancers' legs and arms. The camera follows her closely, even trailing behind as she moves downstage. Sometimes it nestles in the fly space above the stage; other times it sits in the audience and captures waiters passing by. The dancers, providing a silent, almost sinister accompaniment, are shot in unflattering but striking close-up, emphasizing the vaguely lewd chair choreography that recalls *New Girl in Town*'s "Red Light Ballet."

Film is the ideal medium for Fosse's perfectionism, where he can direct the audience's attention to just the detail he wishes it to see. In one telling moment, he shoots Minnelli through the profiles of three dancers. As she sings "The continent of Europe is so wide, Mein Herr / Not only up and down, but side to side, Mein Herr," his camera catches each dancer as she points up, down, or sideways on a specific lyric. The tiny gestures would have little impact onstage, but film captures them in full detail. "If it's right, you should be able to blow up each frame as a picture for your wall," Fosse said, and he demonstrates that here.[35]

The editing of "Mein Herr" captures not only the physical effort of delivering a song and dance (Minnelli lifts her hat and exposes her sweat-soaked hair, the dancers twist themselves into impossibly awkward positions) but also its exhilaration. Through quick cuts and razor-sharp edits, it creates the visceral excitement of a live performance as the number reaches its climax. Shots of the dancers pounding the floor alternate with Minnelli furiously pumping her legs and belting the final note before collapsing over her chair.

"Mein Herr" recalls Marlene Dietrich's "Falling in Love Again" in *The Blue Angel*, but whereas Dietrich was laissez-faire, Minnelli is all high-voltage belting and strutting. (In performance, Sally becomes the devastating man-killer she so desperately strives to be offstage.) Minnelli's gifts are so obvious that when the film opened, her casting as the modestly talented Sally received some criticism, including from Christopher Isherwood himself: "You have this little girl saying, 'Oh, I'll never make it. I haven't really any talent.' Then she comes to the stage and you realize that she's every inch Judy Garland's daughter . . . . The truth is that this cabaret would have attracted half of Europe."[36] It is a fair criticism. But second-rate talent, however true to the source material, is no substitute for genuine star power. Stalking the tiny stage and confidently executing Fosse's angular choreography, Minnelli is indelible. Standing with her long legs apart, bowler hat perched on her head, and staring down the audience, she not only recalls her mother in her famous tuxedo and fedora look but also creates her own iconic image. *Newsweek* put Minnelli on its cover and declared, "A Star Is Born" when *Cabaret* opened.[37] "Mein Herr" is the moment when that became true.

"Mein Herr" made such an impact that both the 1987 and 1998 Broadway revivals of *Cabaret* based their television commercials around the camera and editing style of the number. *Fosse*, the Broadway compendium of his stage and film choreography, included "Mein Herr," and when the show was taped for commercial release in 2001, the camerawork and editing of the number closely followed that of the film. "Mein Herr" also created another Fosse standard: the sexy chair number, preferably with a bowler hat, which has been emulated everywhere from MTV to Cirque du Soleil to Jazzercise routines.

Minnelli's self-described "frantic joie-de-vivre"[38] required Fosse's careful handling to get a nuanced performance from her. Fosse was not above manipulating an actor to get what he wanted. Despite multiple takes, Marisa Berenson, playing the young Natalia Landauer, was unable to come up with just the right expression of shock and revulsion when she finds her dog has been killed and left on her doorstep. Finally, Fosse called for a tray of animal entrails from a local butcher. Without telling Berenson, he placed the entrails on the doorstep and called "Action!" Surprised and shocked, Berenson at last registered the proper degree of disgust.[39]

Fosse quickly came to value Geoffrey Unsworth's ideas, which considerably altered the film's visuals, as he later noted: "Originally, I liked the hard, cold look, sort of a Brechtian flavor. He changed it to give it a softer, smokier feel. It was the right move."[40] *Cabaret*'s diffused look evoked the visual palette of John Huston's *Moulin Rouge*, which had already influenced Fosse's filming of dance numbers. But the executives at ABC Pictures were alarmed by the footage they reviewed and issued angry calls from California. "'What're you doing?! It's so smoky and foggy in the nightclub. If you use one more filter we'll consider it an act of insubordination!'" Fosse recalled with obvious relish. When asked if this threat deterred his use of the filters, he replied, "Hell, no."[41]

The script stitched together from Allen's and Wheeler's contributions, along with those of Fosse, Feuer, and the cast, positioned the cabaret numbers to reflect and comment on the narrative, with scenes and dialogue layered into the numbers. Fosse's sensitivity to music and movement, and his understanding of how to get the best from the actors, gave those moments greater nuance. When Sally returns home after having been stood up by her father, she weeps and is comforted by Brian. His hugs and platonic kisses gradually turn passionate and are matched by Sally's, to the surprise of both. As they pull back, their smiles widen in recognition of the spark between them. At that moment, a clarinet slowly begins the introductory vamp to "Maybe This Time." ("Maybe This Time" was a Kander and Ebb trunk song that Minnelli had recorded in 1964.) Fosse, no fan of ballads, fades in brief scenes of Sally and Brian's growing intimacy as Sally sings the song to a near-empty Kit Kat Klub, perhaps auditioning for one of her sought-after talent scouts from UFA, Germany's major film production studio.

Fosse uses these inserts judiciously before turning the song over to Sally, enveloping her in saturated colors and glowing lights as the camera lovingly circles her. (Thirty years later, director Rob Marshall used a similar setting and camera style for Roxie Hart's "Nowadays" in the film version of *Chicago*.) "Maybe This Time" is Sally's happiest moment, and Fosse finds fresh cinematic methods to convey her joy.

Early in the film, Fosse uses brief musical numbers as counterpoint to the emerging Nazi threat. The mud-wrestling sisters demonstrate their skill while a young Nazi panhandles among the Kit Kat Klub audience. The Klub's owner kicks him out, while onstage the Emcee proclaims the mud-wrestling winner by swiping a streak of mud across his upper lip and giving a Nazi salute. Later, the Emcee and the dancers, dressed in lederhosen, do a comic variation on a German "slap dance," with intricately timed slaps, spanks, and wallops— all contrasted with the Klub owner outside being beaten by the same young Nazi and his cohorts. As the dance's pretend violence escalates, so do the real punches and kicks of the Nazis. The Emcee—always the victor—crows like a rooster as he stands above the vanquished dancers, while the owner is left gasping for breath in an alley.

Other moments require no music or dance to make an impact. Fosse's mise en scène presents the evidence of the rising National Socialist movement as a backdrop for daily life in Berlin. Strolling with Brian as she babbles on about her film ambitions, Sally ignores the posters of Communist messages defaced by the Nazis and sidesteps a legless man, possibly a World War I veteran, wheeling past her with a Nazi flag in his wheelchair. Later, Fosse boldly stages the aftermath of the murder of a Jew by the Nazis as a stage tableau, the camera circling the carnage as German citizens stand silently and Sally, Brian, and Max drive by discussing weekend plans.

The appearance of Max introduces a subplot that sends the film into another dimension of metaphor and comment. When Sally first meets Max and sees his luxurious motorcar, Fosse instantly cuts to close-ups of Sally and the Emcee, eyes glittering, as they each whisper "Money!" The camera then cuts to the pair onstage as they launch into "Money, Money," a new Kander and Ebb song that extols currency in a collapsing economy. Verdon recalled that the original idea was to dress the two as bums, but the resemblance of Minnelli to her mother in her famous tramp number was felt to be too distracting, so instead the pair was outfitted in exaggerated high-style elegance.[42]

It is the only song Sally and the Emcee share in the film, and it gives Minnelli and Grey the opportunity to revel in their mutual showmanship, presenting them in perfect sync as they dance, mime, and cavort in comic venality. Fosse's staging emphasizes the connection of money with sex. Coins are tossed into her cleavage and down his pants. In celebrating that which "makes the world go round," their pelvic swivels and bumping of crotches leave little to the imagination. The number ends with Sally and the Emcee shadow dancing behind a blue-shaded scrim. (Rob Marshall sent Queen Latifah in similar behind-the-screen capering in *Chicago*'s "When You're Good to Mama.")

Sally and Brian's getaway with Max to his estate precipitates two of *Cabaret*'s most powerful sequences, both of which demonstrate Fosse's skill in choreographing the camera absent dance. "Two Ladies," the Emcee's song and dance celebrating the virtues of a ménage à trois, foreshadows the trio's sexual involvement. Following a lavish dinner at which Sally holds court as if she were a regular guest, the three spend the rest of the evening drinking in Max's grand ballroom. As Max and Sally dance intimately, Max bids Brian to join them. Fosse's camera closes in on the trio as they drunkenly dance together, touching foreheads and smiling, the ménage already begun under Max's skilled direction. After Brian passes out, Max and Sally exchange looks, a silent agreement passing between them. Max heads off, and Sally, only momentarily having second thoughts, stumblingly follows. The following day, on the way back to Berlin, the car stops at a beer garden. While Sally, hung over and guilty about the previous evening's events, sleeps in the car, Max and Brian have a glass of wine. Brian offers Max a cigarette from the gold case Max had gifted him and which he had at first refused. With minimal dialogue and a subtle exchange of looks, Fosse makes it clear that Brian is now also open to Max's interest.

Max and Brian listen as a pretty blond boy begins to sing what at first sounds like a lullaby. The boy's sweet tenor rings out as the camera pans down to reveal the Nazi insignia on his uniform. The camera catches the admiring looks of the country people at the tables, some possibly the boy's family. The song's cadence grows more aggressive, taking on a militaristic fervor, as everyone, young and old, stands and joins in. Only an elderly man, looking confused and uncomfortable, sits silently. (Verdon later revealed that much of the footage was done with hidden cameras, and that Fosse had instructed his camera operators to keep filming after he had called "cut" in order to get more candid expressions from the extras.)[43] By the time the boy dons his hat and gives a Nazi salute, the beer garden has become a full-blown Nazi rally. As the camera follows Max's car driving away, Fosse adds a "button," inserting a final, chilling shot of the Emcee, collar unbuttoned and relaxing on a couch, looking up at the camera, smiling and nodding. "Tomorrow Belongs to Me" is the film's only song to escape the confines of the Kit Kat Klub, and its bucolic setting and the ordinariness of the beer garden's patrons only make it more disturbing. (Here, Fosse's eye for casting extras is at its sharpest.)

The "Tiller Girls" number shows Fosse's full command of a dance routine intercut with story elements. Amid streamers and confetti, he stages a precision kick line with more variations than John Tiller's original chorus lineups, while alternating it with shots of hoodlums sneaking over the gates of the Landauer home and painting "Juden" (Jews) on their entryway. The Emcee is soon revealed, in drag, as one of the dancers. He leers at the audience, flaunting his hairy armpits and daring customers to pinch his thighs. The music's sound and rhythm reach a feverish pitch as Natalia opens the door to find her beloved dog dead on the doorstep. Fosse returns to the stage and turns the festive performance sinister. The colorful streamers fall and the lights grow stark and cold as the dancers pull back upstage (ironically, in "Hello Dolly Style," according to his notes)[44] and transform themselves into storm troopers. Their hats become helmets and their canes guns as they goosestep to a military drum roll. The Emcee cackles with menace, and the audience roars with laughter as the vandals run from the Landauer home, shouting "Juden, Juden."

Though she played no role in assisting Fosse with the musical numbers or coaching the performers, Gwen Verdon once again proved to be a steadying and creative presence. Costuming for *Cabaret* was especially problematic, since a general reluctance to recreate an era that many Germans wanted to forget led to much obfuscation regarding wardrobe. When Liza Minnelli asked for clothes from the 1930s, before the war, the German wardrobe crew responded, "What war?"[45] Verdon combed antique stores in Paris to find costumes for Minnelli and Berenson. (It was her idea to dress Minnelli in Fosse's black vest for "Mein Herr.") Later, no suitable head could be found to top off the gorilla costume for "If You Could See Her through My Eyes." In particular, the head required a mouth that could eat a banana and a face with features that would show up under stage lighting. Verdon flew back to New York City, rented the proper gorilla head, and returned to Munich with the head perched on her lap the entire trip.[46]

Cabaret's final musical sequence is its title song. Onstage, Harold Prince used it to show Sally surrendering to the pull of a darkening Berlin. In the film, Fosse presents the song—and Sally—as the ultimate, end-of-the-world showstopper. Fosse films the number simply, isolating Minnelli in pools of darkness that allow the tiniest of facial gestures to register. (Martin Scorsese took a similar approach in filming Minnelli singing "But the World Goes 'Round" in *New York, New York*.) "Cabaret" is the only number in the film that does not cut away from the stage to the audience. It remains self-contained, hermetic. Dressed in a striking purple halter gown with beaded midriff (another Verdon discovery), her breasts barely contained, Minnelli's Sally is an effervescent party girl, swinging along to the song's merry beat. Soon the lights dim, and Sally is alone in the spotlight to contemplate her former roommate, Elsie, who died young "from too much pills and liquor." She barely gives this a second thought before extolling her as "the happiest corpse I'd ever seen." Fosse moves in tight on Minnelli's face and turns the spotlight from cold blue to warm flush. Radiating an obscene heat, she takes up Elsie's advice to "come hear the music play." Sally has already rejected Brian and his offer of respectable domesticity for the world represented by the Kit Kat Klub. Her declaration that "when I go, I'm going like Elsie" is more willful than celebratory. As she rushes to the song's climax, Fosse hastens her demise by capturing her in an inferno of throbbing lights.

"Cabaret" is Sally's final philosophical statement, and Minnelli's performance is so alive with youthful energy and emotional fluidity that the idea Sally would succumb to the coming calamities of the Nazi regime carries a crushing sadness. Those calamities appear almost immediately. The Emcee returns even before her applause ends to remind the audience, as he had at the beginning, that "here, life is beautiful." But now the music is dissonant, the female orchestra blowsier and sweatier, the merriment more forced. The foiled wall reappears, and now reflected from the audience are the insignias of the Nazis, who are not sneaking in to collect money but are enjoying choice seats. They were there when Sally urged them to "come to the cabaret, old chum," and they will remain, deciding the fate of the Kit Kat Klub and other stages like it. It is a simple, silent, and unsettling final image.

Through eleven years of marriage—through *Redhead, The Conquering Hero, Pal Joey, How to Succeed in Business without Really Trying, Little Me, Pleasures and Palaces,* and *Sweet Charity,* through tours, tryouts, and rehearsals—Fosse had never been faithful to Verdon. Still, they remained together, she the faithful helpmate and his most trusted critic, he the loving father to their daughter and the choreographer who showcased Verdon so brilliantly. On *Cabaret,* Fosse's infidelities were his most brazen, including a more serious relationship with a woman who worked on the film as an interpreter. Verdon stayed on the project, but when Fosse returned to New York after completion of filming, they ceased living together as husband and wife.

Cabaret would take its final shape in the editing room, where Fosse was as obsessed with detail as he was on a set or in rehearsal. "I don't understand directors who turn their film over to editors," he said. "It's a very collaborative thing. You go cut by cut, frame by frame right down the line."[47] Here, *Cabaret*'s layered editing was fully realized, aided by Fosse's decision to shoot more film on *Cabaret* than he had on *Sweet Charity.*

Cabaret was previewed less than a month before it was released, indicating the confidence of ABC Pictures and Allied Artists in the film, which was confirmed by the preview audience. Feuer's decision to jettison the book songs and return to Isherwood's original stories was vindicated by many who were asked what they liked best about the film and responded: "The restriction of musical numbers to the cabaret. Intercutting between cabaret and real life" and "It combined the best elements of Berlin stories, *I Am a Camera,* and *Cabaret* brilliantly."[48]

The only significant change *Cabaret* underwent before it officially opened was a single word of dialogue. Brian and Sally learn that they have both slept with Max during an argument in which Brian tells Sally, "Oh, screw Maximilian!" She responds, "I do." After a pause, Brian says, "So do I." Originally, Brian had said, "Oh, fuck Maximilian," and the exchange was filmed twice, once with "fuck" and the other with "screw."[49] Substituting the take with "screw" enabled the film to sidestep an R rating (for those seventeen or older unless accompanied by an adult), which would have limited the film's potential audience, for that of PG (requiring only parental guidance).

(Making the leading male character in an American film bisexual was indeed daring in 1972, and Brian's involvement with Sally was more complex than the romance they shared in the stage musical. But it was an easy opportunity for boldness. Brian's relationship with Sally, including their moments of intimacy, was at the center of the film, while the scenes inferring his liaison with Max were subtle to the point of vagueness. Isherwood himself, who made no claim for the narrator's sexuality in *Berlin Stories,* disliked this characterization. "I felt as though his homosexual side was used as a kink in the film—like bed wetting—and that he was really supposed to be basically heterosexual.")[50]

The film received a celebrity-studded premier at New York City's Ziegfeld Theater on February 13, 1972. Reminding himself of the early enthusiasm for *Sweet Charity*, Fosse was his usual skittish self about his new film's potential reception. He need not have worried. The response from the critics matched those of the preview audience, heralding *Cabaret* not only as an outstanding film but also as a turning point in the history of the movie musical. The *New Yorker*'s Pauline Kael devoted an entire column to extolling its virtues. "'Cabaret' is a great movie musical, made, miraculously, without compromises . . . . the material is hard and unsentimental, and until now there has never been a diamond-hard big American movie musical."[51] While praising Minnelli and others, Charles Champlin of the *Los Angeles Times* was quick to point out the film's greatest asset. "'Cabaret' becomes an all-star vehicle, whose principal star is Fosse."[52]

Fosse's peers also acclaimed his work. His friend Stanley Donen wired, "I thought you would like to know Stanley Cubrick [*sic*] told me that he thinks *Cabaret* is one of the best pictures he ever saw in his life."[53] Joseph L. Mankiewicz, one of the celebrated directors who turned down the film, insisted that Fosse "brought the stink of truth to *Cabaret*. He's one of the few directors I'd write for."[54] Vincente Minnelli accompanied his daughter to a final preview, at the conclusion of which the elder filmmaker said to Fosse, "I have just seen the perfect movie."[55]

Stephen Farber in the *New York Times* put forth the most provocative criticism of *Cabaret*. While saying that it "deserves to be called the first adult film musical,"[56] he asserted that it took a highly moralistic tone by implying that the decadence and hedonism exemplified by the cabaret sequences were a direct cause of the rise of the Third Reich. Farber added, "'Cabaret' may even be read as a cautionary tale for today, a warning that contemporary America, because of its new sexual freedom, is a sick society, comparable to Weimar Germany or the declining Roman Empire—a society on the brink of some kind of horrible apocalypse."[57] Whether or not one agreed with these analogies, they gave *Cabaret* a contemporary currency unusual for a period musical.

Cabaret not only was an invigorating rebuke to all the recent overblown Broadway-to-Hollywood transfers but also was influential across a variety of media. It intersected with both the current nostalgia trend and the gay entertainment scene. "The movie served as an inspirational directive,"[58] said *Village Voice* writer David Tipmore, as the "divine decadence" of its fashions and atmosphere and sexuality found their way into the small nightspots and cabaret rooms that were popping up around Manhattan and in cities like Los Angeles and San Francisco. This loose network of clubs, sometimes referred to as the "K-Y Circuit" (K-Y was a lubricant used by many gay men), was home to many potential male and female Sally Bowleses, both on its stages and in the audiences.

Cabaret influenced at least one other musical. The 1975 Barbra Streisand vehicle, *Funny Lady* (a sequel to *Funny Girl*), directed by Herbert Ross, emerged as a kind of imitation *Cabaret*.[59] In addition to a caustic script by Jay Presson Allen, songs by Kander and Ebb, and Fosse's *Pippin* star, Ben Vereen, in a featured dance role, *Funny Lady* tries to apply *Cabaret*'s sardonic, decadent quality to its romantic musical comedy story. Streisand's big torch song, "How Lucky Can You Get," is performed and filmed in an overwrought manner that emulates "Maybe This Time" but without that song's poignant underpinnings. Echoing Fosse's conflicts with the film studio over his diffused camerawork, *Funny Lady*'s cinematographer, Vilmos Zsigmond, was fired after his early footage was deemed too dark and unflattering. "I wanted the movie to look less like *Funny Girl* and more like *Cabaret*," he later argued. "They wanted the old concept of musicals."[60] One can only wonder whether Geoffrey Unsworth would have survived if *Cabaret* had not been filmed an ocean away from its producing studio.

Cabaret eventually earned more than $42 million at the box office and was one of the few American musicals to do well in foreign film markets. It was still playing in theaters a year later when awards season arrived. The National Board of Review named it Best Film and Fosse, Best Director. The British Film Academy (later known as BAFTA) gave it seven awards, far and away the most for any film, including Best Film and Best Director. At the Golden Globes, *Cabaret* won for Best Picture in the Musical or Comedy category.

Cabaret and *The Godfather* each received ten Academy Award nominations, including for Best Picture and Best Director. *The Godfather* was the prohibitive favorite to sweep the awards, an assumption that was confirmed when Francis Ford Coppola won the Directors Guild of America (DGA) award for Best Director. At that time, only once in the history of the DGA Award had the winner not also won the Oscar for Best Director. But on the evening of the Academy Awards, *Cabaret* won in all the technical categories, Minnelli won as Best Actress, and Grey beat a field that numbered three actors from *The Godfather* to win as Best Supporting Actor.

Fosse looked grim sitting next to Cy Feuer as he listened to the names of the Best Director nominees being read. When his name was called, he jumped up quickly and changed his expression to a broad grin as he accepted the award in what was considered a major upset. In his brief acceptance speech Fosse joked, "Being characteristically a pessimist and cynic, this and some of the other nice things that have happened to me in the last couple of days may turn me into some sort of hopeful optimist and ruin my whole life." (Two days earlier he had won Tony Awards for Best Direction and Best Choreography for *Pippin*.) Among those he thanked was Gwen Verdon, the wife from whom he was now separated, calling her "a dear friend of mine." His remarks were pure Fosse, flip and self-deprecating, referencing his pessimism while allowing just a glimpse of emotion to peek through.[61]

A few minutes later *The Godfather* was named Best Picture, ending *Cabaret*'s streak of wins. Its final tally of eight Oscars set a record for the most wins without capturing the Best Picture honor, a record it still holds. Fosse could not help feeling responsible for the film not capturing the biggest prize. A year later, still smarting over the film's restricted budget, he said, "With just a little more money I could have made a great film. If I'd been able to get the period I think we'd've won best picture."[62]

Despite the foundational contributions of Feuer and Allen, *Cabaret* is identified with Fosse, who insisted that his work varied little from his last film. "If you look closely at the way I shot the numbers in *Sweet Charity*, they are not very different from the numbers in *Cabaret* .... People say I grew so much between those films. It's not so. I just had much stronger material with *Cabaret*."[63] It is possible that Fosse had to direct *Sweet Charity* before he could direct *Cabaret*, passing from experimentation to a new maturity and subtlety.

Cabaret is one of the touchstone films of the 1970s. It brought new life to a moribund film genre and, as musicals seldom do, connected with contemporary politics and sexuality. Like *The Sound of Music* and *Grease*, its film success also redefined its stage antecedent. Subsequent revivals of the stage musical have included some or all of the movie songs, and Sally Bowles and the Emcee are now generally considered the leading roles.

Harold Prince's strict recreation of the original production for a 1987 Broadway revival, with Joel Grey receiving solo star billing above the title, looked tired and dated. But in 1993, Sam Mendes completely re-envisioned the show for an environmental staging at London's Donmar Warehouse, with the audience seated at tables around the playing area. It became the basis for the 1998 Broadway revival produced by the Roundabout Theatre Company that proved a sensation, running six years and returning in 2014. Mendes, who was joined for the Broadway production by choreographer and co-director Rob Marshall, made *Cabaret* blacker and more hellish, with a final image of the Emcee in a concentration camp, wearing both a yellow star (marking him as a Jew) and a pink triangle (for homosexuality). Clifford Bradshaw was now openly gay. Berlin's brutality and dissipation were more explicit than ever. The cabaret dancers wore ragged scraps of clothing and exhibited bruises and needle marks on their arms. But the darker decadence of the cabaret numbers was sweaty and effortful, and never entirely erased memories of the easy panache with which Fosse conjured the alluring amorality of the Kit Kat Klub. No matter how drastically *Cabaret* is revised, Fosse continues to loom over it.

> "What I was struck by mainly was how much work is possible if you don't take vacations and almost kill yourself. You can work a lot."
>
> Bob Fosse, 1973[64]

Prior to *Cabaret*, Liza Minnelli was caught in a show business time warp, identified with the emphatic performing style of her mother while trying to assert her own identity as a young, contemporary woman. *Liza*, her 1970 television special, celebrated her show business lineage with songs associated with her mother but also included sequences of Minnelli singing the work of contemporary composers Jimmy Webb and Randy Newman. *Liza* was developed by Fred Ebb, who did much to shape Minnelli's onstage image, creating her television specials and concert acts, writing specialty material for her with John Kander, and coaching her song delivery and audience interaction. A second television special, *Liza with a Z*, was also Ebb's idea, and like the first it presented her as a youthful trouper, steeped in show business. "This special is a documentary," Ebb's first draft begins, as it follows Minnelli, cinéma-vérité style, through a single performance at Los Angeles's Greek Theatre.[65]

Most television variety specials of the era followed a predictable pattern of guest stars, comedy sketches, and production numbers taped on soundstages. *Liza with a Z*, Fosse's first project after completing *Cabaret*, is something strikingly different: a one-woman stage show filmed to bring the excitement of live performance to the small screen. "We all agreed that the kind of feeling Liza creates when performing for an audience was what we wanted. That meant just one chance," he said.[66]

Fosse not only directed and choreographed *Liza with a Z* but also co-produced with Ebb. He and Ebb switched the show from the West Coast to the East Coast and booked the Lyceum Theater, at 947 seats one of Broadway's most intimate houses, for the "one chance" performance on May 31, 1972. While the industry standard was videotape, Fosse insisted on using film "because there's no way to do my kind of fine cutting with tape."[67] Fosse's choice of cinematographer was equally unusual. Owen Roizman, a recent Oscar winner for the gritty crime drama *The French Connection* who had never worked in television, joined the project to coordinate eight 16mm cameras placed throughout the Lyceum—in the orchestra, balcony, aisles, and wings—and operated one of two handheld cameras himself.

Ebb's original documentary-style ideas were filtered through Fosse, who captures the pre-curtain excitement and anticipation of a live performance. Quick shots of backstage preparations (musicians warming up, dancers stretching) alternate with the audience crowding into the theater lobby and taking their seats. As the lights dim and the orchestra takes its place, the jovial star lightens the mood with a hearty belly laugh as she makes up in her dressing room.

The performance is broken into four discrete acts, each presenting a different facet of Minnelli's talent and building until the final, inevitable *Cabaret* medley triggers a tumultuous ovation. The first act is Liza solo. Fosse uses two sets of curtains, one parting left and right, the other rising from the floor, to frame Minnelli as she is revealed in silhouette. In fedora and oversized fur stole, she looks like a little girl playing dress-up. She soon discards these items, displaying an all-white Halston pantsuit. As in *Cabaret*, Fosse sometimes places the camera low, peering up at her from the front row and catching tops of heads in the audience. Other times he pulls back to isolate her, a tiny figure in white engulfed in darkness.

It is notable how Fosse tames Minnelli's inclination toward hyperactivity. The Minnelli stage personality—girlish, self-deprecating, full of show business banter (her comic exclamation, "Wrong!" is lifted from comedienne Jo Anne Worley of television's *Rowan and Martin's Laugh-In*)—is all there, but it is less manic and more focused. The specialty number, "Liza with a Z," a long-time part of her act, here becomes a tour de force of controlled comic energy and timing. The Jacques Brel–like "It Was a Good Time," about the dissolution of a marriage, includes an emotional "breakdown" ripe for overplaying. But Fosse centers Minnelli's energy, keeps her still, and brings the camera in close to pick up every nuance of feeling flashing across her face. As she builds to the song's climax, his stagecraft underscores her emotions. Backdrop colors go violently red and orange, and when she sings the final note and backs away from the audience, Fosse's curtains descend and merge to swallow her into a black void.

The show's second act is all about presenting Minnelli as a contemporary, sexually forthright young woman. A rock band is onstage, perched on risers (an image Fosse would revisit for the climactic number in *All That Jazz*). From the wings saunter two men in dark glasses and broad-brimmed gaucho hats (dancers Neil Jones and Spencer Henderson), exhaling cigarette smoke in the darkness. Their supercool attitude is disrupted by the entrance of Minnelli, pelvis-pumping in a sparkling red dress cut extra-high to show off her long legs. "I Gotcha," a recent funk hit by Joe Tex filled with macho bluster, is here turned into a feisty feminist workout, as Minnelli asserts her demands for sexual fulfillment ("C'mon, give it to me!") to the two men who follow along silently.

The number is an update on the tight trio dances Fosse created for Gwen Verdon's television appearances a few years earlier, and perhaps because Minnelli is so much younger, "I Gotcha" features his most "now" choreography. She and the two men strut across the stage with "chicken wing arms," according to Fosse's dance notes.[68] They plant their feet, arch their backs, and lock down their arms and legs, alternating awkward shoulder and knee accents. They whip their bodies from one direction to another and, as if unable to control their pelvises, pause briefly to undulate before launching into another step.

Minnelli is surprisingly insouciant as she grinds out the beat in a dress that barely covers her derrière. Fosse's camera follows the trio into the wings as they dance on and off the stage, capturing the men's leaps and slides behind Minnelli. Finally, having vanquished the men, Minnelli exits with an awkward bit of "get down" dancing, but leaving to doubt of who is in control.

The rest of the dancers join Minnelli for "Son of a Preacher Man," the southern soul hit by Dusty Springfield. They execute long, languorous port de bras, eventually falling into prayerful poses. Fosse splits the dancers into small groups, assigning different variations to each for visual variety while always keeping the focus on Minnelli. (Minnelli is frequently joined by two women who mirror her dance moves. At one point the entire ensemble forms a human frame around

Liza gets down in "I Gotcha" from Liza with a Z. *NBC.*

her.) The dancers, dressed in black pants and vests and white shirts, eventually surround and lift Minnelli. They stretch up and out in all directions, creating a Fosse amoeba, and their billowing white sleeves give the impression of Minnelli aloft on a holy cloud. As the number gathers intensity, the dancers rock out in revivalist fervor. Fosse spoke of his desire to insert the camera into his dances, to "make the camera one of the dancers,"[69] and he does so here to stunning effect, catching glimpses of Minnelli in the midst of the frantic activity, her red dress popping out amid the swirling black and white of the dancers' costumes. The number erupts into a final frenzy and concludes with a simple, savvy piece of staging. Fosse brings the curtain down and then quickly raises it as the dancers continue wildly clapping and Minnelli stands singing at center. He brings it down again, but this time brings it up to reveal Minnelli alone onstage, signaling the end of the number and cueing an ovation—the theatrical equivalent of a recording fade-out.

"I Gotcha" and "Son of a Preacher Man" are built on post–"Rich Man's Frug," pre-disco dance moves, but like Minnelli's delivery, they are too precise in conception and execution to be truly contemporary. Instead, in these two numbers Fosse and Minnelli offer a dramatic presentation of popular music and dance—not exactly "hip," but wildly theatrical and riveting.

Fosse highlights the physical effort of Minnelli's performance by keeping the cameras on the sweat-soaked star as she towels herself off while explaining the premise for the next song. Kander and Ebb's "Ring Them Bells" is a one-act musical comedy sketch, with Minnelli voicing a variety of characters while the dancers embody them. In the tale of Shirley Devore, an unmarried thirty-one-year-old still living at home on Manhattan's Riverside Drive who travels the world searching for a husband, the dancers play Shirley's parents, fellow travelers, and assorted romantic possibilities. Outfitted with bells on their extremities (wrists, ankles, hips), they also punctuate the song's refrain ("You gotta ring them bells") to increasingly elaborate and hilarious effect. "Ring Them Bells" contains some of Ebb's most delicious lyrics and tells its anecdotal story with wit and great humor, building to an unexpected comic payoff. When at last Shirley meets Norm Saperstein on the beach in Dubrovnik and learns that he lives in the apartment next door to her in New York, the entire ensemble, in a variety of contortions, stops and shakes every bell on them. The big, applause-earning finish includes a cakewalking kick line. It is, as *Variety* declared, "that tv rarity—a genuine showstopper."[70]

"Ring Them Bells" is the kind of specialty number that could have been written by Minnelli's godmother Kay Thompson for Judy Garland at MGM, and Minnelli plays it like a great sketch comedienne, smoothly switching between characters and socking home its punch lines. Fosse stages it meticulously, shifting the dancers around the stage in rapid-fire arrangements to illustrate Shirley's story and keeping the camera tight on Minnelli before opening wide for its stage-filling finale. In a show overflowing with highlights, "Ring Them Bells" is its comic peak.[71]

The third act of *Liza with a Z* presents the star as a vaudevillian, comfortable with both a soft-shoe routine and an emotive ballad. The soft-shoe was an updated arrangement of the old standard "Bye Bye Blackbird," and Fosse's reworking of it has become one of his most enduring numbers. In their velvet tuxedo jackets, white gloves, and derbies, the dancers look like elegant minstrel performers arranged in geometric groupings under the sculpted stage lighting. They slowly come to life, rolling their hips, snapping their fingers, and slapping their thighs as they whisper the song's lyrics in an easy cadence. Soon Minnelli joins them in chic velvet knickers and ascot, the very picture of a 1972 vaudevillian. She and the dancers gently strut, keeping every movement small and contained, each finger curlicue a tiny grace note. (Two dancers do a diminutive hand flutter above their heads when Minnelli sings her first "blackbird.") Their laid-back attitude gives the song a sense of satire. When the dancers surround Minnelli as she sings, "Oh, what hard luck stories they all hand me," they turn and lift their hats to express mock regrets.

As the music revs up to a rock beat, Minnelli and the dancers retreat upstage, then return in what would come to be the quintessential Fosse walk: arms tight to the sides and jutting out from the elbow, fingers splayed, feet turned in and leading with the pelvis, and staring down the audience as they stalk forward. "Bye Bye Blackbird" is a compendium of Fosse-isms. There are the derbies and white gloves, the mambo steps and hip isolations, the whispered vocals and syncopated whistling. There is the old standard rearranged and given a contemporary pulse. There are the coiled, simmering moves that finally explode into full-out dance. Above all, there is Fosse's ability to split his ensemble into infinite arrangements and create stage pictures of breathtaking symmetry and theatrical power.

In act 4, Minnelli revisits *Cabaret*, singing songs now indelibly linked to her. "Money, Money" is staged with all the male dancers, presenting Minnelli and a sextet of Joel Greys.[72] She ends with "Maybe This Time" and "Cabaret" in full concert form, belting to the top balcony, the sweat flying from her hair and face.

The camera catches the excitement just beyond the stage as it intercuts shots of the dancers taking their bows with Minnelli in the wings drying herself with a towel and waiting for her cue. The audience jumps to its feet (at a time before standing ovations were common) as Minnelli enters, with the cameras swooping back and forth from audience to stage, capturing the exhilaration of the moment for both performer and audience. A camera stationed at the back of the stage charts the rise and fall of the curtain as she acknowledges the ongoing applause.

NBC bumped *Bonanza* from its prime Sunday night slot to broadcast *Liza with a Z* on September 10, 1972. It was a ratings success and a critical stunner. "Ranks with the all-time greats of TV," declared the *Boston Globe*.[73] The soundtrack album became Liza Minnelli's best-selling recording. The awards tally for the show included a Peabody Award and four Emmy Awards, three of which went to Fosse, for his choreography, for his direction, and for Outstanding Single Program–Variety and Popular Music (a shared award for Fosse and Ebb as producers and Minnelli as star). The same year that Fosse lost the Directors Guild Award to Francis Ford Coppola, he won the DGA Award for Best Director of a Television Musical/Variety Special.

Liza with a Z was rebroadcast by NBC twice but then went unseen except for grainy bootleg copies until it was restored and released on DVD in 2006. In a twenty-first-century celebrity landscape where amateurs and poseurs achieve star status, singers are routinely autotuned, and popular female performers from Madonna and Beyoncé to Lady Gaga and Katy Perry appear in special effects–laden stage spectacles, *Liza with a Z* is a revelation of simplicity. To enthrall an audience, it needed only a live performer of consummate skill, first-rate writing, and imaginative, theatrical staging.

The year 1972 was when Liza Minnelli became a true star, and *Cabaret* and *Liza with a Z* were the vehicles that drove her success. The Liza Minnelli that Fosse helped develop in their two films together is the one that came to define her. John Kander, and especially Fred Ebb, created her material and influenced her performing style, but it was Fosse who harnessed her mix of show business bravado and eager-to-please gamine, bringing discipline and polish to both her screen and stage performances.

7

AN ANECDOTIC REVUE

• • •

"I have no interest wasting time and energy doing traditional musicals. I like fooling with new forms, seeing what rules I can break if I push a little harder in different directions."

Bob Fosse, 1978[1]

Fosse's first post-*Cabaret* Broadway musical had its genesis in an undergraduate student production at Carnegie Mellon University five years earlier. *Pippin, Pippin*, a musical drama about the life of the illegitimate son of Charlemagne, king of France in the late eighth century, had music (co-written with fellow student Ron Strauss), lyrics, direction, and choreography by nineteen-year-old drama major Stephen Schwartz. A recording of the score led to Schwartz being signed by a New York agent, and eventually to an offer to write a new score for John-Michael Tebelak's *Godspell*.

Schwartz, who had studied composition and classical piano at Juilliard, was strongly influenced by contemporary music, including everything from Motown to current singer-songwriters like Laura Nyro, James Taylor, and Carole King. Schwartz made *Godspell*'s score both theatrically satisfying and radio-friendly— an effortless amalgam of theater and pop music. *Godspell* was an immediate hit off-Broadway, playing more than two thousand performances and eventually moving to Broadway and spawning multiple US and international companies. "Day by Day," released as a single, was a Top 40 hit, becoming a generations-spanning "soft rock" standard.

It is easy to underestimate the confusion that reigned in the period after *Hair* arrived in 1968 and began to change the rules for what a Broadway musical might sound like. It had a pulsating and eclectic score by Galt MacDermot and topical and often profane lyrics by Gerome Ragni and James Rado. *Hair*'s score produced a number of pop-rock standards, and its cast recording became the first since *Hello, Dolly!* to reach number one on the album charts.[2] Clive Barnes, chief theater critic for the *New York Times*, loved *Hair* and declared that rock was the new sound of Broadway musicals.[3]

There were genuine and sometimes successful attempts to relate musically to a new generation. Galt MacDermot's score for *Two Gentlemen of Verona* (1971), his only post-*Hair* hit, was an entertaining hodgepodge of pop, rock, calypso, and soul with lyrics by John Guare. *Purlie* (1970) had a rousing rhythm and blues–inflected score with music by Gary Geld and lyrics by Peter Udell. Melvin Van Peebles's *Ain't Supposed to Die a Natural Death* (1971) was an urban jazz/fusion song cycle. But the faint-hearted rock rhythms pasted onto Charles Strouse and Lee Adams's conventional score for *Applause* (1970) were typical of most attempts at a new Broadway sound.

One notable hybrid was the score by Burt Bacharach and Hal David for *Promises, Promises*, their 1969 adaptation of the Billy Wilder film *The Apartment*. The team, whose hit records for Dionne Warwick and others included "Walk on By," "I Say a Little Prayer," and "What's New, Pussycat?," brought contemporary pop syncopations and recording studio techniques to Broadway, including a sound environment created by record producer Phil Ramone that used unseen vocalists, electronic instruments in the orchestra pit, and greater reliance on amplification both on- and offstage.

Andrew Lloyd Webber and Tim Rice created a new model for musical theater when their chart-topping concept album *Jesus Christ Superstar* was transferred to the Broadway stage in 1971. It covered similar terrain as *Godspell*, but Lloyd Webber's score was darker, more aggressive, and decidedly more rock-based than Schwartz's, and the show had a relatively modest run. It would take the better part of a decade for Lloyd Webber and Rice to refine the rock-concept-album-to-musical-theater model with *Evita* and for *Jesus Christ Superstar* to gain traction as a popular and venerable arena rock attraction.

It was at this intersection of pop-rock and theater that Stephen Schwartz would prove to be so valuable to the Broadway musical of this period. Unlike MacDermot, Ragni, and Rado, whose various post-*Hair* efforts were mostly incoherent spectacles, he had the discipline to write well-crafted songs that served their shows, advanced plot, conveyed character, and were contemporary and accessible to younger audiences but not threatening to older theatergoers.[4]

Schwartz continued to work on *Pippin* (now with a reduced title), shifting it from melodramatic court intrigue to a story that reflected his own generation's quest for personal fulfillment. Along the way he began collaborating on a new book for the show with Roger O. Hirson, a veteran television writer and playwright who had previously contributed the book for the musical *Walking Happy* (1966). Schwartz and Hirson fashioned an episodic narrative in which Pippin attempts to find meaning in his life through war, revolution, politics, sex, and home life. Pippin's story becomes a "play within a play" acted by a troupe of players who travel by caravan and are led by a senior member called the Old Man. The story is preceded by a telling of the tale of Peregrinus, who wandered the world seeking fulfillment but remained unsatisfied until he saw the eternal flame burning in honor of the gods at the athletic games of Mount Olympus and realized that fire would be the ultimate completion of his life.[5] Pippin finds no gratification in any of his endeavors, including his final attempt at family life with a young widow and her son, and returns to the players in the final scene. They urge him to emulate Peregrinus and set himself on fire in a final glorious blaze, but he resists and ultimately chooses to remain with the widow and seek satisfaction in domestic comforts.

Pippin eventually found its way to producer Stuart Ostrow, whose award-winning *1776* was still running on Broadway. Ostrow had recently been disappointed in his attempts to secure Bob Dylan to write a new musical and was on the alert for a show with a fresh, contemporary score that would appeal to a youth audience.[6] Having previously worked for Frank Loesser, Ostrow knew Bob Fosse from *How to Succeed in Business without Really Trying.* Ostrow approached Fosse, then supervising the editing of *Cabaret,* who agreed to direct and choreograph the show for the following Broadway season.

In an interview before rehearsals began, Fosse expressed unbridled enthusiasm for the show and for his return to the theater. "There were two things about this show which excited me. First, I wanted to get back to Broadway . . . . Some of the best experiences of my life have been on Broadway. And the show! I loved the score of *Godspell. Pippin* has been composed by the same boy, Stephen Schwartz. He's only twenty-five years old [Schwartz was actually twenty-three]," a fond chuckle from Fosse, "and some days he's only twelve. But he's a very talented person. I like his score very much."[7] This fatherly, indulgent observation would prove to be one of Fosse's last favorable comments about Schwartz.

There were several things about the show that must have appealed to Fosse at that moment. *Pippin*'s contemporary score by a young composer and its story of a young man searching for himself probably seemed just the right property to prove that Fosse could connect with newer, more contemporary sounds and themes. What Fosse later referred to as the "small-scaled and fey"[8] nature of the material would make it more easily molded and reshaped to his particular vision. Schwartz might have made a hit with the diminutive *Godspell,* but he was an unproven talent in the Broadway arena. Fosse would not expect him to pose the same kinds of challenges as Cy Coleman or Frank Loesser. As Schwartz's friend David Spangler reflected later, "[Fosse] just thought he'd whip Stephen into shape."[9]

Whereas Schwartz's opinions had been sought and respected by the *Godspell* cast and director, with *Pippin* his role was subsidiary to Fosse's. Schwartz later recalled, "The fact that I had done *Godspell* previously gave me a false impression because it was so much like a bunch of kids getting together in a barn and putting on a show . . . . And so, suddenly encountering how it really worked on Broadway was shocking to me. And it took me quite a while to catch up to it."[10] An early conflict came at the audition for dancers, when Schwartz's insistence on strong voices was rejected by Fosse. "Either I get my dancers or I quit," Fosse demanded, with Ostrow supporting him over Schwartz's objections.[11]

> "The cast will be small for a musical. About eighteen, dancers included. The dancing group will be small, but integrated into the production so they'll all play parts. There won't be any separate dancing chorus."
>
> Bob Fosse, 1972[12]

When Fosse held dance auditions for *Pippin,* he introduced a combination that soon became a talisman for Broadway dancers. In a brief five counts of eight, the dancer executes passé with long, lingering side port de bras; jumps from second position into entrechat quatre before landing in arabesque; and ends with a clean double pirouette. Set to Vincent Youman's "Tea for Two," from the musical *No, No, Nanette* (1925), it serves as a highly concentrated demonstration of basic ballet technique and jazz syncopation, allowing the dancer to reveal his or her individual style and personality.

Each Fosse audition would now begin with "Tea for Two," and dancers continue to marvel at its economy in revealing a dancer's skills. Linda Haberman, who would later dance for and assist Fosse, observed, "It was short, it was fast to teach and easy to pick up. But it showed a lot."[13] Diane Laurenson, who first worked with Fosse on *Dancin'*, said, "It's genius. You have within a fifteen second sound bite a chance to show a fully developed character and a fully trained technique in all aspects of dance."[14]

For *Pippin*, Fosse used improvisation to gauge a dancer's imagination, at one point requiring each to mime catching a bouncing balloon while executing a combination. Ann Reinking, a young dancer from Seattle, later recalled the experience of her first Fosse audition: "Mr. Fosse would guide us, encourage us, help us if we needed it. He told us when the improvisation was right and within the framework of the number, and he would also tell us when we were wrong. He watched our reactions both when we were praised and when we were corrected. He wanted to know if we trusted him. This was the most important criterion of them all. Trust was a big thing with Bob Fosse. Big."[15]

Pippin was conceived as an ensemble show, and the Players, as they were called, are integral to the plot as they tell its story through a series of scenes and songs. "In that show we were no longer chorus people. We were characters. We were in a troupe of strolling players . . . doing different things in the show," recalled dancer Gene Foote.[16] Three years before *A Chorus Line* listed dancers' names on lobby cards and select advertisements, *Pippin* initiated the practice, a breakthrough that gave chorus performers a higher profile than ever before. Fosse's insistence that they bring the same attention to their acting as to their dancing is reflected in a letter to the cast after the show had been running for some time: "Just try to remember all that we talked about as to 'what you represent' and what 'you should be playing' under all the razzle-dazzle & show-biz stuff . . . . So *very* much depends on *each of you acting* the numbers in addition to the singing & dancing— when you do it gives the show so much more weight—and makes it more than just entertaining."[17]

Most of the versatile group of ten dancers (plus two dance alternates, or "swings," who would substitute during absences) hired for *Pippin* would be involved in other Fosse shows during the 1970s. They included Roger A. Bigelow, Candy Brown, Christopher Chadman, Cheryl Clark, Kathryn Doby, Gene Foote, Richard Korthaze, John Mineo, Jennifer Nairn-Smith, Ann Reinking, Paul Solen, and Pamela Sousa. Along with a trusted team of designers and musical directors, they formed a loose repertory company for Fosse throughout the decade.[18]

Reinking's casting proved to be a turning point for both her and Fosse. Her appearance in *Pippin* led to her being cast in increasingly larger roles in several major shows, including the Andrews Sisters musical *Over Here!* (for which she won a Theatre World Award); *Goodtime Charley*, which earned her a Tony Award nomination as Joan of Arc opposite Joel Grey's Dauphin; and as the first replacement for Donna McKechnie in *A Chorus Line*. She would have a five-year personal relationship with Fosse, appear in both *Chicago* and *Dancin'*, and even play a version of herself in *All That Jazz*.[19] For Fosse, Reinking was a new, highly trained dance muse. Her superb technical skills and the precise, elegant line of her dancing influenced a change in Fosse's choreography as he adopted a more lyrical, self-serious approach that his dance vocabulary was not always able to support. Reinking came to embody a new Fosse style, and many of his female dancers appeared to be cast in her image. Icy, earnest, unsmiling—these would increasingly be the touchstones for Fosse's dance style.

In keeping with Schwartz's contemporary pop-rock score and the youthful focus of its story, casting director Michael Shurtleff initially assembled a list of performers seldom seen in the vicinity of Shubert Alley. For the title character, Arlo Guthrie, John Denver, and Mac Davis were sought, along with teen heartthrobs current (David Cassidy of television's *Partridge Family*) and past (Peter Noone of 1960s band Herman's Hermits, and David "Davey" Jones from the Monkees). For Catherine, the widow who eventually persuades Pippin to settle with her and her young son, he envisioned Carly Simon or Judy Collins. Soul and pop singer Freda Payne, Paula Kelly, late of Fosse's *Sweet Charity* film, and rising star Bette Midler were sought to play Pippin's stepmother, the devious Fastrada, a sexy, domestic femme fatale. Ultimately, these roles were cast with more traditional theater performers. Young John Rubinstein, the son of pianist Arthur Rubinstein, and nearly the same age as Schwartz, was cast in the title role. For Catherine, who arrives late in the show, Fosse felt that an actress with "movie star quality"[20] was required in order to make a strong impression, and he selected Jill Clayburgh over more experienced singing actresses. As Fastrada, Fosse cast young dancer-singer Leland Palmer, who resembled Gwen Verdon and had a similarly piquant comic manner.

For the Old Man, the leader of *Pippin*'s Players, a suitable character actor who could dance was sought. Disappointed at the auditions, Shurtleff called in Ben Vereen, a young black singer-dancer who had danced for Fosse in both the Las Vegas company and film version of *Sweet Charity*. Since then he had appeared on Broadway in *Hair* and *Jesus Christ Superstar*. Vereen's audition, for which he crafted dialogue for the Old Man around a series of songs and dances, convinced everyone that their previous conception of the role would have to be adjusted. As Shurtleff later recalled, "For the first time, our 'Old Man' came to life in the person of a young, sexy, humorous black actor who was an irresistible singer and dancer."[21] The Leading Player became the focus for Fosse's reshaping of *Pippin* and proved to be the source of much of the conflict between him and Schwartz.

The Leading Player is, in fact, the first person to appear in "Magic to Do." Rather than the Old Man pulling a caravan onstage from which the Players enter, as in earlier drafts, *Pippin* begins with a blackened stage across which the Players' hands appear to float. The image immediately establishes the mystical, ghostlike world of the Players. Lighting designer Jules Fisher achieved the effect by creating a curtain of light through which the Players would emerge. As he later explained, "There was a case of Bob saying, 'I have a picture, I have an image of their hands floating in space.' And from there, I figured out how to do it. But the idea of lighting just their hands was his."[22] The Players croon to Schwartz's syncopated vamp as the Leading Player's face appears out of the smoky darkness, inviting the audience to join them. Slowly they materialize through the light curtain until all appear across the stage, joyously welcoming the audience to their "anecdotic revue." Their costumes are a blend of contemporary and era-defying elements. The women's flowing scarves and fabric panels open to reveal bare midriffs and plunging necklines. A male dancer appears shirtless with flesh-colored tights and codpiece. Clown white make-up, headpieces, and commedia-style masks complete the circus-like quality of the costumes.

Fosse's direction to the Players for their entrance was to "make love to the audience,"[23] recalled Gene Foote, and from their first appearance they make it clear that the magic they do will include an erotic element. "Magic to Do" establishes the pelvic thrust as *Pippin*'s foundational choreographic movement, to be presented in every possible variation—back to front, side to side, slow grind, or rapid fire pulses—and in a mix of styles, from vintage burlesque to contemporary frug. *Pippin* inaugurated a new phase in Fosse's choreography, highlighted by a slower, more erotic style of movement. As Foote noted, "Bob said, 'When you move, I want you to move as though you're moving against water.' It does something to your body . . . . it's sexy to resist movement."[24] The undulating

Pippin's Players first appear out of darkness as disembodied hands under the direction of Ben Vereen. Photo by Martha Swope © Billy Rose Theatre Division, The New York Public Library for the Performing Arts.

performers in costumes of indeterminate period bring a disconcerting quality to their welcome. They seldom move in unison but instead maintain a loose, improvisational style.

"Magic to Do" is driven by the Leading Player, who stands apart in both dress and demeanor. His entirely black ensemble of tuxedo pants, jacket, vest, and ruffled shirt, with only the whites of his spats breaking the palette, looks like a costume Sammy Davis Jr. might wear on a Las Vegas stage, and mimics Fosse's by-now standard all-black personal attire. He is the only Player who does not wear a mask, facial paint, or headdress, and he always occupies center stage. During an instrumental break, as the Players cross the stage, welcoming the audience and attempting to draw comments and reactions from them, Fosse introduces an element of danger, one that indicates the evening will not be all mischievous playacting. Gene Foote remembered, "Bob told me on the third step to throw my head back and laugh hysterically out of nowhere, and then go right back to my talking . . . . and we scared that audience to death."[25] Soon the stage erupts with sinister laughter as the Players mime magic tricks and circus stunts before the Leading Player pulls them back to center for a final group bow, concluding an opening number that marks *Pippin* as a musical by turns insinuating, erotic, and menacing.

Fosse took *Pippin* out of its medieval setting and turned it into an evening's entertainment performed by the Players for that night's audience. While its story takes place over multiple days and across different locations, it is performed in real time, thus giving it a greater urgency.

The role of the Leading Player was increasingly utilized to introduce new scenes and offer sardonic asides, frequently using contemporary black slang and slogans. This shifts the focus from Pippin to the telling of his story by the Players, emphasizing the episodic nature of the script and the performative aspect of the show. Ben Vereen's performance conjured up an entire gallery of characters both ingratiating and vaguely threatening, including the Emcee in *Cabaret*, *Porgy and Bess*'s Sportin' Life, the Devil from *Damn Yankees*, and Cab Calloway's "Hi De Ho" bandleader, further underscoring *Pippin*'s show business framework.

Until the penultimate "Hearth" sequence that leads into the finale, the episodes in Pippin's life could be presented in any order, and Fosse treats each as a separate set piece with a different staging style. He made continuous use of anachronisms through costumes, dialogue, and movement, borrowing from several decades of entertainment forms, including burlesque, vaudeville, minstrel shows, radio broadcasts, and soap opera. *Pippin* was certainly his most deliberately theatrical and nonrealistic show to date.

Harold Prince's back-to-back collaborations with Stephen Sondheim on *Company* and *Follies*, both of which were told in nonlinear fashion, with songs that commented on the action, and utilized metaphoric production design, marked the full flowering of the concept musical in the 1970s. Musical theater historian James Leve writes that as the musical lost cultural currency to other entertainment forms in the 1960s, it became more self-referential. It was at this moment, he argues, that "the concept musical emerged as a viable means of responding to changes in the status of the musical and of addressing a wider range of social concerns."[26] Theater historian John Bush Jones, who prefers the term "fragmented musicals," has emphasized their "focus on individual characters (pre)occupied with personal introspection."[27] Jones positions fragmented musicals as emblematic of the 1970s, when, weary of political scandals, disappointed by government, and frustrated by economic downturns, Americans turned to introspection rather than public engagement.

Fosse's Broadway musicals of the 1970s are representative of all these ideas. *Pippin*'s protagonist views major issues of war, religion, and social justice through his own narrow perspective. *Chicago*'s Roxie Hart is oblivious to the implications of the roiling tabloid world in which her story takes place. Both shows are constructed around self-conscious, quasi-Brechtian staging concepts that emphasize a show business framework. It was during this period, as musical theater historian Ken Mandelbaum later noted, that "[Fosse's] staging assumed such importance that the work of the composer, lyricist, and librettist was sometimes curtailed or distorted to allow more time for the Fosse magic."[28]

Fosse's most trusted collaborators were now designers. Fosse's preproduction work with Schwartz and Hirson was markedly different from his work with his design team, made up of Tony Walton (sets), Patricia Zipprodt (costumes), and Jules Fisher (lighting), partly because, as Schwartz later remembered, Fosse spoke in visual concepts as opposed to words. As Schwartz explained, "Bob was not a very verbal man, which is odd because he had great friends who were writers. But he was impatient with writers and he didn't really speak our language. So it was hard to actually have a discussion with him about a scene or a concept where you were talking about the underlying ideas of it. It was like talking to someone who spoke a different language."[29]

Nevertheless, Fosse and Hirson did a great deal of work on the book, and it was Hirson whose idea it was to meld bits of dialogue to create the role of the Leading Player for Ben Vereen. The conflicts between Fosse and Hirson stemmed from Fosse's desire to add more contemporary humor to *Pippin*. Hirson later noted that the two words he heard most frequently from Fosse were "'more jokes.' . . . I just couldn't give him what he wanted. He kept looking at me with a look that said, 'Why don't I have Doc [Neil] Simon down here?'"[30] Fosse's drive to make *Pippin* hipper and more impertinent led him to do some rewriting on his own. Hirson pointed to a line of dialogue in which Fastrada tells Charlemagne that her son, Lewis, loves him. Hirson's line for Charlemagne, "Lewis is an ass," was changed by Fosse to "Lewis is an asshole." The change resulted in a much bigger laugh, though it troubled Hirson. He said, "I wince when I hear it. I just don't think it's funny."[31]

In contrast, Fosse's work with his designers was described by Zipprodt as "a marvelously elastic and comfortable relationship."[32] Zipprodt acknowledged that Fosse was not always able to articulate what he wanted, but ironically this worked to her advantage in drawing out his ideas. Fosse wanted the Players' costumes to be "magical" and "anachronistic"; when pressed to elaborate, he responded, "Jesus Christ with tennis shoes."[33] This image gave Zipprodt the freedom to mix styles and historical periods into a grand, theatrical amalgam. Fisher, who would design lighting for all of Fosse's remaining musicals, had an equally positive collaboration with him. As Fisher recalled, "He was keenly aware of light. This is one way that he's different from many other directors . . . . he really understood what it does. And he could offer ideas that would spur me to a better solution."[34]

Walton, who also designed the striking advertising posters for *Pippin* and *Chicago*, described the "extraordinary trust" involved in his working relationship with Fosse.[35] His designs for both shows conveyed Fosse's determination to expand the limitations of the proscenium stage by employing proscenium ladders from which characters appeared (in *Pippin*) and elevators and staircases into the orchestra pit (in *Chicago*).

Walton and Fosse establish *Pippin*'s sense of magic and surprise early in the show with the transition from the opening sequence into Charlemagne's castle. The Leading Player takes out a red handkerchief, balls it up in his fist, and makes it disappear. Immediately from downstage center a spotlight picks up the handkerchief sticking up from the stage. As the Leading Player begins to pull at it, it becomes not a handkerchief but a lavish crimson sash that swiftly rises out of the floor, attached to a loose, ropey frame representing the outlines of the castle and its regal banners. A colorful backdrop descends from upstage as the Players dance in with additional set pieces. In less than a minute, Walton and Fosse transform the bare stage into a lavish royal court.

Fosse gathered a few dancers for preproduction sessions in which he would try out steps and movement patterns, often to music unrelated to the score. Both Stephen Schwartz and Tony Walton remember one of Fosse's favorite pieces of music being "Let the Good Times Roll," written by Shirley Goodman and Leonard Lee and recorded by many singers since its debut in 1956. It was this music that Fosse used to create a trio dance to be featured as an interlude during "Glory," in the show's "War" sequence. When Fosse called in the design team to preview this number, Tony Walton remembers, "Jules and I looked at each other at the end of it, and said to Pat, 'Oh my God. He's going to make this show work after all . . . . His take on it was so mischievous and erotic and inviting and dark— something you didn't get a true sense of from just hearing the score."[36] Stephen Schwartz also admired the dance and wrote a new piece of music whose loping, calliope-style rhythms came to be known as "The Manson Trio" and echoed Harry Nilsson's version of "Let the Good Times Roll."[37]

"The Manson Trio" is just one highlight of the "War" sequence, which follows Pippin's initiation into the planning and execution of battle strategies. Fosse uses a series of show business tropes to stage this sequence of carnage and destruction, effectively mocking the platitudes and contradictions voiced by Charlemagne and, by association, those of the United States in maintaining troops in Vietnam.

"War Is a Science" begins with two dancers entering on opposite sides of the stage performing as minstrel show "tambos" (so called for their performance with tambourines). Their simple cakewalk serves as a crossover scene change into the king's war room, where a tactical meeting is performed as a minstrel show, with the Players as the minstrel line, Charlemagne as interlocutor, and Pippin as an inept end man. The Players perform their synchronized foot tapping and knee slapping with an aggressive, sarcastic energy that frequently erupts into chaos. Fosse punctuates Charlemagne's patter lyrics with interjections from the Players (added against the wishes of both Schwartz and Hirson): "Yuck, yuck," "Doo da, doo da," "Skidoo," "Hotcha," and more.

As the soldiers go off to war (dancing a sprightly soft-shoe) and Charlemagne prays for victory, the Leading Player enters, singing of "battles, barbarous and bloody."[38] Thus begins "Glory," a tour de force set piece that draws on several decades of performance styles for a scathing, if unsubtle, comment on the blood-lust of war. Originally conceived as a kind of *Carmina Burana* chorus number, it was considerably changed to take advantage of Ben Vereen's dancing and singing style.[39] With straw hat and cane, he performs in the full-throated, assertive man-ner of Al Jolson, tossing his head back and throwing open his arms, but punctu-ating each phrase with a series of exaggerated pelvic bumps. The Players form a traveling battle tableau complete with impaled soldier, and they too embellish each musical phrase with pelvic bumps (as does the impaled soldier). As the lyrics become more bloodthirsty ("Shout it out from the highest tower / Shout it out in the darkest hour / Charlemagne, you lead us on to power!"), the staging takes on a frenzied, "hard sell" quality, with aggressive struts and teasing stripper walks. The Leading Player is soon flanked by two female Players using their spears in the style of strip club pole dancers, bumping, grinding, and fondling their spears as they sing, "War is strict as Jesus / War is finer than Spring / Service to Christ and to our King." (For the "War" sequence, Zipprodt designed breastplates made from layers of latex, for ease of movement, with breast-and-nipple details and dangling chains from the crotch.)

The scene soon segues into a mock radio station (call letters, W-A-R), with the Players gathered around microphones for a sprightly verse in the radio-era style of the Andrews Sisters. An applause sign is lowered as the singing fades and a voice-over by the Leading Player lists, *Hit Parade*–style, casualties throughout the history of war.

"The Manson Trio" follows and is the centerpiece of the "War" sequence. Fosse's choice of title is significant. Only the year before, Charles Manson and members of his "family," a loosely formed group of hippies and hangers-on at the fringes of the Los Angeles music scene, had been found guilty of the gruesome 1969 murders of several people, including actress Sharon Tate.

The Leading Player, as a stand-in for Manson, and two female Players take center stage with straw hats and canes, bow to the audience, and assume poses that have come to signify Fosse: feet turned in, hips cocked, shoulders sloped, head turned away from the audience and gazing down at the floor. To Schwartz's insinuating calliope tune, they keep time to the rhythm with their pelvises, first slowly, then in double time. The constantly pulsating pelvis is the engine that drives "The Manson Trio," as Fosse takes vaudeville traveling steps, grapevines, and struts and turns them sinister. Tension builds as the dancers move their shoulders and legs in opposition, sometimes smoothly, other times jaggedly, like broken dolls. As they swivel and glide across the stage, the other Players mime scenes of carnage—stabbings, beheadings, throat slittings. The trio slithers along amid the slaughter, pelvises in continuous motion. Their faces are often cast downward or hidden by their hats, but when fully visible their look is merry, grinning, self-satisfied. Only as the music winds down and their movements begin to slow do they lose their grins and appear apprehensive, as if the import of what they have presided over has slowly dawned on them. The number concludes with a big, hats-off, vaudeville-style bow, but a tentative "ta da!" Staging yet another of his tight trio numbers, Fosse creates a soft-shoe dance of death.

Before this association can settle in, the Leading Player sits, like Judy Garland on the edge of the Palace Theater stage, and begins to sing in a broad, emotive manner, "War is strict as Jesus / War is finer than Spring." But each line is interrupted by loud, carnival sideshow music as body parts (arms, heads, limbs, torsos) are thrown onstage. With the Players sifting through the casualties, he takes center stage to announce, Jolson-style, "You ain't seen nothin' yet, folks!" and leads the Players into one final chorus, in the down-on-one-knee manner of Jolson's performance of "Mammy."[40] As a blood-tinged shadow of Charlemagne is projected against the back wall, the number spirals into a frenzy of bumps, grinds, and burlesque shimmies, with the Players again on one knee amid the body parts, arms outstretched in a "big finish" pose, begging for the thunderous ovation it inevitably receives.

Pippin's "War" sequence revisits the comic mood of Fosse's war ballet from *The Conquering Hero* but reflects a decade's worth of disillusionment. *The Conquering Hero*'s ballet displayed a comic, satiric view of wartime heroics. In 1972, with the Vietnam War slowly grinding down, Fosse chooses to ridicule the pieties surrounding war as a noble and gallant calling. Unlike Truesmith, who is an active, if accidental, participant in a war that still reverberated as one of American triumph, Pippin is largely absent from this battle fought by anonymous soldiers and with no greater good beyond empire-building. The humor is blunt and often sophomoric, but Fosse draws dance, song, and dialogue into a scathing indictment of the folly and hubris of war.

The most blatantly erotic of *Pippin*'s musical numbers arrives in the "Flesh" sequence. Out in the country and encouraged by Berthe to enjoy "sex presented pastorally," the number begins with Schwartz's "With You," a soft rock ballad extolling the pleasures of sexual exclusivity. Working with great simplicity, Fosse uses slow, lyrical movements to create elegant stage pictures for a small ensemble of five dancers. Fosse's effortless shifting of bodies into simple, symmetrical formations carries a graceful inevitability reminiscent of George Balanchine. The girls frame Pippin, lying at his feet or undulating above him. Their arm movements, mirroring each other, create a kind of Kama Sutra environment, at once romantic and licentious. The girls quietly move Pippin onto his hands and knees, and he is slowly mounted by a girl waving a cowboy hat and exclaiming, "Yahoo!" The pace and drive of the number accelerates as it moves into a section referred to as the "Gisella Ballet," after the generic name originally assigned to all the female Players.

A calypso-styled dance for three girls, meant to tease and provoke Pippin, features a full complement of distinctive Fosse moves. The dancers travel restlessly

"Sex presented pastorally." Pippin's initiation into sex begins with a Kama Sutra–like tableau. Left to right: Jennifer Nairn-Smith, Pamela Sousa, John Rubinstein, Candy Brown (rear), Ann Reinking, and Kathryn Doby. Photo by Martha Swope © Billy Rose Theatre Division, The New York Public Library for the Performing Arts.

across the stage, sometimes with flexed arms, shoulder rolls, and neck extensions, and other times using Fosse's favorite traveling mambo step. A number of other familiar Fosse moves can be spotted here; in fact, he references them in his choreographic notes. Many are from his recent *Liza with a Z*: "Lots of 'Preacher Man'— works slowly"; "Liza's in 'Gotcha' (sexy funny) . . . Feet in—out like Charleston. Hands on Hips. Open palms are 'out' with feet"; "Good for sex thing with changes— the 'Gotcha' muscle spasms"; "Half horse prance from 'Preacher Man.'"[41]

With the addition of the male dancers, now stripped to the waist, the dance becomes one of urgent, relentless hedonism. Pippin is positioned in front of a keyhole through which he watches two girls perform a leering, lesbian mating dance. ("You gotta see this!" he gleefully advises the audience.) The girls daintily caress each other's breasts, crotches, and buttocks and writhe in simulated ecstasy. They draw Pippin into a threesome, positioning him on his back so that one can mount him while the other holds a mirror over him, offering a better view. Next, the dancers surround him with a giant opium pipe and, when he is thoroughly stoned, encourage him to spank one of the girls, setting off shrieks of orgasmic bliss. The men pick him up by his arms and legs and rhythmically lower him while the girls roll underneath, to simulate intercourse. One rolls under him on her stomach to simulate anal sex, producing a "What is this?" look from Pippin to the audience.

The music becomes even more frenzied. The dancers surround the increasingly exhausted Pippin as the Leading Player runs through the action dressed as a motorcycle cop and blowing a whistle, as if investigating illicit activity. The dance climaxes with one of Fosse's favorite backward stag leaps, a body roll across the floor, three rapid head rolls, and a final pose on the knees, bracing the upper body on extended arms—as if in anticipation of some undisclosed sexual activity. What began as a gentle, pastoral introduction to sex becomes frantic, anonymous sexual gymnastics that leave Pippin weary and unsatisfied. The near-farcical variety of sexual positions, groupings, and acrobatics that Fosse crowds into this number could be read as both a comment on the new sexual permissiveness of the time and a reflection of his own interests.

(Fosse did create a hilarious and ingenious routine to portray Catherine and Pippin's first sexual encounter. As the pair disappears under the covers, a man and woman enter on either side of the stage. To thundering "Bolero"-style music, they each caress their own bodies, seething with pent-up desire. As the music reaches a crescendo, the woman leaps into the man's arms. But their timing is off, and they collapse in an awkward pile on the floor. As they crawl offstage, Catherine and Pippin sheepishly peer from the covers, each apologizing and promising that next time will be better. Back under the covers they go, as the music begins again and the two dancers reappear, reprising their exaggerated foreplay. But this time the jump and landing are gracefully executed and they exit in triumph, having reached completion. Catherine and Pippin reappear from the covers with a look of contentment on their faces.)

Like many Americans, the now middle-aged Fosse was sampling new freedoms, and his art served as a platform for his experimentation. Fosse was, in the day's parlance, a "swinger." His separation from Gwen Verdon was attributable by many, including Fosse himself, to his affairs and compulsive work habits.[42] He spoke freely of his drug intake and his affairs, and later described this period in detail: "I did cocaine and a lot of Dexedrine. I'd wake up in the morning, pop a pill. After lunch, when I couldn't get going, I'd pop another one, and if I wanted to work all night, still another one. There was a certain romanticism about that stuff. There was Bob drinking and smoking and turning out good work. Still popping pills and screwing around with the girls."[43]

Fosse's always-apparent appreciation for women became more pronounced. His statuesque dancers were costumed more revealingly than those in other musicals of the period. And they exhibited sexually aggressive personas; there were no blushing maidens among his casts. Jules Fisher later evoked "Hogarth and the painters of the flesh" in discussing Fosse's presentation of women onstage.[44] According to Fisher, "He loved women. And he loved the human body, and he wanted it sculpted onstage. And his own personal interest in women came out in the productions."[45]

In all the numerous references by critics to the provocative nature of his choreography, there is seldom criticism of Fosse's presentation of female dancers. Fosse had the luxury of hiring the very best dancers, and his practice of using many of them from show to show meant they were steeped in his dance style. His dances were also dramatically coherent and required an actor's thought process, as Kathryn Doby remembered: "I can't tell you one number of Bob's where there isn't some kind of subtext. That was the wonderful thing about it—he made actors out of dancers."[46] Candy Brown agreed, saying, "We had purpose. He treated us like actors. I always say he was my first acting teacher."[47] While Fosse's female dancers appeared positively Amazonian, he often cast male dancers who were either slight and bore some resemblance to him, or short and pugnacious. It is easy to identify his male dancers as stand-ins for himself and his female dancers as the embodiments of his feminine ideal.

In a coda to the number, as the dancers saunter offstage, one of the men pinches Pippin on his posterior and gives him a look of invitation, thus indicating another sexual option. The moment is indicative of a change in Fosse's approach to working with gay male dancers, as he discussed in an interview soon after *Pippin* opened: "Always before, if I found a male dancer that I knew was homosexual, I would keep saying, no, you can't do that, don't be so minty there. This time, I used the kind of people they were to give the show a kind of individuality, and they were so happy about it I think it helped the show."[48] It was a bold statement considering the casual, unquestioned homophobia of the time. This most heterosexual of director-choreographers was not shy in admitting his own anxieties about homosexuality during his youth: "There were many men I found really attractive. I sometimes thought, 'Is there some latent tendency in me I'm unaware of?' But I never found it a big problem for me, never."[49] Fosse's frankness was startling. No other figure of his stature in the musical theater was discussing this topic, as it pertained either to him or to his dancers.

This did not stop Fosse from indulging in stereotypes or using homosexuality as a punch line. "Ya dumb fruit!" *Chicago*'s Billy Flynn sneers at a limp-wristed tailor.[50] An early draft of *Sweet Charity* featured an effeminate character among its Central Park citizens, and as late as *Big Deal* in 1986, Fosse fell back on stereotypical "fag" humor with a "minty" inmate in a prison scene. In *All That Jazz*, Fosse alter ego Joe Gideon confronts his girlfriend about going out with another man, smugly questioning, "Is he looking to get laid or is he looking for Mr. Right?" Gideon is later challenged about his preoccupation with sex: "That sex thing. Jesus. Listen, I wouldn't say you're a faggot, but you do have a lot of feminine characteristics, right?" Gideon's reply ("Right") allows Fosse to have it both ways by showing that he's capable of being perceived as gay without threat to his ego, while still getting in a "fag" joke—all in an exchange that doesn't entirely make sense. At the same time, Fosse demonstrates a sophistication and perception about the complexities of sexual attraction regardless of orientation. In *All That Jazz*, a single look between a producer and a young male dancer speaks as much about the power dynamic and attraction between them as an entire subplot charting Gideon's involvement with a female dancer.

As warm as his working relationships were with his dancers and designers, Fosse's collaboration with Stephen Schwartz remained one of conflict. Two numbers illustrate much of the creative discord between the two men. Schwartz had written Berthe's "No Time at All" as a song celebrating the pleasures of life regardless of age, intending it to derive its humor from being a rock number performed by an old lady. Fosse's conception was more traditional and age-appropriate. Schwartz later described the conflict over the number: "I walked in one day and she was doing it as straight vaudeville. We had a fight about it and they said, 'If she does it this way she'll stop the show.' I didn't care about her stopping the show. I just didn't like it."[51] "No Time at All" did indeed stop the show, as Fosse's staging transformed it into a sing-a-long for Berthe and the entire audience, complete with lights up in the theater auditorium. Tony Walton flew in a lyric sheet, written in medieval script, and Jules Fisher traced the lyrics with a follow-the-bouncing-ball light. The number was a charmingly old-fashioned highlight of the sexy, high-powered musical.

Catherine's introductory number, "Kind of Woman," allows her to extol her homespun virtues to Pippin ("For I'm just a plain, everyday / Commonplace, come-what-may / Average, ordinary / Wonderful girl!") in a lilting waltz. Fosse was not fond of the number, and after trying various staging ideas, he decided to cut it. As Schwartz later recalled, "We tried a performance without it, and I thought it undercut the character too much. So standing on my right as the author, I insisted it be put back in. And then he did, I thought, quite a campy staging of it, which was not my favorite."[52] In Fosse's staging, Catherine is joined by a haloed trio in Shirley Temple wigs adding chirping vocals. Other Players enter tossing confetti, shooting Cupid arrows at Pippin, and performing mock-ballet moves punctuated with shimmies. The number climaxes with Catherine executing Jeanette MacDonald–style trills and posing inside a large floral display. "Kind of Woman" is just the sort of earnest declaration Fosse disliked, and he undercut its sincerity with parodistic staging. It must have seemed to Schwartz that Fosse was mocking not only the song but also Schwartz.

These scrimmages between Schwartz and Fosse (and Stuart Ostrow, who generally sided with Fosse in artistic disagreements) pointed to a fundamental difference in each man's vision. Schwartz and Hirson's gentle *Pippin* was the antithesis of Fosse's hard-driving Broadway approach. Fosse wanted the show faster, funnier, hipper, more irreverent, and loaded with numbers that "landed." And he was not shy about asserting his prerogative. As Jules Fisher recalled, "Bob's attitude was, 'I've done many shows. This is your first on Broadway. And you're going to follow my lead.'"[53] Fosse was the true "Muscle" on *Pippin*, backed by a producer who shared his vision and wanted a crowd-pleasing hit.

A notable example of congenial collaboration between the two men was a number written at Fosse's request for Pippin and the Leading Player. Schwartz returned with "On the Right Track," a song of encouragement by the Leading Player sung to Pippin. As Schwartz later remembered, "He was in general, critical and not always kindly so, of my lyrics, which he felt were over-wordy and often over-rhymed, and he would sometimes make fun of them."[54] Fosse suggested that Schwartz remove as many lyrics as possible, and he would then fill in the spaces with movement. The number became a syncopated song and dance number staged back and forth across Jules Fisher's light curtain. Fosse interjected dialogue about Pippin's continuing search for meaning in his life, and "On the Right Track" would be the only time in the show that the two characters performed together. Schwartz recalled, "I thought it was a really creative way to deal with the song . . . . I no longer remember what those extra words were, but clearly, they were filler because they weren't necessary. And the whole thing was a pretty happy collaboration."[55]

This momentary detente was in pleasant contrast to the creative battles over *Pippin*'s finale. When Pippin escapes from the confines of a life with Catherine and her son Theo on her estate, he encounters the Players waiting for him. Schwartz and Hirson's script ended with Pippin resisting the Players' call to set himself on fire in a final burst of glory, instead reuniting with his new family. Fosse rejected this sober ending. "I said the boy must be tempted by suicide—I'm fascinated by suicide," he said.[56] Fosse infused the finale with what he called "sexual, tribal insanity"[57] that underscored the Machiavellian purpose of the Players, and especially the Leading Player, in denying Pippin the fulfillment he sought throughout the evening, thus leading him to the "the final affirmation of life . . . death!" (a line provided by Fosse's friend Paddy Chayefsky).[58]

Fosse confirms his conception of the finale and its meaning in a letter to the *Pippin* cast well into the show's Broadway run, in which he gives notes on a recent performance: "Make self-immolation or suicide seem attractive, exciting and extremely sexual . . . . When the finale is right you can make the audience . . . feel that possibly a grand suicide would be a sexual—fulfilling—religious experience. This is not my philosophy (ha ha); it is only what I'm asking you to try to illicite [*sic*] from some part of that audience. I read a statistic somewhere where six people out of every ten have at one point considered suicide. Get me those six!"[59]

(Kathryn Doby recalled that an occasional audience member would heed the Players' invitation and come up onstage. "The first time it happened, we didn't know what to do with the person. So we just kind of surrounded him and we took him offstage. It was pretty wild.")[60]

Sneeringly calling Pippin a "coward" and a "compromiser," the Players strip the stage of all sets and lights—all "magic"—and remove the theatrical costumes and make-up of Pippin, Theo, and Catherine. The Leading Player hastily improvises a final pitch to the audience, encouraging someone to take Pippin's place and set himself on fire. With no volunteers, the Players unceremoniously exit, taking with them the final remnant of theatrical enchantment. ("You try singing without music, sweetheart!") Left in silent darkness with just a work light, Pippin is surrounded by his new family. Catherine asks him how he feels, and his final line of dialogue, for which Fosse took credit,[61] is "Trapped . . . but happy . . . (He looks from one to the other and smiles) which isn't too bad for the end of a musical comedy. Ta da! (They bow as the curtain comes down.)"

Fosse's ending is a tacit acknowledgment that Pippin's new life, while stable and comforting, will never have the theatrical magic and excitement that the Players could provide. It also allows Fosse to present a traditional, boy-gets-girl ending while simultaneously sending it up. Pippin's final line got a laugh when it was used during the show's tryout in Washington, DC. But as the show approached its Broadway opening, Fosse feared that New Yorkers would fault the show for being too soft and sentimental, and he attempted to toughen up *Pippin* during its New York preview period by eliminating the "but happy" in the last line. Predictably, Ostrow approved while Schwartz and Hirson objected strenuously.

The shortened line stayed throughout the entire Broadway run but came to crystallize all the conflicts between Schwartz and Fosse.

Pippin arrived at the Imperial Theater on October 23, 1972, between the openings of *Dude* (with music by Galt MacDermot and lyrics by Gerome Ragni) and *Via Galactica* (with music by MacDermot and lyrics by Christopher Gore). Both were bloated, incoherent spectacles for which even Clive Barnes could muster little enthusiasm. Like *Pippin*, they embraced similar themes of virtuous yet disaffected young men searching for meaning and rebelling against authority. (*Via Galactica* did it in a futuristic setting played on trampolines, *Dude* in a theater transformed into a dirt heap.) Whatever they had to say about contemporary issues was lost in confusion and pretension. In contrast, Bob Fosse trumped Broadway's other "youth musicals" by using his knowledge and understanding of a whole history of show business to stage a story with contemporary themes and a pop-rock score. It was a case of current words and music enriched by old-fashioned theatrical craftsmanship.

Fosse was accustomed to receiving high praise for his work, but *Pippin*'s reviews pointed to a new maturity, a total mastery of staging that he had not previously achieved. Martin Gottfried in *Women's Wear Daily* asserted, "No musical has been so completely choreographed-directed since 'Follies,' every facet timed, meshed and coordinated into a colorful, magical, musical, rhythmic body . . . . a seamless fabric of dance and musical staging."[62]

Pippin was an instant hit, settling in for a run that eventually totaled 1,944 performances—Fosse's longest-running show. While *A Little Night Music* won the Best Musical Tony Award, the 1972–1973 ceremonies were a particular triumph for Fosse, who won for both his choreography and direction. The Tonys were the first of the season's awards presentations that would ultimately bring Fosse the triple crown of show business awards. Days later he would receive the Academy Award for *Cabaret*, and several weeks later he would win three Emmy Awards for *Liza with a Z*. But in a directorial career that started and would end on the Broadway stage and include a total of nine Tony Awards, *Pippin* was Fosse's only win for Best Director.

Pippin ended its run in 1977 as the seventh-longest-running show in Broadway history. The reason for its longevity had much to do with Stuart Ostrow's decision to create a television commercial, something he had previously done with only limited success for 1776.[63] The sixty-second spot, directed by Fosse, focused on one of *Pippin*'s key elements, its sexy dancing. An announcer intones, "Here's a free minute from *Pippin*, Broadway's musical comedy sensation directed by Bob Fosse," as Ben Vereen, Candy Brown, and Pamela Sousa perform a portion of "The Manson Trio" in front of the show curtain. Near the end, the announcer returns and says, "You can see the other 119 minutes live at the Imperial Theater. Without commercial interruption."[64] *Pippin* had already been playing for nearly a year and paid back its investors when, like many long-running shows, its business began to soften. Its box-office rebound was attributable to its commercial, which began airing in September 1973 in the New York metropolitan area.[65] The commercial (which won the advertising industry's Clio Award in 1974) not only increased the show's profits and extend its run but also immediately created a new marketing tool for Broadway. All subsequent Fosse musicals would feature elaborate commercials directed by him.

With *Pippin* firmly established as a hit, and with all the honors coming his way, it might have been expected that Fosse would soften in regard to Schwartz, but that was not the case. He candidly stated, "I had trouble with Schwartz—we fought all the way . . . . He's said he'd never work with me again. Let's just say I wouldn't be eager. I think he's very talented. But not as talented as he thinks he is."[66] Nor was Schwartz shy about airing his grievances to the press, calling the show "one of the worst experiences of my life."[67]

The acrimony was accelerated in early 1973 when Schwartz entered into an agreement to present an Australian production with substantial changes to *Pippin*'s libretto. "None of them represent new material, only previously discarded bits of dialogue and song fragments," Ostrow wrote to his attorney, adding, "The show he envisions is a remnant of his school days and his insistence we return to it has been destructive."[68] These changes sought to "De-Fosse" the show by reducing the size and importance of the role of the Leading Player and placing greater focus on the character of Pippin. Eventually the dispute was taken to arbitration, with Schwartz winning a two-to-one decision allowing him to go forward with the Australian production and upholding his right to make those script revisions.[69] The Australian *Pippin* thus featured Schwartz's revised script with staging by American director-choreographer Sammy Bayes. A London production staged by Fosse adhered to the Broadway script. Neither proved successful.[70]

A posthearing brief prepared by Ostrow's attorneys confirmed that Schwartz's revised script contained 109 changes, all of them initiated by Schwartz. Roger Hirson did not seek the changes to the libretto, nor did he have objections to it being staged in Australia.[71] A copy of Schwartz's revised script with numerous and scathing marginal notations by Fosse underscores the two men's different approaches to the material. Schwartz's changes included the removal of numerous asides and interjections from the Leading Player, many of which were "black slang" expressions.[72] The "War" sequence was heavily cut, including all the "yuck yuck" interjections in "War Is a Science," which Fosse annotates as "essential to minstrel show concept." Many of Schwartz's changes included removing dialogue in which the actors step out of character and highlight the show's concept of a troupe of actors performing Pippin's story.

The most sweeping of Schwartz's changes were to the "Hearth" sequence with Catherine. Most of her out-of-character asides were cut, to which Fosse responded, "Helps create her scatterbrained actress character." The Leading Player's attempt to stop Catherine's final song—"Hey, you haven't got no song here!"—was eliminated, drawing this plaintive comment from Fosse: "Wonderful line—whole concept is inherent—why, why?" Finally, and unsurprisingly, Schwartz reinstated "but happy" into Pippin's final line. Fosse's final note, "The show was the 1st celebration of nihilism—that's new," captures the crux of their clash. Schwartz's youthful story of a boy's quest to go out in the world and find personal fulfillment pushed against Fosse's middle-aged skepticism about the meaning and purpose of life.

There had been no argument about Fosse's contribution to *Pippin*. The post-hearing brief noted that "Mr. Fosse's uncontradicted testimony is that he, himself, collaborated with Roger Hirson in writing text for the libretto, as well as structuring the Play and developing the concept of the Leading Player, described as the central core of the Broadway production."[73] Schwartz's revisions were the basis for the published libretto, which arrived in 1975 while the Broadway production was still running. Despite the changes, enough of Fosse's contributions remained that he wrote to Hirson, demanding to know "if you and Stephen found what I changed or wrote in *Pippin* so disagreeable . . . then why would you allow so much of it to be published under your name?"[74] It surely irked Fosse that despite his significant role in shaping this successful musical, he had no authorial rights over the material. It was a situation he did not take lightly, and *Pippin* would be the last Fosse musical not to carry his name as a writer.

Unlike so many of Fosse's hit shows, *Pippin* has yet to find its way to film, and part of the reason may have been Fosse's reluctance to revisit it for a new medium. As he later reflected, "I made a resolution after *Sweet Charity* never to do on screen what I've done on stage. People want me to make films of *Pippin*, *Chicago*, and *Dancin'*, but they are basically theater pieces not easily adaptable to the screen."[75] Fosse's indifference to a film version did not deter Stuart Ostrow from pursuing the idea, as he described in a memorandum titled, "PIPPIN Motion Picture Impressions."[76] Ostrow's concept of "a boy searching the world over for fulfillment"[77] allowed him to maintain the theatrical nature of the show by setting each sequence in a different, instantly recognizable theatrical venue. "Magic to Do" was envisioned as taking place at the Acropolis or Stonehenge. The "War" sequence would be performed everywhere from the Coliseum of Rome to Bob Hope's Vietnam tours, to the stage of the Palace Theater. Pippin's introduction to sex was set in Las Vegas and at Paris's Crazy Horse Saloon. His life with Catherine and Theo would be played out on an "Andy Hardy Street" on a Hollywood soundstage, evoking old movie images.[78]

Interestingly, Ostrow's concept is similar to that of screenwriter Bill Condon and director Rob Marshall for the 2002 film version of *Chicago* in which Roxie Hart imagines each event in her life played out as a musical number on a vaudeville stage. The self-conscious theatricality of both the Condon-Marshall *Chicago* and Ostrow's proposed *Pippin* film are methods for acknowledging the conceptual underpinnings of their source material.

While there has been no motion picture adaptation, *Pippin* was filmed in 1981 "as the first major Broadway play produced for the home video market."[79] Six cameras filmed three performances of a Hamilton, Ontario, production with Fosse's direction and choreography restaged by original cast member and dance assistant Kathryn Doby. The cast included Ben Vereen reprising his role as the Leading Player and several dancers who had appeared in the show during its Broadway run. The film was directed, produced, and edited by David Sheehan, who disregarded Fosse's editing notes and made indiscriminate cuts to fit a two-hour running time. This resulted in confusing internal cuts to musical numbers and a jarring sense of pace, making the production feel alternately rushed and lethargic. This version of *Pippin* is widely available on DVD, cable television, and the Internet and thus is the one most familiar to the largest audience. The participants disavowed it. Stephen Schwartz called it "frenetic" and "terrible,"[80] and Kathryn Doby said, "It was such a mess, no wonder nobody likes it."[81] It nonetheless captures key Fosse numbers like "Magic to Do" and "The Manson Trio" performed by dancers who had learned them directly from Fosse and his team, features the original designs, and documents the performance of Ben Vereen less than a decade after his creation of the role of Leading Player.

The *Pippin* video featured the Broadway version of the show with the disputed ending, excising "but happy" from Pippin's final lines. Several years later, Schwartz saw a London fringe theater production of the show that offered another alternative. Because of budget limitations, the role of Theo was cast with a teenager so that he could double as an ensemble member. As Schwartz recalled, at the end of the show Pippin and Catherine start to leave the stage, but Theo stays behind. "And then, very softly, acapella, Theo started to sing 'Corner of the Sky.' And then, the vamp for 'Magic to Do' came back in and the Players began to reenter and hold out their hands to Theo. Pippin and Catherine turned and looked startled and horrified that Theo was now going to go through the same journey. And then the lights would black out."[82] Schwartz and Hirson have now incorporated this ending into the official, licensed version of *Pippin*, and Schwartz feels sure Fosse would approve. "It's a much more satisfying ending than either of the ones we came up with."[83]

Remarkably, given their contentious history, Schwartz has restored many of Fosse's contributions to the current libretto, particularly those that underscored *Pippin*'s metatheatrical concept. He recently reflected, "It's only been in retrospect and with my own aging that I've come to appreciate the bigger vision that he brought to the piece, and actually, in an ironic twist, I've become quite an ardent defender of it."[84] He also feels that the conflicts between the two strong-willed men ultimately led to *Pippin*'s success: "I think another thing I didn't understand is that the very tension between my young, somewhat idealistic and naïve vision, and Bob's more hard-bitten cynicism—that very tension which made for creative discomfort sometimes—is why the show works."[85]

Pippin finally returned to Broadway in 2013 in a production that originated at the American Repertory Theater in Cambridge, Massachusetts. Directed by Diane Paulus, this *Pippin* was conceived as a Barnum and Bailey big top parade peopled with acrobats and contortionists. While the 1996 revival of *Chicago* was stripped of its period setting and reduced to an all-black, tights and tuxedo concert, the 2013 *Pippin* was blown up into a nonstop theatrical three-ring circus. (It is one of the few recent Broadway revivals with a larger cast than the original production.) Ben Brantley in the *New York Times* called it "a '*Pippin*' for the 21st century," and its hard sell made it, he said, "ultimately more cynical than Fosse's".[86]

The ghost of Fosse hovered over this new-millennium *Pippin*, choreographed "in the style of Bob Fosse" by former Fosse dancer Chet Walker, starting with its very first image, the Fosse silhouette. Classic Fosse movements, including dance references from *Chicago, Dancin'*, and *All That Jazz*, integrated surprisingly well with the Cirque du Soleil–style staging, emphasizing the presentational elements of Fosse's choreography. The hard-bodied dancers and gymnasts executed every pelvic thrust and undulation, but there was little time to savor the movement amid the breathtaking acrobatics and aerial feats. What was missing was sensuality and simplicity.

Pippin provided a fascinating glimpse, however unintentional, into Fosse's inner conflicts. The struggle between Pippin and the Leading Player gave a preview of the contrast between young Joe Gideon and his older, cynical self in *All That Jazz*. The Leading Player and older Joe are expert purveyors of show business flimflam, never at a loss for a quick line or a big finish. Older Joe ends his life with one final showstopping musical number—in essence, stepping into the box and setting himself on fire—while Pippin turns his back on all that the Leading Player represents. In *Pippin*, the young man rejects the glamour and spectacle of show business (and death) while in *All That Jazz*, the older man embraces both unconditionally. Pippin/young Joe, Leading Player/older Joe: these four characters offer an intriguing prism through which to view Fosse's life and art, making *Pippin* Fosse's most personal show.

8

KEEP IT HOT

• • •

"I dream that somebody is going to knock on the door one day and announce, 'We're taking all those awards back. You didn't really deserve them. Have the statuettes ready when the truck comes.'"

Bob Fosse, 1979[1]

Bob Fosse's triple crown of show business awards in 1973 was unprecedented, and it remains unmatched more than forty years later. In a show business world where winning the EGOT (an acronym for Emmy-Grammy-Oscar-Tony) places an artist in a rarefied group of multiple award winners, Fosse occupied his own exclusive winner's circle of one. For someone who was constantly second-guessing himself, fearful that his work was never good enough, this record winning streak meant only that he was now at a peak from which he would inevitably fall. In May, shortly after collecting the last of his three awards, Fosse checked himself into the Payne Whitney Psychiatric Clinic seeking treatment for depression.[2] His stay was brief—no more than a long weekend. "And then, eventually, I had to say fuck it, it's over, and get back to work. That's the important thing, to *work*," he later recalled.[3] Balancing several projects at once, Fosse kept up a punishing schedule for the next two years.

Liza Minnelli at the Winter Garden was a three-week Broadway stop on a lengthy concert tour that saw Minnelli revisiting much of her *Liza with a Z* repertoire. Fosse directed the entire presentation and downsized the large-ensemble *Liza with a Z* numbers, "Ring Them Bells" and "Bye Bye Blackbird," for a two boy/two girl chorus. Like *Liza with a Z*, Fosse's direction had one goal: to showcase Minnelli's singing, dancing, comedic, and dramatic talents, and while the reviews appropriately focused on Minnelli's performance, Clive Barnes in the *New York Times* lauded "the off-hand ease of mastery" evident in Fosse's staging.[4]

Stanley Donen, his former MGM champion, sought Fosse to play the cameo role of the Snake in his film version of the beloved classic *The Little Prince*, Antoine de Saint-Exupéry's tale of a pilot who crashes in the Sahara and is joined by a child from another planet, presumably representing the pilot's lost innocence. Fosse's Snake first appears as just that: a fat, slimy reptile coiled around a tree limb in the desert. With an exaggerated sibilant "s" sound, Fosse's voice welcomes the Little Prince to this "sunny section of the solar system . . . the Sahara," then is instantly edited into the scene replacing the snake in the tree. Dressed in black pants, shirt, vest, derby, glasses, and leather gloves, and with his customary cigarette (black, of course) dangling from his lips, Fosse looks equal parts snake and pimp as he sings and dances across the Tunisian desert to the slithering tango "A Snake in the Grass." The number includes a witty interlude during which the Snake sprinkles a handful of sand on the desert floor for a soft-shoe routine that is pure Fosse.

"A Snake in the Grass" represents a sourcebook for many of the dance moves Michael Jackson would introduce a decade later in his live performances and videos. Jackson's famous Moonwalk directly echoes Fosse's Joe Frisco backward shuffle. Fosse frequently turns his arched back to the camera, with one hip cocked and the opposite knee bent, with hat pushed far down over his forehead—a move Jackson later adapted and accelerated. Another Jackson signature move— spinning, then stopping abruptly and lifting up on his toes with knees bent—is easily spotted here. Fosse's rhythmic accents, quick shifts of stance, undulating back, and head rolls are all part of Jackson's dance aesthetic. It is little wonder that YouTube features more than one video "mash-up" of Fosse and Jackson performances.[5] "A Snake in the Grass" proves the source for some of the most popular

Desert "Thriller." Fosse as the Snake in The Little Prince *shows off moves later appropriated by Michael Jackson. Paramount Pictures.*

dance moves of the twentieth century—one legendary performer's absorption of a previous generation's art.

"I love camera movement and camera angles. I've spent so many years of my life as a choreographer that pictures and composition are very important to me."

Bob Fosse, 1975[6]

In an interview with his friend Robert Alan Aurthur for the August 1973 issue of *Esquire*, Fosse emerged as a driven multitasker very much aware of his remarkable recent success and not afraid of putting in hard work to bring two ambitious new projects to fruition. His days were tightly scheduled, with mornings spent working on the screenplay for *Lenny* and afternoons collaborating with Fred Ebb on the libretto for *Chicago*.

There are numerous reasons why Bob Fosse felt a kinship with Lenny Bruce. Both were children of show business families (Bruce's mother, Sally Marr, was a comic and emcee in Brooklyn nightclubs), and Fosse was intimately familiar with the world of small-time nightclubs and burlesque houses in which Bruce spent his early career. Both pushed boundaries in their work. Fosse and Bruce both had problems with substance abuse—Bruce's use of narcotics would kill him by age forty, and Fosse's drinking and amphetamine use would lead to near-fatal heart problems during rehearsals for *Chicago* at the end of 1974.

In the 1950s, Lenny Bruce's flouting of sexual taboos and calling out of the hypocrisy of political figures and religious institutions pushed his routines into the area of social satire. His performances could be abrasive as he confronted audiences with jazz-like riffs on double standards surrounding race, sex, and violence. Bruce's routines so outraged church and political figures that he was arrested numerous times on obscenity charges. There were other arrests for narcotics possession. Bruce's legal battles began to consume his performances, which frequently consisted of reading court transcripts and ranting about the legal system. His drug dependency made him an erratic performer. Stripped of his cabaret license, unable to work, and nearly bankrupted by legal fees, Bruce died of a drug overdose in 1966.

By the early 1970s, re-evaluations of Bruce and his legacy had spawned a cottage industry of movies, books, and plays. *Lenny* was first planned as a film with a screenplay by Julian Barry and direction by Tom O'Horgan, who was best known for directing *Hair* onstage. After studio backing was withdrawn, Barry and O'Horgan reshaped the script as a play, which opened on Broadway in May 1971. Starring Cliff Gorman performing a number of signature Bruce routines, *Lenny* presented a cultural hero crushed by the combined forces of organized religion and a corrupt political establishment. Like *Pippin*, *Lenny* touched a chord of Vietnam-era concerns, especially for younger audiences. It was a substantial hit, running more than a year and winning Gorman a Tony Award.

The film version of *Lenny* had been moving forward with Bruce's former manager Marvin Worth producing. However, as soon as he was signed to direct, Fosse exerted his customary control over all elements of the film. He reached out to

David Picker, who had just left United Artists as head of production, and Picker joined the film as its executive producer. Picker's quiet, unobtrusive support allowed Fosse to fully exert his "Muscle" on *Lenny*.

Fosse worked closely with Julian Barry on the screen adaptation, building a *Citizen Kane*–style structure in which persons close to Lenny (his mother, wife, and agent) offer contrasting observations on their subject, creating a multifaceted portrait of the contradictory subject. (Fosse would play the offscreen interviewer, his voice easily recognizable in the film.) Lengthy performance sequences featuring Bruce routines mirror events in his life. Fosse's insistence on shooting in black and white gives the film a gritty, near-documentary quality through the cinematography of Bruce Surtees, the son of Robert Surtees, who had worked with Fosse on *Sweet Charity*.

Dustin Hoffman was Fosse's early choice to play Lenny. The actor immersed himself in research, endlessly listening to recordings of Bruce's routines and speaking to dozens of people who knew and worked with him. After a screen test directed by Fosse, the role of Honey, Bruce's wife, went to Valerie Perrine, a former Las Vegas showgirl who had recently transitioned to film acting.

Lenny got underway in January 1974, with location shooting in Miami, Los Angeles, New York City, and the Catskills. Fosse had kept on schedule and on budget with *Cabaret*, but now with more power came the freedom to shoot until he was completely satisfied with the results. On *Lenny*, he shot and printed five hundred thousand feet of film over its sixteen-week shooting schedule.[7] (Despite numerous takes, he was dissatisfied with Perrine's response in a courtroom scene to the judge's sentencing decision, which was meant to be a devastating surprise to Honey. In a much crueler repeat of his efforts to get the proper reaction from Marisa Berenson in *Cabaret*, Fosse remarked within earshot of Perrine that a man she was seeing had fallen out of a helicopter and died. Only then did he get the effect he was after.)[8]

Fosse worked with a number of collaborators who would be part of his team on subsequent films, including costume designer Albert Wolsky; composer and musical adapter Ralph Burns (who also worked with Fosse on theater projects); and, most important, editor Alan Heim, whose first experience with Fosse was on *Liza with a Z*. It was Heim's job to turn a mountain of footage into the intricate and layered structure of the finished film. As he recalled, "We broke up the comedy routines and found that, the shorter the comedy routines got, the more exciting the film got and the better Dustin's performance was."[9] Heim's fragmented editing paralleled Fosse's fondness in his dances for breaking large groups into smaller and smaller units or shifting tempos to build tension and excitement. But Heim went Fosse one better, inserting shots or dialogue outside the time frame. Fosse loved this; it was another way to control time and space in a way he never could onstage. This bouncing around in time would become the language of all his films.

Fosse's intense collaboration with Julian Barry on *Lenny*'s screenplay led him to write to Barry while editing was underway. In a letter, Fosse acknowledged his nervousness about broaching the subject but said he would like a writing credit on the film: "Obviously I feel I deserve it or I wouldn't be making this quest [*sic*]. I know this is a very delicate and difficult situation, but I do have and have had feelings that I was entitled to it."[10] Barry's response is a respectful "no," though he goes on to praise Fosse's contribution to the film: "There is no question in my mind but that you've made a great film and that it will always be known as Bob Fosse's *Lenny* which is what it should be known as . . . . and I assure you I will continue to make public and private statements about how much of the script is due to your work as director which everybody in the business knows and assumes anyway."[11] The final film credited only Julian Barry for the screenplay.

As respectful and deferential as this exchange was, it marked a pivot point for Fosse. Beginning with *The Pajama Game*, he was never a choreographer who simply staged dances when the dialogue ended and the music began. In *How to Succeed in Business without Really Trying* and *Little Me*, his stylized dances gave physical shape to their shows' comic sensibilities. With *Redhead, Sweet Charity*, and *Pippin*, he used dance to bridge gaps in narrative and create a seamless blend of staging and story. Fosse made authorial contributions to each of his projects that went beyond directing or choreographing. After *Lenny* and his experience on *Pippin*, he was determined to take literal credit for his contributions. Every Fosse film or musical would now include a writing credit for Bob Fosse.

When *Lenny* was released on November 10, 1974, it received split reviews. While praising Fosse as "a true prodigy" ("I don't know of any director who entered moviemaking so late in life and developed such technical proficiency"),[12] the *New Yorker*'s Pauline Kael, in a lengthy review that displayed a deep affinity for Bruce's work, lamented the film that could have been: "Bob Fosse could have made a sensational movie if he had shown the backstage life that shaped Bruce's awareness . . . . Maybe for Fosse that approach seems too close to home and too easy."[13] For Kael, there was show business on display, but the wrong kind: "The black-and-white earnestness of this movie and the youth-culture saintliness laid on Lenny Bruce are the ultimate in modern show-biz sentimentality."[14]

Lenny was a solid commercial hit, and not just with urban moviegoers, its anticipated target audience. By mid-March 1975, it had grossed $11.5 million nationwide, more than $2 million of which was generated from small-town theaters.[15] *Lenny* earned six Academy Award nominations, including for Best Picture and for Fosse as Best Director, but ultimately received no Oscars.

Divorced from the dazzle of the dance numbers in his first two films, *Lenny* highlights Fosse's skill with actors, his ability to capture the energy and detail of low-end show business, and his highly choreographed editing style. The film's strip joints, brick-walled jazz clubs, and Catskills show rooms are captured with vitality and an odd tenderness.

Fosse later reflected that when choreographing for the stage, small movement, or no movement at all, could make a more powerful impact than frenzied activity.[16] Late in the film, he gives a cinematic demonstration of this concept, as he halts all camera movement and pulls back to the top of the Los Angeles nightclub where Bruce makes his last appearance, sick from drugs, incoherent, and barely able to stand. In one uninterrupted take, the camera records every merciless detail of this sad and pathetic performance: the excruciating silences as Bruce mumbles and coughs and tries to gather his thoughts, the ringside revelers determined to laugh however unfunny the routines, the audience walkouts, and Bruce's final, dismal exit off the stage.

Perhaps *Lenny*'s tour de force moment is the strip number that introduces Honey early in the film. At this point, "Hot Honey Harlow," not Lenny, is the headliner, and Fosse showcases her as both a glowing figure of sexual availability and an untouchable beauty on display for a hungry audience. As Honey artfully removes the various panels of her costume, and loosens her long, flowing hair, all to a grinding vamp from the house band, Fosse intercuts shots of the surprisingly diverse audience: bashful young students, sailors, a group of conventioneers, a grinning middle-aged couple, and a few pensive women.

As with the numbers set in *Cabaret*'s Kit Kat Klub, these brief shots vividly establish the performance atmosphere. Heim's editing punctuates Honey's performance with quick shots of cash registers ringing and drinks being served— underscoring the environment of commerce in which Honey's act is only one element. Valerie Perrine brings a confident burlesque swagger to her performance and helps make this striptease one of the best of Fosse's filmed dances.

The era in which Lenny Bruce lived is now more than a half-century in the past. As the controversies surrounding his performances recede, and his cultural importance fades, *Lenny* can be seen now as a fast-paced, richly textured entertainment and a curiously gentle and understanding portrait of one show business provocateur by another, filmed in its director's distinctive style.

> "To tell the truth I'm not too crazy about the original material, but we're just going to do number after number after number. What I want to do is put on a show, a really terrific show!"
>
> Bob Fosse, 1973[17]

It started with the late show. During the Broadway run of *Can-Can*, Gwen Verdon had watched the 1942 film *Roxie Hart* on late-night television. "I loved the movie and I liked the character. But I knew something was wrong with it. I couldn't believe it was written that way," Verdon later recalled.[18] *Roxie Hart*, a star vehicle for Ginger Rogers, was a scrubbed-up adaptation of Maurine Watkins's 1926 play, *Chicago*. It was Verdon's discovery of it that set in motion a two-decade effort to bring to the musical stage Watkins's tale of Cook County Jail murderesses and the corrupt Chicago court system they manipulate.

Maurine Watkins based her play on a pair of sensational murder cases that she covered as a reporter for the *Chicago Tribune*. In the spring of 1924, two similar murders captured the attention of her readers. In March, Mrs. Belva Gaertner, a twice-divorced cabaret singer, was arrested in connection with the killing of a younger man who was found in her car, dead from a pistol wound to the head. Less than a month later, Mrs. Beulah Annan was accused of shooting and killing her lover following an afternoon of drinking in the apartment she shared with her husband. Under questioning, she admitted that she shot the victim because he wanted to break off their affair.[19] (Just prior to the musical's opening in 1975,

Fosse received a note from a Chicago newspaperman who had worked on the Annan story as a young man, claiming that Annan's victim actually bled to death following her biting off the tip of his penis while performing oral sex.)[20]

Both defendants, held without bail in the crowded women's ward of Cook County Jail, became subjects of a series of breathless front-page stories by the enterprising Watkins. With the aid of her defense attorney, Annan, dubbed by Watkins "the prettiest woman ever accused of murder in Chicago,"[21] presented a highly fictionalized image of a demure and loyal wife led astray by the temptations of Jazz Age Chicago. When a jury sentenced another woman to a life sentence for murder, a nervous Annan felt she needed to further burnish her image and suddenly announced that she was pregnant. An all-male jury took less than two hours to return a "not guilty" verdict.[22] Following her acquittal, Beulah left her husband, and the pregnancy was never again mentioned. A few weeks later, the case of Belva Gaertner ("Cook county's most stylish defendant")[23] came to trial and resulted in the same "not guilty" verdict.

Watkins soon transformed her Beulah Annan news stories into a fast-talking comedy about Roxie Hart, who portrays herself as an innocent victim of circumstance in order to win acquittal. Watkins made Roxie a show business wannabe who uses her notoriety to launch a vaudeville career. Belva Gaertner served as a loose prototype for Velma, a "stylish divorcee," also awaiting trial for murder. Billy Flynn, Roxie's defense attorney, was based on W. W. O'Brien, a famous Chicago attorney who devised Annan's self-defense plea. Watkins also created a "sob sister" news reporter named Mary Sunshine, whose enthusiastic reporting of every preposterous detail of Roxie's contrived life story bore a remarkable similarity to the author's account of Annan.

Directed by George Abbott and starring Francine Larrimore as Roxie, *Chicago* was a hit when it opened at the Music Box Theater on December 30, 1926. Burton Davis, in the *New York Daily Telegraph*, described it as "razor-edged satire, caricature in blood."[24] *Chicago* followed its Broadway run with a national tour and then returned to New York. Among its tour stops was the town after which it was named, where Belva Gaertner and W. W. O'Brien happily attended the opening night, posed for photographs with Francine Larrimore, and confirmed that the similarities between them and their onstage counterparts were no coincidence.

Chicago was first adapted for the movies in 1927, produced by Cecil B. DeMille, directed by Frank Urson, and starring Phyllis Haver. Like many a silent movie heroine of dubious virtue, Roxie was required to pay for her sins after capturing headlines and bewitching the all-male jury to win her acquittal. After Roxie wins her freedom, Amos banishes her from their home, and she is last seen slipping into the cold, rainy Chicago night, as a newspaper with her picture on its front page symbolically washes down a street gutter.[25]

Watkins continued writing plays but soon moved to California, taking up screenwriting and contributing to a number of films during the 1930s. By the 1940s, she had abandoned the writing profession and was living with her parents in Florida, where she became a devout Christian.[26] She was not involved with the

1942 *Roxie Hart*, directed by William Wellman, which added a flashback framing device that featured a reformed Roxie, married and with a carful of children.

As early as 1956, producer Robert Fryer sought to obtain the rights to the play as a vehicle for Verdon, following her success in *Damn Yankees*. In the search for a new musical property for Verdon, in the early 1960s additional overtures were made, and Verdon herself appealed to Watkins over the years. But Watkins remained adamantly opposed to selling the rights to her one successful play.[27] Her opposition may have had been fed by guilt over her own complicity in turning cold-blooded killers into tabloid stars, first as reporter, then as playwright. Watkins never relented, though she steadfastly maintained, "All roads lead to Verdon,"[28] and upon her death in 1969, her estate granted Verdon first right of refusal to *Chicago*.

Verdon's last Broadway appearance had been in *Sweet Charity*. By the time *Chicago* opened in 1975, she would be fifty years old, a point clearly on Fosse's mind in a letter to Robert Fryer discussing his work on the project in which he wrote, "The main problem as I see it is the age of Roxy [sic], although I think I may have a solution for that."[29] That solution was to portray Roxie as a woman aware of time moving on, who recognizes that her newfound celebrity is the key to the vaudeville career she covets. Roxie's acknowledgment that "I'm older than I ever intended to be" would be given particular poignancy in Verdon's delivery.[30] (Ann Reinking, who would replace Verdon as Roxie during the Broadway run and then revisit the role two decades later, reflected on the value of having an actress of a certain age in the role: "Because this is the last chance she's got. There's no back-up if she doesn't make this work. So the stakes are higher just because of her age.")[31]

Chicago was the first time Fosse and Verdon had worked together since their separation, but that posed no problem in terms of their professionalism. Verdon remarked, just before the show opened, "It was never husband and wife when we worked together . . . . it was always as actress and director. He has always said I'm the best Fosse dancer, and I believe I am. Why, I'd set my hair on fire if he asked me to."[32] Fosse was equally complimentary of his estranged wife: "I think Gwen is one of the greatest entertainers—*performers*—that I've ever seen in my life. It's like wanting to do something for Jolson, that's how great she is!"[33] To warm up for her return to Broadway, Verdon performed "Who's Got the Pain?" with Harvey Evans on an Ed Sullivan television special and did a summer tour of *Damn Yankees*, reprising her Lola nearly twenty years after she first performed the role.

Following the success of *Cabaret* and *Liza with a Z*, John Kander and Fred Ebb were natural choices to write *Chicago*'s score. Ebb's idea for *Chicago* was to tell Roxie Hart's story as a series of vaudeville numbers that conjured images from popular entertainment acts of the era: a Helen Morgan torch song (Roxie's "Funny Honey," sung perched on a piano while her husband, Amos, takes the rap for her crime); an Eddie Cantor clap-hands number (Roxie's "Me and My Baby," performed after she announces her phony pregnancy); a Sally Rand fan dance (Billy Flynn's introductory "All I Care About," complete with Rudy Vallee–style crooning); a ventriloquist act (Roxie becomes a ventriloquist's dummy on Billy's knee for her press conference in "We Both Reached for the Gun"); a pastiche of Ziegfeld star Marilyn Miller's famous "chin up" number, "Look for the Silver

Lining" (the treacly "A Little Bit of Good," for "sob sister" Mary Sunshine); and a song reminiscent of African American star Bert Williams's signature number, "Nobody" (Amos's "Mister Cellophane"). *Chicago* fully lived up to its subtitle, "A Musical Vaudeville." (Originally, it was to include no dialogue and be told solely through its musical numbers.)[34]

Fosse's concept for *Chicago* took Ebb's idea a step farther. It would be staged, designed, and performed in a distinctly Brechtian manner, forcing the audience to confront and examine the corruption and dishonesty beneath the benign sentiments expressed in the songs. Fosse described Brecht's allegorical play *The Resistible Rise of Arturo Ui*, about a Chicago gangster whose rise parallels that of Adolf Hitler, as inspiration for his approach. (Fosse also used Brecht's device of an unidentified actor stepping forward before the play begins to read a description of what would follow. In *Chicago* it is done mockingly: "Welcome. Ladies and gentlemen, you are about to see a story of murder, greed, corruption, violence, exploitation, adultery, and treachery—all those things we hold near and dear to our hearts.")

Tony Walton, again serving as Fosse's scenic designer, commented on Fosse's interest in conveying his disgust with the recent Watergate scandal through the portrayal of the corrupt media and court system of the 1920s.[35] Fosse himself later admitted, "I'm afraid this show is my image of America right now . . . . It makes some interesting comments on the press, about the way they make celebrities out of killers . . . . *Chicago* isn't just about the '20s."[36]

Bertolt Brecht, one of the most influential figures of twentieth-century theater, created his own unique presentational form of theater that sought to appeal to audiences' reason rather than their emotions. His development of the *Verfremdungseffekt*, or distancing or alienating effect, was essential to his theater.[37] Brecht's collaborations with composer Kurt Weill, beginning with *The Threepenny Opera* in 1928, crystallized his concepts of dramaturgy and stage presentation. Their collaborations featured onstage musicians, use of signs and subtitles, radical separation of dialogue and song, and a cynical presentation aimed at discouraging emotional empathy. Brecht's epic theater was stunningly alive with showmanship. As theater historian Ethan Mordden observed, "It may well be that what keeps his epic theatre fascinating is . . . the style itself, the invigorating theatricality of a performance that keeps saying, Look, I'm a performance. Brecht is, above all, and whether he likes it or not, an entertainer."[38]

Fosse's work as both choreographer and director had always exhibited an element of Brecht's *Verfremdungseffekt*, though Fosse never referenced Brecht or his staging techniques in any way until *Chicago* opened and critics began to make these connections. He frequently disregarded his shows' settings, creating tension by clothing his dancers in stylized, nonperiod costumes, including his by-now trademark derbies and white gloves. He used placards and signs to introduce scenes (as in *Sweet Charity*), placed dance numbers in "limbo" (*Sweet Charity*'s "I'm a Brass Band" and *Redhead*'s "Essie's Vision"), and skillfully utilized lighting to heighten the nonrealism of his stage images (*Sweet Charity* and *Pippin* were two recent examples). *Pippin*'s loose, revue-like look at the life of the son of Charlemagne was set in a kind of permanent limbo, with the story told by an anachronistic troupe of players who frequently interrupted the action to make announcements and offer commentary. *Chicago* would continue and deepen these production and staging techniques.

Moreover, the instantly recognizable Fosse choreography, built around tightly wound, pulled-in, rhythmically charged movement, called attention to itself, creating its own *Verfremdungseffekt*. As film critic Pauline Kael observed: "Arresting the motion at its most distorted—the performers frequently turn their backs to the audience, hips wrenched out—Fosse has made a style of showing us the strain of Broadway's killer feats of movement."[39]

Fred Ebb later revealed that he had written the entire book for *Chicago* himself.[40] Fosse as much as admitted this when discussing his contributions to the script soon after the show opened: "I'm very good at seeing what's wrong, at fixing scenes and dialogue. As a writer, I'm more of a fixer than I am a fellow who comes up with original ideas."[41] Regardless of the authorship, the plot closely followed Watkins's original. The biggest change is the overlay of show business, with Roxie's ride from killer to vaudeville headliner presented as the show's happy ending. In this musical *Chicago*, show business is the pinnacle of achievement, with everyone (save Amos) plugged into its power. Even the prison matron has connections with the William Morris Agency.

In early drafts, the character of Roxie is particularly crude. She literally gives the audience the finger, describes her initiation into sex at the age of fourteen, and displays a pronounced racism, as in this exchange (which was considerably toned down in the final script) when she first meets Velma Kelly:

> ROXIE: Kelly? What's Kelly? She's a spic, ain't she?
> VELMA: I heard that. It happens that I am descended from the de Garcia family which ain't nothin' in this world but a long line of nobeleman [sic] and contessas.
> ROXIE: That's what I said, a spic.[42]

An early ending for the show would have concluded *Chicago* on a chilling note and exposed the full extent of Roxie's coarseness and violent temper. After Roxie and Velma finish their new double act to cheers, they take questions from the audience. One man asks how their consciences allow them to sleep at night and comments, "You're a couple of killers . . . . You're singing and dancing over a couple of coffins, ya know."[43] Roxie savagely screams at the man, "They found us innocent! So, we're innocent. That's the way it is . . . . This is America! America! If you don't like it, get the hell out!" With the man yelling, "Whores! Killers!" and Roxie continuing her harangue, the curtain slowly falls.

This nasty, potentially violent ending was eventually rejected in favor of a brief coda to Roxie and Velma's act. After accepting bouquets of roses, they thank the audience for their role in making them stars:

> VELMA: Roxie and I would just like to take this opportunity to thank you. Not only for the way you treated us tonight, but for before this—for your faith and your belief in our innocence . . . .

ROXIE: Believe us, we could not have done it without you. (As Orchestra plays "Battle Hymn of the Republic")[44]

On a private recording of the show's Philadelphia tryout, the audible gasps from the audience at this dialogue prove that the new ending is equally pointed—drawing a straight line between the corrupt 1920s and the media-drenched post-Watergate audience of 1975. It also had the added advantage of allowing the audience to blur the line between the story and its stars and to applaud Verdon and Chita Rivera, alone together onstage as the curtain came down.

The casting of Rivera was an early decision. Another star dancer in the show would temper audience expectations for the kind of virtuosic dance numbers Verdon had performed in earlier shows. Fosse recalled, "She said, 'I don't want to work as hard as I did on 'Sweet Charity' or 'Redhead.' So I said, 'Let's get some other heavyweights in.' So we got Chita in and took a load off everybody."[45] Rivera and Verdon shared a history. When Rivera was in the chorus of Can-Can and contemplating auditioning to be Verdon's understudy, Verdon advised her to think more ambitiously about her career.[46] In recent years Rivera had moved to Los Angeles, made television appearances, worked in stock and touring productions, and appeared in Fosse's film version of Sweet Charity. But her last appearance on Broadway had been in the disappointing Bajour in 1964. Her Broadway return was almost as momentous as Verdon's.

Another bit of negotiation involved the show's advertising posters. Verdon had always been featured in a solo image on the posters for her shows. But neither Fosse nor Verdon wanted to give the impression that Chicago would be a solo star vehicle. Scenic designer Tony Walton, who was also to design the poster, laughingly recalled, "So Bob said, 'The challenge for you is to do something that feels like the show without featuring Gwen. And the further challenge is that she has poster approval.'"[47] Walton's final poster image, approved by Verdon, owed much to Reginald Marsh's 1920s paintings of burlesque dancers and their male audiences. Its cluster of showgirls languorously grouped together before an exclusively male audience conveyed both the show's gamy milieu and its frank sexuality and became the basis for Chicago's show scrim.

"Every time I do a show, I say I want to make a movie. Every time I make a movie, I think I belong on the stage."

Bob Fosse, 1985[48]

In an era before million-dollar budgets were routine, the lavish Chicago was budgeted at a reasonable $750,000. Because the project had originated with Verdon and she was its raison d'être, she flexed nearly as much "Muscle" as Fosse on Chicago, and her contract confirmed it. She not only had approval over every element of Chicago, including its direction and choreography, libretto, score, designs, orchestrations and dance arrangements, principal cast, and her standby, but also was to receive 10 percent of the box-office gross against a weekly salary of $5,000, as well as 10 percent of all net profits for the run of the show, regardless of how long she stayed with it.[49]

With Verdon and Rivera confirmed, casting focused on the other principal roles and the dance ensemble. Jerry Orbach, who originated roles in the Broadway musicals *Promises, Promises* and *Carnival* and the long-running off-Broadway hit *The Fantasticks*, was cast as Billy Flynn and would receive billing alongside Verdon and Rivera above the title. Amos was cast with the heavyset comedic actor, Barney Martin (who would find national fame twenty years later as Morty, Jerry Seinfeld's father on the television sitcom *Seinfeld*). Talent agent Henry Glassman would be played by David Rounds, and Matron "Mama" Morton by Mary McCarty.

The role of Mary Sunshine changed significantly prior to the start of rehearsals. Notes by casting director Michael Shurtleff indicate that Barbara Cook and operatic soprano Marta Eggerth were being considered for the part, described in the script as "a very sweet-looking woman. Like a suburban den mother."[50] But a later audition list shows the names of drag performers such as Holly Woodlawn, Michael Greer, and Craig Russell auditioning for the role.[51] The South African–born Michael O'Haughey, with a five-octave range, auditioned with an aria from Delibes's *Lakmé* and was promptly cast as Mary Sunshine. He would be billed in all programs and publicity as "M. O'Haughey."

Mary Sunshine in this "musical vaudeville" became a female impersonator whose unmasking at the end of Roxie's trial would illustrate that "things are not always what they appear to be." It is intriguing to imagine the reaction of Maurine Watkins to the character who is her stand-in being played as a female impersonator stripped of her identity at the end of the show.

"Finding a standby for Gwen has always been a major problem for her shows, hasn't it?" Shurtleff noted in a letter to Fosse. "I realized that when I had some of the ladies who stood by for her in the past come in to audition now for Chicago and we saw how they couldn't cut it . . . . I've come up with no one who can DANCE it as well as sing and act it."[52] Finally, a young dancer-singer from Pittsburgh, Lenora Nemetz, was hired as standby for Verdon and, later, for Rivera, as well.

For the dancing ensemble, Fosse looked to many of those who had been with him on his previous show. Of the thirteen dancers cast in *Chicago*, more than half had also appeared in *Pippin*. As with *Pippin*, they received billing on lobby cards and in the program. Michon Peacock, cast in her first Fosse show, remembered the personal attention Fosse was willing to provide to a dancer new to his style. "He was extremely generous, and I learned something very profound in the first day or two of our rehearsals: that he loved to teach what he does. And he would take time on breaks. 'Michon, I'm gonna show you on the break.' And he would work with me one on one."[53]

Tony Walton designed a striking unit set placing the orchestra atop a cylindrical drum above the central playing area. Sliding doors around the drum revealed an elevator for entrances and set changes. Revolving stairs allowed for blocking up to the orchestra level and made the musicians participants in the action. Placing the orchestra onstage allowed Walton to divide the orchestra pit into two sections where he installed another elevator and a flight of stairs, allowing for further variety of entrances and exits. Revolving columns, covered in black vinyl and mylar, surrounded the stage and were covered with 1920s advertising images, artwork, and graphics—all imbued with a faintly threatening quality by Jules Fisher's lighting. These images also covered portions of the floor, into which Fisher installed lights that could be adjusted to give a sinister glow. Walton ringed the entire stage in cold neon tubing, using it also for overhead signs and a giant sunburst "Roxie" logo. Fosse insisted to Walton that *Chicago* must look "stark, hard, and not nice."[54]

As she did with *Pippin*, Patricia Zipprodt attended final dance auditions and sketched costumes based on the dancers' physical proportions and on her discussions with Fosse about what type of characters they were to play.[55] She avoided obvious 1920s styles, opting instead for vaguely unisex tights and leotards mostly in shades of red, black, and silver, with off-kilter touches such as mismatched shoes, stockings rolled to different lengths, and gender-ambiguous accessories— the 1920s through a skewed mirror.

Chicago began rehearsals at the Broadway Arts rehearsal studio on October 26, 1974, with a Broadway opening planned for January 7, 1975, following an out-of-town tryout in Philadelphia. Gene Foote recalled that the first week of rehearsals was exclusively devoted to the dancers, who began work on the opening number, "All That Jazz," and "Roxie," with Verdon and the male dancers.[56] Fosse gave himself an additional choreographic challenge with *Chicago*: "To avoid the Charleston and that whole flapper look, which I'd seen done, and done well so many, many times."[57]

"All That Jazz" shows Fosse's ability to layer song and dance with plot-advancing dialogue. Following a brief overture, the center drum opens to reveal Velma riding up the elevator, back to the audience, with hips pulsating to John Kander's suggestive vamp. She walks to the front of the stage and with her first words ("Come on babe / Why don't we paint the town? / And all that jazz") greets the audience in the style of Prohibition-era celebrity saloon owner Texas Guinan. Velma is the audience's entry into the performance, both part of it and outside it. (She also welcomes the audience back at the top of the second act with Guinan's famous catchphrase, "Hello suckers!")

Velma starts a slow promenade around the stage, bringing the chorus on from the wings, from behind the onstage bandstand, and from below the stage. Jules Fisher described the lighting as "cold and very moody and dark, [with] little sprinkles of light that somehow snuck into the space you saw the performers in."[58] Verdon later recalled that Fosse referred to the ensemble as "worm people" who observe and comment on the action.[59] Each has an individualized sequence of steps that, when performed all together on the stage and in slow motion, create a wave of movement, which in turn shifts into unison steps with startling precision.

In Zipprodt's ambisexual costumes, with the men sometimes exposing as much flesh as the women, and executing Fosse's slowly-moving-through-water choreography, his dancers give *Chicago* an unsettling erotic charge. Their impact still resonated years later when the *New York Times*'s Frank Rich commented on the cautiousness of *La Cage aux Folles*, a musical about two male lovers. The show's drag performances, he wrote, "are less sexually provocative in their use of androgynous sexuality than, for example, the Bob Fosse choreography for Broadway's 'Chicago.'"[60]

Zipprodt provided a trunk of props from which the dancers chose articles to define their particular 1920s character—a gangster, a drunk, a dandy, and so on. Where *Pippin*'s players were directed to make love to the audience, Gene Foote recalled, "Our leading direction in the opening number was, 'When you enter, I want you to confront the audience with murder in your eyes and dare them to look at you.'"[61] Fosse used violent imagery elsewhere to convey the intent of his "worm people." Susan Stroman, a dancer in the show's national company, remembered "a movement where people have their palms flat downstage and they sort of wipe their palms back and forth, and Fosse always told us to make believe we had blood all over our hands and like we were trying to wipe it off on a wall, kind of like the way the Manson family did."[62]

Soon Roxie and Fred Casely drunkenly enter from the staircase in the pit and disappear into the center drum area as the doors close. "All That Jazz" features several Fosse dance tropes, including an amoeba that slowly makes its way across the stage, led and exhorted by Velma. The center drum reopens to reveal Roxie and Fred in bed, in a vaudeville-style performance of sex—frantic, mechanical, and over as soon as it starts. As the dancers surround the bed, Roxie pulls a gun on the quickly departing Fred, shoots him twice, then throws the gun down and exits with a hasty, "I gotta pee." Velma, now on the bandstand atop the stage, finishes the song as the dancers' movements become more frenzied. The number is "buttoned" when the corpse is covered with the bed's sheet, readying it for the next scene of the police investigation of the crime. "All That Jazz" announces that *Chicago* will be swift, bold, and profane.

After rehearsing *Chicago* all day, Fosse would spent the evening on final editing work for *Lenny*, which was nearing its premiere date. The rigor of his schedule quickly took its toll. Alan Heim remembered one editing session when an exhausted Fosse, looking "pale, ghost-like," had to be helped out of his chair.[63] The following week, the entire cast arrived for a read-through of the script, and Verdon was shocked at Fosse's appearance. As she described him, "He was puffed up. He had a funny high voice. I'd never seen him like that."[64] At lunch, Fosse went to New York Hospital complaining of pains in his chest. He never returned to *Chicago* rehearsals. Fosse soon underwent bypass surgery for a blocked artery, but not long afterward, still hospitalized, he suffered a heart attack.

In all, his hospitalization lasted more than a month, followed by recuperation at home. The heartfelt messages he received during his hospital stay confirmed Fosse's standing among his peers in the theater. Director A. J. Antoon wrote, "I pray your heart never has the audacity to even try and attack you. You give so much of it in your work—and for this, thank you."[65] Choreographer Donald Saddler ended his get-well wishes by stating simply, "The theater needs you."[66]

Fosse's health problems and the resulting postponement of such a high-profile new musical were big news in the theatrical community, though the full extent of his illness was not immediately known. (*Variety* referred to it as "physical exhaustion.")[67] Ultimately, the show was suspended for four months before resuming in March 1975. Having faced his own mortality, a weakened but focused Fosse returned to work. His major concession to his illness was a lunch-time nap, and he was back to smoking cigarettes.

For some, his heart attacks and surgery had dramatically changed his approach to the show. John Kander remembered, "The show became more cynical and biting than it started out to be."[68] Always possessed of a dark sense of humor, Fosse's worldview turned truly black. Both Fred Ebb and Tony Stevens, who had joined *Chicago* as assistant choreographer, took to calling him the "Prince of Darkness."[69]

Among the numbers Fosse began staging was "All I Care About," Billy Flynn's introduction, a mawkish, Rudy Vallee–style number in which "the Silver-Tongued Prince of the Courtroom" hypocritically boasts, "I don't care about expensive things / Cashmere coats, diamond rings / Don't mean a thing / All I care about is love." Six statuesque dancers appear at center stage, recreating *Chicago*'s show scrim and poster image. Each wears an abbreviated two-piece costume, little more than a bikini. Their headdresses are bowlers, derbies, or feathers. Each wears only one black stocking above the knee topped by a blood-red garter. As the emcee announces Billy's arrival, the women undulate, roll their heads, and chant, "We want Billy / Where is Billy / Give us Billy." Through the smoky light, the women pull away from the group, each at a different pace and each slowly stepping into a split or lunge until she is on the floor, creating what John Simon termed "a lava of lubricity spreading across the footlights."[70] The women luxuriously stretch out onto their backs and arch their pelvises upward, sighing "We're all his," as they anticipate Billy's longed-for arrival. Finally they rise to full height, strike exultant poses, and breathlessly announce, "Here he is!" before exiting. It may be the most nakedly erotic sixty seconds Fosse ever choreographed.

The center drum opens to reveal Billy, in silhouette, smoking a cigar and dressed in the highest of 1920s fashion. His greeting, "Is everybody here? Is everybody ready?" recalls bandleader Ted Lewis's famous catchphrase, "Is everybody happy?" The dancers return, each carrying two large pink fans, in a nod to Sally Rand's fan dances of the period, and accompany Billy as he proceeds to perform a modified striptease. The more he insists that he cares only for the downtrodden and rejects worldly goods, the fewer clothes he wears. The dancers form a revolving pinwheel around Billy with their fans, dispersing to reveal him with pants gone, clad only in boxer shorts and undershirt.

The dancers are virtuosos of the fans, wielding them with grace and precision. When Billy sings "Show me long, long raven hair / Flowing down, about to there," they immediately move into formation, covering themselves with their fans to create the illusion of luxuriant hair flowing from the head of one dancer. Later, they lock into place to create a giant, feathered fan swaying behind Billy. It is not only Fosse's stage pictures that are so arresting, but also the way in which he transitions from one striking image to another, snapping the dancers into place with an easy inevitability that comes only from methodical planning. "All I Care About" is as much about transitions as it is about evocative stage pictures.

Virtuosos of the fans: Fosse perfected his fan dance with Chicago's "All I Care About."
Center: Jerry Orbach standing, Cheryl Clark, below. Back, left to right: Candy Brown,
Michon Peacock, Graciela Daniele, Charlene Ryan, and Pamela Sousa. Photo by Martha
Swope © Billy Rose Theatre Division, The New York Public Library for the Performing Arts.

The monologue leading into "Roxie," in which she celebrates her impending stardom, was sharpened to provide a tour de force moment for Verdon,
spanning lewd comedy to touching pathos. (Verdon later acknowledged that
the monologue was entirely the work of Herb Gardner.)[71] Roxie's driving ambition to have her own vaudeville act is contrasted with her poignant realization that opportunities are no longer abundant now that she is getting older.
While she admits to cheating on her husband ("I started foolin' around. Then
I started screwin' around, which is foolin' around without dinner"), she also
acknowledges that Amos's steadfastness is increasingly important to her as she
ages. ("Some guys are like mirrors, and when I catch myself in Amos's face I'm
always a kid. You could love a guy like that.") Roxie's confession adds an affecting dimension to her ego and crudeness, while also acknowledging Verdon's
age. In musical comedy Roxie Hart is allowed more dimension than in her previous incarnations.

"Razzle Dazzle," the syncopated number designed to segue into the climactic trial scene, was to be a Fellini-esque, circus-style fantasia with full chorus,
introduced by Billy, who transforms himself into the image of attorney Clarence
Darrow—a winking reference, given Darrow's defense of Leopold and Loeb,
contemporaries of Beulah Annan. John Kander remembered creating the song's
rhythmic structure to please Fosse. "Fred said, 'Put two finger snaps in the middle

of it.' And I thought he was nuts, but I did it. And we went and played it for Bobby, and the moment the fingers got snapped, he was in heaven."[72]

Fosse felt that much of the courtroom scene that followed the number was redundant, with Roxie, under Billy's direction, repeating the details of the crime in much the same way they had been described earlier. Verdon later noted that it was the most difficult scene to write and stage, and that seven different versions were tried before it was set.[73] Fosse assigned dancer Richard Korthaze to play a one-man jury, using items from the by-now indispensable props box. Korthaze chose an outlandish toupee, a woman's cloche hat, a large horn-shaped hearing aid, a gray beard, a large red nosepiece, and other items. Switching between these props inconspicuously while the focus was on Roxie, Korthaze created an entire jury roster and brought a sense of variety and astonishing comedy to the courtroom scene.[74]

Chicago opened at Philadelphia's Forrest Theatre on April 8, 1975, to very mixed reviews. *Variety* noted that its evocations of 1920s performers and musical styles were "piled atop—and frequently overwhelm—a flimsy, sometimes boring book about relentlessly unsympathetic people."[75] Fosse turned his attention to tightening and strengthening the show. The first number to be eliminated was "No," sung by a barbershop quartet to introduce the scene in which Roxie persuades Amos to find $5,000 to hire Billy Flynn as her defense lawyer. Instead, its melody formed the basis for a sinewy "air tap" number (in which tap dance moves are approximated with the feet never touching the floor) to accompany the scene. Renamed "Tap Dance," it was prime Fosse, with four male dancers, shoulders hunkered and hats covering their faces, shifting weight, sometimes nearly falling, but always finding their balance—an illustration in movement of Roxie's verbal tap dance around Amos.

The show's finale, in which Roxie and Velma join forces to star together in a vaudeville act, proved a let-down. "It" and "Loopin' the Loop" were fast-paced specialty numbers that featured the two women playing instruments (Rivera on drums, Verdon on saxophone) and performing a raucous dance number in two-piece dancing costumes with stars on the breasts and a heart attached to the crotch. Fred Ebb remembers Fosse's direction to the songwriters. "He said, 'Couldn't they really get together and do something really elegant and smart and good-looking, so they could be a classy sort of act?' The audience response doubled the minute we put it in.'"[76]

The number was "Nowadays," sung by Roxie after she had been acquitted and then brushed aside for the newest sensational murderess. Starting as a rueful examination of her current status off the front pages, it gradually builds to a celebration of what life in Chicago currently has to offer her. Roxie's solo leads into a grand fanfare introducing the two women in white top hats, tails (over white briefs and black stockings), and canes. "RSVP," Kander's elegant vamp, is the setting for a synchronized strut ("And now, poetry in motion—two moving as one") punctuated with small pelvic bumps and wrist flicks at the breasts, but still fitting Fosse's directive for a "classy" Fred Astaire–style top hat number. Their turn ends with the upbeat "Keep It Hot" as the two, now in fringed skirts, perform a loose-limbed dance set to Peter Howard's escalating dance arrangement and climaxing with cartwheels into splits. Fosse makes it a compendium of all the steps he learned as a young man: the shim sham, the black bottom, the Joe Frisco, snake hips, and even some Little Egypt–inspired cooch dancing, making "Keep It Hot" the ultimate vaudeville dance act.

By the time *Chicago* returned to New York to begin previews, another new musical was poised to steal much of its attention. In early 1974, director-choreographer Michael Bennett had conducted a series of taped conversations with groups of Broadway dancers, or "gypsies." The sessions allowed the dancers to talk about their family backgrounds and early dance training, and their perspectives on

Chita Rivera and Gwen Verdon bring Chicago *to a thrilling conclusion with the ultimate vaudeville dance act in "Keep It Hot," later known as the "Hot Honey Rag." Photo by Martha Swope © Billy Rose Theatre Division, The New York Public Library for the Performing Arts.*

show business and their careers. The tapes were used as the basis for a series of workshops, funded by Joseph Papp's New York Shakespeare Festival, during which the musical was developed. What emerged from these workshops was *A Chorus Line*, a unique mosaic of dialogue, song, and dance told in real time on a bare stage during an audition for a new Broadway musical. *A Chorus Line* was a sensation when it opened on May 21, 1975, and it quickly transferred in July to Broadway's Shubert Theater, where it would remain for fifteen years.

Fosse's sense of competition with *A Chorus Line* and its wunderkind director-choreographer may have fueled his meticulous editing during previews. (Tony Stevens recalls Fosse asking him daily if *Chicago* was as good as *A Chorus Line*.)[77] Verdon's "Me and My Baby" number in the second act featured the male dancers as babies wearing diapers and oversized bonnets backing up the star in an Eddie Cantor–style routine. Knowing the audience's desire to see Verdon do more dancing, Fosse revamped the number as a Dixieland strut with two male dancers, complete with familiar Fosse spats, gloves, and derbies.

"Razzle Dazzle" and the courtroom scene continued to be a problem spot. In detailed notes to Fosse, Fred Ebb called the scene "redundant," urging a stronger burlesque approach and recommending that it "[start] sooner, is short and 'nutty.'"[78] Fosse embellished his staging of the scene to include the cast simulating sex acts and murders around the set, which distracted from the action at center stage. Chita Rivera remembered seeing the number for the first time: "I really was shocked. And I didn't think it was necessary at all. It was just too much."[79]

If this was Fosse's appropriation of Brecht's *Verfremdungseffekt*, it was more distracting than distancing. The staging was later simplified and the explicit sexuality toned down, but Fosse's staging was indicative of a general point of contention between himself and Ebb. In his notes to Fosse, Ebb expressed discomfort with the darker, heavier tone Fosse was projecting onto the show: "I do not think, please forgive me Bobby, that this is a profound show . . . . I don't think it has to be buttressed by overstatement. Laughing and applauding murderesses is an ignoble gesture at best and the folly of our reaction to that celebrity is what underpins the entire enterprise . . . . I think there is no way for this show to be conventional given it's [sic] form and look and basic substance. On the same hand, I don't think it is a 'meaningful' experience . . . . In short (Oh, God, please don't hate me), it ain't Brecht."[80]

One of the key principles Fosse had learned from his work with George Abbott was ruthlessness in delivering a hit show. Regardless of how well he liked a number or a scene or a joke, if it interrupted the flow of the story or slowed down the proceedings, it was out. Now, as *Chicago*'s opening loomed, he cut the role of talent agent Henry Glassman in its entirety. Glassman had one song ("Ten Percent") and also served as emcee, introducing many of the numbers. Cutting the character would allow the show to move more swiftly, and the introductions could be shared among the cast and conductor Stanley Lebowsky from his perch atop the onstage bandstand. This major change happened so late that *Chicago* opened with actor David Rounds's name listed on some advertising materials. The last song written for the show was "When You're Good to Mama," a Sophie Tucker–style number for the Matron, whose character now assumed some of Glassman's mercenary agenting duties.

> "I get fragile when reviews come out and they don't like it. I always thought that would lessen as I got older. It doesn't."
>
> Bob Fosse, 1981[81]

The 46th Street Theater was a lucky house for Fosse and Verdon. They had opened *Damn Yankees, New Girl in Town*, and *Redhead* there, and it was the home of *How to Succeed in Business without Really Trying* for its long run. Now they made a final return when *Chicago* opened on June 3, 1975, carrying a then-record $17.50 top ticket price. The critical reaction was extremely mixed, with many of the reviews noting that *Chicago*'s overall atmosphere drew heavily on Fosse's film version of *Cabaret*. In a double pan of both *Chicago* and *A Chorus Line*, *New Yorker* dance critic Arlene Croce called it "a generally cheap and vicious show" and "the height of theatrical decadence" and had little praise for Fosse's staging.[82] "Many of his images in 'Chicago' are unsteadily supported, because he is trying to force a correspondence between Chicago and pre-Nazi Berlin which has no basis in reality."[83]

More than forty years later, director Harold Prince still feels that Fosse appropriated for *Chicago* the concept, design, and atmosphere of his original Broadway staging of *Cabaret*: "Oh, sure. He stole the whole goddamn thing. Why don't we face it? Everything that Kander, Ebb and he did was just *Cabaret* lite . . . . Everything was the same. He didn't use Boris Aronson. But basically, they just did that show."[84]

However, there were other, more appreciative opinions. *Newsweek*'s Jack Kroll raved, "No one has absorbed Brecht so organically and pertinently as Fosse. His triangulation of 20s Chicago, Brecht and Broadway results in a sneakily contemporary feeling. Behind the garish Weimar–Jazz Age decor we are looking at ourselves."[85]

It was Stephen Farber in the *New York Times* who identified in *Chicago* a darker quality directly linked to Fosse: " 'Chicago' is suffused with a deeply felt sense of horror and outrage that has nothing to do with social protest; the intensity of the musical grows from Fosse's bitterness toward the showbiz world that has nourished him."[86] Billy Flynn, the courtroom showman, and "Razzle Dazzle," his ode to hoodwinking the public, distilled the conflict eating at Fosse. That he could so easily enrapture an audience with his polished staging skills was no longer enough for him; with *Chicago* he was pushing for a bigger, more profound statement. But Fosse the showman ultimately wins out over Fosse the philosopher, and *Chicago* ends with Verdon and Rivera in joyful performance.

There was truth to many of the reviews that found the simple story burdened by *Chicago*'s production concepts. The "musical vaudeville" concept, the "Brechtian staging" concept, the numbers meant to reference song styles of the past, and the staging that evoked still other images sometimes threatened to overpower the story. For instance, Amos's number, "Mister Cellophane," which laments his seeming invisibility ("Cause you can look right through me / Walk right by me / And never know I'm there") is a replica of Bert Williams's famous

"Nobody," but performed with Amos in an oversized tuxedo with clown's hat and collar reminiscent of Emil Jannings's cuckolded husband in *The Blue Angel*. That is a lot of concept for an otherwise straightforward character number. Each of *Chicago*'s numbers is so pointed, so clear in its intent, that heavy-handed references were unnecessary.

A case in point is "Cell Block Tango," a series of musical monologues introducing Roxie's jailhouse neighbors. Scored to a ripe, Rudolph Valentino–style tango, the number starts in darkness with a row of six women behind bars. Each turns on a light attached to the jail cell bars she is carrying as she sings a single catch-phrase related to her crime. Between chants of "He had it comin' / He had it comin' / He only had himself to blame," each steps forward to describe her crime and assert her innocence. Each story is given a comic punch line involving the murder method ("He ran into my knife. He ran into my knife ten times") or motive (bigamy, bisexuality, gum popping). The overarching dance move is a heel dig in time to the insistent tango rhythm as they furiously criss-cross the stage. Michon Peacock remembered, "He wanted us to fight. The image is that you're bulls. That's why we stampeded. Just like bulls charging, marching, jumping, attacking."[87] The heel digs become more insistent, as if digging the graves of the unworthy men they've murdered. At its conclusion, the women retreat to their cell block lineup and, as if in response to a "lights out" command, the stage goes black.

The second act's courtroom scene still feels overextended, and the show does not end so much as stop. There is no real explanation of why Roxie and Velma, who heretofore despised each other, should suddenly team up in a vaudeville act. But these caveats were swept away in the excitement of seeing Gwen Verdon and Chita Rivera dance the high-impact finale. Verdon's dance duties may have been lighter than in the past, but her Roxie Hart was a career highlight, whether growing progressively, and hilariously, drunk while singing atop a piano, doing a knockabout burlesque turn in the courtroom scene, or finding nuances of despair and survival in her "Roxie" monologue. Rivera was all over the show, seemingly in every other number, and her emphatic timing and piercing vibrato gave *Chicago* a distinctive voice. Orbach, Mary McCarty, Barney Martin, Michael O'Haughey, and the *Chicago* dancers matched them in slicked-up style and energy.

Chicago received enough good reviews, including some raves, to settle in as a hit, but that status was endangered when Gwen Verdon was forced to leave the show for vocal cord surgery shortly after its opening. To great astonishment, her temporary replacement was Liza Minnelli, whose sense of personal commitment to Kander, Ebb, and Fosse led her to volunteer to replace Verdon with no billing or advance ballyhoo. Once word of the substitution was public, the show immediately sold out for her five-week stint.

Chicago underwent surprisingly little adjustment for the substitution of Minnelli, primarily a singer, for Verdon, principally a dancer, underscoring the role's relatively light dance demands. "Me and My Baby" reverted to the earlier Eddie Cantor–style staging, but the biggest change was in giving Minnelli a solo spot with "My Own Best Friend." The Verdon-Rivera duet in which they sing their own praises ("And now, Miss Roxie Hart and Miss Velma Kelly sing a song of unrelenting determination and unmitigated ego") was yet another ballad sarcastically reconceived by Fosse, in this case mocking the conventions of torch singers in fedoras and trenchcoats. Minnelli's interpretation dispensed with the mocking attitude to deliver a fully belted star turn, ending the first act with a roar of applause.

Verdon returned to a show that was now a bona fide hit thanks to Minnelli's drawing power. Because of the delay resulting from Fosse's hospitalization, *Chicago* missed the deadline for the 1974–1975 season's Tony Awards, where its principal competition would have been *The Wiz*. The following season's awards were dominated, predictably, by *A Chorus Line*. *Chicago*, which could have used the boost from Tony honors, was left empty-handed. Despite receiving eleven Tony Award nominations, including for Best Musical, *Chicago* lost in all categories—a then-record—and Fosse lost in all three categories in which he was nominated (direction, choreography, and book of a musical).

The results of the Tony Awards placed in sharp relief the dichotomy between the two musicals, both driven by the notion of show business as a metaphor for life. While *A Chorus Line* portrayed a world of competition and disappointment, ultimately, it was an affirming story of life in the theater. *Chicago* offered no such absolution. When Roxie and Velma assure the audience, "We couldn't have done it without you," their words mock the suckers who brought them to fame. *A Chorus Line*'s score was funny, poignant, and reassuring in its contemporaneity. *Chicago*'s patische songs were double-edged, coarse, and slightly off-putting in their echos of a distant past. *A Chorus Line*'s warm bath of understanding reassured audiences, while *Chicago*'s cold shower of cynicism forced them to confront their own complicity in a corrupt culture.

Lenora Nemetz later assumed Chita Rivera's role, and when Gwen Verdon left in January 1977, she was replaced by Ann Reinking, with the press making much of Fosse's replacing his estranged wife with his current girlfriend. For Reinking, Fosse choreographed yet another variation on "Me and My Baby," featuring longer, more lyrical movements for the classically trained star.[88] Jerry Orbach stayed for the entire Broadway run, which ended on August 27, 1977, after more than two years and 936 performances.

Chicago was a hit but not a smash, ending its run without completely paying off its initial investment. A national tour, headlining Orbach, was immediately sent out and played through the following summer. Verdon and Rivera joined the tour when *Chicago* played engagements in Los Angeles and San Francisco as part of the Civic Light Opera Association. A bus-and-truck tour went out at various times for a few years, playing smaller cities. The show was occasionally produced at regional theaters, and in 1985 Chita Rivera headlined an Atlantic City production, playing the role of Roxie. But slowly *Chicago* faded.

It would take two decades for audiences to embrace *Chicago*'s humor and cynicism and relate it to contemporary American life. In May 1996, New York's City Center presented *Chicago* as part of its Encores! series of classic American musicals revived in modest, concert-style stagings. The minimalist production directed by Walter Bobbie and choreographed by Ann Reinking "in the style of

Bob Fosse" proved to be its own tribute to the choreographer, with the Fosse vocabulary as important to the storytelling as the book and score. With Reinking stepping back into the role of Roxie, Joel Grey as Amos, and Bebe Neuwirth, from both the *Sweet Charity* revival and the final cast of *Dancin'* on Broadway, as Velma, there were secure links to Fosse. The show's weekend-long run was a sensation and immediately sparked interest in a Broadway transfer.

Very little was done to embellish the Encores! staging when *Chicago* opened on November 14, 1996 at the 46th Street Theater, now renamed for Richard Rodgers, home of the original production. The cast wore all-black attire, there were minimal props, and the entire action was played directly in front of the onstage orchestra seated in a gold-rimmed jury box. Fosse's spirit was further evoked with the first stage image: a spotlight on an empty chair with a black derby jauntily stationed on the corner, as if the choreographer had left it there only moments earlier.

The gender ambiguity created through costuming and movement in 1975 was jettisoned for a less-threatening Victoria's Secret–style sexuality, with the female dancers in variations on revealing black lingerie. In their all-black costumes and derbies, the men embodied Fosse himself, an impression fortified by the casting of older dancers from earlier Fosse shows. (As these men left the cast and were replaced, the male ensemble came to resemble that of most Broadway musicals, being notably young and muscled.)

Arriving at the end of a cycle of overstuffed, special effects–laden British shows such as *The Phantom of the Opera, Les Misérables,* and *Sunset Boulevard,* the new, stripped-down *Chicago* was a tonic, receiving unanimous acclaim and even landing Neuwirth and the female dancers on the front page of the *New York Times. Chicago* was unfamiliar to many people, and it fit right into a Broadway that had recently welcomed new, youth-focused shows like *Bring in 'Da Noise, Bring in 'Da Funk* and *Rent.*

In 1975, many dismissed Fosse and Ebb's pointed commentary on the collusion between media and the legal system. But by the 1990s, media empires had been built on reporting the salacious crimes and sensational trials of Amy Fisher and Joey Buttafuoco, Lorena and John Wayne Bobbitt, the Menendez Brothers, and, most prominently, O. J. Simpson. The entertainment industry turned them into the kind of media celebrities Roxie Hart only dreamed of becoming. What was vulgar and cynical in 1975 was part of the popular culture landscape by 1996, and *Chicago*'s satire now had the sting of truth about it. The explosion of reality television and social media has kept *Chicago* continuously relevant into the twenty-first century. The media landscape is now littered with Roxie Harts who need only update their Twitter, Instagram, and Snapchat accounts to keep the public interested. Roxie's employment of "alternative facts" and "fake news" contains eerie parallels with contemporary American politics.

Perhaps inevitably amid the revival's admiration, some revisionist history took place. Several critics, like the *New York Post*'s Clive Barnes, praised its less-is-more production and called the original "over-produced and over-pretentious."[89] Others insisted that the stripped-down approach revealed the show's strengths in a way that the original production did not. But setting it in an all-black limbo obliterated Fosse's original concept of telling Roxie's Hart's story in vaudeville performance stylings. It robbed the numbers of their period references and left some of them with little context. (The show's original subtitle, "A Musical Vaudeville," was eliminated.)

The choreography is a loving and respectful homage to Fosse, but it fails to capture his elegance or devastating stage images. Moments that were once startling in their oozing sexuality, like the "We want Billy" introduction to "All I Care About," are now blatantly oversold. A number of Fosse trademarks are revived— the Chaplin walk, the vaudeville strut, the pelvic punctuation—but they lack the organic grounding of his original work. The concluding "Hot Honey Rag," renamed from "Keep It Hot" in the original production, is a recreation of Fosse's own choreography (minus the concluding splits) and features the detail and specificity too often missing from the rest of the staging.

As of its twentieth anniversary in 2016, *Chicago* had run 8,302 performances and is now the second-longest-running show in Broadway history, behind *The Phantom of the Opera*, and the longest-running American musical. Credit for its longevity can be attributed in part to its practice of star replacements, for which name recognition frequently trumps singing and dancing expertise or prior stage experience. Its leading roles have frequently been played, both in New York and on the show's multiple tours, by pop and R & B stars (Usher, Ashlee Simpson, Huey Lewis, Kevin Richardson of Backstreet Boys), country music stars (Billy Ray Cyrus), talk show hosts (Jerry Springer, Wendy Williams), models (Christie Brinkley), reality show personalities (NeNe Leakes of *The Real Housewives of Atlanta*), and sports figures (retired NFL running back Eddie George, Olympic figure skater Elvis Stojko). In 2003, film actress Melanie Griffith joined the Broadway production as Roxie, having never appeared onstage before. Cast solely for her marquee value, Griffith embodied the theme of *Chicago*: that celebrity is its own form of talent, and the public will pay to see anyone famous.

Chicago long ago passed the record of performances by *A Chorus Line*, the show that overshadowed it in the 1970s. *A Chorus Line* was revived in 2006 as an exact replica of its original production. Its seamless blend of music, dance, and dialogue retained its brilliance, but the sentimentality of many of its characters' stories, as well as the 1970s choreography and cultural references, carried a dated quality. The *Chicago* revival's indeterminate, all-black setting gives it a timeless feeling that eases its translation to languages and cultures around the world. It helps explain why it has become an international hit on equal footing with British pop-opera extravaganzas like *Cats* and *Les Misérables*.

The original 1975 production of *Chicago* marked a series of endings. It was the last time Fosse worked with a first-rate score or, indeed, with any writers at all. Fosse achieved his goal of total control, but it would be hard to argue that his work had not benefited from the creative struggle of collaboration with artists like John Kander and Fred Ebb.

Chicago also was the end of the Fosse-Verdon collaboration. This greatest of all Fosse dancers would go on to assist and work alongside him, but she would never again dance his work on the stage. From Lola to Anna Christie to Essie Whimple to Charity Hope Valentine to Roxie Hart, Verdon's indelible gallery of musical theater heroines, all guided by Fosse, was diverse and challenging, making her the unquestioned Broadway dancing star of her era. When Verdon departed the stage, some part of Fosse left with her. A winking humor, a sense of warmth and vulnerability would go missing from his future work.

Finally, *Chicago* was the climax of a particular kind of Broadway musical: the last of the great star vehicles. While its three stars occasionally appeared in movies and on television (long before Jerry Orbach's success on television's *Law and Order*), they earned their above-the-title billing based solely on their work in Broadway musicals. *Chicago*'s lineage extended from *Damn Yankees, West Side Story, Carnival*, and *Sweet Charity* to deliver the larger-than-life star performers that Broadway found it increasingly difficult to create or sustain. Its like would not be seen again, and its rediscovery twenty years later only underscored the great achievement of its original production.

9

DANCIN' SOLO

• • •

"Choreography is writing on your feet."

Bob Fosse, 1978[1]

Bob Fosse expected to begin shooting his new film, *All That Jazz*, during the summer of 1977. But script and casting issues kept pushing the schedule back. "And I said, 'I gotta do what I am supposed to do—which is get in with actors and dancers and *do* something.' And the *fastest* thing was to do something that a book did not have to be written to, that a score didn't have to be written to. All I had to do was go up to a studio myself, prepare and then hire dancers and go in and do it."[2]

A show made up only of musical numbers would be the obvious next step for a director whose breathless pacing and impatience with words made his last two shows play almost like revues. Collaborating with writers and composers would take time, a commodity Fosse felt was now in short supply following his health crisis during *Chicago*. As he told a reporter, "Finally, I thought, 'What the hell, I'm 50. I'd better do it now.'"[3]

A bookless song and dance show held an additional interest for Fosse. More than one ballet company had courted him in recent years. Robert Joffrey was the most persistent, and Fosse had expressed interest in setting a new work on his company. Joffrey went so far as to send Fosse a recording of Cole Porter songs as possible inspiration for a new work for the Joffrey Ballet. However, in their correspondence, Fosse revealed his trepidations. Writing that he was not sufficiently stirred by the Porter music, he added, "I believe there are very strong limitations to my choreographic abilities, but I do feel with proper music, etc. I could do a good one."[4] Perhaps by working away from the ballet world and asserting that his Broadway ballet would be a potpourri of different dance styles, Fosse could have it both ways.

Settling into a studio at Broadway Arts, Fosse played recordings of music from all genres and experimented with bits and pieces of movement. Eventually he brought in a skeleton crew of dancers to try out more extended pieces of choreography. Linda Haberman, one of those dancers, recalled his process: "He would just come up with two counts of eight here and four counts of eight there. It was like creating a vocabulary. And then he would mix and match it and turn it upside down and do the counterpoints to it, and play around with it."[5]

As musical director Gordon Lowry Harrell worked out musical phrasings for songs by Erik Satie, Louis Prima, Cat Stevens, and others, and the dancers learned his movement combinations, Fosse gained confidence that he could create enough varied dances to fill an evening. He could, in other words, "write" a show, using choreography as his words.

In August, *Variety* loftily reported that Fosse was preparing *Dancing*, a plotless musical expected "to create an entirely new kind of theatrical performance."[6] A month later, the trade paper *Back Stage* gave more clues about the new show, now with a different title, when it listed upcoming audition dates. "'Dancers' will consist of *dancing only*. There is no book, no dialogue, no singing," indicating that Fosse was still not entirely sure what form it would take.[7]

Dancin', the show's eventual title, conveyed an earthy, unpretentious approach. Its subtitle, A New Musical Entertainment, would reassure audiences that it was closer in spirit and execution to Broadway than to ballet. Even for a show with no stars or elaborate scenery, *Dancin'* reflected the increased production costs of mounting a Broadway musical. At $900,000, its budget was nearly twice as much as that for *Pippin*, only five years earlier. Half the funding was provided by the Shubert Organization and half by Columbia Pictures, the company producing *All That Jazz*, with both Fosse and Sam Cohn, his agent since David Begelman left CMA's New York agency for Los Angeles, contributing small investments.[8]

By now, a Fosse audition drew practically every dancer in New York, and even some nondancers. "We saw over a thousand people," said Kathryn Doby, once again assisting Fosse. "It actually was like the auditions you see in *All That Jazz*. The whole stage was full of people."[9] Fosse's "Tea for Two" combination was taught to groups of fifty, then ten, and finally performed by three dancers at a time. Those lucky enough to be kept could expect to spend the entire day learning a series of combinations from the new show. As always, Fosse was the most considerate of choreographers, as Ron Schwinn, who appeared in *Chicago*, later recalled. "Fosse gives the fairest audition of anybody. He's right on stage with you . . . . He'll work with you on a combination. He wants you to give it your best shot."[10]

(Fosse had very definite ideas about the kind of individuals he wanted in his shows. Ken Urmston, a dance captain for *Pippin* during its run, recalled a replacement audition for one female dancer. After a day of dancing and singing, the applicants had been reduced to two women. When Fosse chose one over the other, Urmston asked why. "He said, 'I didn't like the way she talked to the piano player. She was very mean to him. I picked up on that right away, and I don't want that in my show.'"[11])

Fosse later held forth on other qualities he looked for in dancers. Trying not to look at faces at first because "I want to see their body lines and to see how well they dance," he kept everyone who danced well "regardless of how they look."[12] He also spent time talking with them to gather hints about their personalities. He later reflected, "I like to work with dancers who are not just *technical* people. They have to be able to act, so it's not just a step they're dancing but an emotion."[13] He added one more important attribute: "There should be a sexuality going on stage, an exchange. It's important that you find those people up there attractive in one way or another."[14]

"He would just get so jaunty," said Gwen Verdon, who remembered the playfulness of Fosse's many flirtations.[15] But a magazine profile of the period painted Fosse as a benign predator, always eager to help female dancers with their stretches and hip placements. "You can assume he's going to try to make you," an unnamed dancer said.[16] When he watched his female dancers rehearse, remembered stage manager Maxine Glorsky, "he would make sexual sounds that they had gotten to him."[17] The sexuality Fosse brought to his work was bracing, but for some female dancers its offstage manifestation was not always welcome.

Ann Reinking's participation was a given, and she would be heavily featured in the ensemble cast. Fosse cast several women similar to Reinking: beautiful and leggy, with a smoky sensuality, like Sandahl Bergman and Vicki Frederick. Broadway stalwarts like Wayne Cilento (an original cast member of A Chorus Line) and Fosse regulars Christopher Chadman, John Mineo, and Richard Korthaze were hired, but Fosse also cast dancers who had worked with ballet and modern dance companies. The most notable cast addition was Charles Ward, a principal dancer with American Ballet Theatre.

Fosse also cast two African American dancers: Edward Love, who had danced with Alvin Ailey's company, and Karen G. Burke. "That's the way it was back then in the 60s and 70s. In a show that was predominantly white, you'd have one black girl and one black guy," said Valarie Pettiford, who would appear in the show's first national tour.[18] At a time when many musicals counted no African Americans among their casts, Fosse had an eye for nontraditional casting. In Pippin, he cast Ben Vereen in a role not specifically requiring an African American. During Chicago's run, when Mary McCarty left the role of the Matron, Fosse replaced her with African American actress Alaina Reed, and he sought Paula Kelly from Sweet Charity as a possible replacement for Chita Rivera. He would hire many African American dancers during this new show's run, and roles would be assigned regardless of race or ethnicity (or, in a few cases, gender). Its first national tour, which opened in early 1979, featured five African American dancers, unusual for the time.

In a break from his last two shows, Fosse assembled an almost new design team. Willa Kim's background as a costume designer for dance companies like American Ballet Theatre and the Joffrey and Eliot Feld companies made her an obvious choice to design wardrobe for a cast of dancers. Scenic designer Peter Larkin created simple fabric louvers along the back wall that could twist and fold and catch Jules Fisher's ever-changing lighting patterns.

Fisher later reflected on the particular challenge of Dancin': "I had to watch Bob Fosse's choreography, spend time with him and get to know intimately what he wanted from each moment. Bob's choreography very frequently consists of small physical movements . . . . if you want to see the person crook a little finger, you have to have a lot of light or very specific light. In 'Dancin,' there are many light sources from multiple directions just to show an arm movement or hand movement."[19] Fisher would also join the Shuberts and Columbia Pictures as producers of *Dancin'*. Fosse proved as apprehensive about producers as ever. "Bob wanted someone who would to some extent be not just a go between, between the Shuberts and himself, but a bit of a protector," Fisher explained.[20]

Fosse's contract guaranteed him 5 percent of every dollar paid at the box office, increasing to 10 percent when the show recouped its costs. The contract granted his direction, choreography, and continuity (referred to as "Fosse material") the same rights as in a standard Dramatists Guild contract, thereby making him not only the sole author of the evening but also its undisputed "Muscle."[21]

"Dancers are exceptional—the most disciplined, hardest-working, most underpaid people in show business. The happiest moments I've ever had have been working with them," Fosse declared.[22] Alone with sixteen dancers, Fosse was in his element when he began rehearsals right after Christmas 1977. Beginning with Neil Diamond's idyllic instrumental "Prologue (Hot Summer Night)," Fosse establishes a pattern that carries through many of the evening's dances, in which a slow, teasing buildup brims with sexual tension before exploding into orgiastic dance.

In silence, a lone female dancer enters the bare stage and stands at center. Only when she begins to move does the music start. Reaching with one arm, she stretches it up from her knee to above her head, slowly, languidly, and then extends the same arm to the side. Her leg is beveled in a showgirl pose with one leg straight and the other bending in slightly, in demi-pointe. This move-ment motif, first seen in Fosse's "Cool Hand Luke" dance for Gwen Verdon, runs through the opening number and is another example of Fosse choreographing without thought to gender. Gwen Verdon later mused, "He's very sensual and he thinks movement is the same for men and women. The only difference is that women wear high heels."[23] In this case, the women are in flat shoes, and the costumes—tights, leotards, leg warmers—are colorful variations on dance class attire. The dancers enter singly or in pairs, earnestly executing pirouettes, lunges, and développés as if examining their form in a classroom mirror.[24]

With the full company onstage and isolated in squares of light, they respond to the building tempo, agitatedly flicking heads, legs, and arms. Linda Haberman described Fosse's direction: "It's like you're a race horse at the gate, right before they leave it. And you just can't wait. You're so jacked up, it's like you're ready to explode."[25] As the beat kicks in, they strike poses with vibrating "jazz hands" and dance a brief combination with go-go headshakes and pulsating frugs, before exiting. From either side of the stage, one dancer runs to meet another as they jump and do a flick kick at center before running off again. The first two danc-ers start downstage, and each successive duo arrives farther upstage. In Fisher's focused lighting, they give the look of dancing in an infinite hallway.

Throughout the number, the dancers regroup upstage, then charge downstage, split apart, then travel back together. As they hit a series of angular poses across the stage, two singers emerge on either side of the stage from the same ladders Fosse used in *Pippin* and begin the vocal for "Crunchy Granola Suite." The dancers do a series of "popcorn jumps" in which, with bodies rigid, they arch up and down, pointing to the floor, first randomly (like kernels popping), then all together.

Fosse continually cross-stitches movement, deploying his dancers in diagonal groupings and swirling patterns. Near the end, they rise from a lunge in a wave of movement that starts upstage and ends with the last dancer downstage. As the number winds down, they return to the showgirl movement, but Fosse holds off the climax by sending them into a sharp series of aerobic moves before ending with the same rump-in-the-air pose from *Pippin*'s "Gisella Ballet."

"Prologue (Hot Summer Night)"/"Crunchy Granola Suite" has no particular point of view other than signaling that *Dancin'* will feature bigger, more virtuosic dances than Fosse's last two shows. Steps that looked current when they were done in *Sweet Charity* or *Pippin* now seem ever-so-slightly dated, and the geometric tableaus the dancers strike have the air of a television variety show. Still, the number demonstrates that Fosse's ability to weave bodies across space and into provocative and imaginative groupings was stronger than ever.

It is no surprise in an evening of song and dance that Fosse would pay tribute to his childhood dance idol, Fred Astaire. In fact, "I Wanna Be a Dancin' Man," from Astaire's film *The Belle of New York* (1952), could be the evening's guiding principle. Its wistful lyric about the impermanence of dance ("I wanna leave my footsteps on the sands of time / If I never leave a dime") had special appeal for Fosse. Ann Reinking called the song his "creed and motto, and it was personal."[26]

As the orchestra strikes up Ralph Burns's jazzy, MGM-style orchestration of the Johnny Mercer–Harry Warren song, the curtain rises on a stageful of Fred Astaires, all dressed in suits the color of vanilla ice cream, white gloves, and Astaire's trademark necktie used as a belt. Clutching straw boaters to their chests, the cast reverently whispers Mercer's lyrics and references Astaire-isms—the debonair walk, the jaunty headshake—before splintering off, leaving a trio center stage. The music transitions to stop time as the trio slides and shuffles, and soon they are supplanted by other small units slithering onstage as the tribute to Astaire becomes filtered through Fosse. Long, extended développés lead into elegant, slow-moving struts. Soft-shoe variations are danced with heads down and hats low over the eyes. Walks lead with the pelvis. Hands hang at the waist. White-gloved hands hold hat brims between thumb and forefinger, with fingers splayed wide.[27]

Oddly enough for a salute to Astaire, "I Wanna Be a Dancin' Man" contains traces of George Balanchine in both its intricate patterns and its self-consciously balletic bearing. As the music slides into rhythmic underscoring and a group of dancers take center stage slapping their thighs in counterpoint, others come and go, dreamily executing adagio pairings and arabesques. These decidedly non-Astaire moves eventually coalesce into two groups surrounding those at center. As their thigh slapping grows more aggressive, the others drop to their knees and shoot their hands to the sky, in a stage picture whose harmonious balance is Balanchine-worthy.

At last, the music dims to an expectant hum. With the utmost gravity, a dancer at center begins a new hand-and-thigh-slapping combination. It builds slowly as, one by one, the others join in. The pace accelerates, and as the music crescendos, the slapping becomes a hypnotic blur. By this time, Fosse has repeatedly edged

A stageful of Astaires in "I Wanna Be a Dancin' Man" from Dancin'.
Photo by Martha Swope © Billy Rose Theatre Division, The New York Public Library for the Performing Arts.

the dance to a climax, only to pull back and start over, each time building tension and anticipation of a final release. When at last it arrives, the result is thunderous. The lights bump up, the music blares, and the dancers explode, high kicking across the stage (though Fosse still cannot resist some hip shaking). They storm the front of the stage in a final coda that feels more like afterglow. Spent, they retreat as a lone dancer pulls an imaginary switch to turn the lights off, earning the dancers and the audience a most satisfied rest. "I Wanna Be a Dancin' Man" is Astaire seen through the lens of Fosse, who uses rhythm erotically, creating a number that teasingly surges, then pulls back endlessly until achieving release— the equivalent of danced foreplay.

"Jack always thought I allowed performers too much freedom . . . . He was a great teacher and a great choreographer. But he would have hated this number," Fosse said about Jack Cole and "Sing Sing Sing."[28] Fosse's emulation of Cole's style is unmistakable in the arrangement made famous by Benny Goodman and His Orchestra in their 1938 Carnegie Hall concert. (Cole himself had famously created a dance to the same arrangement in 1947.) But as with Astaire, Cole is only the starting point for Fosse's full-cast extravaganza.

Less a performance number than a reverie in which dance hall denizens respond to the onstage band, "Sing Sing Sing" opens on a stage filled with dancers in drooping, late-night postures. Only the drummer's tribal beat rouses them, and they move as if possessed by the rhythm. They kick and jerk off the stage, then return in startling gazelle leaps, pausing only to unwind. Hunched over, with their heads and arms flicking to the beat, they regroup at center before

Social dancing, 1940s. Fosse's big-band bacchanal, "Sing Sing Sing," in Dancin'.
Photo by Martha Swope © Billy Rose Theatre Division, The New York Public Library for the Performing Arts.

spilling out across the stage. Here and elsewhere Fosse incorporates variations on the lindy. The men do some of Fosse's most extensive knee work, spinning and sliding across the stage as athletically as any Jack Cole dancer.

Time and again, the dancers undulate and preen, lost in their own response to the beat, only to be snapped back into formation. Arrayed across the stage, they burst into a series of crescent jumps, leaping up with arms high above their head and fingers splayed, arching the torso in one direction while the arms and feet reach in the other, creating a human half-moon.[29]

The group breaks up and drifts off, making way for several variations in which the dancers forge a triangular connection between themselves, the musician, and his instrument, as pointed out by Diane Laurenson, who joined *Dancin'* during its run and later staged numerous tours of the show.[30] "Trombone Solo," danced by a trio of two men and a woman, unfolds with geometric precision. Sitting on the bandstand with the woman in front, hiding the two men directly behind her, they form a Fosse "stack," in which the front person extends her arms out at a downward angle, and the other two extend theirs at ever higher elevations, creating a sunburst effect.[31] The men roll their heads in opposite directions, as if angling for the woman from different vantage points. They wrap their arms around her as she writhes in their embrace. One by one, they fall over on each other, then link arms and slide across the floor. The woman wrests free and dances alone in the spotlight. Soon she brazenly mounts one of the men, who rocks her in a circle as she heaves in ecstasy while the other reaches for her from below. Finally, she falls to the floor, but with her desire still strong, she caresses the men's torsos as they carry her off upside down, hanging by her legs from their arms. Set to the trombone's throbbing rhythm, the dance suggests a wild ménage à trois with the woman the focal point of the men's ravenous attention. It is a moment of frank and unapologetic eroticism.

As the trio disappears into the wings, the spotlight picks up a dancer on the other side of the stage. Her double pirouette signals others to join her in an amoeba formation that becomes a throbbing, luminous organism moving through the sculpted light. When it reaches the center bandstand, it pauses briefly before splitting in two, revealing a dancer reclining in a pool of light. She punctuates the drumbeats with razor-sharp kicks in the air before falling into a swastika position. She hangs from the bandstand as her legs ferociously scissor across each other. Fosse choreographs "Trumpet Solo" around the leonine grace of Ann Reinking. (Reinking later reflected on the union of the trumpet and the dancer in the number. With the trumpet player immediately behind her on the bandstand, the dancer must be his equal in improvisatory gusto while still maintaining the precision of the steps.)[32]

It is a show-off number, built around Reinking's exquisite legs—graceful in repose, yet powerful and authoritative when unleashed. Her body absorbs the beat of the drums as she whips her long hair, jerking and shivering to the rhythms. Every kind of leg extension is featured, from battements to long, lingering développés. She traverses the stage in a series of cannonball jumps, pulling her legs up under her as she jumps, then flicking them out before landing.[33] A breathtaking running slide lands her back on the bandstand. As the trumpet hits a final, piercing tone, she executes a series of layouts, each more extended than the last. With her leg to the sky and her back arched toward the floor, she appears suspended in the air, barely touching the stage. Carried to a side ladder, she stands exultantly, the unquestioned queen of these dance hall revels.

Fosse and Reinking ended their relationship prior to *Dancin'*, but as with Verdon, their split had little bearing on their ability to work together. Reinking's elongated, classically trained body inspired Fosse to extend his choreographic reach, and many moments in *Dancin'* can be attributed to her influence. Like "If My Friends Could See Me Now," "Trumpet Solo" is Fosse showcasing the singular talents of a woman who had influenced his dance style.

Benny Goodman's own "Clarinet Solo," danced by a small ensemble, prompts Fosse's least inspired choreography. Fosse creates striking images as he bends the dancers into hieroglyphic figures, with arms extended high and wrists broken at a sharp right angle as they plié into the floor. But his mostly linear staging becomes monotonous. The climax, in which a lineup of women get their thighs stroked by the men lying below on their backs while the clarinet hits a long, lingering note is too obvious to be arousing.

"Piano Solo" is performed as a tap number, a form of dance unseen in *Dancin'* until now. (Audiences at the time exhaled in pleasure as the sounds of synchronized tapping filled the theater for the first time.) Typical of Fosse, he keeps the movements small. The soft, gentle unison taps by two dancers—who could be the Riff Brothers all grown up—mirror and sometimes work in counterpoint to the delicately swinging piano arrangement. Considering Fosse's early tap dance performances, it is surprising he used so little tap in a show devoted to all forms of dancing. "Piano Solo" is refreshing at the end of a long number driven by so much eroticized athleticism.

"Sing Sing Sing" concludes with a brief reprise of the opening sequence by the full cast, perhaps revealing that Fosse was running dry of ideas. (At fifteen minutes, it is one of his lengthiest pure dance numbers.) The number displays Jack Cole's angular aggression, his elongated arms that grab the air, and what Cole scholar Debra Levine calls "power blocks" or "wedges of power," a recurring motif of Cole's choreography in which unison steps performed by a cluster of dancers in triangular or square arrangements forge an image of power and authority.[34] But it also has a looseness at odds with Cole the disciplinarian and, for that matter, with much of Fosse's previous work. Transitions allow the cast to improvise, underscoring the number's relaxed "last call" feel. "Sing Sing Sing" also exceeds the erotic quotient of Cole's choreography. Driven by the relentless drums, Fosse turns "Sing Sing Sing" into a big band bacchanal.[35]

Some years earlier, Fosse had sketched out an idea for a dance using only "sounds and rhythms."[36] Fosse's truest collaborations were often with percussion, and a suite of dances built around varied and unusual percussion instruments was a natural addition to the new show. Stripped of melody, these four dances, developed by musical arranger Gordon Lowry Harrell to Fosse's specifications, reveal both his choreographic strengths and limitations. As if fearing the dances would not stand on their own, Fosse devised spoken introductions by cast members to establish a light, comic premise for the sequence.

"Percussion I" is danced to only a triangle and clave. The trio number is done in rounds, with one dancer's moves repeated in sequence by the other two. In a pool of light three women softly kneel, sifting sand through their fingers and stretching up toward the sun.[37] Their bodies intertwine, striking simple, graceful poses. Its final image is a reference to George Balanchine's *Apollo*, in which three muses pose in ascending arabesques behind Apollo. Easy, unadorned, and lasting only a moment, "Percussion I" is a grace note in a show of high-powered dance.

Disco bells, tambourines, tom-toms, and—stretching the definition of percussion—electric guitar are added for "Percussion II," a bounding male trio that begins with an entrance by trampoline and body rolls across the stage. The men are equally cocky and goofy in their oversized, baggy pants and sock caps as they trade boxing moves, jump over each other's shoulders, and slide on their stomachs. The start-and-stop rhythm anticipates hip-hop dancing of the next decade as it locks the dancers into one position, then frees them to pop into another. "Percussion II" was given a less playful, more macho performance when it was recreated for *Fosse* in 1999. With the men dressed in black tank tops emphasizing their lean musculature, the dance became a display of athleticism, with higher kicks and jumps and more aggressive sparring. Two decades after its creation, it remained fresh and remarkably contemporary.

Adding exotic instruments like cabasa, vibra slap, finger cymbals, and cuica, "Percussion III" becomes a festival of calypso and Afro-Cuban rhythms. The dance lifts whole chunks of mambo steps from "Who's Got the Pain?" Fosse recycles his old trick of moving a group of dancers into the wings and returning them to the stage before the last dancer exits, making his group of eight dancers look twice as large. This time they mince in from the wings in relevé and plié, with

In "Percussion I" from Dancin', *Fosse references the three muses posed in ascending arabesques in George Balanchine's* Apollo. *Front, Robin Alpert, middle, Rita A. Sullivan, and back, Kim Noor. Photo by Martha Swope © Billy Rose Theatre Division, The New York Public Library for the Performing Arts.*

pelvises pulsing and arms pinned sharply back, giving the body a corkscrew profile. Willa Kim's costumes are at their most fanciful, with curlicues and pom-poms popping out all over the calypso-styled leotards. A wide stance in second-position plié, with arms akimbo and heads tilted downward, is a delightful variation on the Fosse silhouette. Finally, the tempo decelerates and the dancers wind down, bending and drooping until they turn away from the audience, bend over, and balance their hats on top of their hips. "Percussion III" is not Fosse's most original choreography, but its rhythms, costumes, and quirky dance profiles give it a charming folkloric feel and make it one of the most pleasing numbers in *Dancin'*.

Edgard Varèse's "Ionisation," a composition for percussion ensemble, is the final and fitting piece in Fosse's percussion suite. According to Verdon, Fosse was excited by "any dancer who had a unique quality that would extend his capabilities as a choreographer."[38] He must have been pleased to have Charles Ward in the

Fosse works another variation on his Latin-themed dances with "Percussion III" in Dancin'.
*Left to right: Karen G. Burke, Gregory B. Drotar, Ann Reinking, Blaine Savage, Jill Cook
(on floor), Sandahl Bergman, Edward Love, and Gail Benedict. Photo by Martha Swope ©
Billy Rose Theatre Division, The New York Public Library for the Performing Arts.*

Dancin' cast and may have felt that setting a short abstract piece on a celebrated
classical dancer would serve as a warm-up for an extended ballet.

Amid searchlights and wailing sirens, Fosse sends Ward darting across the
stage in a vague paranoia scenario. Fosse throws in familiar hip bumps and
shoulder isolations between pointless slides and knee crawls. Seldom has one
dancer labored so hard to so little effect. (Drummer Allen Herman recalls Ward
requiring oxygen in the wings as soon as he came offstage.)[39] What saves the
number and even makes it a showstopper are Ward's balletic turns and gravity-
defying leaps. But here they come off as tricks bearing little relation to the other
movements.

Fosse was fond of noting his limited choreographic vocabulary, and
"Ionisation" proves his point. "Perfectly dreadful," dance critic Deborah Jowitt
called it.[40] Its overlay of portentousness looks like self-defense, as if Fosse knows
his reach exceeds his choreographic grasp. He wants it both ways: when the self-
serious piece finally ends after several false stops, it is with a mocking exclamation, "That's all, folks!," making it all seem a stunt.

"Ionisation" also created practical problems. A year into the run, and after
the first national tour had begun, general manager Marvin Krauss wrote to the
publishing company that controlled its rights, informing them that the Varèse
composition would be removed from the show as of July 2, 1979. Explaining the
decision, he pointed to the challenge of finding dancers who could follow the difficult piece and the frequent injuries they sustained. Citing the "extraordinary
musicianship the piece requires," he also noted that local musicians along the
tour stops needed more rehearsal time to play it than was available.[41] The dance

was reshaped to new, less complex music by Gordon Lowry Harrell and its title became simply "Percussion IV."

A letter from Fosse to Charles Ward, on tour with the show in Chicago, offers some insight into Fosse's reinterpretation of the dance as a more overt show-off piece. "Obviously, the music is of a much lighter, more playful mood and therefore your performance of it should be along those lines . . . . abandonment, joy and playfulness are the key words and, in straightforward showfolk language, I think you should smile more," he wrote, urging Ward to "[give] the impression of a dancer in a studio with a mirror toying pleasurably with rhythms and steps. I certainly don't think it should retain any of its true seriousness that was in the Varese piece."[42]

Diane Laurenson remembers Fosse visiting the company of the second national tour and restaging "Percussion IV" for herself and another woman. After a few performances, he recast it with two men before finally returning it to a solo for a male dancer.[43] The story demonstrates Fosse's admirable willingness to revisit his work to adjust or improve it. It also reveals his continuing dissatisfaction with a piece that he might have hoped would lead to more challenging work. "Percussion IV" was resurrected for *Fosse* and during its run proved a draw for stars from the ballet world like Desmond Richardson, Julio Bocca, and Damien Woetzel. But it was situated early in the show and lost among more memorable examples of Fosse's choreography.

Jerry Jeff Walker's "Mr. Bojangles" is based on his jailhouse encounter with a street performer who called himself "Bojangles" after Bill Robinson, the great African American tap dancer. The song chronicles the life and times of this itinerant drifter who dances for spare change and free drinks. Bojangles is a type Fosse probably encountered in his early performing days, and one that many performers fear becoming. He gives the character a dance alter ego called "Mr. Bojangles' Spirit," who embodies not his reality but his aspiration. Fosse conceived the number at home, using sliding glass doors in his apartment that allowed reflections to be seen at night. While Fosse danced small steps close to the door, he instructed his daughter, Nicole, now nearly fifteen and a ballet student, to "dance behind me and do the ballet version of what I do."[44] In the reflected darkness, with his daughter as co-choreographer, Fosse began to embody the old man, bent and shuffling, mirrored by a youthful spirit capable of dancing as he could only dream.

More than a dance, Fosse made "Mr. Bojangles" a musical dramatization titled "Recollections of an Old Dancer" and wrote a brief voice-over introduction of a judge sentencing Bojangles to a jail term for public vagrancy and drunkenness. Bojangles is discovered in a debonair stance but stooped over by the years, while his Spirit stands beside him in the erect posture associated with Robinson. "Mr. Bojangles" becomes a dance of idealized remembrance, and Jules Fisher fills the stage with spots of light, through which his Spirit leaps, moving in and out of Bojangles's memory.

Unfortunately, Fosse's invention takes him no further than the number's conception. The Spirit's jetés and balletic postures never connect with the song-and-dance Bojangles. Not unlike "Ionisation," the ballet steps seem random and inorganic to the story Fosse is trying to tell. Only rarely does Fosse forge a dance bond between the two, as when Bojangles crosses the floor in a bent-over strut while his Spirit kicks high and proud beside him. While the number is relatively short, it feels longer, and for someone who shunned sentimentality, it is odd to see Fosse embrace it here.

Prior to starting work on *Dancin'*, Fosse began collecting images of modern dance and ballet performances, many of them from contemporary works featuring dancers wrapping their bodies around each other to create complex shapes, or executing unusual lifts, often with the man on the floor raising a woman above him with either his arms or his legs. Some images include two men partnering each other. Others display dancers topless or nude.

Many of these images found their way into an ambitious ballet with songs by pop songwriters Melissa Manchester and Carole Bayer Sager. "Joint Endeavor" depicts couples in *La Ronde*–style mating. A female singer hangs from a ladder on the side of the stage, breathily crooning "Easy," a song urging a lover to give in to passion ("If you want me / you can have me"). A man and woman perform a pas de deux, as shadowy figures appear from the darkness and offer them puffs of marijuana. Under this influence, one partner leaves and is replaced by another, in an increasingly joyless roundelay, as the music switches to the bluntly titled "If It Feels Good, Let It Ride."[45]

"Joint Endeavor" looks to be Fosse's comment on dead-end promiscuity and drug use, and maybe even a bit of self-flagellation. But his choreography is at its tawdriest here, as the dancers feign wordless passion in a mechanized series of poses more athletic than sensuous. (Some of the movements later found their way into the "Airotica" pas de deux in *All That Jazz*.) One could also reasonably ask what the mysterious chanteuse and the black-coated henchmen have to do with these couples. In "Red Light Ballet," Fosse pushed the limits of frank sexuality by dramatizing in dance both the exuberance and the degradation of Anna Christie's life in a bordello. "Joint Endeavor," lacking a scenario beyond sexual posturing, is merely crude and tedious.

Fosse created several short dances to serve as breathers from the more taxing full-cast numbers. "Big Noise from Winnetka" is nothing more than a crossover done "in one." But as its taut trio fans apart then pulls together like an accordion, it has the sly playfulness of Fosse at his best. The gimmicky "Fourteen Feet" is preceded by a carnival barker–like introduction extolling "An American Musical Foist! . . . And that includes *Oklahoma, West Side Story*, and any of those 'so-called' innovatives . . . . For the first time on any Broadway musical stage, and choreographed by a *professional* choreographer, an entire dance without—I repeat, without moving . . . the feet!"[46] With that, seven dancers nail their wooden clogs to the floor and step into them as Cat Stevens's synthesized "Was Dog a Doughnut" begins percolating. Dressed in dark leotards with two phosphorescent stripes painted down their front, the dancers writhe and shimmy as black lights reduce them to fourteen undulating white strips.

The short number goes down smoothly but was an inventive surprise only to audiences unfamiliar with Alwin Nikolais's pioneering use of costume and lighting to obscure the dancer's body and create new shapes and forms, and of electronic music. In addition, as dance critic Arlene Croce astutely pointed out, "Footwork has about as much to do with Fosse style as lariat-twirling: gyrating bodies are the essence of that style."[47] "Fourteen Feet" is an entertaining novelty, not a work of great originality.

In addition to dialogue and staged introductions, Fosse created what he called "little theatre pieces . . . in the short story form"[48] (some of which were contributed by Herb Gardner and Paddy Chayefsky, it was later revealed).[49] "The Female Star Spot," another "in one" number, featured four women singing Dolly Parton's hit "Here You Come Again." Their discovery that they are all singing about the same cheating man could be Fosse's own comment on his reputation for carrying on affairs with more than one woman at a time. In "A Manic Depressive's Lament," a song and dance solo performed to Jerry Leiber and Mike Stoller's "I've Got Them Feelin' Too Good Today Blues," a man is distrustful of good luck and is truly happy only when informed of bad news. The number becomes a comic riff on the very real anxieties that drove Fosse to check into a psychiatric hospital after his 1973 awards sweep.

One intriguing Fosse idea was a dance choreographed to a soundtrack of television commercials for products like Geritol, Kentucky Fried Chicken, Ban deodorant, Kellogg's Cornflakes, Purina Dog Chow, Hostess Cupcakes, and more. A detailed inventory lists exact timings and music and dialogue cues for sixty-five commercials under consideration. A number of the commercials are for feminine hygiene products; others feature masculine voice-overs for products like automobile tires and men's colognes. The idea was later abandoned, but the presumed satire on American life created by the juxtaposition of the commercials may have found its way into the show's "America" sequence featuring sardonic observations on American men and women and on race.[50]

With celebrations for the United States' Bicentennial still ringing, Fosse ended *Dancin'* on a patriotic note with dances built around American anthems and marches. It could have been his response to Balanchine's *Stars and Stripes* ballet but tilted toward his own brand of satire. As the cast, in sleek black tuxedos, slowly assembles across the stage, Fosse's voice-over quotes a diversity of American opinion, from Thomas Paine ("Those who expect to reap the blessing of freedom must understand the fatigue of supporting it") to Al Capone ("My rackets are run on strictly American lines and they are going to stay that way").[51] The short dances that follow mirror the variety of viewpoints, from somber to smart aleck.

A slow-building "Yankee Doodle Dandy" gives way to "the sexiest hornpipe this side of Scotland," according to the advance publicity for *Dancin'*.[52] "Gary Owen" is Fosse with a flavor of Irish step dancing, along with big arabesque jumps from its trio. He follows it with comments on American gender stereotypes. "Under the Double Eagle" presents a Fosse trio of strutting, muscle-flexing macho men whose satin pastel boxer shorts with hearts on the back mark them as not so tough as they think. "Stout Hearted Men" is slowed to a grinding burlesque beat as three of the longest-legged, long-haired, and most beautiful women in the cast extend their pelvises and suck their thumbs. (Ann Reinking, Sandahl Bergman, and Vicki Frederick were in the number's first cast.) Meant as satire, the number is too short to make more than a superficial impression. In an evening in which his women dancers have been presented as sexually forthright, this brief dance represents a step backward, reducing American women to "infantile sluts," as Arlene Croce put it.[53]

As the orchestra plays a jaunty "Dixie," the show's two African Americans walk onstage in disbelief. "Is that our number?" they ask, before turning the song back on itself. Singing the rewritten lyrics, "Oh, I'm glad I'm not in the land of cotton / Old times there are best forgotten / Get away, get away / Get away, Dixieland,"[54] they dance a witty spoof complete with tongue-in-cheek shuffling, ending in a death pose, with legs flexed in rigor mortis. "When Johnny Comes Marching Home," slowed down and dramatically emoted, is followed by a dance of ebullient welcome before again turning somber with a biting reading of the final lyric, "And we'll all feel gay when Johnny comes marching home." Perhaps intended as Fosse's comment on the futility of war, the brief dance consisted of little more than runs across the stage, and the overall effect was overwrought.

Fosse relied on old-fashioned ballet showmanship for two rousing dances. "Rally 'Round the Flag" and "Stars and Stripes Forever" drew gasps and applause with their fouettés, pirouettes à la seconde, saut de basques, and jetés across the stage. Audiences unfamiliar with ballet performances were stunned to see this caliber of virtuoso dancing on a Broadway stage.

Ladies of burlesque: Fosse's American women. Left to right: Vicki Frederick, Sandahl Bergman, and Christine Colby. Photo by Martha Swope © Billy Rose Theatre Division, The New York Public Library for the Performing Arts.

Finally, the entire company returned for a discofied reprise of "Yankee Doodle Dandy," appropriately called "Yankee Doodle Disco" and choreographed by Christopher Chadman. Fosse generously offered the show's final spot to Chadman, a trusted protégé. "Yankee Doodle Disco" was a prime example of robotic, fast-moving disco moves—*Saturday Night Fever* with dance technique—and ended *Dancin'* with a slice of 1978 social dancing.

> "Staging excites me, the sheer *theatricality* of theater, even though there's something naked and vulgar about it."
>
> Bob Fosse, 1979[55]

Fosse imposed a framing device on *Dancin'* that treated the entire performance as a kind of theatrical ceremony. The audience enters to find a bare stage with rows of overhead lights hanging near the stage floor. Soon a stage manager's voice calls out instructions to lift the stage lights, lower the house lights, and cue the first entrance. At the conclusion of "Yankee Doodle Disco," the stage manager calls out cues to ready the stage for curtain calls. The dancers improvise their individual bows while dance footage of each of them plays on a screen. Unlike a conventional bow, their brief improvisations keep them performing. As they exit, the show's credits roll, as if in a film. Everything is ritualized: the cues, the bows, the credits, the very act of dancing. These metatheatrical devices call attention to *Dancin'* as a self-consciously conceived "show," with even the most lighthearted moments exuding a studied, confined theatricality. It is difficult to imagine any of the show's numbers being performed in daylight.

Dancin' was a marathon for its cast, and to give them opportunities to rest, Fosse structured it in three acts. He was unafraid to start where other directors would end. Each act began with a showstopper: act 1's "Prologue (Hot Summer Night)"/"Crunchy Granola Suite," "I Wanna Be a Dancin' Man" in act 2, and the final act's "Sing Sing Sing"—arguably the show's three best dances. The structure forced him to start at a high level of excitement and then vary the pace, building to a further peak by the end of each act.

When *Dancin'* opened in Boston during a record snowfall, the reviews were as brutal as the weather. *Variety* dismissed it as "an odd collection of Bob Fosse's leftover choreographic ideas, his casual notebook jottings on rock, raunch, and the American flag."[56] The *Boston Phoenix's* Don Shewey accused Fosse of "turning a potentially spectacular, all-dance Broadway show into a lame-brained revue studded with sleazy sex-skits—*Hellzapoppin'* with humpin'."[57]

Much of their criticism focused on two sex-drenched comic dance sketches. In "The Dream Barre," danced to Bach's "Sonata for Violin Solo, No. 4," a bespectacled male ballet student fantasizes about the beautiful girl next to him in class. As the ballet master barks instructions, the two dance a pas de deux of sexual positions that would have closed the burlesque theaters of Fosse's youth. The boy gropes the girl's breasts and simulates cunnilingus. By the time the ballet master commands, "Now, in and out, in and out, in and out. Come, come, come," the boy is predictably pushing up and down on her as if performing intercourse.[58]

Possibly Fosse was trying to get at the fantasies dancers may harbor while doing repetitious barre work surrounded by attractive classmates with beautiful bodies. However, the result is dismayingly juvenile—a single entendre smirk rather than double entendre wit. It is disconcerting to read Fosse's description of "The Dream Barre" as "about falling in love in a ballet class."[59]

The centerpiece of the third act was an elaborate sketch called "Welcome to the Big City," performed to Erik Satie's dreamy "Trois Gymnopédies." A yokel from Dubuque, Iowa, arrives in New York City and is immediately set upon by every hustler in town. He is harassed, propositioned, and masturbated by hookers, massage parlor employees, strippers, and sales clerks. He encounters a dominatrix named Benita Bruise and a hooker who greets him with, "Do you want to pet my poodle, mister?"[60] His New York City experience ends with him mugged and lying on Eighth Avenue, perhaps as a comment on the seediness of 1978 Times Square.

Fosse's sketches are throwbacks to the burlesque routines he watched from the wings as a young performer. But the good-natured raunchiness and comic verve of those old routines is deadened by his insistence on the explicit. These two sketches mark Fosse as surprisingly out of touch, a "dirty old man" of Broadway.

Once again out of town and faced with bad reviews, Fosse got to work on improvements. There was immediate urging from Gerald Schoenfeld and Bernard Jacobs of the Shubert Organization to trim the show's sexually explicit and unfunny moments. (Jacobs scornfully called "The Dream Barre" the "cunnilingus number.")[61] Fosse's instinct was to dismiss criticism from producers. "The fact that he shared with the cast this sort of pushback from the producers made me feel that he kind of enjoyed it, to a degree," Linda Haberman recalled.[62] Nevertheless, midway through the Boston tryout, "Welcome to the Big City" was eliminated, though Fosse held firm on "The Dream Barre," streamlining it but never eliminating its essential crudeness.

Before leaving Boston, an announcement was added at the very top of the show explaining in wisecracking fashion just what the audience could expect: ". . . what you are about to see is an almost plotless musical. Only *once* will 'boy meet girl'. . . 'boy lose girl'. There will be *no* villains tonight . . . *no* baritone heroes, *no* orphanages, *no* Christmas trees, *no* messages . . . . What you will see is dancin' . . . dancin' . . . *some* singin' . . . *and more dancin'*. Ladies and gentlemen, we hope you enjoy our *Dancin'*."[63] Similar to *Chicago*'s opening announcement, the statement clarified the show's purpose and set a light tone for what would follow (and also got in an unsubtle dig at Broadway's family musical hit *Annie*). If it misrepresents Fosse's more serious dance moments, it let audiences know that *Dancin'* would be fast, flip, and not to be taken seriously—a musical entertainment with no profundities.

> "Who knows? This may be my final comeback—Fosse's final farewell musical."
> Bob Fosse, 1978[64]

Aside from the elimination of "Welcome to the Big City," *Dancin'* changed remarkably little between Boston and its New York opening at the Broadhurst Theater on March 27, 1978—barely nine months since Fosse first entered Broadway Arts with a stack of records and an idea for his all-dance musical. Reviews ran the gamut from pans to over-the-top raves like that of Clive Barnes in the *New York Post*, who gushed, "I think it is the most enjoyable musical I have ever seen."[65]

The *New York Times*, which put Fosse and the show on the front page of its Sunday Arts and Leisure section, gave it not one, but two, negative notices. After daily theater critic Richard Eder weighed in ("At its strongest, 'Dancin'' has the qualities of a spectacular recital rather than an integrated musical show"),[66] Walter Kerr zeroed in on what he saw as the differences between ballet and Fosse's style as the basis for an evening of dance: "Dance can stand by itself when it aspires to, and achieves, the interior integrity, the long spiritual spine, of ballet. But this is mainly *show* dancing, these are the steps that have distinguished and/ or set fire to 'Sweet Charity' and 'Cabaret' and 'Pippin' . . . . they are decorative, illustrative, meant for reinforcing something else. They want a book, if only a book to fight with."[67]

Nearly every critic commented on the show's general overlay of sexuality, sometimes positively, like T. E. Kalem in *Time* magazine, who crowned Fosse "the choreographer-king of sensuality."[68] But Linda Winer of the *Chicago Tribune* decried Fosse's "appalling willingness to extend stunted pubescence into an obsession" and the show's "ongoing tedium of sexual heat."[69] Only half in jest, she pleaded, "Somebody should please tie this show's tubes before it makes more."[70]

While "The Dream Barre" and "Joint Endeavor" stayed in *Dancin'* for the entire Broadway run and the first national tour of major cities, neither was included in any of the show's subsequent tours. Fosse may have liked courting controversy, but he finally had to acknowledge the essential weakness of both numbers. Ultimately, the critics mattered less than audience enthusiasm, and in that regard, *Dancin'* was an unqualified success, marketed as a sexy, high-energy experience, a celebration of what Fosse called "the sheer joy of dancing."[71]

With *Dancin'* settled in at the Broadhurst as a hit, Fosse was often asked to contrast his new show with Michael Bennett's *A Chorus Line*, still selling out in its third year next door at the Shubert Theater and long since designated a landmark musical. Fosse called *A Chorus Line* "a great concept for a musical, but if you see it again, watch how much they sing and talk about dancing and how little they do."[72] "There's more dancing in *Dancin'*," he concluded, with just a touch of exasperation with the comparison.[73]

Fosse also may have been defensive about unfavorable comparisons by critics like Wendy Perron, who wrote in the *Village Voice*, "If Bennett started with an idea about gypsy dancers and ended with a work about identity and survival, Fosse started with the 'joy of dancing' and ended with a theatrical equivalent of the *Ed Sullivan Show*."[74] "Fosse was always insanely jealous of Michael," claimed producer Bernard Jacobs, who had a close friendship with Bennett.[75] "He regarded himself as the ultimate creative force in the theater and wanted to receive the accolades which he perceived were appropriate for that person, and the fact that Michael was as successful as he was annoyed the hell out of him."[76]

Dancin' received seven Tony Award nominations, including two for Fosse's direction and choreography. It lost the Best Musical award to *Ain't Misbehavin'*, another musical revue, but Fisher won for his lighting, as did Fosse, to no one's surprise, for his choreography.

The minimal dialogue and lack of plot in *Dancin'* made it the perfect Broadway musical for the growing number of non-English-speaking tourists visiting New York. *Dancin'* ultimately ran more than four years, tallying 1,774 performances. Next to *Pippin*, it was Fosse's longest-running show, as well as his most successful touring property. Two national tours, a bus-and-truck edition, and international companies kept *Dancin'* traveling across the United States and around the world for several years. With his gross percentages as creator and his stake as an investor, it also made Fosse a wealthy man.

Early on, Fosse touted *Dancin'* as a cornucopia of different genres of dancing: "Tap, acrobatic, classical ballet, modern ballet, jazz, rock . . . . Soft shoe. If I could think of anything else, I'd put that in, too."[77] But in its final form, there was considerably less variety. *Dancin'* turned out to be pure Fosse, a genre unto himself, and it revealed more about him than he may have imagined.

At it worst, *Dancin'* displayed both an adolescent, leering vision of sex and a surprising trace of schmaltz. It showed Fosse straining hard to expand his style, successfully with the brawny athleticism of "Sing Sing Sing" but ineffectively in his use of classical dance in numbers like "Ionisation." Fosse was still a bottom-line showman, just like his early mentor, George Abbott. He might have sought to forge a new creative path with this show, but not at the expense of delivering a hit.

But at its considerable best, *Dancin'* brought together the kinetic energy and theatrical flair that sparked every Fosse show from *The Pajama Game* through *Chicago*. Whether *Dancin'* was revue, concert, or recital was finally of no matter. It was the summation of Fosse's gifts as a choreographer, and its success was proof that his brand of theatrical dance (helped along by some singin' and talkin') could carry an entire evening. In a sense, he had finally created his long-awaited ballet.

Though no one knew it at the time, *Dancin'* also marked the end of the line for the kind of all-American Broadway dance that Fosse had helped define and popularize. In the next decade, Broadway movement would be driven by scenery rather than dancers and would speak with a British accent.

10
DANCE OF DEATH
• • •

"It's a little difficult to, you know, think that da-da-ta-da-ta-dum is that impor-
tant, you know, after you've been close to death. But of course, maybe it is.
I don't know. Maybe da-da-ta-da-ta-dum *is* the most important thing in life."
Bob Fosse, 1980[1]

"We sure picked the right subject, didn't we? I'm getting a lot of material here,"
Bob Fosse joked to Robert Alan Aurthur during a phone call from New York
Hospital as Fosse was preparing to undergo bypass surgery.[2] Fosse's hospitali-
zation not only interrupted rehearsals for *Chicago* and editing on *Lenny* but also
halted collaboration with Aurthur on his next project. With Fosse as director,
Aurthur was to write the screenplay for *Ending*, adapted from a recent novel by
Hilma Wolitzer about a woman's response to her husband's cancer diagnosis and
impending death. The irony was not lost on Fosse that he was now trapped in
Ending's hospital setting and facing the possibility of his own mortality.

Fosse and Aurthur picked up their work on *Ending* after *Chicago* opened, con-
ducting interviews with doctors and patients who had been given terminal diag-
noses. To relieve the story's grimness, they inserted on-camera appearances by
doctors, patients, and others who commented on the central story, a device Fosse
had used in *Lenny*. Pete Hamill, another of Fosse's writer friends, read a draft of
the *Ending* script and identified the essential spark that was missing: "I can think
of a dozen directors who could make this film. But from Bob Fosse, I expect something more." He recommended replacing the interviews with musical interludes
and suggested that someone like John Lennon be approached to create a musical "Death Suite" for Fosse to choreograph. "It could be that you can justify that
musical form by . . . making the man closer to you: a dancer or a choreographer
who is dying. That is what the great artists have always done," Hamill continued.
"You're only going to do this subject once, so you might as well make the attempt
at brilliance and originality."[3]

Hamill's suggestions led Fosse and Aurthur to drop *Ending* and use Fosse's
own recent experiences as the basis for a screenplay on the same subject driven by
music and dance. As they did with *Ending*, they began a series of interviews, this
time with Fosse's friends and family; those involved in *Chicago* and *Lenny*; and
the doctors and nurses from his hospitalization. Throughout the summer of 1976,

nearly one hundred interview subjects were urged to share their frank observations about his work methods, his views on death, his insecurities and phobias, his inability to remain faithful to any one woman, and any other topic that would shed light on Bob Fosse, who would be the central character in the new film, now titled *All That Jazz*.

All That Jazz seemed impossible to imagine as a major studio film. Daniel Melnick, the film's eventual executive producer, recalled, "They said it was self-indulgent, that the lead was a bastard, that he died at the end, and that it was about show business. Any one of those four bugaboos alone could kill a movie at the box office, but here was a property that had all four."[4] Melnick persuaded David Begelman, the president of Columbia Pictures and Fosse's former agent, to add *All That Jazz* to Columbia's production roster with a $6 million budget, which eventually ballooned to $9.5 million.[5]

Though Fosse disingenuously denied that *All That Jazz* was based entirely on him, the first draft screenplay was so autobiographical that it used the real names of everyone in Fosse's orbit. All *Chicago* participants are present and accounted for. Alan Heim, *Lenny*'s film editor, is seen cutting footage of Dustin Hoffman's performance; the film's producer, David Picker, arrives, urging Fosse to speed up the editing process; and Valerie Perrine calls Fosse in his hospital room. Fosse's agent, Sam Cohn, along with his friends Paddy Chayefsky and Herb Gardner, accompanied by Gardner's then girlfriend, Marlo Thomas, make appearances. Gwen Verdon, their daughter, Nicole, and his former girlfriend Ann Reinking are present, as is dancer Jennifer Nairn-Smith, who became involved with Fosse when she was cast in *Pippin*. Even actor Jerry Lanning, who was seeing Verdon at the time, shows up. Fosse's doctors are all named, and Harold Prince appears as a director recruited to take over *Chicago* should Fosse be unable to return to work. Sammy Davis Jr. appears as himself on a telethon fundraiser.

By the next draft, real names had been replaced, many with syllabically identical character names:

Bob Fosse	Steve (soon changed to Joe) Gideon
Gwen Verdon	Audrey Paris
Ann Reinking	Kate Jagger
Nicole Fosse	Michelle Gideon
Jennifer Nairn-Smith	Victoria Porter
Fred Ebb	Paul Dann
John Kander	Goddard Harris
Harold Prince	Lucas Sergeant
Dustin Hoffman	Davis Newman
Valerie Perrine	Kimberly Welles
Sammy Davis Jr.	O'Connor Flood
Robert Fryer	Jonesy Hecht
Ira Bernstein	Ted Christopher
Joseph Harris	Larry Goldie
Sam Cohn	Syd Julian

Paddy Chayefsky	Casey Arlinsky
Herb Gardner	Eli Black
Marlo Thomas	Blair Sullivan
David Picker	Joshua Penn
Phil Friedman	Murray Nathan[6]

Characterized as "a man who will allow himself to be adored but not loved," Joe Gideon possesses not only Fosse's professional curriculum vitae but also his ego and drive: "A professional entertainer since age 12, starting in sleazy Chicago nightclubs and burlesque, he has risen to become a leading director-choreographer on Broadway and in films. His success in his profession has been matched by a failure in personal relationships . . . . Alternating between outrageous ego and profound self-doubt he has become a consummate game player, to the point where he no longer can tell where the games end and reality begins. To him the *only* reality is death."[7] It is a raw and excoriating self-portrait. But while this Bob Fosse may be tortured, he is also a riveting character filled with contradictions—an ideal subject for drama.

Fosse's early choice to play his alter ego was Keith Carradine, who had come to prominence through his film roles for director Robert Altman, including the recent *Nashville*. The blond, boyish Carradine bore a resemblance to the young Fosse but was not considered a sufficiently strong box-office name to carry the film.[8] Eventually the role went to Richard Dreyfuss, who was prominent in the cast of the box-office hit *Jaws* and had just completed two high-profile films, Steven Spielberg's *Close Encounters of the Third Kind* and Herbert Ross's *The Goodbye Girl*. Dreyfuss possessed neither a dancer's physique nor the cool, intense Fosse temperament, and there were problems from the beginning. As Fosse later noted, "As soon as we got together, you could smell disaster."[9] After some protracted negotiations, during which Dreyfuss told Melnick, "I can't get up there with my big Jewish ass and try to be a dancer," he left the film just as shooting was about to begin.[10]

Sam Cohn suggested another of his clients, Roy Scheider. While Scheider did not have the marquee value of stars who were considered, like Warren Beatty, James Caan, and Jon Voight, after a week of working with Fosse on the script he was signed to the film. Identified with his tough police officer in *The French Connection* and with action films like *Jaws* and *Marathon Man*, Scheider was seen as a highly peculiar choice. But he proved so convincingly leonine and authoritative in the role, with just the right mix of volatility and weary charm, that it is now hard to imagine anyone other than Scheider playing Joe Gideon.

All That Jazz was filled out with actors who had close associations with Fosse. Ann Reinking was cast as Gideon's girlfriend, essentially playing herself. After Shirley MacLaine rejected the role of Gideon's estranged wife, Fosse reached out to Leland Palmer, from *Pippin*, who resembled a younger Gwen Verdon. In a bit of casting payback, Cliff Gorman, who had originated the role of Lenny Bruce onstage in Julian Barry's play but was bypassed for Fosse's film, played a similar role as the star of *The Stand Up*, the film Joe Gideon edits while rehearsing his new musical, *N.Y./L.A.* Ben Vereen was cast as the Sammy Davis Jr. stand-in, O'Connor Flood. William LeMassena, who went all the way back to *Redhead*, played Jonesy Hecht, the lead producer modeled on Robert Fryer. Alan Heim, Kathryn Doby, Phil Friedman, Stanley Lebowsky, and Jules Fisher all played themselves, and most of the *N.Y./L.A.* dancers, who were addressed by their real names, had been in previous Fosse shows.[11] (The parallels between *Chicago* and *N.Y./L.A.* are emphasized with Mary McCarty and Steve Elmore [a standby for Jerry Orbach] from *Chicago* as cast members in *N.Y./L.A.* The set model Joe displays is Tony Walton's *Chicago* set design. Joe announces conductor Stanley Lebowsky's station on the onstage bandstand, just as it was in *Chicago*.)

Joe Gideon's world is an indoor hothouse environment, with the outdoors merely a pass-through from rehearsal hall to cutting room to home. Broadway Arts, Fosse's favorite rehearsal studio, was recreated in detail at Astoria Studios in Queens, New York. Gideon's apartment was dressed with recreations of items from Fosse's own apartment, and his bottle of Dexedrine carried an address on West Fifty-Eighth Street only doors down from Fosse's residence. Tony Walton, now a trusted member of Fosse's production team, was committed to another film when the original shooting schedule was created; he suggested his associate Phil Rosenberg as production designer. Walton was available to join the film when it finally commenced and was given special billing as fantasy designer.

Walton was instrumental in Fosse's hiring of Giuseppe Rotunno as the film's cinematographer. Rotunno was well known for his work on Federico Fellini's films; this connection was apt, as *All That Jazz* took on the shape and texture of *8½*, Fellini's cinematic rumination on his life and work. Like Joe Gideon, Guido Anselmi from *8½* is a celebrated director at the peak of his career whose struggle to make a film that will live up to critical and popular expectations is interrupted by dreams and memories that reveal his obsessions as both man and artist.

Walton felt that Rotunno would bring cohesion to the disparate visual elements of *All That Jazz*: "It was very tricky because it kept shifting rapidly, at a moment's notice, from reality to fantasy to medical hallucinations, and we were both very conscious that it would be hard to follow, very patchy and hodge-podge."[12] In *All That Jazz*, Fosse borrows freely from Fellini's form and makes it his own. Guido's childhood initiation into the world of the flesh with the prostitute Saraghina and subsequent punishment by his Catholic schoolmasters are mirrored in teenage Joe's merciless teasing by burlesque strippers and his humiliation before a laughing audience when the results of their teasing are unmistakable. (The burlesque theater from Joe's youth is named the Silver Cloud, one of the many joints Fosse once played.) Guido's fantasies of a female harem, with him their whip-wielding master, are transposed to a whirl of showgirls who offer succor and gentle rebukes as they surround Joe's deathbed, cooing, "Who's Sorry Now?" A beautiful woman in white, an angel who offers him the possibility of grace and the renewal of life, interrupts Guido's tortured thoughts. Angelique, Fosse's beautiful woman in white, is an angel of death whose flirtation with Joe grows increasingly intimate, until he delivers himself to her waiting arms.

Gideon's scenes with Angelique, set in a cluttered warehouse of the mind piled with the detritus of a theatrical life, pointedly reveal Fosse's preoccupation with death. To those closest to him it was a familiar subject that came up repeatedly during Fosse and Aurthur's tape sessions. "I think the reason I was never very jealous of other women is that I knew his real affair was with death," Gwen Verdon said.[13] Paddy Chayefsky chalked up Fosse's interest in death to professional ambition: "You want to kill yourself so that people will take you seriously."[14] Fosse's characterization of death as a beautiful woman came directly from his own fantasies: "When you think something's about to happen to you in a car, or on an airplane, coming close to The End, this is a flash I'll get—a woman dressed in various outfits, sometimes a nun's habit, that whole hallucinatory thing. It's like the Final Fuck."[15] Once again, fantasy combined with reality when Fosse cast Jessica Lange, another recent girlfriend, as Angelique.

All That Jazz finally went before the cameras the first week of October 1978, nearly four years after the near-fatal heart problems that precipitated its creation. By now the script had been tightened and several characters eliminated. Goddard Harris, the composer based on John Kander, was gone, and Paul Dann, standing in for Fred Ebb, was now a composer-lyricist. The elimination of the Chayefsky and Gardner characters also meant cutting a scene that had become legendary among Fosse and his friends. The evening before he was to undergo bypass surgery, Fosse summoned Gardner and Chayefsky to his hospital room to witness the signing of his will. After carefully reviewing the document in its entirety, Chayefsky complained, "But I'm your oldest and best friend, and I'm not in your will?" When Fosse responded that his estate would go solely to his wife and daughter, Chayefsky blew up, shouting, "Fuck you! *Live!*"[16]

The company took over the Palace Theater to shoot the film's opening sequence, a cattle call audition for Gideon's new musical. In a wordless montage set to George Benson's live recording of "On Broadway," Fosse does in six minutes what took *A Chorus Line* two hours. He captures the competitive atmosphere of a Broadway dance audition with humor and humanity and in minute detail, as only someone intimately familiar with the process could do.

The sequence begins with brief, eavesdropping shots of the hopefuls on a crowded stage—warming up in the tight space, putting on lipstick, combing their hair, nervously biting their nails. The dancers ultimately chosen will be sleek and attractive, but this large group includes all sizes and shapes, with "real people" looks, and most will be eliminated quickly. The camera pulls up and back to reveal Joe Gideon at the lip of the stage observing a sprawling mass of dancers crowding together to learn Fosse's "Tea for Two" combination being taught by Kathryn Doby. Fosse centers his camera on a spectacularly inept dancer for a quick bit of comic relief. As the field of dancers is winnowed down, quick, overlapping shots of jumps increase the audition's pace and intensity. In the midst of all this activity, Fosse captures the anxiety and dogged focus of those watching intently to pick up the steps. The camera catches a dancer shyly trying to emulate a lyrical arm movement without anyone noticing him.

These were among Scheider's first days of filming after shadowing Fosse through meetings and rehearsals. (Sandahl Bergman remembered Scheider watching performances of *Dancin'* from the wings, as he steeped himself in the dancers' environment.)[17] He had adopted Fosse's shorthand communication style and even perfected his body-wracking smoker's cough, but now he was thrust into running a major Broadway dance audition as Bob Fosse. With Fosse attending to the movements of five cameras placed around the theater, Scheider wore an earpiece so Fosse could feed him directions.[18] Scheider's lean, athletic frame looks comfortable and authoritative in Fosse's all-black work uniform. Like Fosse, Joe Gideon is all over the stage, directing the dancers into formation, giving corrections, applauding an especially graceful move. At one moment, he takes up position at the very back of the stage as dancers criss-cross in front of him. (Much of the choreography for this sequence is taken from "Crunchy Granola Suite" from *Dancin'*.)

In a few brief shots, Fosse establishes Victoria Porter, played by Deborah Geffner, as an early casting favorite. He depicts the resignation and tears as Gideon, like Fosse, delivers the final judgment himself to each dancer. Fosse later commented that much of this footage consisted of "stolen" shots: "A lot of the dancers at that audition did not know whether they were going to be kept in the movie or not . . . . So there was a certain anxiety on their part."[19] A particularly poignant moment shows Gideon offering a handshake to a rejected dancer who looks like a young Bob Fosse. The sequence is "buttoned" with a knowing cutaway to two rejected female dancers heading out the door. "Oh, fuck him, he never picks me," one says, to which the other responds, "Honey, I did fuck him and he never picks me either." "On Broadway" quickly lays out the Gideon/Fosse complexities: driven, womanizing, and forgetful of family obligations, yet also deeply appreciative of the talented people who surround him and painfully aware of his faults.

"We cut to a visual style, and to a rhythm of the shots, but not to the music itself," film editor Alan Heim remembered.[20] Fosse's camera drops to stage level to watch feet strain to learn steps and then gazes up as dancers leap over it. In the most memorable moment, Heim edits a dozen dancers performing a standard pirouette into one dizzying move. "On Broadway" gathers many of the influences that were being felt in film in the 1970s, including the increasingly rapid cutting of television commercials and the use of popular music unrelated to the plot as an accompaniment to montages and action sequences.[21] Fosse absorbs them all and uses them to fresh effect.

In a film full of resplendent dances, the extended sequence marking the development and performance of "Take Off with Us" is both a highlight and a striking example of Fosse's appropriation of his past experiences. Written by Fred Tobias and Stanley Lebowsky in a style similar to that of John Kander and Fred Ebb, "Take Off with Us" is first heard as Paul Dann stridently performs it for Joe, Audrey, and the producers. (Anthony Holland's performance is a wicked suggestion of Fred Ebb, an avid performer of his own songs.) While the producers are enthusiastic, Joe is less than enamored of the song and subsequently struggles with its staging. In scenes that capture the sweaty, repetitive slog of dance rehearsals, Fosse portrays one of his own greatest fears, that of being at a loss for ideas in front of a group of waiting dancers.

When Joe visits Audrey in another rehearsal studio and despairs of his lack of ideas, the scene plays out several strains from the Fosse-Verdon history. Besides referencing a similar moment when he was stuck for ideas staging "Big Spender" in *Sweet Charity*, the parallels to the events surrounding the production of *Chicago* are unmistakable when the talk moves to Audrey's knowledge that Joe thinks she's too old for the role she's playing. She accuses him of doing the show only out of guilt for his unfaithfulness during their marriage. The scene is less an argument than the thrust and parry of two people who have known each other too well and for too long, with old resentments bubbling up as they go about mundane business—in this case, the family business of dance. Audrey's picking at his countless infidelities—so many that he cannot remember their names—triggers an inspiration and sends Joe back to rehearsal.

Fosse stages the first part of "Take Off with Us" almost as a parody of his own work, including whispered vocals, finger snaps, and start-stop rhythms. (It bears some resemblance to Fosse's syncopated revamp of "A Secretary Is Not a Toy.") There are the gloves and hats, the traveling amoeba, the hunched shoulders and flexed pelvises. If the choreography is nothing new, Fosse films it with flair, isolating a wrist snapping to the rhythm, catching legs flexing in and out, and setting his camera low to capture a Fosse "stack" in all its geometric precision. He isolates majestic lead dancer Sandahl Bergman in her own frame as she extends her endless legs and slides across the floor. The bravura camerawork cannot hide the fact that it is all just a bit tacky—energetic but vulgar. (A dancer carrying a snack tray slides through Bergman's open legs. Later, she turns her back to the audience and bends over, singing through her legs.) Predictably, the producers love it.

A few years earlier Fosse had written to Robert Joffrey with an idea for a ballet set on board a coast-to-coast flight. The plane full of business passengers turns into a wild orgy danced to a comedy monologue rather than music. Upon landing, the passengers resume their businesslike comportment and exit.[22] Fosse's airplane orgy ballet becomes the jumping-off point for Gideon's expansion of "Take Off with Us," turning this "Fly the Friendly Skies" jingle into a writhing ode to anonymous sex, featuring nudity and same-sex couplings.

"Welcome aboard Airotica," a dancer announces, as the others peel off their leotards, leaving the men only in dance belts and the women in tights and brief tops. "Flying not only coast-to-coast, but anywhere your desires and fantasies wish to take you," another intones. To a sensuous tango, three couples entwine in the shadowy light. Gideon/Fosse is an equal opportunity sensualist and includes lesbian and gay male couplings, along with a heterosexual couple. The images are arresting, but the dancing is hokey-sexy and mechanical. Similar to "Joint Endeavor" from *Dancin'*, the images derive their interest from the perfection of the dancers' bodies in the sculpted lighting rather than from the choreography. Some of the poses are downright awkward: one half of the male couple threatens to fall from his perch around the other man's torso.

Other dancers join the couples, and they all weave around a large center scaffold. Brief cutaway shots capture the producers' distaste. "Oh!" one mutters as a white female dancer caresses the gleaming torso of a black male dancer. Now the orgy begins, set to a driving rock beat. Atop the scaffold Bergman, on her back, removes her top, as if this alone is a major statement. For good measure, her legs are spread for her. ("Now Sinatra will never record it," sighs Paul Dann.) Bergman awkwardly hangs from the scaffold, at one point balancing precariously on her hands, while the others below dance with a sexual frenzy similar to the climax of *Pippin*'s "Gisella Ballet." They surround the scaffold, beating it as Bergman thrashes about. At last they break away and into the same backward-jump-and-roll combination that ended the "Gisella Ballet," before finally collapsing. Now spent, they bid their sex partners a casual goodbye as Gideon gravely repeats Airotica's motto: "We take you everywhere but get you nowhere." The cast gathers around a light box for ghoulish close-ups as horror movie–style musical chords fade out ominously. Fosse provides his own ovation for the number when Audrey, who has been watching from the side, calls it "the best work you've ever done."

Audrey's praise has to be taken on faith. Fosse's comment on the emptiness of casual, anonymous sex does not get past the emptiness of his choreography. Agnes de Mille could have been referring to "Take Off with Us" when she later wrote of Fosse's choreography, "Most of it is just gymnastics, squirming around seeing what they can try it on with next. I never thought it was possible to take sex out of eroticism, but that's exactly what Fosse does."[23]

The shock and dismay of the producers hark back to Fosse's conflicts with George Abbott and Harold Prince over the "Red Light Ballet" on *New Girl in Town* and to the general unease with his original, sexually explicit "Razzle Dazzle" in *Chicago*. Fosse's original ideas for "Take Off with Us" went even further and included ménages, voyeurism, and a sadomasochistic coupling.[24] An early draft of the script featured all the women topless and in G-strings, and ended with disturbing images that would have been impossible to present in a mainstream film: "The Number finishes with all the dancers in isolated areas; caressing *only* themselves, loving *only* themselves, incapable of making contact with any other person. The final movements simulate masturbation—*there is nothing left but self love*."[25] These are Fosse's *Pippin* Players, each seeking sexual gratification however they can find it. Ultimately, Fosse pulls back, and "Take Off with Us" recreates his subversion of "With You" from *Pippin*, in which Stephen Schwartz's ballad becomes the jumping-off point for a danced display of sexual gymnastics. It is disappointing to realize that Fosse's choreographic statement of sexuality has progressed so little from earlier efforts.

"Take Off with Us" may be a pretentious exposé of sex as sport, complete with faux erotic posturing and "daring" use of selective nudity (besides Bergman, one dancer decorously exposes a single breast), but Fosse the choreographer is bested by Fosse the director, who films and edits it for maximum kinetic impact. The shivery lighting, razor-sharp cutting, and virtuosity of its dancers are what make "Take Off with Us" a showstopper.

"My own inner rhythm is a fast one, a musical rhythm that's bright, not lyrical," he later said.[26] Fosse's internal dance rhythms drive everything in *All That Jazz*. Even domestic scenes with his daughter are built around dance. A father-daughter discussion is conducted while Michelle, a ballet student played by Erzsebet Foldi, assists him as he works out choreography. (Joe communicates best with his daughter and ex-wife while dancing.) Dinner at home concludes with Michelle and Kate giving an informal dance performance to Peter Allen's recording of "Everything Old Is New Again." The charming, strutting dance conveys the warm friendship between his daughter and his girlfriend, and Joe's touching response to their loving effort on his behalf makes it one of the happiest moments in *All That Jazz*. The number also had a basis in reality, according to Gwen Verdon, who described Reinking and Nicole Fosse making up dances to coax Fosse out of his "Norwegian black cloud."[27]

Even Joe's morning ablutions are choreographed and "buttoned" with a jaunty "It's showtime, folks!" The first human sound heard in the film is Joe Gideon's deep cough leading into a jittery montage in which he pumps himself up with Vivaldi, eye drops, Alka-Seltzer, and Dexedrine. Joe can't take his ever-present cigarette out of his mouth, even in the shower. (Gwen Verdon attested that Fosse would often forget he had a cigarette in his mouth: "That cigarette was part of his face.")[28] These morning montages function as chapter breaks throughout the film's first half, each growing, as Alan Heim observed, "more and more grotesque" as they lead up to Joe's hospitalization.[29]

The *N.Y./L.A.* read-though is presented as a pantomime experienced through the eyes and ears of Joe as the world around him recedes. The uproarious laughter of the cast and producers fades out, and he hears only the amplified sounds of his own movement: fingers tapping, a match struck and lighting a cigarette, a pencil breaking and hitting the floor, his own labored breathing. When the film moves to the hospital where Joe awaits surgery, his medical team is introduced as vaude-villians who explain their diagnosis in stand-up comedy fashion. A montage of Joe's flouting of hospital protocol plays like a Fosse musical number, with short scenes of doctors and hospital personnel woven into Ralph Burns's Dixieland rag on the soundtrack. The hospital scenes in Dennis Potter's BBC series *The Singing Detective* (1986), directed by Jon Amiel, carry traces of Fosse's sardonic, burlesque portrait of doctors and hospital life.

The film's most controversial sequence is the juxtaposition of Joe's bypass surgery with a meeting between the *N.Y./L.A.* producers and insurance company representatives to discuss the show's financing in light of his illness. The *All That Jazz* film company contacted doctors at New York's St. Luke's Hospital, who in turn identified a patient who agreed to have his open-heart surgery documented by a film crew.[30] Footage of his chest cavity opened up and the bloody, pains-taking work around his beating heart is intercut with the businesslike budget tally conducted around a cool, shiny conference table. Fosse ignored the urging of many to limit or cut the footage, though in reality it lasts only seconds, and it became the film's most divisive element. Several critics took an almost personal affront to the scene. "People don't go to the movies to watch open-heart surgery . . . . A miscalculation this violent becomes unforgiveable," insisted Janet Maslin in the *New York Times*.[31] But Fosse maintained that critics like Maslin missed the point: "The thing that I like about the scene was the counterpoint . . . . it keeps cutting back and forth to these theatrical producers who are finding out from the insurance company that . . . Joe Gideon . . . might be worth more dead to them than he is alive. And the slight temptation there is with anything when greed and money is involved. That was the point of the scene."[32] (The sequence became so notorious that, according to Fosse, Peter Allen took to introducing "Everything Old Is New Again" as a song heard in "the first open heart surgery musical.")[33]

Joe's delirium under anesthesia naturally becomes a Fosse production number, one done as a film being shot by Joe Gideon. The metacinematic element is set up with a wide panning shot across the Astoria Studios, taking in the Broadway Arts studio set and settling on a vast, lacquered soundstage. As the performers prepare for the camera, a film clapper announces each new take, and Joe Gideon the director confers with Joe Gideon the patient between setups. In Fosse's favorite tight trio arrangement, Joe's wife, mistress, and daughter take turns serenading him with the vaudeville and burlesque standards from Fosse/Gideon's performing past. But the songs take on pointed new meanings when sung by women acting out their complicated histories with Joe. Audrey, the betrayed wife, brightly scats "After You're Gone" before insisting, "Some day / when you grow lonely / your heart will break like mine / and you'll want me only." Kate's supercool, derby-and-strut number, "There'll Be Some Changes Made," issues a dire warning to become "You'd Better Change Your Ways."

The trios are interrupted by the ghosts of girlfriends past. (The film clapper identifies them as "Old Friends.") As lush strings play, the camera pans down their line to introduce them in close-ups, each more beautiful than the next. Glittering, ghostlike apparitions in their white showgirl costumes and headdresses, they weave across the soundstage in elegant configurations. Their ethereal voices, both soothing and accusatory, sing, "Who's Sorry Now?" Spreading their ostrich feather fans, they circle Joe's hospital bed in a Busby Berkeley pinwheel—an audacious image that was reproduced in the film's print and television coverage to represent its mix of musical fantasy and medical scenes. They bid him a final we-told-you-so farewell ("You had your way / Now you must pay") as his heart monitor gives out a last beat.

Finally, Michelle appears in a tight-fitting, grown-up gown and adult make-up, awkwardly smoking a cigarette, to sing the old Sophie Tucker anthem "Some of These Days." As she catalogs all that Joe will miss about being a father if he dies now, she is seconded by Audrey and Kate, who appear showgirl-style, blowing kisses and reclining amid feathers. They take their leave atop a white, limousine-sized hearse, attended by the fan-wielding former girlfriends, as they drive off the soundstage in a cloud of smoke.

Tony Walton recalled Fosse's observations while watching the women dancers during a rehearsal for *Chicago*: "I remember him saying, 'You know, people get into this business for the awards and the glory or whatever. Look at them.

"Who's Sorry Now?," the ghosts of girlfriends past ask as they form a Busby Berkeley–style pinwheel around Joe Gideon's deathbed in All That Jazz. *Twentieth Century-Fox.*

They're why I'm here.' "[34] It was a line he would include in an early draft of *All That Jazz*. Now, without saying it, Fosse stages the last glimpse of his mortality as pure show business of an especially alluring and feminine form. For a man who lived his life surrounded by women onstage, in film, and at home, it is appropriate that they get the final word.

> "I consider myself a showman, and I've tried to make a good show about an offbeat subject."
>
> Bob Fosse, 1979[35]

All That Jazz was a troubled shoot that saw the deaths of Robert Alan Aurthur from lung cancer and "Take Off with Us" dancer Danny Ruvolo in a car accident. The schedule was not helped by Fosse's penchant for shooting large quantities of film. Alan Heim estimated that his ratio of shots filmed versus those used was a staggering ten to one, with dance numbers requiring more coverage.[36]

With the budget now more than $9 million, Columbia Pictures demanded that shooting stop. There were still sequences to be filmed, including Gideon's final number, the opening night performance of *N.Y./L.A.*, and the scenes between Gideon and Angelique. After viewing a selection of scenes, including musical numbers, Alan Ladd Jr., the president of Twentieth Century-Fox, agreed to provide an additional $5 million. Twentieth Century-Fox would distribute the film in the United States, with Columbia handling international distribution.[37]

The additional funding allowed the film to continue shooting for another two weeks, though to film all that remained in the script would have required closer to six weeks of shooting, Tony Walton estimated.[38] The final scene, in which *N.Y./L.A.* has its triumphant Broadway opening after Joe's death, with Lucas Sergeant as its new director and Joe Gideon long forgotten, was eliminated. Instead, the film's climactic scene would be Joe's final farewell performance.

"Oh, boy, do I hate show business," he remarks while watching smarmy telethon host O'Connor Flood. Reminded that in fact the opposite is true, Joe replies, "That's right, I love show business. I'll go either way." His—and Fosse's—conflicted love-hate view of his lifelong profession is played out in what Flood calls "his final appearance on the great stage of life." "Bye Bye Life" is built from "Bye Bye Love," the old Everly Brothers song of teenage angst, with its refrain, "I think I'm gonna die," given an ironic new meaning.

Conceived as a wild rock concert in the style of the then-popular *Midnight Special* television series and staged in a blast of colored spotlights against silver Mylar, "Bye Bye Life" is the finale to end all finales, the ultimate showstopper that only a super-showman like Joe Gideon or Bob Fosse could stage and star in. O'Connor Flood, the very essence of show business mediocrity that Fosse hated, is the emcee of Joe's final performance. His introduction cues a blast of rock guitar that jolts into action the four performers onstage: Joe, O'Connor, and two females in matching bodysuits traced with red and blue veins, perhaps representing the two ventricles of Joe's failing heart. A pseudo-classical fanfare heralds the ascension from below of a rock band dressed in white, with painted faces resembling those of the rock group Kiss. Their make-up matches that of many of the audience members, some with spiderwebs and elaborate patterns painted on their faces. The audience's appearance is confusing. Some audience members sport headdresses and hats that look left over from "Rich Man's Frug." Others have the blank-faced stares of the audiences in *Cabaret*. They light matches as befits a rock concert, but their evening clothes look more appropriate for a classical concert. Sinister gold skulls with lights in their eyes pan the audience. Illuminated skeletons are stationed around the bleachers. If the effect is meant to be Fellini-esque, the result is closer to a self-conscious combination of the Kit Kat Klub and *Night of the Living Dead*.

Fosse, with Ralph Burns's musical help, constructs the number around choruses that build, then pull back, and repeat over and over until the number reaches a frenzy. From a slow start, a rhythmic vamp kicks in, and O'Connor and the two women dance as Joe bodysurfs to the edge of the stage. Kathryn Doby recalled that two other dancers were originally cast in the number: "But they were different heights, different personalities, and it just didn't look right. And the poor ladies were taken out and Annie [Reinking] and myself were thrown into the number three days before we shot it."[39] Reinking and Doby, obviously familiar with Fosse's style, quickly learned the number. However, much of it was adjusted and restaged as Fosse tried a variety of new camera setups to take advantage of the striking set. The final choreography looks cobbled together. The two silent mannequins preen and pose but only rarely connect with the driving rock beat.

They delicately roll on the floor and more than once execute an unfortunate "rabbit hop" step. Vereen joins them for a disjointed, stand-and-pose trio variation. Choreographically, "Bye Bye Life" is hardly Fosse's most inspired work.

The number cycles through rock, pop, and gospel tempos, always pulling back before launching a new phase. At last, it builds to a thunderous climax that finds Joe running through the audience like a rock star, greeting his life's dramatis personae—everyone from his wife and daughter to his youthful "Tops in Taps" self—all while being trailed by a film crew. Even his final performance is fodder for a new posthumous project. "Bye Bye Life" extends itself one last time, and Joe sings the final lyrics with theatrical flourish—and more than a touch of fatigue—as the band crashes into a big crescendo. The audience response is volcanic. The cheering and stomping and crying are everything Joe could wish for. He has created the greatest show business ending of all time. (Fosse, with Gideon as his stand-in, finally stars in one of his own productions.) And then it is over.

Coming at the very end of a two-hour film, "Bye Bye Life" is exhausting. Fosse later wondered why he extended the number to nearly nine minutes, admitting, "I loved it, frankly, so there may have been some weakness in myself that I lost some objectivity."[40] While its music and editing create a visceral thrill, the spectacle is empty and the performances overwrought. (In a role similar to *Pippin*'s Leading Player, but multiplied by ten, Ben Vereen pushes his performing style to such an unctuous extreme that it was difficult for him to entirely shake it off in later performances.) It is Fosse's comment on both his fears of being second-rate and his cynicism about his ability to manipulate an audience. "I hesitate about a movement and think: 'Oh no. They'll *never* buy that. It's too corny, too showbiz.' And then I do it, and they love it," he once observed.[41] "Bye Bye Life" is corny, showbiz Fosse, tarted up with the dynamic cinematic flourishes he had by now mastered.

Alan Heim later recalled that Ralph Burns coined a phrase to describe the unique, time-shifting editing Fosse favored: "Ralph said there's flashbacks, flash forwards, real time. And then there's Fosse time."[42] The editing of *All That Jazz* matches Fosse's own accelerated rhythms—jumping back and forth in time, fracturing scenes with quick inserts, and layering dance images to give his choreography a blast of energy impossible to achieve onstage. Instead of feeling rushed, however, the editing creates its own internal logic. The cutting is often breathless but never frantic, dense but not cluttered, and the storytelling is coherent. In his own amped-up style, Fosse's work as a film director has the discipline and clarity of his early mentor George Abbott. "Fosse time" contains at least a trace of "the Abbott Touch."

All That Jazz is steeped in the ritual and lore of show business. Fosse captures the camaraderie and bonhomie of the theater, as well as the ruthlessness, the start-and-stop creative process, and the ephemeral nature of any show. The responses to Joe's illness and the postponement of *N.Y./L.A.* carry the sting of truth: anger, tears, regret over jobs turned down for this one. "Bullshit," an actor mutters when a producer refers to the cast as "family." Fosse takes particular relish in his portrait of Joe Gideon's Machiavellian rival Lucas Sergeant, acted with purring menace by John Lithgow.

The rehearsal tension between Joe and Victoria, the favored dancer with whom he sleeps, carries a knowing air, as if Fosse had experienced the same dynamic many times before. When Joe tells her, "I can't make you a great dancer . . . . But if you keep trying and don't quit, I know I can make you a better dancer," it echoes Fosse's own acknowledgment of his failings as well as his strengths. "Unfortunately, and I'll never know why, I can't be a faithful husband or lover, but I can be a helpful one," he once admitted.[43] (Fosse was still up to his usual practice of playing tricks on actors to get the emotion he sought. To get the right look of anger from Deborah Geffner as Victoria, he whispered just before a take began, "'By the way, I saw you in *Chorus Line* and you stank. Action.'")[44]

When Kate accusingly tells Joe, "I wish you weren't so generous with your cock," rather than take offense, he mutters, "That's good. I could use that sometime." For Gideon—and Fosse—every experience is filtered through show business. After two hours of dazzle, the final image in *All That Jazz* is of Joe's corpse being zipped into a body bag. For the first time in the film there is a brief moment of silence as the cold reality of Joe's demise sinks in. But it quickly ends as Ethel Merman sounds off with "There's No Business Like Show Business" over the end credits. It is the final, flamboyant flipping of Fosse's middle finger—to death, to sober reflection, to a life without show business.

> "There's a gag going around that I promised to die before the general release of this picture."
>
> Bob Fosse, 1980[45]

All That Jazz was Twentieth Century-Fox's prestige release for Christmas 1979. The studio planned a deliberate rollout of the film, first in New York and Los Angeles, and then slowly expanding into larger markets before opening nationwide to build on what it hoped would be strong reviews and Academy Award nominations in the spring. Fosse embarked on a string of print and television interviews—everything from *Playboy* to NBC's *Today Show*—all to promote his newest and most personal directorial effort.

While denying that Joe Gideon was really him, Fosse candidly held forth on a variety of subjects that linked him to his cinematic doppelgänger. He contemplated his attempts—and failures—to live a more measured life after nearly dying. "You know, after you come close to death . . . you make that deal with God: Let me off and I promise I won't smoke and I won't drink anymore. I'll be nice to the women . . . . And then you live, and suddenly a month later you're right back in the old thing, smoking and drinking and—being dishonest in relationships."[46] About his fanatical devotion to work, he admitted, "The only salvation for me is work—just to keep rehearsing. Only then do I experience absolute happiness."[47] About his new film, he sounded plaintive when he said, "I think it's the best thing I've ever done, but I don't know how good it is."[48]

All That Jazz received a mix of breathless praise and indignant rejection—sometimes in the same review—that brought it attention and strong box-office results in its initial engagements. Vincent Canby in the New York Times praised its "uproarious display of brilliance, nerve, dance, maudlin confessions, inside jokes and, especially, ego. 'All That Jazz' is an essentially funny movie that seeks to operate on too many levels at the same time, but Mr. Fosse, like Barnum & Bailey, believes in giving the customers their money's worth."[49]

"They opened Bob Fosse up and found a case of inoperable ego," Johnny Carson joked in his opening monologue at the Academy Awards presentation,[50] where All That Jazz received nine nominations, including Best Picture, Roy Scheider as Best Actor, and several of the technical categories. Fosse received two nominations, for his directing and his screenplay. While the film was unsuccessful in the major categories, its technical achievements were acknowledged. Ralph Burns won for Best Original Song Score or Adaptation Score; Tony Walton and Philip Rosenberg, along with set decorators Edward Stewart and Gary Brink, won for Best Art Direction; Albert Wolsky received the Best Costume Design award; and, fittingly, Alan Heim won for Best Film Editing. All That Jazz caused a sensation at the 1980 Cannes Film Festival, whose circus-like atmosphere was particularly hospitable to the film's extravagance, and it tied with Akira Kurosawa's Kagemusha for the festival's top prize, the Palme d'Or.

All That Jazz played surprisingly well beyond major urban areas and eventually earned nearly $38 million, allowing it to scrape the low rung of the top twenty highest-grossing films of 1979.[51] "He's not going to release the film with that ending, surely?," Steven Spielberg asked Roy Scheider. When Scheider replied in the affirmative, Spielberg marveled, "Then he's got a lot of guts. Boy, is he some movie maker."[52] Spielberg was only one of many directors who recognized Fosse's maverick achievement. Stanley Kubrick called All That Jazz "the best film I think that I have ever seen."[53]

Just before its opening, Daniel Melnick grandiosely declared, "Regardless of anything else, I believe that All That Jazz will affect future generations of filmmakers as Citizen Kane has."[54] His prediction may have been overstated, but it has proved to have merit. Richard Pryor's autobiographical Jo Jo Dancer, Your Life Is Calling (1986), which he directed and co-wrote, was built on All That Jazz's model of a medical crisis (Pryor's setting himself on fire while freebasing cocaine) as a jumping-off point for the comedian to examine his life, past and present. (Pryor went Fosse one better by starring in his own story.) Recent films like Birdman or (The Unexpected Virtue of Ignorance) (2013), co-written and directed by Alejandro G. Iñárritu, and Top Five (2014), written and directed by Chris Rock, display the influence of Fosse's film in their mix of unvarnished show business machinations and personal retrospection. The rapid, repetitive montages of drug preparation and ingestion in Requiem for a Dream (2000) were drawn from Joe Gideon's morning routine, according to its director, Darren Aronofsky.[55] On its thirtieth anniversary, All That Jazz was still being celebrated, with a lavish appreciation by film critic Matt Zoller Seitz in the New York Times praising it for setting "a new standard for speed and complexity, its structure boasting as many temporal pir-ouettes as the headiest art house fare."[56]

"The Fosse Decade" had already seen *Cabaret, Liza with a Z, Pippin, Lenny, The Little Prince, Chicago,* and *Dancin'.* Now it climaxed with the most daring and revealing project of Fosse's career, one that laid bare the demons and obsessions that had previously lurked at the margins of his work. Its success and notoriety propelled Fosse to a new peak of celebrity. But after this musical comedy *Götterdämmerung,* what could Fosse possibly do as a follow-up?

CONTROL

• • •

In a 1982 television movie, *Portrait of a Showgirl*, a dancer from New York, played by Lesley Ann Warren, instantly impresses a Las Vegas producer when he asks who she has worked with. "Fosse mostly," she says. "Bob Fosse? Heavy hitter," the producer solemnly intones, assuring her of a prime showcase in his new revue, which ends in a dance number featuring Fosse-style strutting with everyone in a derby. As the new decade began, the combined success of *All That Jazz* and *Dancin'* made "Fosse" shorthand for edgy, sexy, high-gloss performance. Fosse now had not only "Muscle" but also status as an iconoclastic artist. After killing himself off on the big screen, one might question what Fosse could possibly do for a follow-up. It would seem that he had exhausted show business as a subject. Yet his next project burrowed even deeper into its bilious dark waters.

Paddy Chayefsky pointed Fosse to Teresa Carpenter's investigative article "Death of a Playmate," published in the *Village Voice*. Carpenter's article, which would win the Pulitzer Prize for Feature Writing, detailed the story of *Playboy*'s 1980 Playmate of the Year, who was murdered by her estranged husband, who then killed himself. Dorothy Hoogstraten was a high school senior in Vancouver, British Columbia, when she met Paul Snider at the Dairy Queen where she was working. Snider was a small-time hustler, a promoter of auto shows and wet T-shirt contests, and a sporadic, not very successful, pimp who was partial to fur coats, fancy cars, and jewelry.

Nine years older than Hoogstraten, Snider cut a worldly figure to the inexperienced teenager. He eventually persuaded her to pose for nude photographs, which he sent to *Playboy*. The magazine was immediately interested in the tall, voluptuous eighteen-year-old, who was summoned to Los Angeles for test shots with a *Playboy* photographer. Along with shortening her name to Stratten, *Playboy* set her up with an agent, and she was quickly cast in several small roles in films and on television.

Snider was devoted to the *Playboy* ethos, with its emphasis on an upwardly mobile enjoyment of women, sex, and high living, and was anxious to be accepted by Hugh Hefner, *Playboy*'s founder, and the celebrities who frequented the Playboy Mansion. But his crass, overbearing manner was a turn-off to the very people whose company he most wanted to join, and he was quickly made unwelcome at the Mansion without Stratten. Around the time Stratten was named Playmate of the Month for August 1979, Snider insisted that they get married. Snider saw himself as the mastermind behind Stratten's career, with marriage part of their "lifetime bargain." Despite misgivings, she went through with the wedding.

Director Peter Bogdanovich, a Mansion regular, met Stratten at a party and later cast her in a featured role in his new film, *They All Laughed*. During filming, Stratten and Bogdanovich began an affair that Snider eventually discovered. Soon, Stratten was named *Playboy*'s 1980 Playmate of the Year. Snider was now well aware that he had lost her, first to the Playboy apparatus and now to a more sophisticated and successful man.

Anxious to end the marriage, Stratten met with Snider at their rented house to discuss a divorce settlement. She arrived around noon on August 14, 1980, and never left. Stratten's and Snider's naked bodies were found later that night. Stratten had died from a gunshot wound to her head and was sodomized either before or after her murder. Next to her body was a homemade bondage chair built by Snider that showed the stains of its use. Snider's body lay near hers. Dorothy Stratten was twenty years old.

The gruesome murder-suicide had all the elements of a tabloid sensation, but Carpenter's article made Stratten only a featured player in her own story, instead focusing on the three men who played key roles in her short life: "In the end, Dorothy Stratten was less memorable for herself than for the yearnings she evoked: in Snider a lust for the score; in Hefner a longing for a star; in Bogdanovich a desire for the eternal ingénue. She was a catalyst for a cycle of ambitions which reveals its players less wicked, perhaps, than pathetic."[1]

Several strands of the Stratten story parallel Fosse's own life and career and may have drawn him to the material, including his identification with the three men at its center. Bogdanovich like Fosse, came to fame as a film director in the 1970s with hits like *The Last Picture Show*, *What's Up, Doc?*, and *Paper Moon*, and had a penchant for beautiful young women. He also was known for providing star-making roles for actresses like Cybill Shepherd, Madeline Kahn, and Tatum O'Neal, just as Fosse had done for Liza Minnelli, Valerie Perrine, and Ann Reinking.

Although Fosse did not embrace the *Playboy* philosophy, the "Muscle" he flexed on any project gave him the power to bestow career opportunities and apply pressure for sex on young women. (Mariel Hemingway, who eventually played Stratten in the film, recalled Fosse's aggressive attempt to have sex with her, literally chasing her around a sofa and insisting that he always slept with his leading ladies. While refusing his advances, she still feared that rebuking him would cost her the role.)[2] Like Hefner, Fosse enjoyed numerous, sometimes simultaneous affairs with women who stayed the same young age even as he got older. He once quipped about his teenage daughter, Nicole, "She loves my girlfriends. Why not? They're all about her age."[3] After his sweep of the Oscar, Emmy, and Tony Awards in 1973, he was pitched to *Playboy* as a potential interview subject, with the enticement, "His many romances now have an endurance of about two weeks, with luck three," marking him as in line with *Playboy*'s values.[4] A photograph accompanying a *Life* magazine profile promoting *All That Jazz* shows Fosse in work shirt opened to midchest and short, cut-off jeans displaying a bulging crotch, holding a glass of wine as a cloud of smoke poured from his mouth. Fosse embodied a 1970s sybarite in a photo that could have been taken at the Playboy Mansion.

Most intriguingly, Fosse felt a kinship with Paul Snider, the story's villain. "I somehow identified with him because he was trying to get in," he said. "It's not that I've been excluded that much, but I know that sense of them all knowing something I don't know. And that makes me very angry."[5] Snider's story touched the part of Fosse that always felt somehow inadequate, as if at any moment he could be exposed as a pretender. When Eric Roberts, cast as Snider, experienced difficulty with a scene during filming, Fosse angrily expressed just how deeply he identified with the story's killer: *"Look at me! . . . If I weren't successful—look at me—that's Paul Snider.* That's what you're playing . . . . Now show me *me."*[6]

Fosse quickly acquired the film rights to Carpenter's *Village Voice* article. Paddy Chayefsky helped his old friend by preparing a nineteen-page outline for the "Dorothy Stratten Project," which Fosse's finished film strongly resembles.[7] Taking off from Carpenter's article, Chayefsky makes Snider the film's focus. Snider's embrace of the *Playboy* philosophy convinces him that the right clothes and cars will grant him entry into *Playboy*'s social circle and the Hollywood power set. But Stratten is the conduit to it all. Without her, he has lost everything, and if he cannot have her, no one else will. Thus, the murder and, to further stake his claim on her, the sexual assault followed by his suicide.

Alan Ladd Jr., who had come up with completion money for *All That Jazz*, quickly agreed to finance and release *Star 80* (its title taken from Snider's customized license plate for his new Mercedes, paid for by Stratten) through the Ladd Company, his new production company headquartered at Warner Brothers. The film was budgeted at $11 million, a million of which would go to Fosse's salary as director, and he would have final cut authority.[8] Fosse not only had full control but also received the biggest salary of his career. Originally Fosse intended to write a first draft and then enlist a collaborator, but after Chayefsky read Fosse's draft, he advised, "You don't need another writer. Write it yourself."[9] It would be Fosse's first solo writing credit.

Fosse suffered a devastating personal blow when Chayefsky died of cancer at age fifty-eight on August 1, 1981. When his turn came to speak at the funeral, Fosse revealed that he and Chayefsky had made a pact to do "this silly thing," a dance routine, at the other's funeral.[10] With that, Fosse began a brief soft-shoe shuffle in honor of his dearest friend, ending with a cry, "I can't imagine my life without you."[11] Somehow fittingly, it would be Bob Fosse's last public performance. *Star 80* would carry a brief dedication to Chayefsky.

As soon as word spread that Fosse would be making a film about Dorothy Stratten, attorneys for all parties made it clear that Fosse and the Ladd Company were wading into deep legal waters. Carpenter's article, along with transcripts of her interviews with Hefner and others and random notes that she shared with Fosse, were the basis for his screenplay. Fosse studied autopsy reports, read obscure interviews with Stratten, and spoke with anyone who knew or had worked with her or Snider. His detailed study allowed him to incorporate actual quotes into the dialogue scenes, which had an additional benefit. To avoid litigation, he was required to document the source of virtually every scene and dialogue exchange in the script.

Bogdanovich, who had taken the Hoogstraten family under his wing, was vehemently opposed to Fosse's film. In a lengthy memo to his attorney, he described the script as "an apologia for a murderer" with only "a comic book outline of the truth." Stratten, he claimed, was characterized as nothing more than a "dumb blonde,"[12] and he took particular exception to Fosse's not portraying her conflicts over the explicit nature of her *Playboy* photographs, as Bogdanovich insisted she had done.

A swirl of letters was exchanged during the summer and fall of 1981 among Fosse, Sam Cohn, Ladd Company attorneys, insurance underwriters, and lawyers for the individuals portrayed in the film. Finally, in May 1982, the script had been sufficiently altered that a Ladd Company attorney was confident that Bogdanovich and the family "would be willing to agree not to sue at this time and if the film as finally released is in accordance with the current script and the few agreed changes, they would agree not to sue at any time in the future."[13]

Fosse agreed to change the names of Bogdanovich and Stratten's younger sister and brother. Stratten's mother would be called simply "Dorothy's Mother." The only party that appeared to have no problem with the script was Hugh Hefner, who even approved the film's use of the *Playboy* logo. Fosse's integrity as a filmmaker surely played a part in securing the cooperation of Hefner, who may have reasoned that an artist like Fosse would offer equitable treatment of the *Playboy* scene.

If any screen role required specific physical attributes, it was Dorothy Stratten. Fosse's original choice was Melanie Griffith. ("Great reading—she understands girl," read a notation from her audition.)[14] But Mariel Hemingway, another client of Sam Cohn and a star of Woody Allen's *Manhattan* and the recent sports film *Personal Best*, pursued the role relentlessly. After Fosse expressed concern regarding her athletic, tomboyish figure, Hemingway had breast augmentation surgery and won the role. In addition to her newly enhanced figure, Hemingway had the requisite fresh-faced, innocent quality Fosse saw in Stratten.

Finalists Richard Gere and Mandy Patinkin were invited to Fosse's apartment for private readings, but the role of Paul Snider ultimately went to Eric Roberts. The boyish Roberts, with only a few film roles to his credit, had the intensity of a young Robert De Niro. Fosse was required to make the Peter Bogdanovich character as different from the real director as possible. Renamed Aram Nicholas, he was cast with the British actor Roger Rees, who had recently played the title role on Broadway in the Royal Shakespeare Company's production of *The Life and Adventures of Nicholas Nickleby*. The small role of Dorothy's mother was played by Carroll Baker, a casting choice that traced a line from Stratten back to Baker's earlier fame as a sex symbol in films like *The Carpetbaggers* and *Harlow*. Fosse originally cast Harry Dean Stanton as Hugh Hefner, but Hefner objected to being played by the saturnine Stanton and threatened to withdraw his cooperation unless he was replaced.[15] To appease Hefner, Fosse substituted the handsome, more benevolent Cliff Robertson.

The threat of lawsuits and the story's harrowing subject matter made Fosse even more detail-driven than usual. On location scouting trips to Los Angeles and Vancouver, Fosse and company visited and exhaustively documented Snider's Vancouver apartment, Stratten's family home, Snider and Stratten's Los Angeles house, and even hotel suites where Dorothy gave *Playboy* interviews. Hugh Hefner would not allow filming at the Playboy Mansion, but he invited visual consultant Tony Walton to take detailed photographs of the interiors and grounds that were then used to dress a large Spanish-style house in Pasadena as a stand-in.

Once again Fosse surrounded himself with trusted colleagues. In addition to Tony Walton, Albert Wolsky handled the costumes, Ralph Burns created the musical scoring, Alan Heim was again film editor, Kathryn Doby was on board to help with the film's few dance requirements, and Wolfgang Glattes and Kenneth Utt, who had worked in production capacities on projects going back to *Cabaret* and *Liza with a Z*, were *Star 80*'s producers. When Giuseppe Rotunno was unavailable, Fosse turned to yet another new cinematographer. Sven Nykvist was celebrated as a key collaborator on Ingmar Bergman's major films, including *The Virgin Spring, Persona, Cries and Whispers*, and the recent *Fanny and Alexander*. He gave *Star 80* the burnished sheen of a *Playboy* pictorial, which proved to be its own comment on the sordid story. Interestingly for someone who prized having a consistent group of collaborators, Fosse never worked with the same cinematographer twice. Consequently, each of his films possessed a strikingly different visual palette.

> "Film is just like music, and acting is dancing. The rhythms . . . and the appeal to the unconscious . . . the drama is all the same. Except in film, through camera angles and cutting, you control the audience's point of view. Some films have snappy rhythms or slow melodies, fast footwork or downbeats. Maybe my films are simply extentions [*sic*] of the choreography. Maybe not."
>
> Bob Fosse, 1983[16]

Star 80 completed its sixteen-week shoot in October 1982, but it would be a year before it was seen by the public—a lengthy postproduction period for a film with no special effects and no musical numbers to score and edit. Fosse was more compulsive than ever in the editing room, where he and Heim crafted *Star 80* into a remarkably complex film.

The first sound heard in the film is a tape recorder being turned on. A montage of Stratten's earnest interview responses narrates the opening credits. Her *Playboy* images are accompanied by a clicking camera shutter that takes on the sickening sound of gunshots. Fosse's screenplay uses a structure similar to that of *Lenny*, with the narrative splintered by observations from interviewees. (As in *Lenny*, Fosse's voice can be heard as the unseen interviewer.)

Fosse begins by quickly establishing Paul Snider and his orbit in 1978 Vancouver. The camera slyly pans past a photograph of Telly Savalas (Snider claimed to be friends with the actor) and across pinups of *Playboy* Playmates and pictorials of the Playboy Mansion as it catches Snider furiously lifting weights to an aerobic beat. He preens in the bathroom mirror, admiring his ripped torso in bikini briefs and practicing ingratiating personal introductions, before his simmering rage catches up with him. (Beefed up for the role and frequently seen in muscle shirts and tight-fitting pants, Eric Roberts is in some ways more fully eroticized than Mariel Hemingway, for all her nude *Playboy*-style shots.) Fosse deftly sketches in scenes of Snider pimping auto show hostesses, promoting his wet T-shirt contests, and humiliatingly, being dangled out the window of a high-rise motel over a murky loan shark deal (a scene Martin Scorsese later borrowed for *The Wolf of Wall Street* [2013]).

Dorothy Stratten's working-class Vancouver, with its salad bar restaurants and prom nights, is portrayed without condescension. In one of the film's wittiest moments, Stratten is seen during a *Playboy* interview describing her first meeting with Snider. She describes "this gentleman" and "this gorgeous blonde" who came into the Dairy Queen where she worked, both wearing fur coats. (Fosse shot scenes in the actual Dairy Queen where Stratten and Snider met.) Fosse then cuts to Snider and a tough, bleached blonde, both in bedraggled fake fur and dripping wet from the rain. Fosse is careful to depict Snider's initial attentiveness and gallantry toward Stratten, leading to his skillful maneuvering of her into posing nude.

"In *Star 80*, I tried to make it like a musical, with one slow scene, then a staccato scene. I put in moments of sheer entertainment just to break the tension," Fosse later said.[17] Fosse stages a pole dancer's explicit performance as a rebuke to Stratten's wholesome recounting of her treatment by *Playboy*. A Playboy Mansion roller disco party is scored to Benny Goodman's recording of "Sing, Sing, Sing," as Aram Nicholas first glimpses Stratten among the skaters. The period recording frames the sequence as a tribal spectacle, with swarms of barely dressed Playmates skating in circles, ogled by Mansion denizens.

Snider's Hollywood makeover is scored to a brassy Ralph Burns beat and paced like a dance number as the camera follows him trying on sunglasses and jewelry, being fitted for a new wardrobe, and going from slicked-down "tango dancer," as Dorothy's mother calls him, to California blow-dried stud. His new look is less gauche than his Vancouver wardrobe, but there is no change in Snider's peacock manner.

In a detailed recreation of the couple's house, Fosse uses dance discipline to stage the film's harrowing and inevitable climax. A tense marital discussion begins in front of a wall-sized Stratten portrait, its soft-focus glamour serving to mock the domestic drama being played out in the foreground. Snider is alternately belligerent and collared, shyly pleading with Stratten one moment and angrily cursing her the next. Fosse builds in several opportunities for Stratten to walk out, yet she remains to try to comfort and reason with the man to whom she still feels some loyalty. Hearing him take out the rifle brings her into their bedroom. From here, Fosse choreographs the action like a dance number, building to a peak of near violence before backing away and starting again. Snider tries to rape Stratten, but her cries send him into retreat. When Stratten removes her clothes and offers herself to him, his rage renders him impotent. With snapshots of their early days in Vancouver flashing in his mind, Snider reaches for the rifle. "They did this," he mutters before blasting away at Stratten.

Fosse intercuts shots of others in Stratten's life going about routine business oblivious to the carnage taking place. Now Snider takes his homemade bondage rack from the closet and straps Stratten's corpse to it as her most provocative *Playboy* poses run through his mind, their pert glossiness a sharp contrast to the grim scene. Fosse's camera closes in on Roberts's face, as Snider presumably sodomizes her. Afterward, Snider takes the gun and shoots himself. The camera pulls back to show the bloody tableau, its two victims reduced to pitiful, doll-sized figures. *Star 80* ends as it began, with Dorothy Stratten in voice-over cheerfully responding to yet another interview inquiry about her *Playboy* fame.

In a cinema landscape filled with slasher films like the *Halloween* and *Friday the 13th* series, *Star 80*'s violence is a model of restraint, all the more powerful for its refusal to show every detail of the killing. But Fosse got no credit for his cinematic discretion, perhaps because he had telegraphed the violence within the film's first minutes. He insisted that setting up the murder first and then cutting back to it periodically gave the story a feeling of classical tragedy.[18] But the repeated shots of Eric Roberts with blood-ringed eyes cursing Hefner and others, the bloody walls, the knifing of Stratten's photographs—all scored to portentous, horror movie music—weigh the film down with gloom and dread and give Paul Snider a murderous edge from his very first appearance.

The film that opened on November 10, 1983, in limited release is lean and tightly paced. "Fosse time" editing packs in a dizzying number of scenes, some lasting mere seconds, ricocheting through Stratten's short career and pushing the story to its sad conclusion. The *Lenny*-style interviews help telescope the story, though it is unclear just who the interviewees are talking to, or why. *All That Jazz*'s Broadway rehearsal halls and the smoke-filled nightclubs of *Cabaret* and *Lenny* were alive with vitality and the thrill of performance. But in *Star 80*'s desultory auto shows, wet T-shirt contests, and roller skating parties, the talent and training required of Fosse's show business world count for little. Perhaps that is why Dorothy Stratten generates so little enthusiasm for Fosse. While men flock around her like a disco-era Belle Poitrine from *Little Me*, Stratten has no skills beyond her beauty and desirability. Despite her newly enhanced breasts, Hemingway lacks Stratten's voluptuous sexuality, more coltish than curvaceous.

Eric Roberts easily dominates the film not only because of the script's focus but also by force of personality. He has the power and confidence of a young Montgomery Clift or Marlon Brando and skillfully conveys Snider's contradictions: his easily wounded bravado, the sweaty realization when he is trying too hard to please, and the vulnerability that turns in a flash to violence.

With legal threats from Bogdanovich hanging over his head, Fosse neutered the film's Aram Nicholas, whose scenes with Stratten give the impression they are roommates rather than lovers. Fosse may have avoided a lawsuit by Bogdanovich but not his scorn. Bogdanovich decried the film's "showy mediocrity and repressed misogyny," calling Fosse's staging of the final murder-suicide scene "preposterous and obscene."[19]

Despite Cliff Robertson's benign portrayal, Hefner faulted the film for its focus on Snider and its implicit moral tone, insisting, "The biggest lie in the movie is the way it links sex to violence by repeatedly giving us Dorothy's photo sessions intercut with flashbacks of the murder scene."[20] Hefner's opinion did not, however, prevent *Playboy* from capitalizing on its Stratten connection. *Star 80* was highlighted in the magazine's annual "Sex in Cinema" feature, and photographs taken for the film of Hemingway-as-Stratten were given their own multipage layout.

Hefner was correct in his assessment of Fosse's linking of *Playboy* with violence toward women. But *Star 80*'s terse, uninflected recounting of the Dorothy Stratten and Paul Snider story carries a subtler condemnation. The camera clicks that sound like gunshots when they accompany Stratten's *Playboy* images are only part of it. By pulling back and letting his carefully composed images tell the story, Fosse connects the culture of *Playboy* and Hollywood with the possibility of degradation and violence lurking just under the surface. The only time Stratten is seen in an acting role is when she is filming an exploitation film in which she is beaten until blood comes out of her mouth.[21] Hefner may appear warm and paternal, but he presides over parties where Stratten and other young women are offered up to Mansion regulars. He exercises control over everyone in his circle, authorizing background checks on Snider and exiling him from the Mansion, and surrounding Stratten with chaperones and spokespeople who direct her responses in interviews. Without overstatement, Fosse makes it clear that Snider's violent possessiveness toward Stratten is at the extreme end of a continuum that Hefner also occupies.

Star 80 received a number of positive reviews and made the "ten best" lists of several critics, including Richard Schickel in *Time* magazine, who wrote, "[Fosse] has stripped away his self-indulgence, and he emerges here as a masterly director in full possession of a terrible vision."[22] But the negative responses were particularly vitriolic, faulting Fosse for even filming the story. "Bob Fosse's *Star 80* is about the degradation of everything and everybody," insisted the *New Yorker*'s Pauline Kael, who questioned Fosse's personal morality in making the film.[23] "Fosse piles on such an accumulation of sordid scenes that the movie is nauseated by itself."[24]

Released in a marketplace dominated by blockbuster action and science fiction hits like the *Star Wars* and *Indiana Jones* series, *Star 80* barely registered. It was a "downer," a film with no payoff or resolution that would have been better received in the previous decade of more freewheeling and adventurous filmmaking. Audiences stayed away, and the film grossed only $6.5 million, far short of expectations. Before its release, *Star 80*'s pedigree and subject made it a talked-about film for Academy Award consideration, but following its negative reviews and poor box-office performance, the Oscars wanted nothing to do with it.

For a film made thirty-five years ago, *Star 80* looks remarkably contemporary. Its costumes and production design avoid garish 1970s styles, and its music score includes only a few recognizable disco staples, relying instead on Ralph Burns's jazz-based instrumentals, all of which allow it to escape the feel of a period film. Its story of male exploitation of, and violence against, women remains dismayingly timely. Its dense, rapid-fire editing, which confused some viewers at the time, has now become an accepted standard for film and television storytelling.

Star 80 may have been unappreciated when it first appeared, but its impact is noteworthy. Fosse's use of disparate interview subjects to break up and tell a story from multiple angles has been expanded upon by other filmmakers like Richard Linklater, who used a similar device for his film *Bernie* (2011), also based on a true story. Fosse's presentation of the murder-suicide as the film's climax, without resolution or moralizing, was discomfiting at the time. Since then, other films have led up to similarly grisly crimes, such as Bennett Miller's *Foxcatcher* (2014), based on another true story. *Star 80* is the lost Fosse project that deserves reassessment.

> "One reason I would come back is I would get angry. They're lionizing all these other people and I'd think: 'You want to see some dancing? *I'll* show you some dancing!' Part of the work ethic is probably a way of saying, 'You forgot me, folks. I want to remind you I'm here.'"
>
> Bob Fosse, 1986[25]

Fosse had given up his office at 850 Seventh Avenue following Paddy Chayefsky's death. In the aftermath of *Star 80*, he retreated to his Manhattan apartment and, increasingly, to his house in Quogue, in the town of Southampton on Long Island, though he was still much in demand. The Nederlander Organization courted him to film *Dancin'*. Billy Joel and Michael Jackson wanted him to helm their upcoming music videos. He was everyone's first choice when a film musical was planned. Earlier he had turned down *Saturday Night Fever* and *The Rose*. Now he passed on *Flashdance* and the film versions of *Annie* and *A Chorus Line*. Fosse had already created his own abbreviated version of *A Chorus Line* with his "On Broadway" sequence in *All That Jazz*, but that did not stop him from making his own contributions to that 1985 film. "I can't tell you how many people he coached for the movie," Gwen Verdon recalled, including their daughter, Nicole.[26]

Nicole, who had followed her parents into dance, was the catalyst for her father's late attempt at a ballet. A brief *New York Times* article in May 1982 announced her appearance in a short reworking of "The Firebird" as a solo created especially for her by Fosse. "Magic Bird of Fire (Nepotism)," danced to a disco arrangement of Stravinsky's music, was one of several premieres at a benefit performance for the company Ballet Today.[27] Dance critic Mindy Aloff recalled, "In this solo for the adult Nicole—the woman who had once danced so charmingly at home as a child . . . Fosse's taste, training, expertise, good intentions, and personal feelings were all cycling around together, like clothes in a washing machine."[28] The dance was not reviewed and was performed only a few times as part of gala events for Ballet Today before disappearing. Attendees at Fosse's memorial found "Magic Bird of Fire (Nepotism)" listed among his credits as his sole ballet. (The reference to nepotism was likely a nod to a father's affectionate gift to his dancing daughter.)

Fosse returned to the role of "show doctor" when Ben Vereen reached out to him to stage his second-act solo, "New Man," in *Grind*, a new musical directed by Harold Prince and choreographed by Lester Wilson. Fosse agreed to step in only with Prince's approval. "It was the beginning of our resolving some of the old problems we'd had in past years and it gave me pleasure," Prince later recalled.[29] *Grind* took place in a 1930s Chicago burlesque house, a comfortable milieu for Fosse, and the dance became a compendium of his favorite steps from the era, like snake hips, Joe Frisco, and the "mess around."[30] The lengthy number was filled with Fosse-isms: the hip accents, shoulder swivels, and signature Vereen moves from *Pippin*.

By now, Fosse was a respected éminence grise of Broadway. He was sought for his feedback on *Smile*, a musical adaptation of the 1975 film about a teen beauty pageant. A transcript of his discussion with the show's composer, Marvin Hamlisch, and lyricist, Howard Ashman in 1985, is a fascinating glimpse of both Fosse's analysis of the material and the eagerness of the show's creators to have him involved. Hamlisch sees the show's pageant as a metaphor for the corruption of the American dream while Ashman hopes it will expose the false optimism pedaled by the current Republican administration. Fosse agrees with both, likening it to his own *Chicago*. "That's why I called you," Hamlisch exclaims.[31] Ashman is even more to the point: "I would give my right arm to have you do it." *Smile* opened on Broadway a year later, directed by Ashman himself, and closed after forty-eight performances.

> "*Big Deal* was never meant to be anything more than a sweet and entertaining evening."
>
> Bob Fosse, 1986[32]

A brief article in the *New York Times* on March 2, 1967, noted that Fosse had optioned the stage rights to the Italian film *Big Deal on Madonna Street* (1958) for a musical adaptation.[33] Directed and co-written by Mario Monicelli, *I Soliti Ignoti* (or *The Usual Unknown Persons*, in its original Italian title) was a gently comic takeoff on popular heist films like Jules Dassin's *Rififi* (1955). In postwar Rome, a group of hapless hoods and thieves plot to rob a jewelry store safe by sneaking into an apartment next door while the occupants are away and breaking through the connecting wall. Though they methodically plan what they expect to be a perfect crime, they ultimately bungle the job, breaking through the wrong wall, bursting a water pipe, and blowing up a stove. They pause only to raid the apartment's refrigerator before fleeing the scene and slowly dispersing, their grand scheme having come to nothing.

"I adored the movie," Fosse later said. "It was about fumblers trying to do something bigger than they were capable of doing and never giving up. That thread appealed to me—that desire to keep trying all the time."[34] Fosse changed the story's locale from Rome to Tijuana, Mexico, the better to use a musical palette similar to that of the upbeat, horn-driven Herb Alpert and the Tijuana Brass sound he favored at the time. He soon produced a first draft of *Big Deal* that resembles his initial adaptation of *Nights of Cabiria*: diligent in following the plot and creative in adapting the material to the stage, but lacking in humor and spots for musical numbers.

Perhaps anticipating *Big Deal* as his follow-up film to *Sweet Charity* for Universal Pictures, Fosse also adapted the material as a screenplay. He created "The Big Deal Ballet," an Agnes de Mille–derived imagining of the perfect crime, featuring a visual palette similar to the stylized musical sequences in the *West Side Story* film. Dancers standing in for the gang members gracefully carry out each complex step of the heist—in stark contrast to its eventual execution.[35] "I couldn't get Universal on the phone," Fosse later recalled after the failure of *Sweet Charity*,[36] and he was unsuccessful in interesting others in the project. Soon he was involved with *Cabaret* and left *Big Deal* to languish.

After *Dancin'* and *All That Jazz*, Fosse discovered a new affection for *Big Deal*. He said, "It's not just straight dancing; it's the chance for me to do a story again. And it's sweet. Most of the stuff I've been doing is kind of hard-edged and cynical, particularly the movies."[37] By the time *Big Deal* was announced for Broadway, Fosse had settled on a score made up entirely of popular songs of the 1930s.[38] This would be his second show to forgo an original score in favor of old songs. As he explained, "I wanted to use old elements, and to see if I could work something new out of [them] . . . . And there were all these songs that I grew up with as a kid that I loved . . . . And I had this project for many years in mind and so I thought, I can marry these two things . . . and it would be a wonderful score."[39]

On one hand, it seemed that Fosse was no longer interested in the creative back-and-forth of collaboration. On the other, he may have felt that time was running down, and he was in a hurry to create as quickly as possible. He later estimated that *Big Deal* took just over a year—with the exception of *Dancin'*, the shortest amount of time he had spent putting a show together. "But still it's a big chunk of your time, especially when you're going to be 59 in June," he said after the show opened. "You start thinking, how many of those chunks can I . . . ," as his thoughts trailed off.[40]

The period songs reflected the show's new setting and time frame. Instead of Tijuana, the story's big deal would be carried out in Chicago in the 1930s by a struggling group of unemployed African American men on Chicago's South Side during the height of the Depression. The songs and the setting would bring Fosse full circle to his hometown roots.

> "I had such nice memories of the show that I was afraid of ruining them. It's sort of like the girl you had a crush on in high school. You're really not sure you want to see her again 20 years later."
>
> Bob Fosse, 1985[41]

After a staged reading of *Big Deal* in the spring of 1985, Sam Cohn began pitching the show as Fosse's long-awaited return to Broadway. But another project temporarily intruded. Joseph Harris, one of the original producers of *Sweet Charity*, was co-producing a revival for the Los Angeles Civic Light Opera. Fosse discouraged the idea, fearing that the show—and his choreography—would appear dated after twenty years. "Everyone thinks this is the best work I've ever done. What if it's not?" he confided to dancer Chet Walker.[42] But when the producers signaled their intention to go forward regardless of his involvement, he relented and took part in the project.

The show was to be a vehicle for Debbie Allen, currently the star of the popular musical television series *Fame*. Before her television success, Allen had established herself as an accomplished stage performer. As Anita in Jerome Robbins's 1980 revival of *West Side Story*, she danced with fiery energy and bravura technique. Allen was more than qualified to take on Gwen Verdon's legendary role, though her personality was brasher than that of the aimless Charity.

Fosse cast the show in New York and then assumed his role as overall supervisor. John Bowab, an associate producer on the original Broadway production who had directed stock and regional revivals over the years, would be the official director. Verdon would restage Fosse's choreography and personally coach Debbie Allen. This revival would be not a rethinking but a recreation, down to Robert Randolph's original sets. Cy Coleman would update some of his music, but the score would remain intact. Patricia Zipprodt would design new costumes, but Charity's little black dress was retained as a kind of official uniform. The difference was that *Sweet Charity* was now a period piece, and the setting was clearly identified as the mid-1960s.

The revival's immediate problem was that *Sweet Charity*'s original choreography did not exist in any notated form. "There were no notes. They had the film. And they had Gwen's memory, which was damn good," remembered dance captain Mimi Quillin.[43] Verdon, Quillin, and Christopher Chadman recreated the numbers with the assistance of a videotape of the film in constant play in the rehearsal room. (Quillin recalled Verdon laying out the patterns for "Rich Man's Frug" using salt and pepper packets. "The men were the pepper and the women were the salt.")[44]

When Fosse flew to Los Angeles to see a run-through three weeks before the first performance, he jumped in and began reworking the show. He sharpened the dances and applied his director's eye to every nuance of their performance. Rehearsing "Big Spender," "Bob would walk down the line and lean in and whisper to each one of us, 'Pick me,'" Quillin recalled.[45] According to Verdon, Fosse's work on "Big Spender" was like "a needlepoint tapestry that he just kept weaving," said Quillin.[46]

"I've redone some of my own work, and I've shortened it, made it a bit swifter," Fosse said just before the show, which now carried his name as director, opened on July 19, 1985.[47] This new twentieth-anniversary *Sweet Charity* clocked in at a streamlined hour and fifty-nine minutes, plus intermission. Instead of Verdon's Chaplinesque pathos, Allen supplied a feisty up-for-anything ebullience that gave the show a brighter feel. "Everyone seems a little younger and nicer than in previous 'Sweet Charity' casts," Dan Sullivan observed in the *Los Angeles Times*.[48]

What most delighted audiences were Fosse's dances, the kind of confident, emphatic show dancing seldom seen on Broadway in recent years. The witty satire of "Rich Man's Frug" was even funnier two decades later. "If My Friends Could See Me Now" and "Big Spender" re-emerged as canny, character-based numbers brimming with theatrical ingenuity and surprising reservoirs of emotion. It was the kind of dancing identified with its original star, and Gwen Verdon's work on the show was celebrated as the vital link to that earlier era.

Verdon once observed that dancers die twice, "the first time when they realize they are no longer the kind of athletes they were."[49] Her perspective on the passage of time and the diminution of strength was remarkably clear-eyed. "Oh it's hard," she said. "I don't like it, but what are you going to do about it?"[50] Verdon had entered that period of her career in which she was celebrated for her past accomplishments. When she made a surprise appearance at the 1984 Tony Awards, in a brief reprise of "Nowadays" with Chita Rivera, the audience response was overwhelming.

Verdon made an elegant transition from dancing star to character player, often cast as a former dancer or actress. She guest-starred on television series like *M*A*S*H*, *Trapper John, M.D.*, and *Magnum, P.I.* She was the Rockettes' resident choreographer in *Legs*, a television movie, and filmed a small role as Richard Gere's mother in Francis Ford Coppola's film *The Cotton Club*. Verdon was part of an ensemble cast of older actors in Ron Howard's *Cocoon*, which opened while *Sweet Charity* was rehearsing. The science fiction comedy-drama proved a surprise hit and introduced Verdon to a large audience that had no idea of her celebrated dancing past.

A 1982 guest appearance on *Fame* resulted in a delightful challenge dance with future Charity, Debbie Allen. Verdon's effortless high kicks, saucy hip extensions, and piquant comic timing demonstrated that her inimitable star power was undimmed. More significantly, there was the continuing connection with Fosse. Her duties on *Sweet Charity* confirmed her status as the living repository for Fosse's work, the woman who held within her body and brain his classic repertoire.

> "I do see shows having more special effects, more like Spielberg movies. Everybody's into short-term concentration, like MTV, with hyped-up sound and lights. I used to get criticized for doing dazzling effects. Now it's in."
>
> Bob Fosse, 1985[51]

When *Dancin'* finished its Broadway run in the summer of 1982, the Winter Garden Theater was already undergoing renovations to accommodate the environmental staging of Andrew Lloyd Webber's London sensation *Cats*, which opened later that year. *Cats* was the start of a decade defined by extravagant London imports that minimized dance. While the revue-like *Cats* featured nonstop movement, its dancers were lost in costumes and make-up that blended into the gargantuan scenery as they performed repetitive, gymnastic routines.

Rather than creating new excitement around dance, as *A Chorus Line* and *Dancin'* had done, *Cats* ushered in a depressed period for choreography on Broadway. Danny Daniels's high-energy tap numbers for *The Tap Dance Kid* and Scott Salmon's splashy showgirl routines for *La Cage aux Folles* were the exceptions, as many musicals featured only brief patches of movement. For the first time in its history, the Tony Awards eliminated the category for Best Choreography in the 1984–1985 season. A new show by one of the architects of the modern dance-oriented musical was highly anticipated.

In 1978, Fosse said, "You see, for my kind of dancing there is no vocabulary . . . . The stuff I do has to be demonstrated, which means I have to get up and feel it in my body before I can teach it. I figure I have a few more years, with luck."[52] When he began preproduction work on *Big Deal*, those years were mostly behind him. He brought on two choreographic associates to demonstrate what he could now only describe. Christopher Chadman, who had been in every Fosse show since *Pippin*, served as associate choreographer, with prominent billing and a small royalty. Fosse's showcasing of Chadman's choreography in *Dancin'* pointed his career in a new direction. Since then Chadman had choreographed the Broadway musical *Merlin*, starring Doug Henning and Chita Rivera, staged an extravagant production for Peter Allen and the Rockettes at Radio City Music Hall, and directed and choreographed revues off-Broadway. Linda Haberman, who appeared in *Dancin'* and the video version of *Pippin*, came on board as assistant to the choreographer. They were soon joined by a skeleton team of dancers on whose bodies Fosse would work out the painstaking details of his dances.

Virtually every available African American singing actor was seen for one of *Big Deal*'s principal roles. Cleavant Derricks, a Tony Award winner for *Dreamgirls*, was cast over Ben Vereen as Charley, the peacockish failed boxer and leader of the bumbling group of robbers. His *Dreamgirls* costar, Loretta Devine, was cast as Lilly, the housemaid in the apartment next to the pawnshop (changed from the film's jewelry store) who inadvertently supplies the keys to the robbers. The other gang members—the diminutive, perpetually famished Otis; family man Willie; Slick, the strict disciplinarian who keeps his sister Phoebe locked in their apartment; and Sunnyboy, a good-natured young drifter—were played by Alde Lewis Jr., Alan Weeks, Larry Marshall, and Mel Johnson Jr., respectively. Young Desiree Coleman, with a multi-octave voice, was cast as Phoebe, a role mentioned as a possibility for Whitney Houston.[53]

Big Deal's dance roles were drawn from the Broadway and touring companies of *Dancin'*. Gary Chapman was Dancin' Dan, a veteran safecracker who counsels the gang, and his accomplices were played Valarie Pettiford and Barbara Yeager. The racially mixed dance ensemble included *Dancin'* stalwarts like Cisco Bruton II, Lloyd Culbreath, Diane Laurenson, Frank Mastrocola, and Roumel Reaux, along with several first-time Fosse dancers. Wayne Cilento and Bruce Anthony Davis, both from the *Dancin'* Broadway company, were cast as two narrators. (A third narrator, to be played by Vanessa Williams, was eliminated before rehearsals began.)

Jules Fisher was again on board as both lighting designer and executive producer. Peter Larkin, the scenic designer for *Dancin'*, was back. Patricia Zipprodt was designing costumes for her fourth Fosse show. Once again, Gordon Lowry Harrell was musical arranger and conductor, with Ralph Burns in charge of orchestrations. Fosse's favorite stage manager, Phil Friedman, who went as far back with him as *The Conquering Hero*, returned for what he said would be his last show before retirement.

His design team and music staff gave *Big Deal* a unique look and sound. Fosse and Harrell revisited popular songs of the 1930s before settling on the twenty-three that would make up *Big Deal*'s score. Harrell's arrangements and Burns's orchestrations gave them a contemporary 1980s sound that, in several instances, radically changed their tone and meaning. The orchestra included four synthesizers and four percussionists, contributing to the show's heavily amplified sound. (Charlie's courtroom testimony before a judge is even scored as a rap sequence.) Harrell's synthesized sound effects and musical underscoring were heard over the show's elaborate sound system, designed by recording engineer Phil Ramone, with speakers installed throughout the theater to give *Big Deal* a cinematic, surround-sound feel.[54]

By now, Jules Fisher had worked with Fosse numerous times. He noted, "Each subsequent theater piece was more influenced by his movie experience. He saw in movies that he could control everything. But he couldn't command it in the theater, so that was frustrating to him."[55] Fosse relied heavily on film techniques in staging *Big Deal*, even going so far as to storyboard the entire script, like a screenplay. The script was structured to frequently play two scenes against each other on different parts of the stage, with dissolves and cross-fades to segue cinematically back and forth. "A lot fell to lighting to try to give him the freedom that he had in motion pictures," Fisher said.[56]

This meant that the stage had to be kept dark to highlight the alternating scenes, which only played to Fosse's fondness for darkness. "To him, the perfect picture was nothing but a single spot of light on the performer," Fisher remembered.[57] In fact, Fosse starts and ends the show with an effect reminiscent of Busby Berkeley's "Lullabye of Broadway" in *Gold Diggers of 1935*, in which the face of singer Wini Shaw appears as a tiny speck of light in an all-black screen. *Big Deal*'s curtain rises on a pitch-black stage with a single spotlight illuminating a singer high atop a platform, seemingly floating in the darkness as she sings a down-tempo rendition of the Depression era staple "Life Is Just a Bowl of Cherries."[58]

Peter Larkin was challenged to create a black box set open and airy enough to accommodate Fisher's lighting effects. A unit with stairs leading to a platform upstage left served as a variety of locations, from bandstand to boxing ring to movie theater balcony. Set pieces moved on and off to create the show's forty-three scenes. Plexiglass platforms slid on from high in the wings, giving the impression their occupants were suspended in the air. Fosse frequently used these platforms to interject a character into a scene, commenting on or explaining a point, like a "thought bubble" in a cartoon.[59]

With his designers' help, Fosse pushed his staging past the proscenium more aggressively than ever. Larkin built girders out over the orchestra pit for additional playing areas. Entrances and exits were made through the theater aisles. In act 2, Fosse staged the run-up to the heist as environmental theater, sending his actors through the air and under the stage. The gang's first access point from the street to the apartment is through a coal chute. A large slide was attached to the top of the stage platform, and each gang member slid down and into an opening in the stage (where they landed on cushions below). They then re-entered up through the orchestra pit. Fosse's most daring stunt took the men through the theater's side boxes and up to a catwalk along the mezzanine from which they grabbed hold of a zip line and sailed over the audience and down to the stage. Fosse's three-dimensional staging, all accompanied by synthesizer sound effects, not only surpassed that of *Cats* but presaged the elaborate aerial effects of *Spider-Man Turn Off the Dark* twenty-five years later.

Larkin created a porous deck underneath which Fisher installed lighting equipment. In the second-act opening, "Now's the Time to Fall in Love," featuring the dancers in a sultry version of one of Fosse's Latin-flavored numbers, the stage appeared to be smoking from below. For "Ain't We Got Fun?," set in a prison yard, illumination from under the stage looked like lights shining through prison bars.

The Shubert Organization, along with Roger Berlind and Jerome Minskoff, were the lead producers on *Big Deal*, budgeted at a sizable $5 million. Fosse had previously wrangled with the Shubert's Gerald Schoenfeld and Bernard Jacobs on *Dancin'*. But *Dancin'* was a long-running moneymaker, and the Shuberts were happy to be back in business with him, even refurbishing their Broadway Theater for the occasion. Fosse's financial deal on *Big Deal* was potentially highly lucrative. In addition to an up-front fee of $35,000, he would receive pre-recoupment royalties of 3½ percent as author of the libretto, 1½ percent as director, and ⅔ percent as choreographer, for a total of 5⅔ percent, rising to 9½ percent after recoupment.[60] (It must have pleased him that his author's royalty was more than his combined royalties for directing and choreographing.)

Given the small-scale nature of its story, it is ironic that *Big Deal*'s forty-three scenes, twenty-three songs, and cast of twenty-three made it Fosse's biggest show since the original *Sweet Charity*. With the entire responsibility for the show's script and staging on his shoulders, the strain on Fosse was apparent.

"Where there's smoke, there's Fosse," promised Big Deal's *television commercial. Here, Jules Fisher lights Peter Larkin's porous stage deck from below, creating an erotic inferno for "Now's the Time to Fall in Love." Photo by Martha Swope © Billy Rose Theatre Division, The New York Public Library for the Performing Arts.*

"He really lived at the rehearsal hall," said Linda Haberman.[61] She and Chadman arrived each morning ahead of the cast to find Fosse already working alone in front of the mirror. At times his memory failed him. "He couldn't do or remember the sequences," Haberman recalled. "He wanted to be able to do it so he could feel it and maybe come up with the next step or sequence. And he would get really pissed off."[62]

Fosse was in constant physical pain, suffering with sciatica in his lower back, and wore a foam brace under his shirt. "I can hardly move. I can't even tie my own shoes," he confessed.[63] He looked every day of his fifty-eight years. The goatee was now gray, the hair barely there. Rehearsal photographs show him in baggy sweater and wearing reading glasses on a chain, looking more like an aging professor than the intense, driven dance master of even a few years earlier. And always, the ever-present cigarette hung from his lips. Having stopped smoking briefly after his surgery in 1974, he had long since returned to multiple packs per day. "It gets so embarrassing, coughing all day during rehearsals," he said, only half-jokingly. "The actors are looking at you like, 'Gee, I hope you stay alive to get us to the opening.'"[64]

Big Deal's story was simple but fed by numerous subplots and characters. Attempting to clarify the action, Fosse fell back on the use of the two narrators, but their precise function continued to thwart him. Unlike the interview subjects who pushed the story along in Star 80 and Lenny, or the Leading Player who commandeered the action in Pippin, they stood outside the narrative, with no connection to the plot or characters. Wayne Cilento admitted, "I still haven't figured out why the narrators are integral to the show, and that's a fundamental problem when you're examining character motivation. I'm not sure I even have a character."[65] (The narrators were introduced at the top of the show singing "For No Good Reason at All," an unfortunately apt song title.)

The show's songs did little to define Big Deal's large cast of characters. Aside from his establishing number, "Charley My Boy," and a later fantasy number, Cleavant Derricks's Charley had scant opportunities to reveal himself through song. Loretta Devine began and ended the show with "Life Is Just a Bowl of Cherries," but otherwise, despite star billing, her role remained peripheral. The gang members had little to sing about, and Fosse was unable to sketch out distinct and vibrant characters through dialogue. Big Deal was Sweet Charity without Neil Simon, who could have brightened the characters and quickened its pace. "I think he knew it wasn't where it needed to be, and he was just extremely frustrated," recalled Linda Haberman.[66] But with no collaborators with whom to work—or even fight—there was no one to point out what to others was obvious. Fosse's "Muscle" was strongest when rigorously exercised against the ideas of others.

Big Deal's small-time characters did not easily lend themselves to dance, and the bulk of the choreography is given over to the narrators and ensemble. Several numbers are suggestive of earlier Fosse efforts. "Ain't We Got Fun?," performed early in the show by shackled prisoners, has the same ironic punch as "Big Spender." Dressed in prison stripes, the full ensemble (including the women, some in mustaches) performs a deadpan version of the cheery tune, singing in

Fosse's favorite whisper vocals and rattling their shackles in time to the synco-pated rhythm. Their witty soft-shoe, performed on a platform with the sound and texture of a sandbox, is Fosse at his slyest. Dancin' Dan and his two partners in crime are introduced in act 2 with "Me and My Shadow," an exceptionally sinuous example of Fosse's tight trios. Like cat burglars dressed in gray against the black set, the three are all slicing legs and slithering torsos as they sail across the stage to the brassy musical arrangement.

In the film, after the gang has broken into the apartment and are slowly and diligently drilling through the wrong wall, each briefly remarks on what he will do with his share of the money. Fosse transforms the moment into four fantasy musical numbers. Family man Willie dreams that his baby grows up to graduate from college, and Little Willie sings the sweet "Daddy, You've Been a Mother to Me" to his proud father. The ever-hungry Otis imagines life as an international all-you-can-eat feast. Accompanied by four female dancers, he sings and tap dances through the old Andrews Sisters swing hit "Hold Tight, Hold Tight." Though spirited, the number made little impression, and the electronic dance rhythms worked against Alde Lewis Jr.'s intricate tapping. Slick dreams of an elaborate wedding for his sister Phoebe and Sunnyboy, and the trio sings a gospel-styled

Fosse works one final variation on his tight trio formations for Big Deal's *"Me and My Shadow." Left to right: Valarie Pettiford, Gary Chapman, and Barbara Yeager.*
Photo by Martha Swope © © Billy Rose Theatre Division, The New York Public Library for the Performing Arts.

"Happy Days Are Here Again." The fantasy allowed Peter Larkin to brighten the set by revealing a striking blue cyclorama and stained glass windows, but the overblown number focused on two minor characters to little effect.

Finally, Charley dreams of life as a celebrated movie star, mobbed by paparazzi when he arrives at the premiere of his latest film. Surrounded by the full company of dancers, he sings a slow-building rhythm-and-blues version of "I'm Sitting on Top of the World," highlighted by Jules Fisher's rock concert lighting. Fosse's staging was surprisingly limp, with the dancers arrayed on the stairs and platform, doing music video–style, step-touch choreography. "It was so not him," remembered Linda Haberman. "That was one number that we didn't have completely worked out."[67] Designed as the show's eleven o'clock number, it relied solely on Cleavant Derricks's ingratiating personality and full-throated vocals for its impact.

Staging these musical numbers all in a row was a static concept and robbed the story of momentum at a crucial moment. They all fell short of Fosse's usual standards, when only back-to-back showstoppers could have justified the arrangement. The numbers were also letdowns because they signaled that *Big Deal* was about to end without one final dance number.

A Fosse show meant a dancing show, but in *Big Deal* Fosse staged only one full-out dance number. "Beat Me Daddy, Eight to the Bar," with its pulsating pelvises and its slow ooze, looks like a Fosse number, but here he works in a more muscular style than ever. The punishing knee work recalls that of Jack Cole and Michael Kidd. Big, brawny chunks of movement alternate with minute, stop-action isolations. A simmering, percolating arrangement of the boogie-woogie standard is the basis for a full-strength ensemble number that Fosse constructs with mathematical precision. Built around rising and falling sequences that escalate to a thunderous climax, the number's orchestration turns the song inside out, finding notes and rhythms where none previously existed, rendering it unrecognizable from famous renditions by Glenn Miller and the Andrews Sisters. A pulsing synthesizer keeps the tempo edgy and nervous, and the amplified percussion gives the music a techno–big band drive.

In a ballroom called Paradise, working-class revelers gather, the women in their print dresses, the men in delivery-boy caps. As an orchestra plays atop a bandstand and a mirror ball spins, the narrators swagger with sharp-edged shoulders and thrusting pelvises in friendly one-upmanship for the attentions of the flirtatious Lilly. Like Fosse and Tommy Rall in *My Sister Eileen*'s "Alley Dance," they dare each other to spin and slice through the air faster and higher. Reaching a stalemate, they fall to their knees as the music hits an early peak and pulls back.

In the shadows behind them the dancers twist and unwind. They lock their feet into the floor, throw their arms above their heads and convulse to the beat. Their tiny, individual moves—a shoulder roll, a wrist flick—accent different percussive beats and create a jittery, rolling web of stage movement. They seep upstage, pausing to hit an accent before falling almost imperceptibly into a Jack Cole "power block."[68] From there, they stalk forward, pelvises first, before bursting apart and melting to the floor.

Social dancing, 1930s. The last great Fosse number, "Beat Me Daddy, Eight to the Bar" from Big Deal. *Left to right: Roumel Reaux, George Russell, Wayne Cilento, Bruce Anthony Davis, and Frank Mastrocola. Photo by Martha Swope © Billy Rose Theatre Division, The New York Public Library for the Performing Arts.*

Back on their feet, pools of light capture them in sharp, angular writhing, jerking as if possessed by the rhythm. The music pulls back one last time before beginning its final build. The men crash to the floor, paddling in place on one knee. Throughout the number, movements frequently mirror the orchestra solo-ists, spotlighted on the bandstand. Here, the women's stuttering steps and the men's fluttering fingers echo the piano's riffs.[69] At last, the music's coiled ten-sion explodes. Spread across the stage, the dancers turn on themselves, lunging out and extending their arms in a wide second position. Suddenly they stop in place, skittishly marking time like racehorses at the starting gate. They dash back upstage, jump with arms in the air, then fan out across the stage before ending with backs to the audience and arms upraised, genuflecting to the band whose instruments they have just embodied in dance.

"Beat Me Daddy, Eight to the Bar" has much in common with other large-scale Fosse numbers like "Sing Sing Sing" (set in the 1940s), "Two Lost Souls" (1950s), and "Rich Man's Frug" (1960s) in which Fosse weaves together a ritualized series of steps that suggest period dance but convey a brash, contemporary sexuality.[70] The movements are virile yet economical. This is Fosse as minimalist, confident in the power of his images. Regardless of his physical ailments, Fosse demonstrates that his ability to create a showstopper is undiminished. "Beat Me Daddy, Eight to the Bar" stands as the last great Fosse number.

"Broadway's changed and I don't much like it anymore."

Bob Fosse, 1986[71]

The *Boston Herald*'s headline summed up the local response to *Big Deal* when it opened its out-of-town tryout on February 15, 1986: "Super Musical Hurt by Clumsy Script."[72] Indeed, most of the criticism focused on the inadequacy of Fosse's book, while praising the dance numbers and performers. Boston's top critic, Kevin Kelly, of the *Boston Globe*, offered suggestions for improvements: "What 'Big Deal' needs is to tell us less, tell it quicker and funnier. It needs more dancin', less plottin.'"[73]

There was additional criticism of the two narrators ("useless and distracting")[74] and the placement of the four fantasy numbers at the very end of the show ("arbitrary, totally out of proportion with the plot").[75] In the past, when faced with bad out-of-town reviews, Fosse got right to work with changes. But this time his changes were only minor. Herb Gardner came up to Boston to help brighten the script with added humor. The producers offered suggestions, but in a replay of the Boston tryouts for *Dancin'*, Fosse disregarded them—and not with good grace. "I'm the director. You're the producer. Let me make my show, so shut the fuck up," Fosse reportedly snapped in response to their notes.[76] Audiences appeared to take the reviews at their word and mostly stayed away. *Big Deal*'s box-office figures never went much above 50 percent of capacity.

In a painfully diplomatic letter to Fosse just as the show was loading into the Broadway Theater for its New York opening, the Shuberts gingerly enumerated several key concerns. After opening with extravagant praise ("you have created an exciting musical, and The Shubert Organization is proud to be its producer"),[77] they respectfully asked that the lighting be brightened on the all-black set. "Your work is too good not to be fully seen . . . . Also, the fact that a large number of the cast are dark complected prevents the audience from seeing their faces and fully comprehending their words and appreciating their acting." "Could you possibly choreograph an acrobatic dance number which would be a sure showstopper?," they pleaded, to replace the "Hold Tight, Hold Tight" fantasy number. "We must get them out of their seats at the curtain call," they beseeched, asking Fosse to expand the full-cast reprise of "I'm Sitting on Top of the World." Continuing to tread carefully, they signed the letter, "With great affection and friendship." The suggestions were not only reasonable but also astute in light of the show's eventual New York reception. Yet they fell on deaf ears. "Cocksuckers," Fosse called the Shuberts.[78]

When *Big Deal*, Fosse's first new show in eight years, opened on April 10, its reviews were remarkably similar to those in Boston, with the chief criticism directed at Fosse the writer. Frank Rich, in his all-important *New York Times* review, wrote, "The cinematic staging techniques are of little use when the story being told is static and mirthless."[79] He went on to lament, "The dizzying sense of levitation that Mr. Fosse achieves in ['Beat Me Daddy, Eight to the Bar'] is one of those unquantifiable elements . . . that defined the Broadway musical when it really was a going concern. The disappointment of 'Big Deal' is that even Mr. Fosse, one of the form's last magicians, can conjure up that joy so rarely."[80] Not only did *Big Deal*'s New York reviews deem it a disappointment, but its failings—all laid at the feet of its singular creator—were seen as embodying all that ailed the Broadway musical in 1986.

(Even *Forbidden Broadway*, the long-running cabaret spoof of Broadway and its personalities, piled on with "Hey, Bob Fosse," to the tune of "Hey, Big Spender," in which a trio stumbles through a dance number in gloomy, dark lighting. They lament their show's lack of plot and laughs, and beg their director, "Hey, Bob Fosse, spend a little time on the book.")[81]

This judgment was further underscored by enthusiastic reviews for the revival of *Sweet Charity* when it opened a few weeks later. The Debbie Allen–starring production was brought to New York and installed in the cavernous Minskoff Theater, a half dozen blocks from *Big Deal*. With two Fosse shows opening so close together, comparisons were inevitable—and not to *Big Deal*'s favor. "Next to the full-throttle pyrotechnics of *Sweet Charity*, even the two or three dance numbers that have been praised in *Big Deal* appear lame and derivative," mused David Kaufman in *Downtown* magazine.[82]

After both shows had opened, a defensive Fosse discussed *Big Deal* and its critical reception with Kevin Grubb of *Dance Magazine*. He railed against critics John Simon ("sarcastic" and "cruel")[83] and Frank Rich ("elitist" and "so separated from what the audience likes"), and offered harsh opinions of current shows. The Stephen Sondheim–James Lapine musical *Sunday in the Park with George* was "a boring experience for most people," and the book for Tommy Tune's *My One and Only* (like *Big Deal*, a new musical using a score of existing songs) was "a piece of shit."

Fosse was particularly proud of the techniques he brought from films to the stage. "I think it's the first musical . . . that really is done with cinematic techniques," he insisted. "And that there are such things on that stage as dissolves. I mean, there is simultaneous action, which you don't see in musicals . . . . There's such things as quick cuts, where you pick up a person here, and go out on him, and then pick up another person over there, which is like a quick cut in film. So it is full of what I know about cinema, for years, that I've heard about people saying, 'Why can't we get that technique on stage.' Well, I think I did it and then they didn't notice it."

But the techniques Fosse described had been in use by other directors for some time. Harold Prince used dissolves and simultaneous action in *Follies* fifteen years earlier. Michael Bennett's staging of *Dreamgirls* in 1981 involved at least as many scenes as *Big Deal* on a bare stage defined by a series of moving light towers. In fact, Fosse's work on *Big Deal* was not unlike *Dreamgirls*' fluid, cinematic mix of song, dance, and dialogue. That he was not aware of, or chose to ignore, innovations by his peers that he now claimed for himself made Fosse appear disengaged from what was happening elsewhere in the theater.

Fosse directed the show's commercial, which emphasized its dancing and carried the voice-over "Where there's smoke, there's Fosse." But neither the commercial nor five Tony nominations kept *Big Deal* from playing to half-empty houses. In addition to Best Musical and Best Actor in a Musical for Cleavant Derricks, *Big Deal*'s nominations included three for Fosse, for choreography, direction, and, surprisingly, his book. The nominees in the latter category included the quick flop *Wind in the Willows* and Betty Comden and Adolph Green's retread of their film script for *Singin' in the Rain*. It appeared that Fosse's maligned book for *Big Deal* was similarly designated to fill out the sparse category, and Rupert Holmes was the easy winner for *The Mystery of Edwin Drood*.

Big Deal looked like a winner during the awards telecast when the dancers performed "Beat Me Daddy, Eight to the Bar," and few could begrudge Fosse's award for choreography. It was his ninth Tony Award and the only one received by *Big Deal*. (In comparison, *Sweet Charity* won four Tony Awards, including for Best Revival.) But the win came too late. When *Big Deal* closed on June 11 after only seventy performances, the once unthinkable had occurred: Bob Fosse had his first Broadway flop.

Big Deal was truly a mixed bag, its failure regrettable but predictable. The film's characters resisted musicalization in a way that Fellini's *Cabiria* did not. Its dark, film noir look was out of step with its essentially comedic story. Moreover, *Big Deal* appeared to be two shows at odds with each other. The simple, low-key characters and plot were disconnected from the high-powered narrators and dance ensemble in sleek, black tuxedos who looked to be holdovers from *Dancin'* and whose various appearances played more like interruptions.

But numbers like "Ain't We Got Fun?," "Me and My Shadow," and "Beat Me Daddy, Eight to the Bar" showed Fosse extending and refining his style of movement. Regardless of whether others had used the techniques before, his cinematic staging was swift and seamless, and he pushed against the boundaries of the proscenium in new, inventive ways. Fosse's use of old pop songs for *Big Deal*'s score foreshadowed the "jukebox musical" that would become popular in the twenty-first century with shows like *Mamma Mia!* and *Jersey Boys*. His repurposing of unsophisticated popular songs, often in ironic counterpoint to their original meanings, was unusual for the time and gave *Big Deal* a sense of wit and surprise. And the show's electrified orchestrations gave the 1930s songs a contemporary flair, fusing the past with the present.

During the show's Boston tryout, Fosse reflected ruefully on where he now found himself at this point in his life and career: "If I had my life to live over again, I would have gone the route of Jerry (Jerome Robbins), would have gone into ballet, choreographed ballets. God, it's too late, too late now to do that."[84] In a sense, *Big Deal* was a full-length ballet, created from Fosse's own libretto—a continuous flow of music and dance, with its period score part of a unique soundscape and his now-classic dance style emerging gracefully from stage movement. Like *Star 80*, *Big Deal* was the purest distillation of Fosse's creative vision. It was a cruel irony that just at the moment when he had the full control he so desired, his work was rejected.

FOSSEVILLE

* * *

Sweet Charity's success was bittersweet for Bob Fosse: an old show celebrated while his new work was snubbed. There was a memorial air to the awards and honors that now came his way. When Fosse and Gwen Verdon appeared together as presenters on the 1987 Tony Awards, his tribute sounded like his own final summation of her importance to his work. Describing the choreographer's art as "only about fifty percent conception," he proposed "that the real test of your talent is getting five or six . . . people in a room who are just a little crazier than you are, and who can try to live out that thing in your head." After a pause, he continued, "And sometimes, if you're very lucky, you can find someone who dances it better than you ever dreamed it . . . and for me, that someone was Miss Verdon."[1]

Fosse and Verdon worked together rehearsing first Ann Reinking, as Debbie Allen's Broadway replacement, and then Donna McKechnie for *Sweet Charity*'s national tour in the summer of 1987. By now, Verdon had coached two generations of dancing actresses in the role she had originated. The bond between Fosse and Verdon remained strong, driven by mutual respect and the desire to see his work performed to its highest capacity. A photograph taken in East Hampton during this period signals their complex, continued intimacy. Verdon faces directly out with a warm and satisfied smile, as if basking in Fosse's presence, while his gaze is downward and contemplative, both comforted and conflicted by her closeness.

Fosse, along with Verdon and Cy Coleman, made the unusual practice of traveling to each stop on the *Sweet Charity* tour to work with the cast. There was a particular urgency to the rehearsal just before the show opened at the National Theater in Washington, DC, on September 23, 1987. "He worked us to the knuckle that day, because this was a turning point," remembered Diane Laurenson.[2] Business had been soft in earlier tour stops. Strong reviews in Washington would hopefully lead to improved business; if not, the tour could end. Following rehearsal, Fosse returned to his hotel to change. On the way back to the theater, he suddenly collapsed on the street. With Verdon beside him, he was rushed to the hospital, where he died in the emergency room of a massive heart attack at 7:23 p.m., just as the curtain was going up on *Sweet Charity*.[3] At the end of the show, the opening-night audience stood and cheered, unaware that its star director had just expired. It was a moment steeped in theatrical irony that Fosse would have appreciated.

A memorial was held on October 30 at the Palace Theater. The speakers were all male, and almost entirely writers. No dancers appeared except in film clips, and all were overshadowed by images of Fosse, who seemed to laugh at death as he glided across the screen. The memorial was followed that evening by a kind of wake, produced and directed by Fosse himself. In his will, he had earmarked $25,000 as a gift for sixty-six friends to "go out and have dinner on me."[4] Held at Central Park's Tavern on the Green, the dinner guests included Fosse's writer friends, dancers and actors, his agent, his doctor, his daughter, his wife, and various girlfriends from over the years. "They all have at one time or other during my life been very kind to me. I thank them," Fosse wrote.[5] His thanks provided a lavish spread, endless drinks, and an orchestra. "Dance like you're going to percussion heaven," he exhorted the *Sweet Charity* cast on the last day of his life,[6] and as the evening wore on and the dance floor filled, his friends fulfilled his directive, dancing one last Fosse showstopper.

A wave of AIDS-related fatalities was devastating the theatrical community, and Fosse's death was somewhat overshadowed by that of another important figure who had recently succumbed to the disease. Michael Bennett, whose landmark musical *A Chorus Line* was still going strong on Broadway and around the world, died of the disease on July 2, 1987. He was forty-four years old. Coverage of Fosse's death at sixty implied that perhaps his best work was behind him. Bennett was in the prime of his career, and his death left major projects to languish; unlike for Fosse, a sense of promises unfulfilled infused the mourning for the younger man.

At the 1988 Tony Awards, Bennett was afforded a lengthy tribute, featuring numbers from several of his shows. Nothing was mentioned of Fosse until Chita Rivera, presenting the choreography award, paused to remember Fosse's words from the previous year about the art of choreography: "So from all of the dancers and all of the people who have ever worked with Bobby, I would just like to take a moment and remember, and say that he did make us deliriously crazy, very happy, and very proud."[7]

> "I have two major fears in life. One is that I'll be asked to do things like appear on those talk shows where famous old people talk about their careers and that I'll be asked to choreograph toy store commercials. The other fear is that I'll accept both of those."
>
> Bob Fosse, 1984[8]

At Fosse's memorial service, Pete Hamill defined his art as a spot "where corrosive wit and cynical style always play against the most darkly glamorous backdrops" and called that spot "Fosseville."[9] *Chicago*'s 1996 revival served as a return trip to Fosseville, celebrating his spirit and the theater he embodied. At the same time, another musical salute to Fosse was being developed. In 1985, Chet Walker, who had danced in *Pippin* and *Dancin'* and would be part of the *Sweet Charity* revival, approached Fosse with an idea for a television retrospective of his work, but with a difference. As Walker later recalled, "The impetus was for people in this business to say, 'thank you' to him."[10] In Walker's concept, Fosse travels down the hallway of a rehearsal studio. Each door he opens reveals a familiar face—Verdon, Shirley MacLaine, Joel Grey, Chita Rivera, Ben Vereen—teaching young dancers the Fosse numbers that made each a star, demonstrating his influence on multiple generations of dancers. Fosse, always ambivalent about looking backward, threw up several caveats. "I don't want anyone on the show that's worked with me before," he demanded. When asked why, he replied, "Because I don't want to be told what I did. I want to do."[11]

With Fosse's death, the tribute was placed on hold. In the early 1990s, Walker reached out to Verdon with the idea of reviving the project as homage to Fosse's body of work. With her blessing, Walker began teaching classes in Fosse style, eventually reconstructing entire numbers. A new generation of dancers was eager to learn the Fosse repertoire, and Walker and Verdon not only taught Fosse's style but also provided provenance and historical context for his signature movements.

Livent, a Canadian theatrical producing organization, funded a series of workshops during which the show was refined. Richard Maltby Jr., who had directed the celebrated revue *Ain't Misbehavin'*, was eventually brought in to unify this anthology of dances into a loosely biographical form. Ann Reinking came aboard to create the connective tissue between the many numbers. When *Fosse* opened at the Broadhurst Theater on January 14, 1999, its cumbersome credits listed Maltby as director; Reinking as co-director and co-choreographer; Walker as responsible for choreographic recreation; Verdon as artistic adviser; and Maltby, Walker, and Reinking for overall conception.

Fosse's three-act structure resembled *Dancin'*, and indeed, that later Fosse show was heavily represented. The cast of thirty-two served as a versatile dance company performing a repertoire of twenty-six full-length numbers. *Fosse* included such now-iconic numbers as "Steam Heat," "Big Spender," and "Rich Man's Frug" and rediscoveries like "Cool Hand Luke" and the spirited "I Gotcha" from *Liza with a Z*. But Fosse's early, lively work with Mary Ann Niles was hastily dispensed with, and numbers conceived for film, like "Mein Herr," looked static without quick-cut editing. The three pas de deux from "Take Off with Us" were strenuous rather than sexy and, worse, appeared dated.

As in *Big Deal*, *Fosse* was bookended by "Life Is Just a Bowl of Cherries." ("Sing Sing Sing" was its rousing encore number.) The song set a reverential and somber tone for the show, with the dancers often adopting a dead-eyed sultriness. One would never imagine that Fosse had staged some of the funniest dances ever seen on Broadway, like "Rich Kids' Rag" and "A Secretary Is Not a Toy," nor that he satirized sex so deliciously in "Whatever Lola Wants," one of several prime Gwen Verdon numbers that were not included.

By focusing so heavily on Fosse's later, more self-consciously serious work, the show inadvertently exposed what Fosse had always admitted: that he had a limited dance vocabulary. Ingeniously recycling those steps into fresh patterns and formations, he made them look both new and reassuringly familiar from one show to the next. Now, so many similar numbers in quick succession threatened monotony. By the time "The Manson Trio" was performed in the third act, it was only the latest in a long series of tight trio numbers that began to look alike.[12]

In a weak season for musicals, *Fosse* won the Best Musical Tony Award. Chet Walker's original idea of including Fosse stars in a tribute show was partially realized when Ann Reinking, Bebe Neuwirth, and Ben Vereen joined the Broadway cast at various times during its run. With virtually no dialogue, the show was a hit with foreign tourists and ran for more than two years, closing after 1,093 performances. Fittingly, the show was the final work of Gwen Verdon, the indefatigable keeper of the Fosse flame. She died in her sleep at her daughter's home on October 18, 2000, at the age of seventy-five.

With *Fosse* and *Chicago* both playing on Broadway, a Fosse renaissance was in full swing, capped by the worldwide success of *Chicago*'s 2002 film adaptation. The film restores *Chicago* to color from the revival's black-and-white palette and preserves its original conception as a series of 1920s vaudeville turns. Rather than try to shoehorn the presentational numbers into a realistic setting, *Chicago* wittily embeds them in the narrative as fantasies seen through the eyes of Roxie Hart.

Chicago was the feature film–directing debut of Rob Marshall, a former dancer and one of Broadway's busiest choreographers. He was clearly influenced by Fosse's direction of *Cabaret*, and *Chicago*'s visuals are strongly reminiscent of that film's foreboding glamour. Fosse's staging concepts form the foundation for much of Marshall's work, but he actively avoids references to Fosse's famous style. The film's choreography is strenuously sexy, giving off flickers of Fosse but no real heat. As with the *Chicago* revival, what is missing is the atmosphere of sensuality Fosse could so effortlessly create.

Chicago was criticized for its overly aggressive editing, but as the first full-fledged dance musical in years, it bears the hallmarks of Fosse's musical films filtered through two decades of music videos, a new medium for filmed dance. *All That Jazz* appeared just two years before MTV broadcast its first music video, but its impact was almost immediately apparent in the dance-oriented videos that became a staple of the network. For many first-generation MTV stars, like Michael and Janet Jackson, Madonna, and Paula Abdul, *All That Jazz* was the first Fosse they had experienced. Their visual approximation of that film's posed, locked-down choreography, captured in hurriedly edited, arresting images, would come to define dance for a new era. "Fosse" was now its own brand.[13]

Less felicitously, musicals that followed *All That Jazz*, from *Flashdance* and *Staying Alive* to the more recent *Magic Mike* and the *Step Up* series, reflect what dance critic Joan Acocella called the "MTV trickle-down" of Fosse's influence.[14] Fosse constructed his film dances as if they were to be performed onstage, but in these new musicals, frantic editing allows dancers to perform superhuman feats of gymnastics that accelerate Fosse's more layered, nuanced editing methods to the point of incoherence. (Fosse saw how others had distorted his techniques, commenting in 1983, "I'm embarrassed to say that what's happening now is part of my doing. I think it's being carried to the extreme where it's not interesting anymore.")[15]

So thoroughly has Bob Fosse's dance and theatrical aesthetic been absorbed into the popular culture that it feels as if it has always been here, available to be scavenged without regard for its underlying structure. YouTube is filled with videos of amateur dance groups performing faux Fosse routines. Dance studios emblazon images of derbied dancers snapping their fingers in white gloves to advertise classes in theater dance. Televised dance competitions like *So You Think You Can Dance?* offer Fosse-style posturing as "Broadway" routines. Fosse's work is reduced to a generic category of dance that anyone can do, regardless of skill or training—trading on the image and mystique of Fosse but without the underpinnings of context and intent.

Lately, the Fosse hold on American theater dance has loosened. Acrobatics and spectacle were deemed necessary to the revival of Fosse's *Pippin*. Frantic a-move-on-every-beat staging and gratuitous gymnastics, much of it popularized by television dance competitions, have found their way into every type of musical regardless of historical or stylistic appropriateness. "TRUST . . . RELAX . . . ARTISTRY," Fosse advised in a note to the cast of *Chicago*.[16] Reviving Fosse in today's frantic dance environment requires both dancers and audiences to slow down and savor the nuances.

Maintaining the integrity of his work is the driving force of the Verdon-Fosse Legacy LLC, established by Fosse and Verdon's daughter, Nicole. The organization sponsors master classes of classic Fosse repertoire taught by a core group of final-generation Fosse dancers. A new generation is learning his key works from those who are Fosse's primary source material: the dancers who hold within their bodies his unique choreographic language.

Yet while his original dances are being preserved and passed on, in postmodern fashion others are harvesting and repurposing key elements of them. Beyoncé sifts "Rich Man's Frug" through a gaudy hip-hop sensibility in her video "Get Me Bodied," while her "Single Ladies" is an aggressive, twenty-first-century translation of Verdon's "Mexican Breakfast" (1969). Hip-hop dancing captures the tiny movement slivers associated with Fosse and, when performed in unison by dance crews, takes on a hypnotic quality similar to that of Fosse's trio numbers. Andy Blankenbuehler's densely layered hip-hop-inspired choreography for Lin-Manuel Miranda's *Hamilton* (2015) is built on isolations and surprising start-stop rhythms that a new-century Fosse might have created. Young Charles "Lil Buck" Riley is an influential proponent of "Memphis Jookin,'" a form of street dance that in his interpretation combines Michael Jackson's Moonwalk (itself a reincarnation of Fosse) with both Fosse's isolations and his slithering, liquid movements. These artists reference Fosse in innovative new ways that make their work feel fresh and forward-looking.

Three decades after his death, Fosse's "Muscle" shows no signs of weakening. He remains both a touchstone for American theater dance, recognizable around the world, and a continuing source of inspiration for new artists.

NOTES

FOREWORD

1. The first volume in the series on a choreographer is Kara Anne Gardner's *Agnes de Mille: Telling Stories in Broadway Dance* (2016).

INTRODUCTION

1. William Goldman, *The Season: A Candid Look at Broadway* (New York: Harcourt, Brace, 1969), 285–298.

2. George Abbott, *Mister Abbott* (New York: Random House, 1963), 254.

3. See Richard Kislan, *Hoofing on Broadway: A History of Show Dancing* (New York: Prentice Hall, 1987), 42.

4. See Ned Wayburn, *The Art of Stage Dancing: The Story of a Beautiful and Profitable Profession* (New York: Belvedere, 1980), 42.

5. Ibid., 90–91.

6. See Barbara Stratyner, *Ned Wayburn and the Dance Routine: From Vaudeville to the Ziegfeld Follies*, Studies in Dance History No. 13 (Madison: University of Wisconsin Press for the Society of Dance Scholars, 1996), ix.

7. See Mark N. Grant, *The Rise and Fall of the Broadway Musical* (Boston: Northeastern University Press, 2004), 229.

8. In addition to staging the dances and ensembles for *Whoopee!*, Felix is credited with directing the show, while the dialogue direction is attributed to William Anthony McGuire, a typical breakdown of responsibilities on musicals of the time.

9. Seymour Felix, quoted in Kislan, *Hoofing on Broadway*, 57.

10. Larry Stempel refers to Lee, along with Felix, Busby Berkeley (1895–1976), and Bobby Connolly (1896–1944), as "part of the Big Four group of young Broadway dance directors in the 1920s." Stempel, *Showtime: A History of the Broadway Musical Theater* (New York: Norton, 2010), 230. *Show Boat* was one of eight Broadway productions Lee choreographed in a busy twelve-month period. The others included the Gershwins' *Oh, Kay!*, Harry Tierney and Joseph McCarthy's *Rio Rita*, Rodgers and Hart's *Betsy*, and the latest edition of the *Ziegfeld Follies*, with songs by Irving Berlin. Berkeley staged numerous musical comedies and revues, including Rodgers and Hart's *A Connecticut Yankee* (1928) and *Present Arms* (1928), before moving on to films, where he stretched the John Tiller model of precision dance to geometric extremes. Connelly provided Ray Henderson, B. G. DeSylva, and Lew Brown's *Good News* (1927) and the Gershwins' *Funny Face* (1927) with cheerfully energetic tap and Charleston numbers, but he is best remembered for his dances for the 1939 film version of *The Wizard of Oz*.

11. Ethan Mordden, *Broadway Babies: The People Who Made the American Musical* (New York: Oxford University Press, 1983), 132.

12. Sammy Lee did not choreograph every number in *Show Boat*. African American dancer, choreographer, producer, and teacher Aaron Gates was engaged to stage at least

one number for the separate black chorus. See Todd Decker, *"Show Boat": Performing Race in an American Musical* (New York: Oxford University Press, 2013), 108, 119–120.

13. It should be noted that Mamoulian, who also directed the premiere production of the Gershwins' *Porgy and Bess* (1935), confidently staged musical numbers not requiring dance. He smoothed transitions from dialogue to song and brought fluidity to his direction of crowd scenes.

14. To understand how startling and new "Laurey Makes Up Her Mind" was at the time, a look at Robert Alton's ballet "Joey Looks into the Future," for Rodgers and Hart's *Pal Joey* (1940), is instructive. Joey is about to realize his dream of owning and starring in his own nightclub thanks to his new, wealthy female patron. While Joey chafes at her control over him ("What do I care for a dame? / Every damn dame is the same"), he quickly surrenders to the anticipation of fame and success ("I'm gonna own a night club / It's gonna be the right club"). Alton lacked de Mille's dramatic imagination and was satisfied to present a crowd-pleaser. Joey's internal conflicts are soon dispensed with, and the number concludes as a celebration of his future. De Mille later complimented his work as "slick, finished, and speedy" and noted, "There were no great moments of dramatic revelation, but each routine was solidly built and effective." Agnes de Mille, *Dance to the Piper* (Boston: Little, Brown, 1951), 184.

15. De Mille, *Dance to the Piper*, 86.

16. See Carol Easton, *No Intermissions: The Life of Agnes de Mille* (Boston: Little, Brown, 1996), 179–180, 252–253.

17. Kara Anne Gardner, *Agnes de Mille: Telling Stories in Broadway Dance* (New York: Oxford University Press, 2016), 40.

18. Grant, *The Rise and Fall of the Broadway Musical*, 267.

19. Agnes de Mille secured the *Oklahoma!* assignment on the strength of her recent American West ballet, *Rodeo* (1942). Its sodbusters and pioneer women are direct antecedents for *Oklahoma!*'s farmers and cowboys, and de Mille's now-familiar movement vocabulary is much in evidence. But de Mille was hired to fashion dances for the already-developed property, whereas Robbins's *Fancy Free* served as the primary source material for *On the Town*, with his collaborators bending to his conception.

20. See Abbott, *Mister Abbott*, 221.

21. See Arthur Laurents, *Original Story By: A Memoir of Broadway and Hollywood* (New York: Knopf, 2000), 348.

22. Frank Rich, *Hot Seat: Theater Criticism for The New York Times, 1980–1993* (New York: Random House, 1998), 26.

23. Ibid.

24. John Martin, "Dance: Broadway," *New York Times*, October 27, 1957.

25. John Corry, "Robbins Weighs the Future—Ballet or Broadway?," *New York Times*, July 12, 1981.

CHAPTER 1: BOY DANCER

1. Paul Gardner, "Bob Fosse Off His Toes," *New York*, December 16, 1974, 59.

2. Glenna Syse, "Triumphs of a 'Chicago Boy,'" *Chicago Sun-Times*, April 22, 1973.

3. Fosse Genealogy by Margaret Sell Fosse, Hurlock, Maryland, 1976, box 52B, Bob Fosse and Gwen Verdon Collection, Music Division, Library of Congress, Washington, DC.

4. Syse, "Triumphs of a 'Chicago Boy.'"

5. Chris Chase, "Fosse, from Tony to Oscar to Emmy?," *New York Times*, April 29, 1973.

6. Gaby Rogers, "Bob Fosse: 'Choreography Is Writing with Your Body,'" *Newsday*, October 1, 1978.

7. Ibid.

8. See Ronna Elaine Sloan, "Bob Fosse: An Analytic-Critical Study" (PhD diss., City University of New York, 1983), 59.

9. Bernard Drew, "Life as a Long Rehearsal," *American Film*, November 1979, 28.

10. See Arnold Zeitlin, "The Inhibited Choreographer from Chicago," *Chicago Daily News*, March 26, 1966.

11. Arthur Laurents, *Gypsy* (New York: Theatre Communications Group, 1994), 73.

12. Rachel Shteir, *Striptease: The Untold History of the Girlie Show* (New York: Oxford University Press, 2004), 43. Fosse referenced Little Egypt's brand of cooch dancing years later in *Chicago*, when Chita Rivera stripped down to display her toned torso in a series of undulations during "I Can't Do It Alone," which included displays of burlesque and vaudeville performance tropes, including "Oriental" dancing, sister act precision steps, and acrobatics.

13. *The South Bank Show*, March 8, 1981, on *All That Jazz*, directed by Bob Fosse (Twentieth Century-Fox and Columbia Pictures, 1979), DVD (Criterion Collection, 2014).

14. Linda Winer, "Bob Fosse: The Razzle-Dazzle Director Is Planning to Jazz Up Broadway with His New 'Deal,'" *USA Today*, October 30, 1985.

15. Undated clipping, "Scrapbook, Fosse," box 56B, Bob Fosse and Gwen Verdon Collection.

16. Marian Zailian, "Dancin' Bob Fosse Still Flirts with Death," September 2, 1979, box 52D, Bob Fosse and Gwen Verdon Collection.

17. See "Vaudeville on Broadway," November 1, 1944, advertisement in "Scrapbook, Fosse," box 56B, Bob Fosse and Gwen Verdon Collection.

18. Robert Alan Aurthur, "Hanging Out," *Esquire*, August 1973, 8.

19. Ibid.

20. Zailian, "Dancin' Bob Fosse Still Flirts with Death."

21. Moira Hodgson, "When Bob Fosse's Art Imitates Life, It's Just 'All That Jazz,'" *New York Times*, December 30, 1979.

22. Bruce Williamson, "All That Fosse," *Playboy*, March 1980, 250.

23. Zailian, "Dancin' Bob Fosse Still Flirts with Death."

24. *Paul Draper on Tap*, Camera Three, WGBH Boston, aired 1979, Jerome Robbins Dance Division, The New York Public Library for the Performing Arts.

25. "Bob Fosse and Gwen Verdon," *American Musical Theater with Earl Wrightson*, CBS, aired January 1, 1962.

26. Navy Liaison Unit press release, undated, "Scrapbook, Fosse," box 56B, Bob Fosse and Gwen Verdon Collection.

27. Bob Fosse *Call Me Mister* contract, September 13, 1946, box 43A, Bob Fosse and Gwen Verdon Collection.

28. Robert Pollak, "Pick of Chicago's 1946–47 Stage Season," *Chicago Sunday Times*, June 8, 1947.

29. Untitled and undated review, *Windsor Daily Star*, "Scrapbook, Fosse," box 56B, Bob Fosse and Gwen Verdon Collection.

30. See John Anthony Gilvey, *Before the Parade Passes By: Gower Champion and the Glorious American Musical* (New York: St. Martin's Press, 2005), 22–33.

31. Martin Gottfried, *All His Jazz: The Life and Death of Bob Fosse* (New York: Bantam Books, 1990), 56.

32. Mary Ann Niles quoted in Sloan, "Bob Fosse," 65.

33. Ibid., 67.

34. Anna Kisselgoff, "Jack Cole Is Dead; A Choreographer," *New York Times*, February 20, 1974.

35. See Glenn Loney, *Unsung Genius: The Passion of Dancer-Choreographer Jack Cole* (New York: Franklin Watts, 1984), 11.

36. Walter Terry, *I Was There: Selected Dance Reviews and Articles, 1936–1976*, comp. and ed. Andrew Mark Wentink (New York: Audience Arts, 1978), 149.

37. Constance Valis Hill, "From Bharata Natyam to Bop: Jack Cole's 'Modern' Jazz Dance," *Dance Research Journal* 33, no. 2 (Winter 2001–2002): 31.

38. Ibid., 32, 34–35.

39. Dance analysis of "Limehouse Blues" based on footage from *The Colgate Comedy Hour* with Dean Martin and Jerry Lewis, aired February 4, 1951, accessed December 5, 2013, https://www.youtube.com/watch?v=Rq44ql5cPDY.

40. Abel, "New Acts: Fosse and Niles," *Variety*, December 15, 1948, 56.

41. Eileen Casey, telephone interview by author, January 31, 2016.

42. A photograph from *Call Me Mister* featuring the pair in a midair leap was used as a publicity photograph for their act, with Fosse in particular barely contained by gravity. His choreography for the "Alley Dance" in the film *My Sister Eileen* (1955) features several displays of the Fosse stag leaps by Fosse and Tommy Rall.

43. Display ad, *Variety*, October 26, 1949, 66.

44. Drew, "Life as a Long Rehearsal," 29.

45. See Lisa Jo Sagolla, *The Girl Who Falls Down: A Biography of Joan McCracken* (Boston: Northeastern University Press, 2003), 1–4, for a detailed choreographic analysis of McCracken's appearance in this number.

46. Michael Kidd quoted in ibid., 57–58.

47. Ibid., 108.

48. Ibid.

49. Gwen Verdon interview, WNET/13 *Dance in America*, Bob Fosse and Gwen Verdon Collection.

50. Bone, "Plays Out of Town: *Dance Me a Song*," *Variety*, December 28, 1949, 44.

51. Gwen Verdon interview, WNET/13 *Dance in America*, Bob Fosse and Gwen Verdon Collection.

52. Dance analysis for "Steppin' Out with My Baby" based on footage from *The Colgate Comedy Hour* with Dean Martin and Jerry Lewis, aired April 29, 1951, accessed December 5, 2013, https://www.youtube.com/watch?v=6rqxlIoFimM. Dance analysis for "Get Happy" based on footage from *The Colgate Comedy Hour* with Dean Martin and Jerry Lewis, aired May 20, 1951, accessed December 5, 2013, http://www.youtube.com/watch?v=mtqXsME2kus.

53. Chase, "Fosse, from Tony to Oscar to Emmy?"

54. See ibid.; Dick Anderson, "The Dancin' Man," *The Hamptons*, August 1, 1986, box 52E, Bob Fosse and Gwen Verdon Collection; "Bob Fosse," *The Dick Cavett Show*, aired July 8, 1980; and "American Theatre Wing School Steps Up TV Curriculum in Show Biz Upbeat," *Variety*, February 13, 1952, 28, 48.

55. See Sanford Meisner and Dennis Longwell, *Sanford Meisner on Acting* (New York: Vintage Books, 1987), and Peter B. Flint, "Sanford Meisner, a Mentor Who Guided Actors and Directors toward Truth, Dies at 91," *New York Times*, February 4, 1997.

56. Contract between Loews International and Robert Fosse, April 19, 1951, box 51A, Bob Fosse and Gwen Verdon Collection.

57. Correspondence between Metro-Goldwyn-Mayer and Robert Fosse, May 16, 1951, box 51A, Bob Fosse and Gwen Verdon Collection.

58. Lionel Chetwynd, "Except for Bob Fosse," *Penthouse*, January 1974, 90.

59. Marjory Adams, "Stage Show: Carol Bruce Shines in Clever 'Pal Joey' at Boston Summer Theatre," *Boston Globe*, August 7, 1951.

60. Richard L. Coe, "One on the Aisle: Group at Olney Does Corking 'Pal Joey,'" *Washington Post*, September 13, 1951.

61. See "Equity Fines Ms. Morrow; Stage Mgrs. Show Up," *Billboard*, March 29, 1952, 45; Sam Zolotow, "'The Victim' Bows to Rialto Tonight," *New York Times*, May 2, 1952; and "Legit Bits," *Variety*, May 7, 1952, 56.

62. See Gottfried, *All His Jazz*, 64–65, and Sam Wasson, *Fosse* (Boston: Houghton Mifflin Harcourt, 2013), 67–68.

63. Dance analysis based on *Cavalcade of Stars*, aired June 20, 1952, the Paley Center for Media.

64. Clifford Terry, "Home Town Boy Bob Fosse Makes Good," *Boston Globe*, April 20, 1969.

65. Gilvey, *Before the Parade Passes By*, 53.

66. Stanley Donen interviewed by Michael Kantor, August 26, 2003, Theatre on Film and Tape Archive, The New York Public Library for the Performing Arts.

67. See Donald Duncan, "They Flip for Joe Price," *Dance Magazine*, August 1964, 10.

68. See Stephen M. Silverman, *Dancing on the Ceiling: Stanley Donen and His Movies* (New York: Knopf, 1996), 184, for Donen's discussion of filming the number in *Give a Girl a Break*.

69. This story has been retold frequently by Donen and others and has passed into Fosse legend. For a full retelling, see Peter Stone's comments in the *Bob Fosse Memorial*, Palace Theater, October 30, 1987, Theatre on Film and Tape Archive.

70. Transcript of Bob Fosse interview with Kevin Kelly, *The Ten O'Clock News*, WGBH-TV, February 24, 1986, *Big Deal* clipping files, Shubert Archive, New York City.

71. *The Dick Cavett Show*, July 8, 1980.

72. "Bob Fosse: Steam Heat," *Great Performances: Dance in America*, PBS, aired February 23, 1990.

73. Paul Rosenfield, "Fosse, Verdon and 'Charity': Together Again," *Los Angeles Times*, July 21, 1985.

74. See John Franceschina, *Hermes Pan: The Man Who Danced with Fred Astaire* (New York: Oxford University Press, 2012), 186.

CHAPTER 2: APPRENTICESHIP

1. "Bob Fosse," *The Dick Cavett Show*, PBS, aired July 8, 1980.

2. See Hal Prince, *Contradictions: Notes on Twenty-Six Years in the Theatre* (New York: Dodd, Mead, 1974), 8–9.

3. Harold Prince, interview by author, September 11, 2013.

4. See Samuel L. Leiter, *The Great Stage Directors: 100 Distinguished Careers of the Theater* (New York: Facts on File, 1994), 1–4; and unpublished interview with Bob Haddad, box 49A, Bob Fosse and Gwen Verdon Collection, Music Division, Library of Congress, Washington, DC.

5. Brooks Atkinson, "'The Pajama Game': Ministrations of George Abbott Evident in Lively New Musical Production," *New York Times*, May 30, 1954.

6. See employment agreement between Loew's Incorporated and Robert Fosse, September 14, 1953, box 51A, Bob Fosse and Gwen Verdon Collection.

7. Harold Prince, interview by author.

8. Kevin Boyd Grubb, *Razzle Dazzle: The Life and Work of Bob Fosse* (New York: St. Martin's Press, 1989), 41.

9. Harold Prince, interview by author.

10. Bob Fosse contract for *The Pajama Game*, February 26, 1954, box 167, Harold Prince Papers, Billy Rose Theatre Division, The New York Public Library for the Performing Arts.

11. Contract Digest, *The Pajama Game* Company, box 167, Harold Prince Papers.

12. See Jerome Robbins contract for *The Pajama Game*, March 29, 1954, and Statement from Bob Fosse, March 1954, box 167, Harold Prince Papers.

13. Glenn Loney, "The Many Facets of Bob Fosse," *After Dark*, June 1972, 24.

14. See Shirley MacLaine, *My Lucky Stars: A Hollywood Memoir* (New York: Bantam Books, 1995), 165.

15. Walter Terry, "The Dance World: 'Pajama Game'; A Ballet Concert," *New York Herald Tribune*, June 6, 1954.

16. See Arnold Zeitlin, "The Inhibited Choreographer from Chicago," *Chicago Daily News*, March 26, 1966.

17. Interview with Kenneth Geist quoted in Deborah Jowitt, *Jerome Robbins: His Life, His Theater, His Dance* (New York: Simon and Schuster, 2004), 243.

18. Jerome Robbins letter to David Hocker, December 6, 1955, box 65, Jerome Robbins Papers, Jerome Robbins Dance Division, The New York Public Library for the Performing Arts.

19. Floria V. Lasky memo to Jerome Robbins, December 12, 1973, box 65, Jerome Robbins Papers.

20. Unpublished interview with Bob Haddad, box 49A, Bob Fosse and Gwen Verdon Collection.

21. See Jerry Adler interviewed by Michael Kantor, March 29, 1999, Theatre on Film and Tape Archive, The New York Public Library for the Performing Arts.

22. Unpublished interview with Bob Haddad, box 49A, Bob Fosse and Gwen Verdon Collection.

23. George Abbott and Richard Bissell, *The Pajama Game* (New York: Random House, 1954), 107.

24. See Trav S.D., *No Applause—Just Throw Money* (New York: Faber and Faber, 2005), 170.

25. Unpublished interview with Bob Haddad, box 49A, Bob Fosse and Gwen Verdon Collection.

26. Martin Gottfried interview with Jerome Robbins, May 17, 1988, Jerome Robbins Dance Division.

27. Leo Lerman, "Broadway '53–54: No Gains," *Dance Magazine*, June 1954, 53.

28. Jerome Robbins quoted in Martin Gottfried, *All His Jazz: The Life and Death of Bob Fosse* (New York: Bantam Books, 1990), 79.

29. Richard Watts Jr., "Factory Life in Musical Comedy," *New York Post*, May 14, 1954.

30. Stephen Sondheim quoted in Jowitt, *Jerome Robbins*, 243.

31. Frances Herridge, "Curtain Cues: The 'Steam Heat' in 'Pajama Game,'" *New York Post*, May 28, 1954.

32. See Tim Carter, *Oklahoma! The Making of an American Musical* (New Haven, CT: Yale University Press, 2007), 246.

33. Ann Reinking, telephone interview by author, April 29, 2016.

34. See Gene Siskel, "Who Killed Dorothy Stratten? 'STAR 80' Says Today's Values . . . ," *Chicago Tribune*, November 6, 1983.

35. Loney, "The Many Facets of Bob Fosse," 26.

36. "Gwen Verdon and the American Dance Machine," *The Dick Cavett Show*, PBS, aired December 5, 1977.

37. Rex Reed, "I Never Wanted to Be Special," *New York Times*, February 6, 1966.

38. *The Dick Cavett Show*, December 5, 1977.

39. See Robert Rice, "New Star in Town: Gwen Verdon," *New York Post*, June 3, 1957; "The Devil's Disciple," *Time*, June 13, 1955, 63; and Reed, "I Never Wanted to Be Special."

40. Suzanne Daley, "Stepping into Her New Shoes," *New York Times*, June 21, 1981.

41. Robert Rice, "New Star in Town: Gwen Verdon," *New York Post*, June 5, 1957.

42. "Bob Fosse and Gwen Verdon," *American Musical Theater with Earl Wrightson*, CBS, aired April 1, 1962.

43. John Martin, "The Dance: In the Broadway Musical Sector," *New York Times*, February 26, 1950.

44. Cy Feuer interviewed by Michael Kantor, February 23, 1999, Theatre on Film and Tape Archive.

45. Ibid.

46. Cy Feuer with Ken Gross, *I Got the Show Right Here: The Amazing, True Story of How an Obscure Brooklyn Horn Player Became the Last Great Broadway Showman* (New York: Simon and Schuster, 2003), 171.

47. See Radie Harris, "Broadway Ballyhoo," *Hollywood Reporter*, May 12, 1953, 4.

48. Murray Schumach, "'Can Can' Dancer: Gwen Verdon Says Ballet and Burlesque Contributed to Her Current Role," *New York Times*, May 31, 1955.

49. Art Buchwald, "Some Advice from a Can-Can Expert," *New York Herald Tribune*, October 3, 1954.

50. Chita Rivera, telephone interview by author, February 11, 2016.

51. Paul Rosenfield, "Fosse, Verdon and 'Charity': Together Again," *Los Angeles Times*, July 21, 1985.

52. Bob Fosse contract for *Damn Yankees*, January 20, 1955, box 57, Harold Prince Papers.

53. See Prince, *Contradictions*, 17.

54. Harold Prince, interview by author.

55. Interviews with Geraldine Fitzgerald, Gwen Verdon, Marian Seldes, and Elizabeth McCann, *CUNY Spotlight*, CUNY-TV, 1991, Theatre on Film and Tape Archive.

56. All quotes from interviews with Geraldine Fitzgerald, Gwen Verdon, Marian Seldes, and Elizabeth McCann, *CUNY Spotlight*.

57. George Abbott and Douglass Wallop, *Damn Yankees* (New York: Random House, 1956), 145.

58. Ibid., 85.

59. "The Theater: New Musical in Manhattan," *Time*, May 16, 1955, 104.

60. Gwen Verdon quoted in Herb Gardner, "Eulogy," *Time*, October 30, 2000, 31.

61. Rosenfield, "Fosse, Verdon and 'Charity.'"

62. Interviews with Geraldine Fitzgerald, Gwen Verdon, Marian Seldes, and Elizabeth McCann, *CUNY Spotlight*.

63. Gwen Verdon interview, WNET/13 *Dance in America*, Bob Fosse and Gwen Verdon Collection.

64. Interviews with Geraldine Fitzgerald, Gwen Verdon, Marian Seldes, and Elizabeth McCann, *CUNY Spotlight*.

65. Cyrus Durgin, "The Stage: 'Damn Yankees,' Baseball Musical at the Shubert," *Boston Globe*, April 13, 1955.

66. See Margery Beddow, *Bob Fosse's Broadway* (Portsmouth, NH: Heinemann, 1996), 7.

67. Hobe, "Shows on Broadway: *Damn Yankees*," *Variety*, May 11, 1955, 64.

68. Ibid.

69. Unpublished interview with Bob Haddad, box 49A, Bob Fosse and Gwen Verdon Collection.

70. Harold Prince, interview by author.

71. Dance analysis based on "The George Abbott Tribute," *The Colgate Variety Hour*, aired December 11, 1955, the Paley Center for Media.

72. Dance analysis based on *The Ed Sullivan Show*, accessed October 21, 2015, https://www.youtube.com/watch?v=pCFoWIt7Mac.

73. Frank Derbas quoted in Greg Lawrence, *Dance with Demons: The Life of Jerome Robbins* (New York: Putnam's, 2001), 243.

74. Leo Lerman, "Dance On and Off Broadway: 56–57," *Dance Magazine*, 30. Peter Gennaro and Ellen Ray performed "Mu-Cha-Cha" (without Judy Holliday) on *The Steve Allen Show*, April 28, 1957, the Paley Center for Media.

75. Jerome Robbins letter to Tanaquil Le Clerq, December 3, 1956, box 1, Jerome Robbins Papers.

76. See Stephen M. Silverman, *Dancing on the Ceiling: Stanley Donen and His Movies* (New York: Knopf, 1996), 246–247, for Donen's remembrance of his arrangement with Abbott. See also Judith Crist, "The Roxy Reopens with 'Damn Yanks,'" *New York Herald Tribune*, September 21, 1958.

77. Articles extolling the efficiency of the production noted that *The Pajama Game* was completed fifteen to twenty days ahead of schedule at a savings of between $200,000 and $300,000, including $30,000 saved when color tests confirmed that the cast could appear without makeup. Additional savings were realized when Fosse choreographed all the dances completely before filming began, rather than in bits and pieces throughout production. See John Allen, "'The Pajama Game' Was Played Swiftly," *New York Herald Tribune*, Mar 17, 1957, and "Pre-production Rehearsals Speed 'Pajama Game'; Also Helps That Most of Cast from Broadway," *Variety*, January 2, 1957, 3, 15.

78. Harold Prince telegram to Bob Fosse, October 23, 1956, box 168, Harold Prince Papers.

79. See Silverman, *Dancing on the Ceiling*, 247.

80. Jean-Luc Godard, *Godard on Godard*, trans. and ed. Tom Milne (New York: Viking Press, 1972), 87–88.

81. Robert Griffith letter to George Abbott, March 13, 1958, box 58, Harold Prince Papers.

82. Patricia Ferrier Kiley, telephone interview by author, November 9, 2013.

83. Gwen Verdon quoted in Silverman, *Dancing on the Ceiling*, 256.

84. Gwen Verdon interview, WNET/13 *Dance in America*, Bob Fosse and Gwen Verdon Collection.

85. Bosley Crowther, "A Season Come to Life: 'Damn Yankees,' 'The Defiant Ones' Lead a Lively Fall Film Parade," *New York Times*, October 5, 1958.

86. Ibid.

87. Loney, "The Many Facets of Bob Fosse," 26.

88. See Sam Zolotow, "A Very Rewriting Novel for Stage," *New York Times*, July 11, 1956.

89. See Seymour Peck, "'Anna Christie' Sings: O'Neill in Song," *New York Times*, May 12, 1957.

90. "Budget 'Girl' at $242,750; Loew's, Inc., Has Option; Due May 8 at 46th St.," *Variety*, January 16, 1957, 67.

91. See Frederick Brisson, Robert Griffith, and Harold Prince letter to Robert Fosse, September 27, 1956, box 163, Harold Prince Papers.

92. Interviews with Geraldine Fitzgerald, Gwen Verdon, Marian Seldes, and Elizabeth McCann, *CUNY Spotlight*.

93. Harold Prince, interview by author.

94. Bob Fosse interview with Stephen Harvey, September 1983, box 60F, Bob Fosse and Gwen Verdon Collection.

95. Interviews with Geraldine Fitzgerald, Gwen Verdon, Marian Seldes, and Elizabeth McCann, *CUNY Spotlight*.

96. Patricia Ferrier Kiley, telephone interview by author.

97. Harvey Evans, interview by author, September 6, 2013.

98. Ibid.

99. See Steven Suskin, *The Sound of Broadway Musicals: A Book of Orchestrators and Orchestrations* (New York: Oxford University Press, 2009), 489. Robert Russell Bennett orchestrated "There Ain't No Flies on Me" and all its dance variations, as well as "Roll Yer Socks Up."

100. Philip K. Scheuer, "Verdon Dynamic 'Yankee,'" *Los Angeles Times*, May 11, 1958.

101. Ibid. Fosse and Verdon performed a portion of the "Pony Dance" on *American Musical Theater with Earl Wrightson*, April 1, 1962.

102. Peck, "'Anna Christie' Sings."

103. The description of the "Red Light Ballet" is based on interviews with dancers Harvey Evans, David Gold, Patricia Ferrier Kiley, and Alton Ruff; Beddow, *Bob Fosse's Broadway*, 12–13; photographs from the Billy Rose Theatre Division, The New York Public Library for the Performing Arts; and scrapbooks in the Bob Fosse and Gwen Verdon Collection.

104. Dance scholar Liza Gennaro's analysis of the presentation of the female body in the work of de Mille and Fosse briefly considers *New Girl in Town*'s "Red Light Ballet" as a precursor to his stylization of the Fan-Dango Ballroom Girls in *Sweet Charity*. See Gennaro, "Broken Dolls": Representation of Dancing Women in the Broadway Musical," accessed August 12, 2013, http://www.bodiesofwork.info/Bob%20Fosse.html, and Gennaro, "Evolution of Dance in the Golden Age of the American 'Book Musical,'" in *The Oxford Handbook of the American Musical*, ed. Raymond Knapp, Mitchell Morris, and Stacy Wolf (New York: Oxford University Press, 2011), 50–51, 56–57.

105. George Abbott, *Mister Abbott* (New York: Random House, 1963), 254.

106. Harold Prince, interview by author.

107. Harvey Evans, interview by author.

108. Unpublished interview with Bob Haddad, box 49A, Bob Fosse and Gwen Verdon Collection.

109. Abbott, *Mister Abbott*, 254.

110. Sidney Fields, "Four Are Needed to Replace Gwen," undated, unsourced article, box 44E, Bob Fosse and Gwen Verdon Collection.

111. Don Ross, "O'Neill Set to Music in Abbott's 'New Girl,'" *New York Herald Tribune*, May 12, 1957.

112. Brooks Atkinson, "The Theatre: Singing Anna Christie," *New York Times*, May 14, 1957.

113. Leo Lerman, "Dance On and Off Broadway: 56–57," *Dance Magazine*, June 1957, 68–69.

114. Unpublished interview with Bob Haddad, box 49A, Bob Fosse and Gwen Verdon Collection. See also Gwen Verdon quoted in Ronna Elaine Sloan, "Bob Fosse: An Analytic-Critical Study" (PhD diss., City University of New York, 1983), 114.

115. See Robert Griffith letter to George Abbott, February 10, 1958; Harold Prince letter to George Abbott, February 11, 1958; Harold Prince letter to George Abbott, February 13, 1958; Robert Griffith letter to George Abbott, February 21, 1958; and Harold Prince letter to George Abbott, March 18, 1958, all in box 57, Harold Prince Papers, for discussion of the efforts to find a replacement for Gwen Verdon.

116. Robert Griffith letter to George Abbott, March 14, 1958, box 57, Harold Prince Papers.

CHAPTER 3: UNCLE SAM RAG

1. Jack Viertel, "Bob Fosse Supervises L.A. 'Charity' Event," *Los Angeles Herald-Examiner*, July 14, 1985.

2. For the genesis and development of *Redhead*, see Bill Smith's series of articles, "A Show Is Born," *Newark Evening News*, June 22–25, 1959; Charlotte Greenspan, *Pick Yourself Up: Dorothy Fields and the American Musical* (New York: Oxford University Press, 2010), 195–197; and Sidney Sheldon, *The Other Side of Me: A Memoir* (New York: Grand Central Publishing, 2005), 292–293.

3. Lionel Chetwynd, "Except for Bob Fosse," *Penthouse*, January 1974, 91.

4. Bob Fosse notes, "Murder Musical: Things to be included," box 46B, Bob Fosse and Gwen Verdon Collection, Music Division, Library of Congress, Washington, DC.

5. Bob Fosse agreement with Dorothy Fields, Albert Hague, David Shaw, and the Estate of Herbert Fields, October 1, 1958, box 46B, Bob Fosse and Gwen Verdon Collection.

6. Patricia Ferrier Kiley, telephone interview by author, November 9, 2013.

7. David Gold, telephone interview by author, January 11, 2014.

8. Harvey Evans, interview by author, September 6, 2013.

9. Chris Chase, "Fosse, from Tony to Oscar to Emmy?," *New York Times*, April 29, 1973.

10. "Bob Fosse and Gwen Verdon," *American Musical Theater with Earl Wrightson*, CBS, aired April 1, 1962.

11. Robert Alan Aurthur, "Hanging Out," *Esquire*, December 1972, 80.

12. *American Musical Theater with Earl Wrightson*, April 1, 1962.

13. Dance analysis based on "'Erbie Fitch's Twitch," accessed November 12, 2013, https://www.youtube.com/watch?v=MxdmCL9XJ64. Verdon performed "Erbie Fitch's Twitch" October 4, 1959, on *The Dinah Shore Chevy Show*, a rare example of her recreation of a number from one of her vehicles during its initial run.

14. The term "eleven o'clock number," coined when curtains were at 8:30, refers to a rousing song or dance that energizes the second act just before a show's conclusion. Perhaps the most famous such number is "Rose's Turn" from *Gypsy*. Examples from Fosse's shows include "Two Lost Souls" in *Damn Yankees*, Judy Holliday's bravura "I'm Goin' Back" from *Bells Are Ringing*, and Roxie and Velma's "Nowadays/R.S.V.P./Keep It Hot" in *Chicago*.

15. Leo Lerman, "Close-Up of 'Redhead,'" *Dance Magazine*, May 1959, 40–45.

16. Margery Beddow, *Bob Fosse's Broadway* (Portsmouth, NH: Heinemann, 1996), 15.

17. Harvey Evans, interview by author.

18. Paul Gardner, "Whither the Dream Ballet?," *New York Times*, September 20, 1959.

19. All dialogue quotes and stage directions from Dorothy and Herbert Fields, Sidney Sheldon, and David Shaw, *Redhead* typescript, NCOF+, Billy Rose Theatre Division, The New York Public Library for the Performing Arts.

20. David Gold, telephone interview by author.

21. Harvey Evans, interview by author.

22. Don Ross, "Gwen Verdon on Broadway in New Musical 'Redhead,'" *New York Herald Tribune*, February 1, 1959.

23. Beddow, *Bob Fosse's Broadway*, 17.

24. See Martin Gottfried, *All His Jazz: The Life and Death of Bob Fosse* (New York: Bantam Books, 1990), 112.

25. Gwen Verdon interview, WNET/13 *Dance in America*, Bob Fosse and Gwen Verdon Collection.

26. Ibid.

27. Untitled review, *Cue*, February 21, 1959, *Redhead* clipping file, Billy Rose Theatre Division, The New York Public Library for the Performing Arts.

28. Jan Herman, "Up Close: Bob Fosse," *New York Daily News*, April 6, 1986.

29. *Redhead* dance rehearsal remembrances from author interview with Harvey Evans.

30. Richard Watts Jr., "Another Triumph for Gwen Verdon," *New York Post*, February 6, 1959.

31. Brooks Atkinson, "The Theatre: 'Redhead,'" *New York Times*, February 6, 1959.

32. Gilbert Millstein, "New Girl in Town—And How," *New York Times*, February 15, 1959.

33. "'Redhead,' Show Snubbed for 10 Years, to Pay Off Its Investment by June," *Variety*, February 11, 1959, 1.

34. Hobe, "Shows on Broadway: Redhead," *Variety*, February 11, 1959, 72.

35. Greenspan, *Pick Yourself Up*, 199.

36. "Gwen Twists Ankle, Gets to See 'Redhead,'" *Variety*, August 5, 1959, 2.

37. Jess, "Legit Followup: Redhead," *Variety*, August 19, 1959, 60.

38. John Chapman, "'Redhead' Is a Tip-Top Musical," *New York Daily News*, February 6, 1959.

39. Paul Rosenfield, "Fosse, Verdon and 'Charity': Together Again," *Los Angeles Times*, July 21, 1985.

40. Descriptions and dance analyses of all numbers based on "The Wonderful World of Entertainment," *Ford Startime*, NBC, aired October 6, 1959, the Paley Center for Media.

41. Clive Barnes, "Floss, Fosse & Fosseland," *Dance Magazine*, May 1999, 110.

42. Sam Zolotow, "Fund Drive Set by Arena Stage," *New York Times*, October 15, 1959.

43. Buzz Halliday quoted in Sam Wasson, *Fosse* (Boston: Houghton Mifflin Harcourt, 2013), 152. Fosse was uncredited in the program and publicity for *The Girls against the Boys*, which opened on November 2, 1959, and closed after sixteen performances.

44. Barry Rehfeld, "Fosse's Follies," *Rolling Stone*, January 19, 1984, 44.

45. Letter from? to Oscar Oleson, May 4, 1960, box 43B, Bob Fosse and Gwen Verdon Collection (letter is incomplete).

46. See Otis L. Guernsey Jr., ed., *Broadway Song and Story: Playwrights/Lyricists/Composers Discuss Their Hits* (New York: Dodd, Mead, 1985), 45.

47. Letter from? to Oscar Oleson, May 4, 1960.

48. Richard Korthaze, interview by author, January 20, 2014.

49. Larry Gelbart quoted in Gottfried, *All His Jazz*, 126.

50. Ibid., 124.

51. Bernard Drew, "Life as a Long Rehearsal," *American Film*, November 1979, 31.

52. Beddow, *Bob Fosse's Broadway*, 22.

53. Ibid., 23.

54. Ibid.

55. *The Conquering Hero* script synopsis, box 43B, Bob Fosse and Gwen Verdon Collection.

56. The description of "The Battle," as it was called in the program for the New Haven and Washington, DC tryouts, is based on interviews with dancers Patricia Ferrier Kiley and Richard Korthaze; Beddow, *Bob Fosse's Broadway*, 23–24; and "Sketch for Narrative of Ballet" and Fosse's dance notes, box 43B, Bob Fosse and Gwen Verdon Collection. All quotes are taken from "Sketch for Narrative of Ballet" and Fosse's dance notes.

57. Robert Whitehead quoted in Gottfried, *All His Jazz*, 126–128.

58. Mervyn Rothstein, "Is There Life after 'M*A*S*H'?," *New York Times*, October 8, 1989.

59. F.R.J., "The Theater in Review: 'The Conquering Hero' Big, Brassy Musical," *New Haven Journal-Courier*, November 22, 1960.

60. Morris (Moose) Charlap deposition, March 14, 1961, box 43B, Bob Fosse and Gwen Verdon Collection.

61. Larry Gelbart, *Laughing Matters: On Writing M*A*S*H, Tootsie, Oh, God!, and a Few Other Funny Things* (New York: Random House, 1998), 204–205.

62. Charlap deposition, March 14, 1961, box 43B, Bob Fosse and Gwen Verdon Collection.

63. All quotes from Bob Fosse telegram to the *New York Times*, December 14, [1960], *The Conquering Hero* clipping file, Billy Rose Theatre Division.

64. See American Arbitration Association, Theatrical Arbitration Tribunal, Robert Fosse, Claimant v. Producer's Theatre, Inc., Respondent, February 16, 1961, box 43B, Bob Fosse and Gwen Verdon Collection.

65. Gelbart, *Laughing Matters*, 205.

66. Untitled review, *Cue*, January 28, 1961, *The Conquering Hero* clipping file, Billy Rose Theatre Division.

67. A.T., "The Conquering Hero," *Dance Observer*, April 1961, *The Conquering Hero* clipping file, Billy Rose Theatre Division.

68. See Stuart W. Little, "Theater News: Fosse Awarded 6 Cents in Suit on Use of Dances," *New York Herald Tribune*, September 22, 1961; Sam Zolotow, "Novel by Sneider Will Be Musical," *New York Times*, September 22, 1961; "Bob Fosse Wins Award of 6c for 'Hero' Dances," *Variety*, October 4, 1961. An envelope containing six pennies, Fosse's full award, is included in *The Conquering Hero* files in the Bob Fosse and Gwen Verdon Collection.

CHAPTER 4: COMIC RELIEF

1. "Dance On: Ann Reinking," *Dance On: With Billie Mahoney*, Video Workshop for Dance and Theatre, August 31, 1983, Jerome Robbins Dance Division, The New York Public Library for the Performing Arts.

2. Fosse performed "The Narcissistic Tango" on "Bob Fosse and Gwen Verdon," *American Musical Theater with Earl Wrightson*, CBS, aired April 1, 1962.

3. See Louis Calta, "'Pal Joey' a Hit; Run Is Extended," *New York Times*, June 2, 1961.

4. Glenn Loney, "The Many Facets of Bob Fosse," *After Dark*, June 1972, 24.

5. Shepherd Mead, *How to Succeed in Business without Really Trying* (New York: Simon and Schuster, 2011), 3.

6. "Officemanship," *Time*, October 27, 1961, 79.

7. Richard Korthaze, interview by author, January 20, 2014; Donna McKechnie with Greg Lawrence, *Time Steps: My Musical Comedy Life* (New York: Simon and Schuster, 2006), 39–40.

8. Unpublished interview with Bob Haddad, box 49A, Bob Fosse and Gwen Verdon Collection, Music Division, Library of Congress, Washington, DC.

9. Leo Lerman, "At the Theatre," *Dance Magazine*, January 1962, 12.

10. Loney, "The Many Facets of Bob Fosse," 24.

11. Steven Suskin, *The Sound of Broadway Musicals: A Book of Orchestrators and Orchestrations* (New York: Oxford University Press, 2009), 434.

12. *The South Bank Show*, March 8, 1981, on *All That Jazz*, directed by Bob Fosse (Twentieth Century-Fox and Columbia Pictures, 1979), DVD (Criterion Collection, 2014).

13. Gagh, "Shows Out of Town: *How to Succeed in Business without Really Trying*," *Variety*, September 6, 1961, 54.

14. Cy Feuer with Ken Gross, *I Got the Show Right Here: The Amazing, True Story of How an Obscure Brooklyn Horn Player Became the Last Great Broadway Showman* (New York: Simon and Schuster, 2003), 229.

15. Ibid.

16. McKechnie with Lawrence, *Time Steps*, 41.

17. Lerman, "At the Theatre," 13.

18. Previous musicals to receive the Pulitzer Prize for Drama were *Of Thee I Sing* (1931), *South Pacific* (1950), and *Fiorello!* (1960). Future winners would include *A Chorus Line* (1976), *Sunday in the Park with George* (1985), *Rent* (1996), *Next to Normal* (2010), and *Hamilton* (2016).

19. Jack Perlman letter to Brian Brook, January 20, 1964, box 44C, Bob Fosse and Gwen Verdon Collection.

20. Unpublished interview with Bob Haddad, box 49A, Bob Fosse and Gwen Verdon Collection.

21. "Wit and Wisdom at the Dance Magazine Awards Presentation," *Dance Magazine*, June 1963, 32.

22. Ervin Drake quoted in Sam Wasson, *Fosse* (Boston: Houghton Mifflin Harcourt, 2013), 175.

23. Percy Shain, "Night Watch: Seasons of Youth Pasted Together," *Boston Globe*, October 26, 1961; Barbara Delatiner, "On Television: 'Premise' Players Sparkled in Dull Show," *Newsday*, October 26, 1961.

24. Dance analysis of "I Don't Think I'll End It All Today" and the audition sequence is based on *Seasons of Youth*, ABC, aired October 25, 1961, the Paley Center for Media.

25. Bernard Drew, "Life as a Long Rehearsal," *American Film*, November 1979, 75.

26. Quotes from *Cleveland, U.S.A.*, box 53B, Bob Fosse and Gwen Verdon Collection.

27. Leo Lerman, "At the Theatre: 'Nowhere to Go but Up,' 'Little Me,'" *Dance Magazine*, January 1963, 26.

28. Cy Feuer quoted in Richard Lenon, "Conquest of the Seven Caesars," *Newsweek*, November 26, 1962, 52.

29. See Feuer with Gross, *I Got the Show Right Here*, 235.

30. Unpublished interview with Bob Haddad, box 49A, Bob Fosse and Gwen Verdon Collection.

31. See Sam Zolotow, "Directors' Union Enters Broadway: Feuer and Martin Are First to Recognize Society," *New York Times*, February 21, 1962; Milton Esterow, "Stage Directors Await Vote Today," *New York Times*, August 2, 1962.

32. David Gold, telephone interview by author, January 11, 2014.

33. Feuer with Gross, *I Got the Show Right Here*, 231.

34. All quotes from "Fosse Notebook," box 44D, Bob Fosse and Gwen Verdon Collection.

35. See Margery Beddow, *Bob Fosse's Broadway* (Portsmouth, NH: Heinemann, 1996), 33.

36. "Fosse Notebook," box 44D, Bob Fosse and Gwen Verdon Collection.

37. See Mark Knowles, *Tap Roots: The Early History of Tap Dancing* (Jefferson, NC: McFarland, 2002), 143–145.

38. See Robert Wahls, "Something's Afoot on Broadway," *New York Sunday News*, April 21, 1963.

39. Ibid.

40. Kevin Kelly, "'Little Me' in New York: Broadway Musical Rolls Nowhere on Soft Tires," *Boston Globe*, January 17, 1963.

41. See Katrina Hazzard-Gordon, *Jookin': The Rise of Social Dance Formations in African-American Culture* (Philadelphia: Temple University Press, 1990), 122–123.

42. All quotes and descriptions of "I've Got Your Number" from "Fosse Notebook," box 44D, Bob Fosse and Gwen Verdon Collection.

43. Rudolf Nureyev performed "I've Got Your Number" with Julie Andrews on her television special "Julie Andrews' Invitation to the Dance, with Rudolf Nureyev," *CBS Festival of Lively Arts for Young People*, CBS, aired November 30, 1980.

44. Wahls, "Something's Afoot on Broadway."

45. See Lerman, "At the Theatre: 'Nowhere to Go but Up,' 'Little Me,'" 26.

46. All quotes and descriptions of "Rich Kids' Rag" from "Fosse Notebook," box 44D, Bob Fosse and Gwen Verdon Collection.

47. Thomas R. Dash, "Hail Conquering Caesar! Sid a Wonder in 'Little Me,'" undated, unsourced article, *Little Me* clipping files, Billy Rose Theatre Division, The New York Public Library for the Performing Arts.

48. Norman Nadel, "'Little Me' at Lunt-Fontanne," *New York World-Telegram*, November 19, 1962.

49. Walter Terry, "Torrid Man on Broadway," *New York Herald Tribune*, December 2, 1962.

50. Gwen Verdon interview, WNET/13 *Dance in America*, Bob Fosse and Gwen Verdon Collection.

51. "'Little Me' Breaks Philadelphia Records," undated press release, *Little Me* clipping files, Billy Rose Theatre Division.

52. See Richard Gehman and Betsy Gehman, "The Seven Caesars," *Theatre Arts*, November 1962, 75.

53. Lerman, "At the Theatre: 'Nowhere to Go but Up,' 'Little Me,'" 26.

54. "The Theater: Hail Caesar," *Time*, November 30, 1962, 53.

55. Gwen Verdon interview, WNET/13 *Dance in America*, Bob Fosse and Gwen Verdon Collection.

56. Jesse Gross, "Three Exit with $265,000 Loss," *Variety*, July 8, 1963, 53.

57. Lerman, "At the Theatre: 'Nowhere to Go but Up,' 'Little Me,'" 24.

58. Jerry Tallmer, "On Tour with 7 Caesars," *New York Post*, November 11, 1962.

59. See Alfred T. Hendricks, "Sid Caesar Faints on Stage," *New York Post*, June 13, 1963.

60. See "3 Original Leads Will Tour 'Little,'" *Variety*, January 23, 1964, 37.

61. See "London 'Little Me' May Recoup Loss from U.S. Venture," *Variety*, January 20, 1965, 61; "'Little Me' Folds Sat. (4), London; Hasn't Recouped," *Variety*, September 1, 1965, 57.

62. The 1982 revival, directed by Robert Drivas and choreographed by Peter Gennaro, starred James Coco and Victor Garber splitting the roles of Belle's suitors, and Mary Gordon Murray as Belle. It played thirty-six performances. The 1998 Roundabout Theatre Company revival, directed and choreographed by Rob Marshall and starring Martin Short and Faith Prince (as both younger Belle and her older self) played ninety-nine performances as part of the theater's subscription season.

63. Leo Lerman, "Lament for Broadway," *Dance Magazine*, June 1963, 25.

CHAPTER 5: RHYTHM OF LIFE

1. Lionel Chetwynd, "Except for Bob Fosse," *Penthouse*, January 1974, 91.

2. Richard P. Cooke, "The Theater: Variations on an Old Subject," *Wall Street Journal*, June 3, 1963.

3. *Pal Joey* choreography notebook, box 45C, Bob Fosse and Gwen Verdon Collection, Music Division, Library of Congress, Washington, DC.

4. Sam Zolotow, "Musical Planned for Gwen Verdon," *New York Times*, April 26, 1963.

5. See Jerome Robbins letter to Ray Stark, [September 1962], box 18, Jerome Robbins Papers, Jerome Robbins Dance Division, The New York Public Library for the Performing Arts. See also William J. Mann, *Hello Gorgeous: Becoming Barbra Streisand* (New York: Houghton Mifflin Harcourt, 2012), 260–266, 284–287, for a discussion of the Streisand versus Bancroft arguments and details of Robbins's departure.

6. See Bob Fosse letter to *Funny Girl* creators, [September 1963], box 44A, Bob Fosse and Gwen Verdon Collection.

7. See Chetwynd, "Except for Bob Fosse," 91, and Robert Wahls, "Bob Who? Bob Fosse," *New York Sunday News*, November 26, 1972, for Fosse's assertions of his choice of Barbra Streisand for the role of Fanny Brice.

8. See Fosse's notes and cuts to the *Fanny Brice* (working title) script, dated June 19, 1963, box 44A, Bob Fosse and Gwen Verdon Collection.

9. See *The Funny Girl*, "Marked script, notes of contributions," August 1963, box 19, Jerome Robbins Papers.

10. On one point Fosse and Robbins were in agreement. Neither was in favor of keeping "People" in the show, feeling that the song was at odds with Fanny's show business confidence. The new director, Garson Kanin, felt similarly, and Jule Styne and Bob Merrill fought to retain it, reasoning that the song would be a major hit

record for Barbra Streisand, which it was. See Theodore Taylor, *Jule: The Story of Composer Jule Styne* (New York: Random House, 1979), 242–243.

11. Martin Gottfried interview with Jerome Robbins, May 17, 1988, Jerome Robbins Dance Division.

12. See Bob Fosse letter to *Funny Girl* creators, [September 1963], box 44A, Bob Fosse and Gwen Verdon Collection.

13. Ibid. See also Bob Fosse's *Funny Girl* employment agreement, August 1, 1963, box 44A, Bob Fosse and Gwen Verdon Collection.

14. Ibid.

15. Bob Fosse *Funny Girl* withdrawal letter, September 19, 1963, box 44A, Bob Fosse and Gwen Verdon Collection.

16. "Loesser's New One," *New York Herald Tribune*, February 9, 1965.

17. Sam Zolotow, "Fosse Quits 'Funny Girl' Post to Work for Lerner and Lane," *New York Times*, September 23, 1963.

18. Chetwynd, "Except for Bob Fosse," 91.

19. Ibid.

20. Bob Fosse's *Pleasures and Palaces* choreographic notebook, box 46A, Bob Fosse and Gwen Verdon Collection.

21. Kathryn Doby, interview by author, October 17, 2012.

22. Richard Korthaze, interview by author, January 20, 2014.

23. Ibid.

24. Jay Carr, "Palaces Da, Pleasures Nyet," *Detroit News*, March 12, 1965.

25. Ibid.

26. Bob Fosse's *Pleasures and Palaces* choreographic notebook, box 46A, Bob Fosse and Gwen Verdon Collection.

27. Kathryn Doby, interview by author.

28. Alice Evans, telephone interview by author, January 24, 2016. Many of the *Pleasure and Palaces* dancers had worked on the recent *Little Me* and *How to Succeed in Business without Really Trying*, while others had danced for Fosse multiple times, going back to his first show as a choreographer. They included Don Emmons (*Bells Are Ringing, How to Succeed* in Business without Really Trying), Gene Gavin (*How to Succeed* in Business without Really Trying, *Little Me*), David Gold (*New Girl in Town, Redhead, Little Me*), Richard Korthaze (*The Conquering Hero, How to Succeed* in Business without Really Trying), and Dale Moreda (*The Pajama Game, New Girl in Town, Redhead, The Conquering Hero, How to Succeed* in Business without Really Trying).

29. Ibid.

30. Paul Rosenfield, "Fosse, Verdon and 'Charity': Together Again," *Los Angeles Times*, July 31, 1985.

31. See John D'Emilio and Estelle B. Freedman, *Intimate Matters: A History of Sexuality in America*, 2nd ed. (Chicago: University of Chicago Press, 1997), 301–318; Mark Hamilton Lytle, *America's Uncivil Wars: The Sixties Era from Elvis to the Fall of Richard Nixon* (New York: Oxford University Press, 2006), 194–216, 269–282.

32. Bob Fosse quoted in Shaun Considine, *Mad as Hell: The Life and Work of Paddy Chayefsky* (New York: Random House, 1994), 245.

33. *The South Bank Show*, March 8, 1981, on *All That Jazz*, directed by Bob Fosse (Twentieth Century-Fox and Columbia Pictures, 1979), DVD (Criterion Collection, 2014).

34. Undated Writing, box 53B, Bob Fosse and Gwen Verdon Collection.

35. Descriptions and quotes taken from "Early Notes on Show Called 'Dance Hall' Done before Seeing 'Cabiria,'" box 26D, Bob Fosse and Gwen Verdon Collection.

36. According to news articles published around the time of *Chicago*'s eventual musical adaptation, Fryer and Lawrence Carr had sought the stage rights to the play as early as 1956. See Lewis Funke, "'Chicago' Saga," *New York Times*, January 28, 1973; Louis Calta, "Musical 'Chicago' Due on Broadway," *New York Times*, July 28, 1974.

37. Martin Gottfried, *All His Jazz: The Life and Death of Bob Fosse* (New York: Bantam Books, 1990), 160–161.

38. Ibid., 161.

39. Discussion of Martin Charnin's involvement with the *Cabiria* musical is based on "Fosse Account of Events," Jack Perlman's notes on Charnin's lawsuit, box 26C, Bob Fosse and Gwen Verdon Collection.

40. Bob Fosse deposition, 466–468, box 26C, Bob Fosse and Gwen Verdon Collection.

41. Fosse discarded an early scene in which Charity tries prostitution, but after going to the hotel room of a traveling businessman and spying a picture of his wife and children, she thinks better of it and leaves.

42. Gagh, "Shows Out of Town: Sweet Charity," *Variety*, December 8, 1965, 68.

43. Neil Simon, *Rewrites: A Memoir* (New York: Simon and Schuster, 1996), 215.

44. "Seek 395G Capital for 'Sweet Charity' Musical; 25G Wks SRO to Recoup," *Variety*, October 6, 1965, 73.

45. Kathryn Doby, interview by author.

46. David Gold, telephone interview by author, January 11, 2014.

47. Dick Anderson, "The Dancin' Man," *The Hamptons*, August 1, 1986, box 52E, Bob Fosse and Gwen Verdon Collection.

48. "Bob Fosse: Steam Heat," *Great Performances: Dance in America*, PBS, aired February 23, 1990.

49. "Gwen Verdon and the American Dance Machine," *The Dick Cavett Show*, PBS, aired December 5, 1977.

50. Ibid.

51. All dialogue and lyrics (by Dorothy Fields) from Neil Simon, *Sweet Charity*, in *The Collected Plays of Neil Simon*, vol. 2 (New York: Random House, 1991), 2–113.

52. Gwen Verdon interview, WNET/13 *Dance in America*, Bob Fosse and Gwen Verdon Collection.

53. David Gold, telephone interview by author.

54. Suzanne Charny, telephone interview by author, August 6, 2015.

55. Ibid.

56. *Broadway Beat with Richard Ridge*, Manhattan Neighborhood Network, aired June 22, 1999.

57. Descriptions of "Rich Man's Frug" taken from Bob Fosse's *Sweet Charity* choreographic notes, box 30B, Bob Fosse and Gwen Verdon Collection.

58. Kevin Kelly, "Gwen Verdon Great, 'Charity' a Humdinger," *Boston Globe*, January 31, 1966.

59. Diane Laurenson, interview by author, September 14, 2015.

60. Ibid.

61. Arthur Todd, "Sweet Charity on Broadway," *Dancing Times*, March 1966, 298, in Bob Fosse clipping file, Jerome Robbins Dance Division.

62. Gwen Verdon interview, WNET/13 *Dance in America*, Bob Fosse and Gwen Verdon Collection.

63. Ibid.

64. Dance analysis of "If My Friends Could See Me Now" based on footage from *The Ed Sullivan Show*, CBS, aired March 5, 1967, accessed August 15, 2015, https://www.youtube.com/watch?v=nAHvLPWZkr8.

65. John McMartin, interview by author, January 19, 2015.

66. "I'm a Brass Band" choreography notes, box 30B, Bob Fosse and Gwen Verdon Collection.

67. Dance analysis of "I'm a Brass Band" based on footage from *The Ed Sullivan Show*, CBS, aired October 2, 1966, accessed August 17, 2015, https://www.youtube.com/watch?v=pzoRFhnvtJ8.

68. John Kobal, *Gotta Sing Gotta Dance: A Pictorial History of Movie Musicals* (London: Hamlyn, 1971), 299.

69. Robert Viagas, ed., *The Alchemy of Theatre—The Divine Science: Essays on Theatre and the Art of Collaboration* (New York: Playbill Books, 2006), 33.

70. "Is the Director-Choreographer Taking Over?," roundtable discussion broadcast by radio station WEVD, New York, March 30, 1966, Rodgers and Hammerstein Archives of Recorded Sound, The New York Public Library for the Performing Arts.

71. John Anthony Gilvey, *Before the Parade Passes By: Gower Champion and the Glorious American Musical* (New York: St. Martin's Press, 2005), 131.

72. Chita Rivera quoted in Dennis McGovern and Deborah Grace Winer, *Sing Out Louise! 150 Stars of the Musical Theatre Remember 50 Years on Broadway* (New York: Schirmer Books, 1993), 128.

73. Larry Stempel, *Showtime: A History of the Broadway Musical Theater* (New York: Norton, 2010), 572.

74. Hobe, "Show on Broadway: Sweet Charity," *Variety*, February 2, 1966, 58.

75. Ibid.

76. Kelly, "Gwen Verdon Great, 'Charity' a Humdinger."

77. Henry Hewes, "Broadway Postscript: Charity Springs Eternal," *Saturday Review*, February 12, 1966, *Sweet Charity* clipping file, Billy Rose Theatre Division.

78. "Gwen Verdon," *Eye on Dance: Great Performers*, April 2, 1984, Jerome Robbins Dance Division.

79. Michael Iachetta, "The Sexiest Granny in Town," *Sunday News*, April 17, 1966.

80. See Douglas Watt, "Gwen Verdon May Get Her 'Charity' Man Yet," unsourced, undated article, *Sweet Charity* clipping file, Billy Rose Theatre Division.

81. See "'Charity' Now Earning 8G a Week, Still Needs $308,966 to Recoup; Production Cost $496,608 to Open," *Variety*, September 28, 1966, 61.

82. See Jack Pearlman letter to Joseph P. Harris, February 23, 1967, box 26C, Bob Fosse and Gwen Verdon Collection.

83. See John Hallowell, "Theater: Rebellion on Broadway as Stars Balk at Lengthy Runs," *Life*, July 21, 1967, 42.

84. *Sweet Charity* Playbill, May 1967, accessed September 3, 2015, http://www.playbillvault.com/Show/Detail/Whos_who/9184/41465/Sweet-Charity.

85. Hallowell, "Theater: Rebellion on Broadway as Stars Balk at Lengthy Runs," 42.

86. Joseph Harris letter to Bob Fosse, December 12, 1967, box 26C, Bob Fosse and Gwen Verdon Collection.

87. Marjory Adams, "Stars Share a Husband's Gift," *Boston Globe*, February 2, 1969.

88. For a book-length consideration of the short-lived cycle of 1960s big-budget Hollywood musicals, see Matthew Kennedy, *Roadshow! The Fall of Film Musicals in the 1960s* (New York: Oxford University Press, 2014).

89. See Shirley MacLaine, *My Lucky Stars: A Hollywood Memoir* (New York: Bantam Books, 1995), 175.

90. "Bob Fosse," *The Dick Cavett Show*, PBS, aired July 8, 1980.

91. See *Sweet Charity* Step Outline by I. A. L. Diamond, July 28, 1967, box 30A, Bob Fosse and Gwen Verdon Collection. In Diamond's outline, Charity, like Cabiria, is fearful of the police and is tougher and more streetwise than onstage. At the conclusion, she gives all her money to Oscar so that he can buy a gas station they plan to run together in New Jersey. He rushes off to make the down payment while Charity waits, but after several hours, Charity calls both his apartment building and his office and discovers that there is no record of him in either place.

92. Peter Stone, "The Evolution of 'Sweet Charity,'" *Los Angeles Times*, March 31, 1968.

93. Charles Champlin, "Finest Hour for Bob Fosse and Feet in General," *Los Angeles Times*, May 11, 1969.

94. "'Sweet Charity' Exit of Ross Hunter a Victory for Fosse (& MacLaine?)," *Variety*, November 8, 1967, 4.

95. Discussion of *Sweet Charity* casting taken from casting notes, box 30B, Bob Fosse and Gwen Verdon Collection.

96. John McMartin, interview by author.

97. Quotes from Fosse's camera notes, box 30B, Bob Fosse and Gwen Verdon Collection.

98. John Ware, "How Fosse Went to Hollywood," *Today's Cinema*, February 24, 1969, 10.

99. Paul D. Zimmerman, "Song and Dance Man," *Newsweek*, May 7, 1973, 104.

100. *From Stage to Screen: A Director's Dilemma*, on *Sweet Charity*, directed by Bob Fosse (Universal Pictures, 1969), DVD (Universal, 2003).

101. Fosse's camera notes, box 30B, Bob Fosse and Gwen Verdon Collection.

102. Alastair Macauley, "They Seem to Find the Happiness They Seek," *New York Times*, August 14, 2009.

103. Moira Hodgson, "When Bob Fosse's Art Imitates Life, It's Just 'All That Jazz,'" *New York Times*, December 30, 1979.

104. Joan McCracken, "Thoughts While Dancing," *Dance Magazine*, April 1946, 41.

105. Shirley MacLaine quoted in Kevin Boyd Grubb, *Razzle Dazzle: The Life and Work of Bob Fosse* (New York: St. Martin's Press, 1989), 132.

106. Gwen Verdon interview, WNET/13 *Dance in America*, Bob Fosse and Gwen Verdon Collection.

107. The alternate happy ending can be seen as an extra on the film's DVD release.

108. Fosse's camera notes, box 30B, Bob Fosse and Gwen Verdon Collection.

109. Chetwynd, "Except for Bob Fosse," 92.

110. Dance analysis of "Cool Hand Luke" and "Mexican Shuffle" based on footage from *The Bob Hope Special*, NBC, aired October 14, 1968, accessed September 12, 2015, https://www.youtube.com/watch?v=oXrblSn2ZsU&list=PLwhgYWVMXqimnMoCV1yr9xxHy9hcYCwl5.

111. Audience responses taken from *Sweet Charity* preview tallies in Phoenix, Arizona, December 6, 1968, and Chicago, Illinois, December 7, 1968, box 30A, Bob Fosse and Gwen Verdon Collection.

112. See Viola Hegyi Swisher, "Bob Fosse Translates Sweet Charity from Stage to Screen," *Dance Magazine*, February 1969, 25.

113. John Mahoney, "Universal's 'Sweet Charity' Smash: One All-Time Boxoffice Champions," *Hollywood Reporter*, January 29, 1969, 3.

114. Murf, "Film Review: 'Sweet Charity,'" *Variety*, January 29, 1969, 6.

115. *Sweet Charity* advertisement, *Variety*, January 8, 1969, 44.

116. Vincent Canby, "Screen: A Blow-Up of 'Sweet Charity,'" *New York Times*, April 2, 1969.

117. Maria Harriton, "Film: 'Sweet Charity,'" *Dance Magazine*, July 1969, 26.

118. Peter Stone, *Sweet Charity* screenplay, revised September 4, 1968, box 114, Peter Stone Papers, Billy Rose Theatre Division, The New York Public Library for the Performing Arts.

119. "Universal Stressing Sex Angles in New 'Charity' Campaign," *Variety*, October 15, 1969, *Sweet Charity* (Motion Picture) clipping files, Billy Rose Theatre Division.

120. Ibid.

121. See "All-Time Film Rental Champs," *Variety*, January 7, 1976, 50. Shorn of most of its soulful photo montages, and with scenes trimmed and tightened, *Sweet Charity*'s general release print, which was the version widely available on television for years afterward, is actually an improvement on the original release. No numbers were eliminated, though "Rhythm of Life" and "I Love to Cry at Weddings" feature internal edits. The currently available DVD features the film's original uncut road show release.

CHAPTER 6: WILLKOMMEN

1. Bruce J. Schulman, *The Seventies: The Great Shift in American Culture, Society, and Politics* (New York: Free Press, 2001), 48.

2. Beth Bailey and David Farber, eds., *America in the Seventies* (Lawrence: University Press of Kansas, 2004), 6.

3. See David Frum, *How We Got Here: The 70s: The Decade That Brought You Modern Life (for Better or Worse)* (New York: Basic Books, 2000), 188–189.

4. Shirley MacLaine, *My Lucky Stars: A Hollywood Memoir* (New York: Bantam Books, 1995), 182.

5. David Begelman letter to Bob Fosse, May 14, 1969, box 51B, Bob Fosse and Gwen Verdon Collection, Music Division, Library of Congress, Washington, DC. See also Sam

Wasson, *Fosse* (Boston: Houghton Mifflin Harcourt, 2013), 239–240, for a discussion of Fosse's break with MCA and signing with CMA.

6. Gwen Verdon interview, WNET/13 *Dance in America* (Used for *Bob Fosse: Steam Heat*, aired September 6, 1989), Bob Fosse and Gwen Verdon Collection.

7. Dance analysis of "Mexican Breakfast" based on *The Ed Sullivan Show*, CBS, aired June 1, 1969, accessed December 20, 2015, https://www.youtube.com/watch?v=lnQosST-6Y4. Beyoncé appropriated the choreography and low-tech set design of "Mexican Breakfast" for her "Single Ladies" video in 2008. Consequently, all footage of "Mexican Breakfast" available on YouTube has been outfitted with different, more contemporary music tracks.

8. Dance analysis for "A Fine, Fine Day" based on *The Ed Sullivan Show*, CBS, aired February 1, 1970, accessed December 20, 2015, https://www.youtube.com/watch?v=1bpUfphm-nw.

9. See "New Era? ABC Splits Costs with AA, WB on Musicals," *Independent Film Journal*, February 4, 1970, 10.

10. "Bob Fosse," *The Dick Cavett Show*, PBS, aired July 8, 1980.

11. See Hal Prince, *Contradictions: Notes on Twenty-Six Years in the Theatre* (New York: Dodd, Mead, 1974), 125.

12. Joe Masteroff, Fred Ebb, and John Kander, *Cabaret*, in Stanley Richards, ed., *Great Musicals of the American Theatre*, vol. 2 (Radnor, PA: Chilton, 1976), 581.

13. *Cabaret*'s published libretto includes the "meeskite" lyric, with the Jewish reference listed as an alternate lyric. When the libretto was revised for revivals, the Jewish reference was reinstated.

14. Larry Stempel, *Showtime: A History of the Broadway Musical Theater* (New York: Norton, 2010), 518–519.

15. Prince, *Contradictions*, 131.

16. See "'Cabaret' to Roll April 2 in Bavaria; AA Handles U.S., 20th in Cont'l Mkt.," *Variety*, December 9, 1970, 23.

17. See *Cabaret* "Cost and Budget," July 10, 1970, box 16B, Bob Fosse and Gwen Verdon Collection.

18. Harold Prince, interview by author, September 11, 2013.

19. Cy Feuer with Ken Gross, *I Got the Show Right Here: The Amazing, True Story of How an Obscure Brooklyn Horn Player Became the Last Great Broadway Showman* (New York: Simon and Schuster, 2003), 241.

20. Ibid., 243.

21. *Cabaret: A Legend in the Making*, on *Cabaret*, directed by Bob Fosse (Allied Artists and ABC Pictures Corporation, 1972), Blu-Ray (Warner Brothers, 2013).

22. Feuer with Gross, *I Got the Show Right Here*, 242.

23. See ibid., 239–242, and Cy Feuer interviewed by Michael Kantor, February 23, 1999, Theatre on Film and Tape Archive, The New York Public Library for the Performing Arts, for Feuer's discussion of his early plans for *Cabaret*'s screen adaptation.

24. Paul Gardner, "Bob Fosse," *Action*, May–June 1974, 24.

25. See Bill Davids, "Director Bob Fosse: Sweet on 'Charity' and 'Cabaret,'" *Kingsman*, March 10, 1972, 11, box 52D, Bob Fosse and Gwen Verdon Collection.

26. Bob Fosse letter to Mary Dorfman, December 11, 1971, box 16B, Bob Fosse and Gwen Verdon Collection.

27. See Radie Harris, "Hugh Wheeler Role in 'Cabaret' Told," *Hollywood Reporter*, April 5, 1972, 6.

28. Feuer with Gross, *I Got the Show Right Here*, 244.

29. All quotes from Bob Fosse handwritten notes and letter to Martin [Baum], undated, box 16B, Bob Fosse and Gwen Verdon Collection.

30. Cy Feuer interviewed by Michael Kantor.

31. Gardner, "Bob Fosse," 24.

32. C. Robert Jennings, "Divine Decadence Provides the Theme for German 'Cabaret,'" *Los Angeles Times*, June 27, 1971.

33. Hollis Alpert, "Willkommen, Bienvenue, Welcome!," *Saturday Review*, March 4, 1972, 66.

34. Kathryn Doby, interview by author, October 17, 2012.

35. Gardner, "Bob Fosse," 27.

36. David J. Gehrin, "An Interview with Christopher Isherwood," in *Conversations with Christopher Isherwood*, ed. James J. Berg and Chris Freeman (Jackson: University Press of Mississippi, 2001), 78.

37. *Newsweek*, February 28, 1972. The same week, *Time* magazine also put Minnelli on its cover, announcing her as "The New Miss Show Biz." *Time*, February 28, 1972.

38. Kathleen Carroll, "Minnelli and Grey Star in 'Cabaret,'" *New York Sunday News*, June 13, 1971.

39. See Stephen Tropiano, *Cabaret* (Milwaukee, WI: Limelight Editions, 2011), 77.

40. Betty Spence, "Bob Fosse—He'll Take the Risks," *Los Angeles Times*, May 17, 1981.

41. Robert Alan Aurthur, "Hanging Out," *Esquire*, August 1973, 8.

42. Gwen Verdon interview, WNET/13 *Dance in America*, Bob Fosse and Gwen Verdon Collection.

43. Ibid.

44. "Old Tiller" dance ideas, box 16B, Bob Fosse and Gwen Verdon Collection.

45. See Rex Reed, "Liza Minnelli—Queen of Decadent Berlin," *Baltimore Sun*, July 25, 1971.

46. Gwen Verdon interview, WNET/13 *Dance in America*, Bob Fosse and Gwen Verdon Collection.

47. Davids, "Director Bob Fosse: Sweet on 'Charity' and 'Cabaret,'" 12.

48. Audience responses taken from *Cabaret* preview cards, Anaheim and Westwood, January 21–22, 1972, box 16B, Bob Fosse and Gwen Verdon Collection.

49. See Jay Presson Allen and Hugh Wheeler, *Cabaret*, final draft, February 15, 1971, box 15C, Bob Fosse and Gwen Verdon Collection; Michael York, *Accidentally on Purpose: An Autobiography* (New York: Simon and Schuster, 1991), 276.

50. Christopher Isherwood quoted in Vito Russo, *The Celluloid Closet: Homosexuality in the Movies* (New York: Harper and Row, 1981), 191.

51. Pauline Kael, "Grinning," *New Yorker*, February 19, 1972, 84.

52. Charles Champlin, "'Cabaret' a Yardstick for Future Musicals," *Los Angeles Times*, April 2, 1972.

53. Stanley [Donen] telegram to Bob Fosse, May 4, 1972, box 47A, Bob Fosse and Gwen Verdon Collection.

54. Jay Scott, "Fosse's Legacy Nears Perfection," *Globe and Mail*, September 25, 1987.

55. Martin Gottfried, *All His Jazz: The Life and Death of Bob Fosse* (New York: Bantam Books, 1990), 228.

56. Stephen Farber, "'Cabaret' May Shock Kansas . . . ," *New York Times*, February 20, 1972.

57. Ibid.

58. David Tipmore quoted in James Gavin, *Intimate Nights: The Golden Age of New York Cabaret* (New York: Grove Weidenfeld, 1991), 303.

59. See Pauline Kael, "Talent Isn't Enough," *New Yorker*, March 17, 1975, 112–117, for her lengthy review of *Funny Lady*, in which she compares its screenplay, direction, choreography, and score to those of *Cabaret* and Barbra Streisand's performance to that of Liza Minnelli.

60. Vilmos Zsigmond quoted in James Spada, *Streisand: Her Life* (New York: Crown, 1995), 328.

61. "Bob Fosse Wins Best Directing: 1973 Oscars," accessed January 19, 2016, https://www.oscars.org/oscars/ceremonies/1973.

62. Aurthur, "Hanging Out," 8.

63. Kenneth Geist, "Skirting Death: The Trials of Bob Fosse," unpublished interview, box 52D, Bob Fosse and Gwen Verdon Collection.

64. Mary Campbell, "After Winning the Triple Crown Where Can Fosse Go?," *Philadelphia Inquirer*, September 16, 1973.

65. *Liza with a Z*, first draft, May 27, 1971, box 45A, Bob Fosse and Gwen Verdon Collection.

66. Barbara Goldsmith, "Brilliant Television Concert, Liza Minnelli," *Harpers Bazaar*, September 1972, 186.

67. Ibid.

68. "Liza TV" dance notebook, box 45A, Bob Fosse and Gwen Verdon Collection.

69. *The South Bank Show*, March 8, 1981, on *All That Jazz*, directed by Bob Fosse (Twentieth Century-Fox and Columbia Pictures, 1979), DVD (Criterion Collection, 2014).

70. Bok., "Television Review: *Liza with a Z*," *Variety*, September 13, 1972, 54.

71. The song was revisited often by Minnelli in later concert appearances and was the basis for *Ring Them Bells!*, an unproduced screenplay by Paul Zindel that strictly followed the song's story, from Riverside Drive to the beach of Dubrovnik where Shirley and Norm meet on the sand. See Paul Zindel, *Ring Them Bells!*, first draft, November 15, 1974, box 70, Fred Ebb Papers, Music Division, The New York Public Library for the Performing Arts.

72. Minnelli and the female dancers recreated the staging of "Mein Herr," and Fosse shot it in an approximation of the film, but the number was cut from the final broadcast. The excised "Mein Herr" can be seen as a bonus feature on *Liza with a Z: A Concert for Television*, DVD (Showtime Entertainment, 2006).

73. Percy Shain, "Liza's Special—All-Time Great TV," *Boston Globe*, September 11, 1972.

CHAPTER 7: AN ANECDOTIC REVUE

1. Linda Winer, "For 'Chicago''s Fosse, Life Is a 'Cabaret' of Musical Hits," *Chicago Tribune*, February 19, 1978.

2. See Elizabeth L. Wollman, *The Theater Will Rock: A History of the Rock Musical from Hair to Hedwig* (Ann Arbor: University of Michigan Press, 2006), 53.

3. Clive Barnes called *Hair* "the first Broadway musical for some time to have the authentic voice of today rather than the day before yesterday." Barnes, "Theater: 'Hair'—It's Fresh and Frank," *New York Times*, April 30, 1968.

4. In *The Rise and Fall of the Broadway Musical* (Boston: Northeastern University Press, 2004), Mark N. Grant writes that Stephen Schwartz, not Galt MacDermot or Andrew Lloyd Webber, was "the first composer to bring into the Broadway musical the notated back-phrasing of melodic rhythm that was characteristic of recorded Motown music, but he superimposed it on the non-Motown eight eighth-notes groove" (155). By formalizing this songwriting approach and the accompanying singing style it demands, according to Grant, Schwartz was "an unheralded Broadway revolutionary; his unconscious influence on young musical writers of the 1990s like Jonathan Larson is just as evident as that of Sondheim" (156).

5. See *Pippin*, undated script, box 24A, Bob Fosse and Gwen Verdon Collection, Music Division, Library of Congress, Washington, DC.

6. See Stuart Ostrow, *Present at the Creation, Leaping in the Dark, and Going against the Grain: 1776, Pippin, M. Butterfly, La Bete and Other Broadway Adventures* (New York: Applause Theatre and Cinema Books, 2006), 64.

7. Glenn Loney, "The Many Facets of Bob Fosse," *After Dark*, June 1972, 26.

8. Douglas Watt, "How Bob Fosse Made 'Pippin' a Pip of a Play," *Pippin* clipping file, Billy Rose Theatre Division, The New York Public Library for the Performing Arts.

9. David Spangler quoted in Carol De Giere, *Defying Gravity: The Creative Career of Stephen Schwartz from Godspell to Wicked* (New York: Applause Theatre and Cinema Books, 2008), 87.

10. Stephen Schwartz, interview by author, June 12, 2012.

11. Ostrow, *Present at the Creation*, 66.

12. Loney, "The Many Facets of Bob Fosse," 27.

13. Linda Haberman, interview by author, November 17, 2015.

14. Diane Laurenson, interview by author, September 14, 2015.

15. Ann Reinking, "Auditioning for Fosse," *Dance Magazine*, February 2007, 90.

16. Gene Foote, telephone interview by author, June 6, 2010.

17. Letter from Bob Fosse to the cast of *Pippin*, undated, box 25A, Bob Fosse and Gwen Verdon Collection.

18. Candy Brown, Christopher Chadman, Cheryl Clark, Gene Foote, Richard Korthaze, Paul Solen, and Pamela Sousa would all appear in *Chicago*, with Ann Reinking later replacing Gwen Verdon as Roxie Hart. Chadman, Korthaze, Reinking, and John Mineo would appear in *Dancin'*, with Chadman also contributing choreography and later serving as dance supervisor. Kathryn Doby would assist Fosse on both *Chicago* and *Dancin'*, and essentially play herself in *All That Jazz*.

19. See Richard Philp, "Spotlight On: Ann Reinking," *Dance Magazine*, February 1978, 76–77; Joanne Ney, "Ann Reinking: Dance Sensation," *Cue*, January 5, 1979, 25–26; Jennifer Dunning, "High-Stepping into Stardom," *New York Times*, April 2, 1978; Bernard Carragher, "Ann's Way Isn't Donna's," *New York Daily News*, August 8, 1976.

20. Stephen Schwartz quoted in De Giere, *Defying Gravity*, 88.

21. Michael Shurtleff, *Audition: Everything an Actor Needs to Know to Get the Part* (New York: Walker, 1978), 171.

22. Jules Fisher, telephone interview by author, October 24, 2011.

23. Gene Foote, telephone interview by author.

24. Ibid.

25. Ibid.

26. James Leve, *Kander and Ebb* (New Haven, CT: Yale University Press, 2009), 28–29.

27. John Bush Jones, *Our Musicals, Ourselves: Social History of the American Musical Theatre* (Hanover, NH: Brandeis University Press, 2003), 269.

28. Ken Mandelbaum, *"A Chorus Line" and the Musicals of Michael Bennett* (New York: St. Martin's Press, 1989), 15.

29. Stephen Schwartz, interview by author.

30. Roger O. Hirson quoted in Jerry Parker, "For Stephen Schwartz Success Unspoiled 'Pippin,'" *Newsday*, May 20, 1973.

31. Ibid.

32. Patricia Zipprodt, "Designing Costumes," in *Contemporary Stage Design U.S.A.*, ed. Elizabeth B. Burdick, Peggy C. Hansen, and Brenda Zanger (Middletown, CT: Wesleyan University Press, 1974), 29.

33. Patricia Zipprodt interview, Oral History Program, Fashion Institute of Technology, November 11, 1979, box 13, Patricia Zipprodt Papers and Designs, Billy Rose Theatre Division, The New York Public Library for the Performing Arts.

34. Jules Fisher, telephone interview by author.

35. Tony Walton, telephone interview by author, December 17, 2011.

36. Ibid.

37. Stephen Schwartz, interview by author. Schwartz also cites "All That Jazz" from *Chicago* as a similar reinterpretation of "Let the Good Times Roll."

38. All lyric quotations from Roger O. Hirson and Stephen Schwartz, *Pippin* (New York: Drama Book Specialists, 1975).

39. Stephen Schwartz, interview by author.

40. It is a rich irony that Fosse gave the African American Ben Vereen so many gestures and slogans associated with Al Jolson, who was indelibly linked to blackface performance. However, Jolson was so popular and his style so identifiable that their use instantly conjures a whole era of popular entertainment. Performed by a young African American, they add yet another layer of satire and sarcasm to the "War" sequence.

41. *Pippin* choreographic notes, box 25A, Bob Fosse and Gwen Verdon Collection.

42. Fosse and Verdon were always discreet in discussing their separation. See Chris Chase, "Fosse, from Tony to Oscar to Emmy?," *New York Times*, April 29, 1973, and Suzanne Daley, "Gwen Verdon: Stepping into Her New Shoes," *New York Times*, June 21, 1981, for their respective versions of their marital problems. In the interviews, each speaks admiringly of the other, and each assumes responsibility for the separation.

43. Berry Rehfeld, "Fosse's Follies," *Rolling Stone*, January 19, 1984, 49.

44. Jules Fisher, telephone interview by author.

45. Ibid.

46. Kathryn Doby, interview by author, October 17, 2012.

47. Candy Brown, interview by author, June 26, 2015.

48. Chase, "Fosse, from Tony to Oscar to Emmy?"

49. Kenneth L. Geist, "Fosse Reflects on Fosse," *After Dark*, February 1980, 32.

50. Fred Ebb and Bob Fosse, *Chicago: A Musical Vaudeville* (New York: Samuel French, 1976), 34.

51. May Okon, "'Pippin,' 'Godspell,' and Schwartz," *New York Sunday News*, December 3, 1972.

52. Stephen Schwartz, interview by author.

53. Jules Fisher, telephone interview by author.

54. Stephen Schwartz, interview by author.

55. Ibid.

56. Laurie Johnstone, "Fosse Discusses Creation of 'Pippin,'" *New York Times*, November 7, 1972.

57. Letter from Bob Fosse to the cast of *Pippin*, June 13, 1974, box 25A, Bob Fosse and Gwen Verdon Collection.

58. See Ostrow, *Present at the Creation*, 67.

59. Letter from Bob Fosse to the cast of *Pippin*, June 13, 1974, box 25A, Bob Fosse and Gwen Verdon Collection.

60. Kathryn Doby, interview by author.

61. See Watt, "How Bob Fosse Made 'Pippin' a Pip of a Play."

62. Martin Gottfried, *Pippin* review, *Women's Wear Daily*, October 25, 1972, in *Pippin* clipping file, Billy Rose Theatre Division.

63. Philip H. Dougherty, "'A Chorus Line' Commercial," *New York Times*, July 1, 1975.

64. *Pippin* commercial, accessed September 15, 2012, http://www.youtube.com/watch?v=bo4Tz-4rkvs.

65. Hobe Morrison, "TV Spots Boosting 'Pippin' B.O.; Musical Has Paid $800G Profit," *Variety*, January 23, 1974, 59.

66. Johnstone, "Fosse Discusses Creation of 'Pippin.'"

67. Jerry Parker, "The Birth Pangs of a Broadway Hit," *Newsday*, September 10, 1972.

68. Stuart Ostrow letter to Alvin Deutsch, January 25, 1973, box 25A, Bob Fosse and Gwen Verdon Collection.

69. Hobe Morrison, "Authors Win 'Pippin' Dispute: Consider Anti-Trust vs. Guild," *Variety*, November 14, 1973, 63.

70. Reviewing the production in Adelaide, Australia, Clive Barnes said that Bayes "seems to have imitated the Fosse staging but quite missed the vitality and liveliness of the original." "Musicals Thrive in Australia, but Accent Is Broadway," *New York Times*, July 26, 1974. The London critics were merciless. Robert Cushman called it "merely loathsome" (*Observer*, November 4, 1973), while Harold Hobson disparaged it as "childish," "simple-minded," and looking like "a No. 2 touring version of 'The Vagabond King'" (*Sunday Times*, November 4, 1973).

71. Post-Hearing Brief on Behalf of Stuart Ostrow, In the Matter of the Arbitration between Stephen Schwartz and Stuart Ostrow, American Arbitration Association, Case No. 1310 0504 73, undated, box 25A, Bob Fosse and Gwen Verdon Collection.

72. All quotes from undated *Pippin* script featuring revisions and cuts initiated by Stephen Schwartz and marginal notations by Bob Fosse, box 24B, Bob Fosse and Gwen Verdon Collection.

73. Post-Hearing Brief on Behalf of Stuart Ostrow, box 25A, Bob Fosse and Gwen Verdon Collection.

74. Bob Fosse letter to Roger O. Hirson, October 22, 1975, box 25A, Bob Fosse and Gwen Verdon Collection.

75. Geist, "Fosse Reflects on Fosse," 32.

76. Stuart Ostrow letter to Bob Fosse, March 3, 1973, box 25A, Bob Fosse and Gwen Verdon Collection.

77. Ibid.

78. Ibid.

79. Morrie Gelman, "'Pippin' Cassette Travels TWA: First Airborne Stage Show?," *Variety*, February 24, 1982, 111.

80. Stephen Schwartz, interview by author.

81. Kathryn Doby, interview by author.

82. Stephen Schwartz, interview by author.

83. Ibid.

84. Ibid.

85. Ibid.

86. Ben Brantley, "The Old Razzle-Dazzle, Fit for a Prince," *New York Times*, April 26, 2013.

CHAPTER 8: KEEP IT HOT

1. C. Lee Jenner, "In Fosse's Nightmare He Loses His Oscars," *Philadelphia Bulletin*, December 16, 1979.

2. See Sam Wasson, *Fosse* (Boston: Houghton Mifflin Harcourt, 2013), 345–347, and Martin Gottfried, *All His Jazz: The Life and Death of Bob Fosse* (New York: Bantam Books, 1990), 282–285, for discussions of Fosse's brief self-imposed hospitalization.

3. Lionel Chetwynd, "Except for Bob Fosse," *Penthouse*, January 1974, 90.

4. Clive Barnes, "Stage: A Gifted and Exciting 'Liza,'" *New York Times*, January 7, 1974.

5. Among several such video mash-ups, these are two of the most persuasive: "Bob Fosse vs. Michael Jackson" places clips from *The Little Prince* (incorrectly identified as 1971) next to footage of Michael Jackson in a performance dated 1982 to draw similarities between their choreography. https://www.youtube.com/watch?v=1LE_TYTxRxg, accessed December 2, 2016. "Bob Fosse + Michael Jackson" syncs his "Snake in the Grass" performance to Jackson's "Billie Jean" recording for a startlingly smooth combination of dance and music. https://www.youtube.com/watch?v=QUlEBhGgEeo, accessed December 2, 2016.

6. Scott Hornstein, "The Making of *Lenny*: An Interview with Bob Fosse," *Filmmakers Newsletter*, February 1975, 32.

7. Ibid.

8. "Bob Fosse," *The Dick Cavett Show*, PBS, aired July 8, 1980.

9. "Plus Cameraimage: A Conversation with Alan Heim," December 7, 2012, CommingSoon.net, accessed March 3, 2016, http://www.comingsoon.net/movies/features/97675-plus-camerimage-a-conversation-with-alan-heim.

10. Bob Fosse letter to Julian Barry, June 6, 1974, box 47B, Bob Fosse and Gwen Verdon Collection, Music Division, Library of Congress, Washington, DC.

11. Julian Barry letter to Bob Fosse, undated, box 47B, Bob Fosse and Gwen Verdon Collection.

12. Pauline Kael, "When the Saints Come Marching In," *New Yorker*, November 18, 1974, 194.

13. Ibid., 201–202.

14. Ibid., 202.

15. "'Lenny' Hits $11.5-Mil," *Variety*, March 19, 1975, 3.

16. "Bob Fosse: Steam Heat," *Great Performances: Dance in America*, PBS, aired February 23, 1990.

17. Robert Alan Aurthur, "Hanging Out," *Esquire*, August 1973, 6.

18. *Broadway Beat with Richard Ridge*, Manhattan Neighborhood Network, aired November 19, 1996.

19. See Maurine Watkins, "Woman Plays Jazz Air as Victim Dies," *Chicago Tribune*, April 4, 1924, reprinted in Maurine Watkins, *"Chicago," with the Chicago Tribune Articles That Inspired It*, edited and with an introduction by Thomas H. Pauly (Carbondale: Southern Illinois University Press, 1997), 122–123.

20. Curtis L. Peterson letter to Bob Fosse, May 20, 1975, box 47B, Bob Fosse and Gwen Verdon Collection.

21. Maurine Watkins, "Demand Noose for 'Prettiest' Woman Slayer," *Chicago Tribune*, April 5, 1924, reprinted in Watkins, *"Chicago," with the Chicago Tribune Articles That Inspired It*, 126.

22. Maurine Watkins, "Jury Finds Beulah Annan Is 'Not Guilty,'" *Chicago Tribune*, May 25, 1924, reprinted in Watkins, *"Chicago," with the Chicago Tribune Articles That Inspired It*, 143–148.

23. Maurine Watkins, "Jury Finds Mrs. Gaertner Not Guilty," *Chicago Tribune*, June 6, 1924, reprinted in Watkins, *"Chicago," with the Chicago Tribune Articles That Inspired It*, 154.

24. Burton Davis, "'Chicago' Opens at Music Box," *New York Daily Telegraph*, January 1, 1927.

25. See Robert S. Birchard, "Who Directed *Chicago*?," liner notes, *Chicago*, directed by Frank Urson (A Cecil B. DeMille Studio Production, 1927), DVD (Flicker Alley, 2010). Though credited to Frank Urson, who had been assistant director on DeMille's previous film, *King of Kings*, there was speculation that DeMille chose not to be officially listed as the director of the racy *Chicago* immediately following his biblical epic's overwhelming box-office success.

26. Thomas H. Pauly, "Murder Will Out, and It Did in 'Chicago,'" *New York Times*, December 22, 1996.

27. See Lewis Funke, "Remarque's Play Comes 'Full Circle,'" *New York Times*, January 28, 1973, and Louis Calta, "News of the Stage: Musical 'Chicago' Due on Broadway," *New York Times*, July 28, 1974.

28. *Broadway Beat with Richard Ridge*, Manhattan Neighborhood Network, aired November 19, 1996.

29. Bob Fosse letter to Robert Fryer, April 15, 1972, box 47A, Bob Fosse and Gwen Verdon Collection.

30. All dialogue and lyric quotations from Fred Ebb and Bob Fosse, *Chicago: A Musical Vaudeville* (New York: Samuel French, 1976).

31. Ann Reinking, telephone interview by author, April 29, 2016.

32. Robert Wahls, "Gwen Verdon, the Eternal Gypsy," *New York Sunday News*, June 1, 1975.

33. Chetwynd, "Except for Bob Fosse," 93.

34. See Richard Philp, "Bob Fosse's 'Chicago': Roxie's Razzle Dazzle and All That Jazz," *Dance Magazine*, November 1975, 40. Kander and Ebb discuss the song and performance references in John Kander and Fred Ebb as told to Greg Lawrence, *Colored Lights: Forty Years of Words and Music, Show Biz, Collaboration, and All That Jazz* (New York: Faber and Faber, 2003), 127–128. Detailed overviews of *Chicago*'s song antecedents can be found in James Leve's *Kander and Ebb* (New Haven, CT: Yale University Press, 2009), 77–103; Ethan Mordden's *One More Kiss: The Broadway Musical in the 1970s* (New York: Palgrave Macmillan, 2003), 128–131; and Scott Miller's *Deconstructing Harold Hill: An Insider's Guide to Musical Theatre* (Portsmouth, NH: Heinemann, 2000), 24–36.

35. See Patricia MacKay, "*Chicago*: Tony Walton Designs in Black Vinyl and Neon," *Theatre Crafts*, October 1975, 36.

36. Marilyn Stasio, "A Tough 'Chicago' Is Where Bob Fosse Lives," *Cue*, July 7, 1975, 64.

37. See Bertolt Brecht, *Brecht on Theatre: The Development of an Aesthetic*, ed. and trans. John Willett (New York: Hill and Wang, 1992), for his full discussion of and rationale for his theatrical aesthetic.

38. Ethan Mordden, *The Fireside Companion to the Theatre* (New York: Knopf, 1989), 51.

39. Pauline Kael, "Talent Isn't Enough," *New Yorker*, March 17, 1975, 117.

40. See Didier C. Deutsch, "A Look Back," liner notes for *Chicago: A Musical Vaudeville*, CD reissue, Arista 07822-18952-2, 1996.

41. Philp, "Bob Fosse's 'Chicago,'" 40.

42. Bob Fosse and Fred Ebb, *Chicago*, first draft, August 3, 1973, box 17A, Bob Fosse and Gwen Verdon Collection.

43. All quotes from Bob Fosse and Fred Ebb, *Chicago*, first draft, April 1973, box 53, Fred Ebb Papers, Music Division, The New York Public Library for the Performing Arts.

44. Ebb and Fosse, *Chicago: A Musical Vaudeville*, 91.

45. Unpublished interview with Bob Haddad, box 49A, Bob Fosse and Gwen Verdon Collection.

46. See Jan Hodenfield, "Gwen Verdon & Chita Rivera: 2 from the Chorus," *New York Post*, May 31, 1975.

47. Tony Walton, telephone interview by author, December 17, 2011.

48. Linda Winer, "Bob Fosse: The Razzle-Dazzle Director Is Planning to Jazz Up Broadway with His New 'Deal,'" *USA Today*, October 30, 1985.

49. Gwen Verdon *Chicago* contract, September 27, 1974, box 18C, Bob Fosse and Gwen Verdon Collection.

50. *Chicago* casting notes, July 16, 1974, box 18B, Bob Fosse and Gwen Verdon Collection.

51. *Chicago* audition list, August 21, 1974, box 18B, Bob Fosse and Gwen Verdon Collection.

52. Michael Shurtleff letter to Bob Fosse, October 27, 1974, box 18B, Bob Fosse and Gwen Verdon Collection.

53. Michon Peacock, telephone interview by author, January 21, 2016.

54. MacKay, "*Chicago*: Tony Walton Designs in Black Vinyl and Neon," 34.

55. Gene Foote, telephone interview by author, June 6, 2010.

56. Ibid.

57. Philp, "Bob Fosse's 'Chicago,'" 40.

58. Jules Fisher, telephone interview by author, October 24, 2011.

59. Gwen Verdon interview, WNET/13 *Dance in America*, Bob Fosse and Gwen Verdon Collection.

60. Frank Rich, "'La Cage' Has That Old-Time Appeal," *New York Times*, August 28, 1983.

61. Gene Foote, telephone interview by author.

62. Susan Stroman quoted in Wasson, *Fosse*, 447–448.

63. Alan Heim commentary, *All That Jazz*, directed by Bob Fosse (Twentieth Century-Fox and Columbia Pictures, 1979), DVD (Criterion Collection, 2014).

64. Moira Hodgson, "When Bob Fosse's Art Imitates Life, It's Just 'All That Jazz,'" *New York Times*, December 30, 1979.

65. A. J. Antoon letter to Bob Fosse, November 9, 1974, box 47B, Bob Fosse and Gwen Verdon Collection.

66. Donald Saddler letter to Bob Fosse, undated, box 47B, Bob Fosse and Gwen Verdon Collection.

67. "Fosse Fatigue Causes Delay in Start of 'Chicago' Rehearsals," *Variety*, November 6, 1974, 61.

68. Kander, Ebb, and Lawrence, *Colored Lights*, 123.

69. See Tony Stevens, oral history interview, conducted by the author, November 20, 2007, Jerome Robbins Dance Division, The New York Public Library for the Performing Arts, and "The Music of Kander and Ebb: Razzle Dazzle," *Great Performances*, PBS, aired December 3, 1997.

70. John Simon, *John Simon on Theater: Criticism, 1974–2003* (New York: Applause Theatre and Cinema Books, 2005), 52.

71. Gwen Verdon interview, WNET/13 *Dance in America*, Bob Fosse and Gwen Verdon Collection.

72. "The Music of Kander and Ebb: Razzle Dazzle, December 3, 1997."

73. Gwen Verdon interview, WNET/13 *Dance in America*, Bob Fosse and Gwen Verdon Collection.

74. Richard Korthaze, interview by author, January 20, 2014.

75. Hari, "Shows Out of Town: *Chicago*," *Variety*, April 16, 1975, 86.

76. "The Music of Kander and Ebb: Razzle Dazzle, December 3, 1997."

77. Tony Stevens, oral history interview, Jerome Robbins Dance Division.

78. Fred Ebb, "Notes on *Chicago*," undated, box 18C, Bob Fosse and Gwen Verdon Collection.

79. Chita Rivera, telephone interview by author, February 11, 2016.

80. Fred Ebb, "Notes on *Chicago*," undated, box 18C, Bob Fosse and Gwen Verdon Collection.

81. J. Wynn Rousuck, "Acclaimed Choreographer Bob Fosse Would Chuck It All to Be Fred Astaire," *Baltimore Sun*, March 29, 1981.

82. Arlene Croce, "The End of the Line," *New Yorker*, August 25, 1975, 81–82.

83. Ibid., 81.

84. Harold Prince, interview by author, September 11, 2013.

85. Jack Kroll, "My Kind of Town," *Newsweek*, June 16, 1975, 89.

86. Stephen Farber, "Bob Fosse's Acid Valentine," *New York Times*, August 3, 1975.

87. Michon Peacock, telephone interview by author.

88. Ann Reinking performed this revamped version of "Me and My Baby" on "Julie Andrews' Invitation to the Dance, with Rudolf Nureyev," *CBS Festival of Lively Arts for Young People*, CBS, aired November 30, 1980, accessed December 20, 2016, https://www.youtube.com/watch?v=Df3UNn7CCx4.

89. Clive Barnes, "'Chicago' Second to None," *New York Post*, November 15, 1996.

CHAPTER 9: DANCIN' SOLO

1. "Bob Fosse Talks about *Dancin'*," *New York Theatre Review*, March 1978, 9.

2. Unpublished interview with Bob Haddad, box 49A, Bob Fosse and Gwen Verdon Collection, Music Division, Library of Congress, Washington, DC.

3. Robert Berkvist, "'This Show Is about the Sheer Joy of Dancing,'" *New York Times*, March 26, 1978.

4. Bob Fosse letter to Robert Joffrey, May 24, 1976, box 47D, Bob Fosse and Gwen Verdon Collection.

5. Linda Haberman, interview by author, November 17, 2015.

6. "Fosse Planning 'Dancing' Musical," *Variety*, August 10, 1977, 65.

7. "General Casting: Equity for 'Dancers,'" *Back Stage*, September 16, 1977, 46.

8. See Memorandum from Franklin R. Weissberg to Alan J. Hartnick, December 30, 1977, *Dancin'* materials, box 2A, Shubert Organization Legal Papers, Shubert Archive, New York City.

9. Kathryn Doby, interview by author, October 17, 2012.

10. "The Real Chorus Line: Broadway Dancers," *The David Susskind Show*, WNTA-TV, October 18, 1981, Jerome Robbins Dance Division, The New York Public Library for the Performing Arts.

11. Ken Urmston, interview by author, August 9, 2014.

12. Berkvist, "'This Show Is about the Sheer Joy of Dancing.'"

13. Ibid.

14. Unpublished interview with Bob Haddad, box 49A, Bob Fosse and Gwen Verdon Collection.

15. Gwen Verdon interview, WNET/13 *Dance in America*, Bob Fosse and Gwen Verdon Collection.

16. Barbara Rowes, "After Three Coronaries and Critical Surgery, Bob Fosse Puts His Heart and Soul into 'All That Jazz,'" *People*, March 3, 1980, 70.

17. Maxine Glorsky, oral history interview, September 29, 2001, conducted by Jennifer Dunning, Jerome Robbins Dance Division.

18. Valarie Pettiford, interview by author, October 26, 2015.

19. Leah D. Frank, "Light Is the Love of His Life," *New York Times*, November 12, 1978.

20. Jules Fisher, telephone interview by author, October 24, 2011.

21. Bob Fosse employment contract for *Dancin'*, January 12, 1978, *Dancin'* materials, box 2A, Shubert Organization Legal Papers.

22. George Perry, "I Wanna Be a Dancin' Man," *Sunday Times* (London), June 8, 1980.

23. Jay Scott, "Fosse's Legacy Nears Perfection," *Globe and Mail*, September 25, 1987.

24. My thanks to Kathryn Doby for pointing out this scenario.

25. Linda Haberman, interview by author.

26. Ann Reinking, telephone interview by author, April 29, 2016.

27. This movement is often referred to as "teacup fingers." See Debra McWaters, *The Fosse Style* (Gainesville: University Press of Florida, 2008), a book-length instruction, with photographs, of signature Fosse moves.

28. Stephen M. Silverman, "Bob Fosse Dances to His Own Kind of Musical," *New York Post*, March 24, 1978. The listing for "Sing Sing Sing" in the program for *Dancin'* included Fosse's dedication, "For Gwen and Jack. The latter would have hated it."

29. See McWaters, *The Fosse Style*, 107–108, for further discussion of the crescent jump and landing.

30. Diane Laurenson, interview by author, September 16, 2015.

31. See McWaters, *The Fosse Style*, 166, for further discussion of the stack.

32. Ann Reinking, telephone interview by author.

33. My thanks to Diane Laurenson for pointing out the cannonball jumps in "Trumpet Solo." See McWaters, *The Fosse Style*, 135–138, for a discussion and demonstration of this step.

34. "All That Jack: Hollywood's Genius Choreographer Reemerges," presentation by Debra Levine, January 25, 2016, Museum of Modern Art, New York City.

35. Since *Dancin'*, other Broadway director-choreographers have set dance numbers to "Sing Sing Sing." In 1999, Susan Stroman used it to conclude her dance play, *Contact*; it also was part of the finale of *Swing*, Lynn Taylor-Corbett's singing and dancing revue.

36. "Clear Day and Other Ideas," box 45b, Bob Fosse and Gwen Verdon Collection.

37. My thanks to Diane Laurenson for sharing with me the imagery for this number.

38. Gwen Verdon interview, WNET/13 *Dance in America*, Bob Fosse and Gwen Verdon Collection.

39. Allen Herman, interview by author, January 7, 2016.

40. Deborah Jowitt, "In and Out of Bounds," *Village Voice*, May 15, 1978, 81.

41. Marvin H. Krauss letter to Franco Colombo, June 27, 1979, *Dancin'* materials, box 2A, Shubert Organization Legal Papers.

42. Bob Fosse letter to Charles Ward, May 22, 1979, box 48A, Bob Fosse and Gwen Verdon Collection.

43. Diane Laurenson, interview by author.

44. Nicole Fosse interview, WNET/13 *Dance in America*, September 6, 1989, Bob Fosse and Gwen Verdon Collection.

45. My thanks to James Horvath for discussing with me the intricacies of the various pas de deux in "Joint Endeavor." James Horvath, interview by author, May 27, 2016.

46. *Dancin'*, unmarked production script, box 4, Phil Friedman Papers, Museum of the City of New York.

47. Arlene Croce, "Broadway Downbeat," *New Yorker*, April 24, 1978, 150.

48. "Bob Fosse Talks about *Dancin'*," 9.

49. John Corry, "Broadway: Morosco to Get 'Da,' Story of an Irishman as Told by His Son," *New York Times*, March 31, 1978.

50. See Inventory, "Fosse Commercials," *Dancin'* materials, box 2A, Shubert Organization Legal Papers.

51. *Dancin'*, unmarked production script, box 4, Phil Friedman Papers.

52. *Dancin'* publicity, *Dancin'* materials, box 2A, Shubert Organization Legal Papers.

53. Croce, "Broadway Downbeat," 150.

54. *Dancin'*, unmarked production script, box 4, Phil Friedman Papers.

55. Marilyn Stasio, "In Step with Bob Fosse, 'Dancin'' Man," *Los Angeles Times*, June 3, 1979.

56. Snyd., "Shows Out of Town: *Dancin'*," *Variety*, February 22, 1978, 92.

57. Don Shewey, "Throwin' the Night Away," *Boston Phoenix*, February 28, 1978.

58. *Dancin'*, unmarked production script, box 4, Phil Friedman Papers.

59. "Bob Fosse Talks about *Dancin'*," 9.

60. Linda Haberman, interview by author.

61. Martin Gottfried, *All His Jazz: The Life and Death of Bob Fosse* (New York: Bantam Books, 1990), 363.

62. Linda Haberman, interview by author.

63. *Dancin'*, unmarked production script, box 4, Phil Friedman Papers.

64. Berkvist, "'This Show Is about the Sheer Joy of Dancing.'"

65. Clive Barnes, "How Dance Took Over Musicals," *New York Post*, March 31, 1978.

66. Richard Eder, "'Dancin', Fosse's Musical, Opens at the Broadhurst," *New York Times*, March 28, 1978.

67. Walter Kerr, "'Dancin'' Needs More Than Dancing," *New York Times*, April 9, 1978.

68. T. E. Kalem, "Corybantic Rites on Broadway," *Time*, April 10, 1978, 94.

69. Linda Winer, "Curtain Rises on Variety and Broadway Comes into View," *Chicago Tribune*, May 28, 1978.

70. Ibid.

71. Berkvist, "'This Show Is about the Sheer Joy of Dancing.'"

72. Ibid.

73. Mel Gussow, "Broadway to Hear Sound of Musicals," *New York Times*, January 11, 1978.

74. Wendy Perron, "The New Broadway: Dance Takes Center Stage," *Village Voice*, May 8, 1978, 36.

75. Bernard B. Jacobs, oral history interview, April 8, 1993, conducted by Suki Sandler, Dorot Jewish Division, New York Public Library.

76. Ibid.

77. Linda Winer, "For Chicago's Fosse, Life Is a 'Cabaret' of Musical Hits," *Chicago Tribune*, February 19, 1978.

CHAPTER 10: DANCE OF DEATH

1. *Tomorrow with Tom Snyder*, January 31, 1980, on *All That Jazz*, DVD (Criterion Collection, 2014).

2. "Bob Aurthur phone call to Fosse before operation," November 15, 1974, box 1A, Bob Fosse and Gwen Verdon Collection, Music Division, Library of Congress, Washington, DC.

3. All quotes from Pete Hamill letter to Bob Fosse, April 25, 1976, box 14B, Bob Fosse and Gwen Verdon Collection.

4. Daniel Melnick quoted in Bernard Drew, "Life as a Long Rehearsal," *American Film*, November 1979, 75.

5. Paul Rosenfield, "Long, Winding Road to 'Jazz,'" *Los Angeles Times*, January 6, 1980.

6. *All That Jazz* screenplay, September 8, 1976, box 1A, Bob Fosse and Gwen Verdon Collection.

7. Ibid.

8. See Bob Fosse letter to Michael Shurtleff, August 25, 1976, box 5C, Bob Fosse and Gwen Verdon Collection.

9. Drew, "Life as a Long Rehearsal," 75.

10. *All That Jazz*, Academy of Motion Picture Arts and Sciences screening, May 7, 2007, Margaret Herrick Library, Beverly Hills, California.

11. Among the *N.Y./L.A.* principal dancers who had appeared in Fosse shows on Broadway or on tour were Sandahl Bergman (*Pippin* and *Dancin'*), Eileen Casey (*Pippin* and *Dancin'*), Bruce Anthony Davis (*Dancin'*), Gary Flannery (*Pippin* and *Dancin'*), Jennifer Nairn-Smith (*Pippin*), Danny Ruvolo (*Pippin*), Candace Tovar (*Chicago*), and Rima Vetter (*Dancin'*).

12. Tony Walton, telephone interview by author, December 17, 2011.

13. "Bob Aurthur's Notes on *All That Jazz* Tapes," June 14, 1976, box 1A, Bob Fosse and Gwen Verdon Collection.

14. Ibid.

15. Bruce Williamson, "All That Fosse," *Playboy*, March 1980, 250.

16. Shaun Considine, *Mad as Hell: The Life and Work of Paddy Chayefsky* (New York: Random House, 1994), 297.

17. Sandahl Bergman, telephone interview by author, April 27, 2016.

18. Roy Scheider commentary on *All That Jazz*, directed by Bob Fosse (Twentieth Century-Fox and Columbia Pictures, 1979), DVD (Criterion Collection, 2014).

19. Ruth Hamilton, "Bob Fosse: It's a Tough Life but a Good One," *Globe and Mail*, February 1, 1980.

20. Alan Heim interview on *All That Jazz*, directed by Bob Fosse (Twentieth Century-Fox and Columbia Pictures, 1979), DVD (Criterion Collection, 2014).

21. See Marco Calavita, "'MTV Aesthetics' at the Movies: Interrogating a Film Criticism Fallacy," *Journal of Film and Video*, 59, no. 3 (Fall 2007), 15–31.

22. See Bob Fosse letter to Robert Joffrey, June 24, 1976, box 47C, Bob Fosse and Gwen Verdon Collection.

23. Peter Buckley, "The Fiery Miss de Mille," *Horizon*, September 1980, 31.

24. "Fosse Notebook—Fire Bird-Rock, *All That Jazz*, 1," box 3B, Bob Fosse and Gwen Verdon Collection.

25. *All That Jazz* screenplay revised, April 14, 1977, box 2B, Bob Fosse and Gwen Verdon Collection.

26. Betty Spence, "Bob Fosse—He'll Take the Risks," *Los Angeles Times*, May 17, 1981.

27. Gwen Verdon interview, WNET/13 *Dance in America*, Bob Fosse and Gwen Verdon Collection.

28. Ibid.

29. Alan Heim commentary on *All That Jazz*, directed by Bob Fosse (Twentieth Century-Fox and Columbia Pictures, 1979), DVD (Criterion Collection, 2014).

30. See "Doc Stars in a Reel Drama," *New York Daily News*, December 21, 1979.

31. Janet Maslin, "Sifting Flaws for Flashes of Genius," *New York Times*, January 13, 1980.

32. "Bob Fosse," *The Dick Cavett Show*, PBS, aired July 8, 1980.

33. Bob Fosse interview with William Wolf, October 24, 1983, NYU's School of Continuing Education class "The Filmmakers," William Wolf Film and Theater Interview Collection Sound Recordings, 1972–1988, Rodgers and Hammerstein Archives of Recorded Sound, The New York Public Library for the Performing Arts.

34. Tony Walton, telephone interview by author.

35. Stephen M. Silverman, "'Jazz'—All That Agony!," *New York Post*, December 20, 1979.

36. See Spence, "Bob Fosse—He'll Take the Risks."

37. See Rosenfield, "Long, Winding Road of 'Jazz'"; Drew, "Life as a Long Rehearsal," 74–75.

38. Tony Walton, telephone interview by author.

39. Kathryn Doby, interview by author, October 17, 2012.

40. Spence, "Bob Fosse—He'll Take the Risks."

41. Marilyn Stasio, "In Step with Bob Fosse, 'Dancin'' Man," *Los Angeles Times*, June 3, 1979.

42. Alan Heim commentary on *All That Jazz* DVD.

43. Drew, "Life as a Long Rehearsal," 29.

44. Michael Musto, "Whatsername and All That Jazz," *Soho Weekly News*, January 10, 1980, 35.

45. James Lardner, "Bob Fosse: 'All That Jazz' Puts His Private Life on the Screen . . . ," *Washington Post*, February 10, 1980.

46. Marian Zailian, "Dancin' Bob Fosse Still Flirts with Death," unidentified clipping, September 2, 1979, box 52D, Bob Fosse and Gwen Verdon Collection.

47. Drew, "Life as a Long Rehearsal," 77.

48. Ibid.

49. Vincent Canby, "The Screen: Roy Scheider Stars in 'All That Jazz,'" *New York Times*, December 20, 1979.

50. George Peary, "I Wanna Be a Dancin' Man," *Sunday Times* (London), June 8, 1980.

51. http://www.worldwideboxoffice.com/index.cgi?start=1979&finish=1979&order=domestic, accessed May 17, 2016.

52. Roderick Mann, "Roy Scheider: Talent, Luck and 'All That Jazz,'" *Los Angeles Times*, November 18, 1979.

53. Stanley Kubrick quoted in John Baxter, *Stanley Kubrick: A Biography* (New York: Carroll and Graf, 1997), 12.

54. Daniel Melnick quoted in Drew, "Life as a Long Rehearsal," 26.

55. See John Anderson, "The Many Worlds of Darren Aronofsky," *Directors Guild Quarterly*, Fall 2013, accessed May 17, 2016, http://www.dga.org/Craft/DGAQ/All-Articles/1304-Fall-2013/Darren-Aronofsky.aspx.

56. Matt Zoller Seitz, "All That Fosse: All Those Echoes of 'All That Jazz,'" *New York Times*, December 27, 2009.

CHAPTER 11: CONTROL

1. Teresa Carpenter, "Death of a Playmate," *Village Voice*, November 5–11, 1980, 1, 12–14, 16–17.

2. See Mariel Hemingway, *Finding My Balance: A Memoir* (New York: Simon and Schuster, 2003), 82–85, and Mariel Hemingway with Ben Greenman, *Out Came the Sun: Overcoming the Legacy of Mental Illness, Addiction, and Suicide in My Family* (New York: Regan Arts, 2015), 131–132.

3. Chris Chase, "Fosse's Ego Trip," *Life*, November 1979, 96.

4. Maurice Peterson letter to Murray Fisher, June 22, 1973, box 47A, Bob Fosse and Gwen Verdon Collection, Music Division, Library of Congress, Washington, DC.

5. Barry Rehfeld, "Fosse's Follies," *Rolling Stone*, January 19, 1984, 44.

6. Martin Gottfried, *All His Jazz: The Life and Death of Bob Fosse* (New York: Bantam Books, 1990), 413.

7. See "Dorothy Stratten Project," box 156, Paddy Chayefsky Papers, Billy Rose Theatre Division, The New York Public Library for the Performing Arts.

8. Film Director Deal Memorandum, signed by Bob Fosse, April 27, 1982, box 31B, Bob Fosse and Gwen Verdon Collection.

9. Roderick Mann, "Bob Fosse—Writing 'Star 80' Was Easy, Filming It Wasn't," *Los Angeles Times*, November 13, 1983.

10. Bob Fosse quoted in Shaun Considine, *Mad as Hell: The Life and Work of Paddy Chayefsky* (New York: Random House, 1994) , 398.

11. Ibid. See also "Soft-Shoe Tribute at Playwright's Funeral: Chayefsky Mourned with Laughter and a Dance," *Los Angeles Times*, August 5, 1981.

12. All quotes from Peter Bogdanovich memo to Bob Powsnwer [sic], March 3, 1982, box 35A, Bob Fosse and Gwen Verdon Collection.

13. Kenneth Meyer letter to Jay Kanter, May 11, 1982, box 31C, Bob Fosse and Gwen Verdon Collection.

14. "Bob Fosse Film" casting schedule, September 23, 1981, box 35C, Bob Fosse and Gwen Verdon Collection.

15. Frank Sanello, "Bob Fosse Finds Compassion in a Tragic Tale," *L.A. Life*, November 10, 1983, 5.

16. Michael Bowen, "Will Gritty 'Star 80' Glitter at the Box Office?," *Boston Globe*, November 6, 1983.

17. Rehfeld, "Fosse's Follies," 49.

18. See Bob Fosse interview with William Wolf, October 24, 1983, NYU's School of Continuing Education class "The Filmmakers," William Wolf Film and Theater Interview Collection Sound Recordings, 1972–1988, Rodgers and Hammerstein Archives of Recorded Sound, The New York Public Library for the Performing Arts.

19. Peter Bogdanovich, *The Killing of the Unicorn: Dorothy Stratten (1960–1980)* (New York: William Morrow, 1984), 173.

20. Hugh Hefner quoted in Gene Siskel, ". . . But Hugh Hefner Finds a Different Villain," *Chicago Tribune*, November 6, 1983.

21. The scene is a reference to *Autumn Born*, a low-budget Canadian film made in 1979 with a plot that featured Stratten in scenes of beatings and bondage. Never released while she was alive, the film carried ghoulish associations with the actress following her murder and was later quietly relegated to the home video market.

22. Richard Schickel, "A Centerfold Tragedy of Manners," *Time*, November 14, 1983, 98.

23. Pauline Kael, "The Perfectionist," *New Yorker*, November 28, 1983, 176.

24. Ibid., 177.

25. Leslie Bennetts, "Bob Fosse—Dancing with Danger," *New York Times*, April 6, 1986.

26. Gwen Verdon interview, WNET/13 *Dance in America*, Bob Fosse and Gwen Verdon Collection.

27. See Ruth Robinson, "Future Events: Performance the Ploy," *New York Times*, May 16, 1982.

28. Mindy Aloff, email communication with author, August 5, 2016.

29. Carol Ilson, *Harold Prince: A Director's Journey* (New York: Limelight Editions, 2000), 330.

30. Dance notes for "New Man," box 51B, Bob Fosse and Gwen Verdon Collection.

31. All quotes from http://www.psclassics.com/cd_ashman_transcript.html, accessed July 31, 2016.

32. Dick Anderson, "The Dancin' Man," *The Hamptons*, August 1, 1986, box 52E, Bob Fosse and Gwen Verdon Collection.

33. Sam Zolotow, "Musical 'Big Deal,'" *New York Times*, March 2, 1967.

34. Bennetts, "Bob Fosse—Dancing with Danger."

35. See Bob Fosse, *Big Deal*, first draft screenplay, July 1, 1969, box 66A, Bob Fosse and Gwen Verdon Collection.

36. Kevin Kelly, "Fosse, at 58, Finds No Security in Success," *Boston Globe*, February 9, 1986.

37. Bennetts, "Bob Fosse—Dancing with Danger."

38. In a 1972 letter to producer Robert Fryer, Fosse described his plan for *Big Deal* to have an original score, possibly by John Kander and Fred Ebb, and his new Roxie Hart musical to have a score composed entirely of preexisting period songs. The opposite scenario eventually played out for each show. Bob Fosse letter to Robert Fryer, April 15, 1972, box 47A, Bob Fosse and Gwen Verdon Collection.

39. Bob Fosse audio interview with Kevin Boyd Grubb, May 18, 1986, Bob Fosse and Gwen Verdon Collection.

40. Ibid.

41. Steven Winn, "Fosse Almost Didn't Do It Again," *San Francisco Chronicle*, September 21, 1985.

42. Chet Walker, interview by author, December 28, 2012.

43. Mimi Quillin, interview by author, December 9, 2015.

44. Ibid.

45. Ibid.

46. Ibid.

47. Jack Viertel, "Bob Fosse Supervises L.A. 'Charity' Event," *Los Angeles Herald-Examiner*, July 14, 1985.

48. Dan Sullivan, "Stage Review: Allen Puts Sweetness Back in 'Charity,'" *Los Angeles Times*, July 22, 1985.

49. Suzanne Daley, "Stepping Into Her New Shoes," *New York Times*, June 21, 1981.

50. Ibid.

51. Linda Winer, "Bob Fosse: The Razzle-Dazzle Director Is Planning to Jazz Up Broadway with His New 'Deal,'" *USA Today*, October 30, 1985.

52. Gaby Rogers, "Bob Fosse: 'Choreography Is Writing with Your Body,'" *Newsday*, October 1, 1978.

53. See Bob Fosse letter to Howard Feuer, October 1, 1985, box 8A, Bob Fosse and Gwen Verdon Collection. See also *Big Deal* casting notes, undated, box 1, Christopher Chadman Papers, Billy Rose Theatre Division, The New York Public Library for the Performing Arts.

54. My thanks to Gordon Lowry Harrell for sharing with me his experiences working with Fosse on the musical arrangements for *Big Deal*, as well as his reflections on the show's sound design. Gordon Lowry Harrell, telephone interview by author, September 1, 2016.

55. Jules Fisher, telephone interview by author, October 24, 2011.

56. Ibid.

57. Ibid.

58. During the "Roxie" number in the film version of *Chicago*, director Rob Marshall isolates Roxie in the upper-right corner, a tiny, shimmering image in the screen's velvety blackness—precisely the cinematic image Fosse labored to achieve onstage.

59. My thanks to Lloyd Culbreath for discussing the use of these platforms with me. Lloyd Culbreath, interview by author, October 18, 2015.

60. See Robert Fosse *Big Deal* employment agreement, December 24, 1985, box 9A, Bob Fosse and Gwen Verdon Collection.

61. Linda Haberman, interview by author, November 17, 2015.

62. Ibid.

63. Kelly, "Fosse, at 58, Finds No Security in Success."

64. Bennetts, "Bob Fosse–Dancing with Danger."

65. Wayne Cilento quoted in Kevin Boyd Grubb, *Razzle Dazzle: The Life and Work of Bob Fosse* (New York: St. Martin's Press, 1989), 256.

66. Linda Haberman, interview by author.

67. Ibid.

68. "All That Jack: Hollywood's Genius Choreographer Reemerges," presentation by Debra Levine, January 25, 2016, Museum of Modern Art, New York City.

69. My thanks to Lloyd Culbreath and Valarie Pettiford for pointing out how the choreography in this number mirrors the various instruments in the onstage band.

70. My thanks to Diane Laurenson for pointing out the number's parallels to other Fosse dances.

71. Bob Fosse audio interview with Kevin Boyd Grubb, May 15, 1986, Bob Fosse and Gwen Verdon Collection.

72. Arthur Friedman, "Super Musical Hurt by Clumsy Script," *Boston Herald*, February 17, 1986.

73. Kevin Kelly, "'Big Deal': Pleasures and Problems," *Boston Globe*, February 17, 1986.

74. Friedman, "Super Musical Hurt by Clumsy Script."

75. Ibid.

76. Rick Elice quoted in Michael Riedel, *Razzle Dazzle: The Battle for Broadway* (New York: Simon and Schuster, 2015), 335.

77. All quotes from Gerald Schoenfeld letter to Bob Fosse, March 19, 1986, box 8B, Bob Fosse and Gwen Verdon Collection.

78. Name withheld, interview by author, December 20, 2015.

79. Frank Rich, "Theater: 'Big Deal,' from Bob Fosse," *New York Times*, April 11, 1986.

80. Ibid.

81. "Hey, Bob Fosse," music by Cy Coleman and lyrics by Gerard Alessandrini, in *Forbidden Broadway: Unoriginal Cast Album, Volume 2*, DRG, 1991.

82. David Kaufman, "The Sweet Nostalgia of a Revival," *Downtown*, May 21, 1986, 8A.

83. All quotes from Bob Fosse audio interview with Kevin Boyd Grubb, May 15, 1986, Bob Fosse and Gwen Verdon Collection.

84. Kelly, "Fosse, at 58, Finds No Security in Success."

FOSSEVILLE

1. *1987 Tony Awards*, CBS, aired June 7, 1987.

2. Diane Laurenson, interview by author, September 14, 2015.

3. See Charles W. Hall and Douglas Stevenson, "Bob Fosse Dies after Collapsing on D.C. Street," *Washington Post*, September 24, 1987; Clyde Satterwhite, "Bob Fosse Dead at 60," *New York Daily News*, September 24, 1987.

4. Aaron Shapiro letter to Jerome Robbins, October 5, 1987, box 507, Jerome Robbins Papers, Jerome Robbins Dance Division, The New York Public Library for the Performing Arts.

5. Ibid.

6. Patricia Ben Peterson quoted in Irvin Molotsky, "Bob Fosse, Director and Choreographer, Dies," *New York Times*, September 24, 1987.

7. *1988 Tony Awards*, CBS, aired June 5, 1988.

8. Kevin Gault and Tom Hinckley, "Bob Fosse: *Star 80*, Show Business and All That Jazz," *The Cable Guide*, November 1984, A24.

9. *Bob Fosse Memorial*, Palace Theater, October 30, 1987, Theatre on Film and Tape Archive, The New York Public Library for the Performing Arts.

10. Chet Walker, interview by author, December 28, 2012.

11. Chet Walker, interview by author, March 18, 2013.

12. Fred Ebb imagined a different, thematic celebration of Fosse. An outline for *Bob Fosse: A Dancin' Man* sketches in a series of dance suites to create a biographical picture of the choreographer. As a narrator introduces each section with observations about Fosse, dancers pay tribute to his sense of humor ("Uncle Sam Rag" and "Ain't We Got Fun"); his cynicism ("Razzle Dazzle," "Manson Trio," and "Cell Block Tango"); his beginnings in burlesque ("All I Care About") and vaudeville ("Mr. Bojangles"); his interest in sex ("Big Spender" and "Mein Herr"); his problems with censorship ("Red Light Ballet"); his work with Verdon ("If My Friends Could See Me Now," "Cool Hand Luke," and "Roxie"); and his influences (Jack Cole with "Sing Sing Sing," and Fred Astaire with "I Wanna Be a Dancin' Man"). Ebb even envisioned ending the first act

with *New Girl in Town*'s "There Ain't No Flies on Me," including its full-cast cakewalk as the curtain comes down, and raising the second-act curtain with the cast still dancing, just as Fosse did in 1957. Some of Ebb's ideas parallel Chet Walker's, including ending with the full cast applauding a Fosse stand-in as he performs a sand dance to "Life Is Just a Bowl of Cherries." See box 95, Fred Ebb Papers, Music Division, The New York Public Library for the Performing Arts.

13. In the 1989 music video for Abdul's "Cold Hearted," a record producer describes to his associates the dance number they are about to see. "It's a Bob Fosse kind of thing. It's going to be really, really hot." "Yeah, but tastefully—it's tastefully hot," says another. In setting, costuming, lighting, choreography, camerawork, editing, and overall tone, the video is both homage to and rip-off of "Take Off with Us."

14. Joan Acocella, "Dancing and the Dark," *New Yorker*, December 21, 1998, 100.

15. Ed Blank, "Why Don't They 'Dance' in Films Anymore? Ask Fosse," *Pittsburgh Press*, September 8, 1983.

16. "Fosse's notes to company," undated, box 95, Fred Ebb Papers.

SELECTED BIBLIOGRAPHY

Abbott, George. *Mister Abbott*. New York: Random House, 1963.

Aurthur, Robert Alan. "Hanging Out." *Esquire*, August 1973, 6–8, 20.

Bailey, Beth, and David Farber, eds. *America in the Seventies*. Lawrence: University Press of Kansas, 2004.

Beddow, Margery. *Bob Fosse's Broadway*. Portsmouth, NH: Heinemann, 1996.

Bogdanovich, Peter. *The Killing of the Unicorn: Dorothy Stratten (1960–1980)*. New York: William Morrow, 1984.

Brecht, Bertolt. *Brecht on Theatre: The Development of an Aesthetic*. Edited and translated by John Willett. New York: Hill and Wang, 1992.

Calavita, Marco. "'MTV Aesthetics' at the Movies: Interrogating a Film Criticism Fallacy." *Journal of Film and Video* 59, no. 3 (Fall 2007): 15–31.

Carpenter, Teresa. "Death of a Playmate." *Village Voice*, November 5–11, 1980, 1, 12–14, 16–17.

Chetwynd, Lionel. "Except for Bob Fosse." *Penthouse*, January 1974, 89–93.

Considine, Shaun. *Mad as Hell: The Life and Work of Paddy Chayefsky*. New York: Random House, 1994.

Decker, Todd. *"Show Boat": Performing Race in an American Musical*. New York: Oxford University Press, 2013.

De Giere, Carol. *Defying Gravity: The Creative Career of Stephen Schwartz from Godspell to Wicked*. New York: Applause Theatre and Cinema Books, 2008.

D'Emilio, John, and Estelle B. Freedman. *Intimate Matters: A History of Sexuality in America*. 2nd ed. Chicago: University of Chicago Press, 1997.

De Mille, Agnes. *Dance to the Piper*. Boston: Little, Brown, 1951.

Drew, Bernard. "Life as a Long Rehearsal." *American Film*, November 1979, 26–31, 75, 77.

Easton, Carol. *No Intermissions: The Life of Agnes de Mille*. Boston: Little, Brown, 1996.

Feuer, Cy, with Ken Gross. *I Got the Show Right Here: The Amazing, True Story of How an Obscure Brooklyn Horn Player Became the Last Great Broadway Showman*. New York: Simon and Schuster, 2003.

Franceschina, John. *Hermes Pan: The Man Who Danced with Fred Astaire*. New York: Oxford University Press, 2012.

Frum, David. *How We Got Here: The 70s: The Decade That Brought You Modern Life (for Better or Worse)*. New York: Basic Books, 2000.

Gardner, Kara Anne. *Agnes de Mille: Telling Stories in Broadway Dance*. New York: Oxford University Press, 2016.

Gehrin, David J. "An Interview with Christopher Isherwood." In *Conversations with Christopher Isherwood*, edited by James J. Berg and Chris Freeman, 74–89. Jackson: University Press of Mississippi, 2001.

Gelbart, Larry. *Laughing Matters: On Writing M*A*S*H, Tootsie, Oh, God!, and a Few Other Funny Things*. New York: Random House, 1998.

Gennaro, Liza. "Evolution of Dance in the Golden Age of the American 'Book Musical.'" In *The Oxford Handbook of the American Musical*, edited by Raymond Knapp, Mitchell Morris, and Stacy Wolf, 45–61. New York: Oxford University Press, 2011.

Gilvey, John Anthony. *Before the Parade Passes By: Gower Champion and the Glorious American Musical*. New York: St. Martin's Press, 2005.

Goldman, William. *The Season: A Candid Look at Broadway*. New York: Harcourt, Brace, 1969.

Gottfried, Martin. *All His Jazz: The Life and Death of Bob Fosse*. New York: Bantam Books, 1990.

Grant, Mark N. *The Rise and Fall of the Broadway Musical*. Boston: Northeastern University Press, 2004.

Greenspan, Charlotte. *Pick Yourself Up: Dorothy Fields and the American Musical*. New York: Oxford University Press, 2010.

Grubb, Kevin Boyd. *Razzle Dazzle: The Life and Work of Bob Fosse*. New York: St. Martin's Press, 1989.

Hamilton Lytle, Mark. *America's Uncivil Wars: The Sixties Era from Elvis to the Fall of Richard Nixon*. New York: Oxford University Press, 2006.

Hazzard-Gordon, Katrina. *Jookin': The Rise of Social Dance Formations in African-American Culture*. Philadelphia: Temple University Press, 1990.

Hemingway, Mariel. *Finding My Balance: A Memoir*. New York: Simon and Schuster, 2003.

Hemingway, Mariel, with Ben Greenman. *Out Came the Sun: Overcoming the Legacy of Mental Illness, Addiction, and Suicide in My Family*. New York: Regan Arts, 2015.

Hill, Constance Valis. "From Bharata Natyam to Bop: Jack Cole's 'Modern' Jazz Dance." *Dance Research Journal* 33, no. 2 (Winter 2001–2002): 29–39.

Jones, John Bush. *Our Musicals, Ourselves: Social History of the American Musical Theatre*. Hanover, NH: Brandeis University Press, 2003.

Jowitt, Deborah. *Jerome Robbins: His Life, His Theater, His Dance*. New York: Simon and Schuster, 2004.

Kander, John, and Fred Ebb as told to Greg Lawrence. *Colored Lights: Forty Years of Words and Music, Show Biz, Collaboration, and All That Jazz*. New York: Faber and Faber, 2003.

Kennedy, Matthew. *Roadshow! The Fall of Film Musicals in the 1960s*. New York: Oxford University Press, 2014.

Kislan, Richard. *Hoofing on Broadway: A History of Show Dancing*. New York: Prentice Hall, 1987.

Knowles, Mark. *Tap Roots: The Early History of Tap Dancing*. Jefferson, NC: McFarland, 2002.

Kobal, John. *Gotta Sing Gotta Dance: A Pictorial History of Movie Musicals*. London: Hamlyn, 1971.

Lawrence, Greg. *Dance with Demons: The Life of Jerome Robbins*. New York: Putnam's, 2001.

Leiter, Samuel L. *The Great Stage Directors: 100 Distinguished Careers of the Theater*. New York: Facts on File, 1994.

Leve, James. *Kander and Ebb*. New Haven, CT: Yale University Press, 2009.

Loney, Glenn. "The Many Facets of Bob Fosse." *After Dark*, June 1972, 22–27.

———. *Unsung Genius: The Passion of Dancer-Choreographer Jack Cole*.
New York: Franklin Watts, 1984.

MacLaine, Shirley. *My Lucky Stars: A Hollywood Memoir*. New York: Bantam
Books, 1995.

Mandelbaum, Ken. *"A Chorus Line" and the Musicals of Michael Bennett*. New York: St.
Martin's Press, 1989.

Mann, William J. *Hello Gorgeous: Becoming Barbra Streisand*. New York: Houghton
Mifflin Harcourt, 2012.

McGovern, Dennis, and Deborah Grace Winer. *Sing Out Louise! 150 Stars of the
Musical Theatre Remember 50 Years on Broadway*. New York: Schirmer Books, 1993.

McKechnie, Donna, with Greg Lawrence. *Time Steps: My Musical Comedy Life*.
New York: Simon and Schuster, 2006.

McWaters, Debra. *The Fosse Style*. Gainesville: University Press of Florida, 2008.

Meisner, Sanford, and Dennis Longwell. *Sanford Meisner on Acting*.
New York: Vintage Books, 1987.

Miller, Scott. *Deconstructing Harold Hill: An Insider's Guide to Musical Theatre*.
Portsmouth, NH: Heinemann, 2000.

Mordden, Ethan. *Broadway Babies: The People Who Made the American Musical*.
New York: Oxford University Press, 1983.

———. *The Fireside Companion to the Theatre*. New York: Knopf, 1989.

———. *One More Kiss: The Broadway Musical in the 1970s*. New York: Palgrave
Macmillan, 2003.

Ostrow, Stuart. *Present at the Creation, Leaping in the Dark, and Going against
the Grain: 1776, Pippin, M. Butterfly, La Bete and Other Broadway Adventures*.
New York: Applause Theatre and Cinema Books, 2006.

Prince, Hal. *Contradictions: Notes on Twenty-Six Years in the Theatre*. New York: Dodd,
Mead, 1974.

Rehfeld, Barry. "Fosse's Follies." *Rolling Stone*, January 19, 1984, 42, 44, 46, 49, 64.

Riedel, Michael. *Razzle Dazzle: The Battle for Broadway*. New York: Simon and
Schuster, 2015.

Russo, Vito. *The Celluloid Closet: Homosexuality in the Movies*. New York: Harper and
Row, 1981.

Sagolla, Lisa Jo. *The Girl Who Fell Down: A Biography of Joan McCracken*.
Boston: Northeastern University Press, 2003.

Schulman, Bruce J. *The Seventies: The Great Shift in American Culture, Society, and
Politics*. New York: Free Press, 2001.

Sheldon, Sidney. *The Other Side of Me: A Memoir*. New York: Grand Central
Publishing, 2005.

Shteir, Rachel. *Striptease: The Untold History of the Girlie Show*. New York: Oxford
University Press, 2004.

Shurtleff, Michael. *Audition: Everything an Actor Needs to Know to Get the Part*.
New York: Walker, 1978.

Silverman, Stephen M. *Dancing on the Ceiling: Stanley Donen and His Movies*.
New York: Knopf, 1996.

Simon, Neil. *Rewrites: A Memoir*. New York: Simon and Schuster, 1996.

Sloan, Ronna Elaine. "Bob Fosse: An Analytic-Critical Study." PhD diss., City University of New York, 1983.

Stempel, Larry. *Showtime: A History of the Broadway Musical Theater.* New York: Norton, 2010.

Stratyner, Barbara. *Ned Wayburn and the Dance Routine: From Vaudeville to the Ziegfeld Follies.* Studies in Dance History No. 13. Madison: University of Wisconsin Press for the Society of Dance Scholars, 1996.

Suskin, Steven. *The Sound of Broadway Musicals: A Book of Orchestrators and Orchestrations.* New York: Oxford University Press, 2009.

Terry, Walter. *I Was There: Selected Dance Reviews and Articles, 1936–1976.* Compiled and edited by Andrew Mark Wentink. New York: Audience Arts, 1978.

Trav S. D. *No Applause—Just Throw Money.* New York: Faber and Faber, 2005.

Tropiano, Stephen. *Cabaret.* Milwaukee, WI: Limelight Editions, 2011.

Viagas, Robert, ed. *The Alchemy of Theatre—The Divine Science: Essays on Theatre and the Art of Collaboration.* New York: Playbill Books, 2006.

Wasson, Sam. *Fosse.* Boston: Houghton Mifflin Harcourt, 2013.

Watkins, Maurine. *"Chicago," with the Chicago Tribune Articles That Inspired It,* edited and with an introduction by Thomas H. Pauly. Carbondale: Southern Illinois University Press, 1997.

Wayburn, Ned. *The Art of Stage Dancing: The Story of a Beautiful and Profitable Profession.* New York: Belvedere, 1980.

York, Michael. *Accidentally on Purpose: An Autobiography.* New York: Simon and Schuster, 1991.

Zipprodt, Patricia. "Designing Costumes." In *Contemporary Stage Design U.S.A.,* edited by Elizabeth B. Burdick, Peggy C. Hansen, and Brenda Zanger, 29–33. Middletown, CT: Wesleyan University Press, 1974.

INDEX

"Joan McCracken types," 24
marriage to Fosse, 30, 54, 55, 69, 76
professional support for Fosse, 36, 95
thoughts on filming dance, 132
McGuire, William Anthony, 277n8
McKayle, Donald, 75
McKechnie, Donna, 92, 167, 271
McLerie, Allyn Ann, 78
McMartin, John, 108, 117, 123, 126, 129
Me and Juliet, 36, 50
"Me and My Baby," 192, 203, 205, 206, 308n88
"Me and My Shadow," 264, 269
Meet Me After the Show, 47
"Mein Herr," 65, 148–150, 153, 273, 300n72, 316n12
Meisner, Sanford, 24, 26, 62, 64
Melnick, Daniel, 232, 233, 245
Memphis Jookin', 275
Mendes, Sam, 157
Menendez Brothers, 207
Mercer, Johnny, 16, 215
"Merely Marvelous," 73
Meri, La, 46
Merlin, 260
Merman, Ethel, 60, 128, 244
Merrick, David, 105
Merrill, Bob, 61–62, 105, 292n10
Merry Widow, The, 47
"Mexican Breakfast," 140–141, 275, 298n7
"Mexican Shuffle," 135–136
MGM, 3, 26, 27, 30, 31, 36, 37, 42, 43, 46, 47, 58, 61, 94, 185, 215
Middle of the Night, 111
Midler, Bette, 167
Midnight Cowboy, 137
Midnight Special, 242
Mielziner, Jo, 9–10
Milk and Honey, 93
Miller, Ann, 31–32
Miller, Bennett, 255
Miller, Buzz, 36, 40, 41, 46
Miller, Glenn, 265
Miller, Marilyn, 192

Mineo, John, 166, 213, 301n18
Minnelli, Liza, 4, 143, 145, 148–150, 151, 153, 155, 156, 157–162, 185, 205–206, 248, 299n37, 300n59, 300n71, 300n72
Minnelli, Vincente, 143, 155
Minskoff, Jerome, 262
Minskoff Theater, 268
Miranda, Lin-Manuel, 275
Misérables, Les, 207, 208
Miss Liberty, 78
"Mister Cellophane," 193, 204
Mitchell, Julian, 7, 12
Moiseyev, Igor (Moiseyev Dance Company), 109
"Money, Money," 151, 161
Monicelli, Mario, 256
Monkees, the, 167
Monroe, Marilyn, 67
Montgomery, Robert, 118
Moonwalk, 186, 275
Moore, Garry, 115
Mordden, Ethan, 7–8, 193
Moreda, Dale, 74, 93, 293n28
Moreno, Rita, 129
Morgan, Helen, 192
Morse, Robert, 88, 91, 93
Most Happy Fella, The, 88
Mostel, Zero, 103
Motown, 301n4
Moulin Rouge (1952), 132, 150
"Mr. Bojangles" (Jerry Jeff Walker), 222–223, 316n12
MTV, 150, 259, 274
"Mu-Cha-Cha," 56–57, 92, 94, 141
Murray, Mary Gordon, 2, 292n62
"Muscle, the," 1, 2, 3, 6, 9, 12, 69, 86, 87, 91, 106, 107, 129, 177, 188, 195, 247, 248, 263, 275
Music Box Theater, 191
Music Man, The, 78
My Fair Lady (musical), 78, 93, 102
My Fair Lady (film), 128
"My Heart Belongs to Daddy," 48
My One and Only, 268
"My Own Best Friend," 205–206

"My Personal Property," 136–137
My Sister Eileen (Joseph Fields and
    Jerome Chodorov), 42
My Sister Eileen (Ruth McKenney), 42
My Sister Eileen (film), 42–44, 50, 99,
    128, 265, 280n42
Mystery of Edwin Drood, The, 269

Nadel, Norman, 101
Nairn-Smith, Jennifer, 166, 174,
    232, 311n11
"Narcissistic Tango, The," 87, 99
Nash, Ogden, 9
Nashville, 233
National Board of Review, 156
National Theater, 271
Native Dancer, 70
NBC, 77, 161–162, 244
Nederlander Organization, 255
Neighborhood Playhouse, 24, 26
Nemetz, Lenora, 196, 206
Neuwirth, Bebe, 121, 207, 274
New Girl in Town, 3, 61–67, 73,
    78, 80, 98, 105, 110, 135,
    149, 154, 204, 238,
    286n104, 317n12
  background and plot, 61
  budget, 61, 114
  casting, 61–62, 67, 293n28
  choreography, 62–67
  critical reception, 66
  Fosse's conflicts with Abbott and
    Prince, 3, 63–67, 69, 238
  Tony Awards, 67
  understudies and replacements for
    Verdon, 66, 67
New Group, The, 127
"New Man," 256
"New Town is a Blue Town, A," 39
New York City Center, 87, 105
New York City Center Encores!, 206–207
New York Drama Critics' Circle Award,
    93, 144
New York, New York, 153
New York Shakespeare Festival, 202
Newman, Randy, 157

Next to Normal, 290n18
Nicholas Brothers, The, 15
Nichols, Mike, 132
Nichols, Nichelle, 129
Night of the Living Dead, 242
Nights of Cabiria, 110, 112, 113, 129,
    130, 256
Nikolais, Alwin, 223–224
Niles, Mary Ann (Marian), 3, 19–20,
    21–22, 24–25, 29, 33, 54,
    69, 273
Nilsson, Harry, 171
"No," 201
No, No, Nanette, 166
No Strings, 93
"No Talent Joe," 47
"No Time at All," 176–177
"Nobody," 193, 205
Noone, Peter, 167
North, Sheree, 67
"Nothing is Impossible," 29
"Nowadays," 151, 201, 259
"Nowadays/R.S.V.P./Keep It Hot,"
    201, 287n14
"Now's the Time to Fall in Love," 262
Nureyev, Rudolf, 291n43
Nykvist, Sven, 251
N.Y./L.A., 234, 239, 241–243
Nyro, Laura, 163

O'Brien, W. W., 191
Of Thee I Sing, 290n18
Oh, Kay!, 277n10
O'Haughey, Michael, 196, 205
O'Horgan, Tom, 187
Oklahoma! (musical), 8–9, 23, 53, 63, 64,
    80, 120, 223, 278n19
Oklahoma! (film), 42
Oliver! (musical), 103
Oliver! (film), 117
Oliver, Thelma, 117, 129
On a Clear Day You Can See Forever, 107,
    144
"On Broadway," 235–236, 255
"On the Right Track," 177–178
On the Riviera, 46